HENRIK JOHAN IBSEN

was the pioneer who opened the new frontiers of the modern drama and violated all the unwritten taboos of the nineteenth-century theatre. In **A DOLL'S HOUSE** he fought against the subjugation of modern woman. In **GHOSTS** he introduced the theme of venereal disease to the stage and anatomized the provincial and puritanical repressiveness of middle-class life. In **AN ENEMY OF THE PEOPLE** he vented his spleen on the vested interests and their opportunistic minions in the intelligentsia. And in **THE WILD DUCK** he poured his scorn on moralistic meddlers in people's lives.

Whatever theme he touched, Ibsen brought light into the dark corners of the soul and society, and with it his grim humor, his scathing irony, and his wealth of compassionate understanding for weak and fallible humanity.

FOUR GREAT PLAYS
BY HENRIK IBSEN

Translated by R. Farquharson Sharp

**With an Introduction and Prefaces to each Play
by John Gassner**

FOUR GREAT PLAYS BY IBSEN

A Bantam Book / published by arrangement with
E. P. Dutton & Co., Inc.

Bantam Classic edition / March 1958

2nd printing .... January 1960	6th printing .. February 1963
3rd printing ..... March 1961	7th printing .. September 1963
4th printing .... October 1961	8th printing ...... June 1964
5th printing .... October 1962	9th printing .... January 1965
10th printing .... October 1965	

Bantam Library of World Drama edition / January 1967

12th printing ..... May 1967	14th printing . November 1968
13th printing ..... May 1968	15th printing .... August 1969
16th printing ... February 1970	

Bantam edition / May 1971

18th printing . December 1971	21st printing .. August 1974
19th printing . November 1972	22nd printing . February 1975
20th printing . November 1973	23rd printing . November 1975
24th printing .... August 1976	

ISBN 0-553-10195-1

Published simultaneously in the United States and Canada

*Bantam Books are published by Bantam Books, Inc. Its trade-
mark, consisting of the words "Bantam Books" and the por-
trayal of a bantam, is registered in the United States Patent
Office and in other countries. Marca Registrada. Bantam
Books, Inc., 666 Fifth Avenue, New York, New York 10019.*

PRINTED IN THE UNITED STATES OF AMERICA

Contents

❧

Introduction

BY JOHN GASSNER

Henrik Ibsen: A Sceptic in a China-Shop

Henrik Ibsen, who was born in Norway in 1828, has long held the unofficial title of "father of the modern drama," and for sufficiently good reasons. Historians have certainly discovered no earlier dramatist for whom they could advance rival claims. Great reputations, it is true, have to be paid for as well as merited, and Ibsen paid for his fame *twice*. He was granted only notoriety by conservative contemporaries, who accused him of immorality and subversion, and he began to be patronized by sophisticated individuals within a decade after his death in 1906 as a worthy but rather humdrum and old-fashioned playwright. It would seem that Ibsen was fated to be misunderstood in two centuries; he was too radical for the nineteenth and too conservative for the twentieth. Whether or not he is still somewhat misunderstood, however, his importance to the modern theatre has long been accepted. He impressed so many important contemporaries with the power of his writing that even conventional nineteenth-century playwrights began to pay him the compliment of imitation. And continuing to affect the course of the theatre after 1900, he won the allegiance of many of its leaders from Galsworthy to Arthur Miller.

The plays in this volume represent the middle and most influential period of Ibsen's career, which started in 1877 with his attack on pseudo-respectability *The Pillars of Society* and ended in 1884 with *The Wild Duck*. He was in his fifties then and had a long career in the theatre as a stage manager, director, and playwright behind him. He had suffered many deprivations and disappointments, but had also enjoyed some triumphs, especially with the publication of two plays in verse, *Brand* and *Peer Gynt*, in 1865 and 1867 respectively. He had also been at odds with the Norwegian middle-class for many years, preferred to live abroad, in Italy and Germany, and was already known as an intransigent social critic.

With *The Pillars of Society* and *The Wild Duck*, but especially with the three plays that came between them—*A Doll's House* in 1879, *Ghosts* in 1881, and *An Enemy of the People* in 1882—Ibsen established realism as the ruling principle of modern drama. Problems of the day had been aired on the stage for some decades before he began presenting them, but nobody before Ibsen had treated them without equivocation or without stressing secondary matters while ignoring primary ones. Ibsen's social dramas supplanted the contrived, often melodramatic, construction of earlier European problem plays with a dramatic technique that was at once natural and penetrative. "Drama of ideas" was largely Ibsen's creation because the idea was made flesh in his work and sympathy was, at the same time, secured against deterioration into sentimentality by an acutely critical mind.

Stupidity or cowardice often moved Ibsen to anger, yet it was, above all, his sceptical and sardonic spirit that made plays such as *A Doll's House, Ghosts,* and *An Enemy of the People* original, that really made them distinguishable from the ordinary thesis-drama or tract. No pretence or delusion was safe from his quizzical scrutiny, not even liberalism or reform itself, and no institution or cherished notion was exempt from his scorn in this "destructive" phase of his career. To overawed friends and irritated foes Ibsen was either a heroic image-breaker or an iconoclast gone berserk. In view of the fragility of the objects of his rampage, the bric-a-brac of conventional beliefs, it might have been more correct to describe him as a sceptic in a china-shop.

Still, his rebelliousness was no trivial matter in an age that cherished the bric-a-brac, and even his least weighty protests had far-reaching consequences. With the plays of his middle period, as well as with a few pieces written before and after, Ibsen enabled the stage to recover much of the prestige it had lost to the modern novel in the nineteenth century. After *A Doll's House* and *Ghosts* it became increasingly difficult for a playwright to make an impression unless he directed his attention to the realities of modern life and brought to bear upon them at least some semblance of intelligence. .

Today it seems incredible that *A Doll's House* should have created the furor it did. In exploding Victorian ideals of feminine dependency the play seemed revolutionary in 1879. When its heroine Nora left her home in search of self-development it seemed as if the sanctity of marriage had been flouted by a playwright treading the stage with cloven-feet. That Nora's marriage might be reestablished on sounder foundations than those she had repudiated, that Ibsen's aims were essentially reconstructive rather than destructive, eluded Ibsen's critics not so much because his plea for feminine emancipation was new (others had made it before him), but because he was not content with pleading. He took the offensive instead, stripping masculine egotism to the bone and depriving a conventional "doll's house" type of marriage of all its romantic and sentimental frippery. And he climaxed the awakening of his heroine not with the expected reconciliations of domestic drama, but with Nora's closing the door on her husband, home, and marriage. An anarchist's pistol shot could not have reverberated more frighteningly in the Victorian world than the closing of that door.

In the plays of the middle period Ibsen's *manner* was mainly destructive. His methods of exposing a situation were those of a strategist calculated to disturb the playgoer and startle him into thought. Ibsen used the stratagem of starting innocently with a convincing introduction to commonplace life and then dealing it a shattering blow. The very prosiness of the writing (he had deliberately made prose his medium after having gained distinction as a poet) contributed to the efficacy of his tactics. The spectator was apt to be caught napping when respectability was invalidated by mounting disclosures of inconsistency, error, and evil in its fabric. For all his seriousness, moreover, Ibsen also employed humor as a means for unsettling a settled opinion or discrediting a public oracle. Ibsen never tired of treating the proponents of vested interest and convention with irony.

The classic example of Ibsen's method is *Ghosts*. Although the play is somber enough in substance to be regarded as a tragedy, it devastates Pastor Manders, the representative of conventional morality, with humor and irony. Ibsen shows him to be such a fool at times that one cannot even hate him; he is so gullible and so ignorant of life that we can only agree with Mrs. Alving in the play when she calls him a big baby. Yet the results of his conventionality are so dreadful as to make his moral thinking immoral. In adhering to his rigid code, Pastor Manders forced Mrs. Alving to return to an incurably unfaithful husband. The good man thinks he saved a home when he actually preserved a façade behind which her life was a mockery of marriage and a travesty of love. Appearances were preserved at the cost of happiness, and the ultimate reward of "virtue," of Mrs. Alving's return to her husband, is her son's collapse into feeble-mindedness as a result of inherited venereal disease. It was as if Ibsen the devilishly sharp ironist had inverted the axiom that the wages of sin are death in a dramatic statement to the effect that the wages of virtue were paresis and imbecility. Having been condemned for letting Nora leave her husband in *A Doll's House*, Ibsen seemed to be saying "I'll give you a woman who did *not* leave her husband." It is no wonder that *Ghosts* raised an outcry against its author second to none in the history of the theatre, that public productions of the play were forbidden or long delayed, and that it became mandatory for advanced theatrical groups to stage the play early in their career.

It remains to be said that Ibsen made an innovation in dramatic technique that also served him well in his assault on conventional minds. It might be called the method of frontal attack, and it consisted of direct statements by characters involved in the action of the play. Direct statements were hardly new in the European theatre, but Ibsen used them in a new and singularly effective way. He developed them in the form of a dramatic discussion. Ibsen made controversy an important element in the drama, and incorporated it in the central situations. It was the nimble mind of Shaw that first detected the transformation of dramatic structure that accompanied Ibsen's transvaluation of values. In the little book *The Quintessence of Ibsenism*, originally given as a lecture for the Fabian Society in 1890, Shaw pointed out that "Up to a certain point in the last act, *A Doll's House* is a play that might be turned into a very ordinary French drama," if a few lines were excised and a sentimental reconciliation were substituted for the conclusion. But "at just that point," Nora unexpectedly stopped reacting emotionally and sat down to discuss the meaning of her marriage with her husband. This discussion scene, which Ibsen had in mind from the beginning, carried the full charge of a climax in the play and was also the resolution of its action. Discussion, in brief, superseded the familiar unravelling of the plot or the "denouement" in the conventional type of "plotty" drama that had come to be known as "the well-made play." It was with the addition of this technical feature, which is vastly more important than the realism of detail that abounds even in meretricious movies, that the distinctly modern drama was born.

In *Ghosts*, Ibsen extended the element of discussion, introducing it early and allowing it to permeate the play. And in the comedy *An Enemy of the People* Ibsen made controversy the very core of the action once he pitted his idealistic hero Dr. Stockmann against an entire community determined to defend its vested interests. The conflict was by its very nature a debate between Stockmann and his opponents on the issue of conscience and integrity *versus* opportunism. Written with broad, slashing strokes of satire and supplied with a vigorous plot, *An Enemy of the People* was also an effective piece of standard theatre. In this scornful work, in which some of the characterization is so subordinated as to verge on caricature, the controversy was no less an action than the action was a controversy.

An Enemy of the People apparently purged its irritated author of his resentments, for he reversed his aim completely in his next work. In *The Wild Duck*, he directed his fire against a would-be reformer. But it would have been an error to assume that Ibsen had renounced "discussion" in a work that actually discussed and demonstrated the fallacy of inflexible idealism. And it would have been equally wrong to assume that Ibsen had made his peace with convention simply because he discredited Gregers Werle, the neurotic truth-seeker of the play. Ibsen, in short, remained the same individualist, the same enemy of dogmatism and proponent of moral relativism, he had been in *Ghosts*.

Essentially, it was not his matter but his manner that had changed by 1884. But it was enough to reveal him in *The Wild Duck* as a compassionate observer of humanity as well as the sceptic now engaged in scattering the chinaware of idealism rather than the common porcelain of conservatism. Ibsen revealed the most attractive side of his personality in wishing to temper the keen wind of truth to those who could subsist only on benign illusion. And, above all, he brought to the foreground of his work his considerable understanding of people, his talent for character-creation. That talent had been sufficiently apparent in his portraits of Nora and Mrs. Alving and in the minor characterizations of *A Doll's House* and *Ghosts*, as well as in the comic delineation of Dr. Stockmann in *An Enemy of the People*. But "character-drama" had been necessarily overshadowed by argument in these plays. In *The Wild Duck*, instead, the characters drew attention to themselves as living persons, and they dictated Ibsen's argument with their lives. The accent naturally fell on psychological reality the moment Ibsen rejected moral absolutes in favor of the view that the "truth" is relative to the realities of the individual situation—that is, to the character and emotional needs of the person. The concentrated logic of development so effective in *Ghosts* had to give way to a more fluid type of dramatic movement than Ibsen had used in earlier realistic plays. With *The Wild Duck*, in 1884, Ibsen was on the threshold of the new naturalistic style of playwriting for which Chekhov became celebrated nearly a score of years later.

An important concomitant of the altered technique of *The Wild Duck* was the heightened poetic texture of the work. In this masterpiece of the realistic drama, Ibsen concluded his middle period with a characteristic departure from humdrum journalism and flat problem-play dramaturgy. When Ibsen abandoned verse-drama in the 1870's it was clearly not his intention to deprive the theatre of all poetry. He remained an imaginative writer and a poet of the theatre, although an unobtrusive one in whose work poetic atmosphere blended with common reality, as it does in the last, "sunrise," scene of *Ghosts*. And Ibsen began to give new scope to his poetic imagination through symbolism, actually using it to sharpen, rather than to soften, his argument in *Ghosts*, where the burning of the orphanage erected by Mrs. Alving in memory of her husband symbolized the end of deception and the idea of "ghosts" served as a symbol for the dead beliefs that continue to haunt the living. Nor was an educated playgoer likely to miss the parallel between that play and a classic tragedy of Fate, the main difference being that for the modern realist Fate lay in the environment that tied Mrs. Alving to her dismal marriage as well as in the genes that gave her a syphilitic son. In *The Wild Duck* the symbolism of the bird in the Ekdal garret was especially well marked. (Ibsen was soon to move into his so-called Symbolist phase with such plays as *The Lady from the Sea* and *The Master Builder*.) The compulsive reformer Gregers, who suffers, we are told, from "an acute attack of integrity," talks about "marsh vapors" when he means family secrets. Aroused by the possible illegitimacy of little Hedvig, he says he would like to be "an amazingly clever dog" that "goes to the bottom after wild ducks when they dive and bite themselves fast in tangle and sea-weed, down among the ooze." And Hedvig herself may be likened to her strange pet, the captive wild duck with the broken wing: "Nobody knows her, and nobody knows where she came from either." But the most compelling poetry of *The Wild Duck* will be found not so much in the symbolism as in the movement of life itself in the play, in the mingled comedy and pathos and in the moods and day-dreaming of the characters.

All things considered, it becomes evident, then, that this small collection of plays represents various facets of a complex talent. We see Ibsen, in the four masterpieces of his middle period, as a realist who went beyond realism of detail to establish a realism of character analysis and social criticism. We encounter in the plays an early master of disputation (Shaw was his great successor) who, nevertheless, did not stint on dramatic action and character drawing. We discover a severely honest playwright who was relentless in exposing error and falsehood, but who could dissolve severity with humor and substitute irony for denunciation without losing his quarry. Ibsen's talent had a comic as well as tragic bent,—

a fact not often enough stressed by his critics. And he was characteristically modern in blending elements of comedy and tragedy in such plays as *A Doll's House* and *The Wild Duck* to form an intermediate type of play serious in action but uninflated with the grandeur or grandiloquence of past ages. (The French term *drame* is perhaps the most suitable for this largely modern type of play.) Ibsen was, besides, both prosaic and poetic, both specific and universal, just as he was clear in argument yet complex, even enigmatic, in his dealings with human nature. And he made no rigid commitment to a single philosophy or even to a single dramatic style even in the closely related work of his middle period. In these and other respects, he was plainly independent and followed his own course as an observer and judge of reality. He made his character Dr. Stockmann declare that "the strong stand alone." Whether or not this is always true, there can be no doubt that Ibsen was "strong" and that he stood alone.

Ibsen continued to compose realistic and symbolic plays until 1899 when he published his last work, the poetic drama *When We Dead Awaken*. Although he lived on until the spring of 1906, he produced nothing after 1899; by chronology he belonged entirely to the nineteenth century. Several of the late plays—the somber tragedy *Rosmersholm* (1886), the incisive character-portrait *Hedda Gabler* (1892), and two bitter studies of spiritual failure, *The Master Builder* (1892) and *John Gabriel Borkman* (1896)—became justly celebrated. After *The Wild Duck*, Ibsen's work was largely *reprise*, and even before his creative fires were completely banked he had begun to share his domination of the modern stage with younger men such as Strindberg in Sweden, Maeterlinck in France, Shaw in England, and Chekhov in Russia. As long as he was able to write, however, Ibsen remained a formidable figure in literature and the theatre, a man for whom the creative life was a passionate inquiry into truth and falsehood, right and wrong. It is entirely fitting that as he lay dying his last statement should have been *"On the contrary."*

A Doll's House

A Doll's House was not the first of Ibsen's plays to make enemies for him; but it was the first to spread his reputation as a subversive playwright abroad, and arouse enmity toward him in foreign lands. Ibsen's subject was no longer local politics, as in the earlier *Love's Comedy*, but the miseducation and subjugation of the European middle-class woman. It is difficult to overestimate the significance, and, indeed, the novelty of such a theme for Victorian readers and audiences.

Although *A Doll's House* no longer arouses such burning topical interest, it remains a vital drama of character. Ibsen's strong-willed heroine, Nora, is no mere case history in a suffragette bill of particulars. Far from being a typical victim of male domination, Nora is master of the domestic world she calls her doll's house. She has the initiative to nurse her husband through a long illness, the courage to forge his name to a promissory note in order to get the money for his convalescence, and she is even able, in the face of enormous difficulties, to meet the payments on her loan. Only when a disgruntled employee of her husband's bank tries to blackmail Nora's husband into restoring him to the job from which he has been fired is Nora's deception revealed.

The play's turning point is based far less on Nora's supposed innocence of the realities of the world than on her husband's understandable fear of scandal in their provincial bourgeois world. Because her notion that marriage could protect her from all eventualities is shattered, and because she had romantically expected heroic sacrifices from him, Nora resolves to find some basis for her marriage other than bourgeois convention and girlish romanticism: she decides to leave her "doll's house" to seek independence in the "outside world." Although her example might be cited as an object lesson by feminists, Ibsen took great pains to make her disenchantment and climactic decision the result of her unique personal character and experience.

At the very end of the play Ibsen is forced to push his argument very hard to convince us that Nora really believes she can leave her young children behind when she deserts her husband. But precisely this drastic conclusion, no matter how it stretches credibility, has secured polemical importance for the play. As George Bernard Shaw concluded in *The*

Quintessence of Ibsenism, the most original part of the play was the discussion Nora initiated once the threat of prosecution for forgery was completely removed by the blackmailer's repentance. In a conventional "well-made" drama, Torvald's eagerness to forget the entire unpleasant crisis would have been followed by a quick reconciliation and an unclouded dénouement. In rejecting such a conventional climax, Ibsen was transcending Scribe and the nineteenth-century commercial theatre. At the same time, he was trying to ground his play in the psychological realities of human character, in the tradition of such great masters of nineteenth-century realism as Balzac, Flaubert and Turgenev, rather than in mere theatrical contrivance. Finally, Ibsen wanted to advance the cause of "the drama of ideas," which he had already begun to promote in such early, more romantic, plays as *Brand, Peer Gynt* and *Emperor and Galilean,* and to root it firmly in the everyday social and domestic middle-class world of Europe. That Ibsen himself seems to have been uncertain about the validity of his unconventional climax was revealed when he permitted a German production of *A Doll's House* to revise the ending and to show Nora remaining with her husband.

A Doll's House was completed and published late in 1879. It was so successful that it had to be reprinted twice within three months of publication. Translations followed in German, Finnish, English, Polish, Russian and Italian. The play was successfully presented in Copenhagen in the same year of publication, and then in Stockholm and Christiania (Oslo). In March of the same year the play had its German premiere in Munich. The first public production in England was entitled *Breaking a Butterfly,* and was presented in London in March 1884. According to Ibsen's early advocate and translator, William Archer, this severely mangled adaptation presented the husband as "an ideal hero, instead of the sensual, self-righteous weakling of Ibsen." The first acceptable British production, which starred Janet Achurch, came much later, in June 1889. It was repeated by the same actress in 1892. The first American production was presented at Milwaukee in 1882 in an adaptation entitled *The Child Wife.* Not until 1889 did Americans see an unadulterated version of the play. Ultimately, with the exception of *Ghosts,* Ibsen's *A Doll's House* became the most frequently performed of his plays in England and the United States.

DRAMATIS PERSONÆ

Torvald Helmer.
Nora, his wife.
Doctor Rank.
Mrs. Linde.
Nils Krogstad.
Helmer's three young children.
Anne, their nurse.
A Housemaid.
A Porter.

(*The action takes place in Helmer's house.*)

ACT I

(SCENE.—*A room furnished comfortably and tastefully, but not extravagantly. At the back, a door to the right leads to the entrance-hall, another to the left leads to Helmer's study. Between the doors stands a piano. In the middle of the left-hand wall is a door, and beyond it a window. Near the window are a round table, arm-chairs and a small sofa. In the right-hand wall, at the farther end, another door; and on the same side, nearer the footlights, a stove, two easy chairs and a rock-ing-chair; between the stove and the door, a small table. Engravings on the walls; a cabinet with china and other small objects; a small book-case with well-bound books. The floors are carpeted, and a fire burns in the stove. It is winter.*

A bell rings in the hall; shortly afterwards the door is heard to open. Enter NORA, *humming a tune and in high spirits. She is in out-door dress and carries a number of parcels; these she lays on the table to the right. She leaves the outer door open after her, and through it is seen a* PORTER *who is carry-ing a Christmas Tree and a basket, which he gives to the* MAID *who has opened the door.*)

NORA. Hide the Christmas Tree carefully, Helen. Be sure the children do not see it till this evening, when it is dressed. (*To the* PORTER, *taking out her purse.*) How much?

PORTER. Sixpence.

NORA. There is a shilling. No, keep the change. (*The* PORTER *thanks her, and goes out.* NORA *shuts the door. She is laughing to herself, as she takes off her hat and coat. She takes a packet of macaroons from her pocket and eats one or two; then goes cautiously to her husband's door and listens.*) Yes, he is in. (*Still humming, she goes to the table on the right.*)

HELMER (*calls out from his room*). Is that my little lark twittering out there?

3

NORA (*busy opening some of the parcels.*) Yes, it is!

HELMER. Is it my little squirrel bustling about?

NORA. Yes!

HELMER. When did my squirrel come home?

NORA. Just now. (*Puts the bag of macaroons into her pocket and wipes her mouth.*) Come in here, Torvald, and see what I have bought.

HELMER. Don't disturb me. (*A little later, he opens the door and looks into the room, pen in hand.*) Bought, did you say? All these things? Has my little spendthrift been wasting money again?

NORA. Yes but, Torvald, this year we can really let ourselves go a little. This is the first Christmas that we have not needed to economise.

HELMER. Still, you know, we can't spend money recklessly.

NORA. Yes, Torvald, we may be a wee bit more reckless now, mayn't we? Just a tiny wee bit! You are going to have a big salary and earn lots and lots of money.

HELMER. Yes, after the New Year; but then it will be a whole quarter before the salary is due.

NORA. Pooh! we can borrow till then.

HELMER. Nora! (*Goes up to her and takes her playfully by the ear.*) The same little featherhead! Suppose, now, that I borrowed fifty pounds to-day, and you spent it all in the Christmas week, and then on New Year's Eve a slate fell on my head and killed me, and—

NORA (*putting her hands over his mouth*). Oh! don't say such horrid things.

HELMER. Still, suppose that happened,—what then?

NORA. If that were to happen, I don't suppose I should care whether I owed money or not.

HELMER. Yes, but what about the people who had lent it?

NORA. They? Who would bother about them? I should not know who they were.

HELMER. That is like a woman! But seriously, Nora, you know what I think about that. No debt, no borrowing. There can be no freedom or beauty about a home life that depends on borrowing and debt. We two have kept bravely on the straight road so far, and we will go on the same way for the short time longer that there need be any struggle.

NORA (*moving towards the stove*). As you please, Torvald.

HELMER (*following her*). Come, come, my little skylark must not droop her wings. What is this! Is my little squirrel out of temper? (*Taking out his purse.*) Nora, what do you think I have got here?

NORA (*turning round quickly*). Money!

HELMER. There you are. (*Gives her some money.*) Do you

think I don't know what a lot is wanted for housekeeping at Christmas-time?

NORA (*counting*). Ten shillings—a pound—two pounds! Thank you, thank you, Torvald; that will keep me going for a long time.

HELMER. Indeed it must.

NORA. Yes, yes, it will. But come here and let me show you what I have bought. And all so cheap! Look, here is a new suit for Ivar, and a sword; and a horse and a trumpet for Bob; and a doll and dolly's bedstead for Emmy,—they are very plain, but anyway she will soon break them in pieces. And here are dress-lengths and handkerchiefs for the maids; old Anne ought really to have something better.

HELMER. And what is in this parcel?

NORA (*crying out*). No, no! you mustn't see that till this evening.

HELMER. Very well. But now tell me, you extravagant little person, what would you like for yourself?

NORA. For myself? Oh, I am sure I don't want anything.

HELMER. Yes, but you must. Tell me something reasonable that you would particularly like to have.

NORA. No, I really can't think of anything—unless, Torvald—

HELMER. Well?

NORA (*playing with his coat buttons, and without raising her eyes to his*). If you really want to give me something, you might—you might—

HELMER. Well, out with it!

NORA (*speaking quickly*). You might give me money, Torvald. Only just as much as you can afford; and then one of these days I will buy something with it.

HELMER. But, Nora—

NORA. Oh, do! dear Torvald; please, please do! Then I will wrap it up in beautiful gilt paper and hang it on the Christmas Tree. Wouldn't that be fun?

HELMER. What are little people called that are always wasting money?

NORA. Spendthrifts—I know. Let us do as you suggest, Torvald, and then I shall have time to think what I am most in want of. That is a very sensible plan, isn't it?

HELMER (*smiling*). Indeed it is—that is to say, if you were really to save out of the money I give you, and then really buy something for yourself. But if you spend it all on the housekeeping and any number of unnecessary things, then I merely have to pay up again.

NORA. Oh but, Torvald—

HELMER. You can't deny it, my dear little Nora. (*Puts his*

arm round her waist.) It's a sweet little spendthrift, but she uses up a deal of money. One would hardly believe how expensive such little persons are!

NORA. It's a shame to say that. I do really save all I can.

HELMER (*laughing*). That's very true,—all you can. But you can't save anything!

NORA (*smiling quietly and happily*). You haven't any idea how many expenses we skylarks and squirrels have, Torvald.

HELMER. You are an odd little soul. Very like your father. You always find some new way of wheedling money out of me, and, as soon as you have got it, it seems to melt in your hands. You never know where it has gone. Still, one must take you as you are. It is in the blood; for indeed it is true that you can inherit these things, Nora.

NORA. Ah, I wish I had inherited many of papa's qualities.

HELMER. And I would not wish you to be anything but just what you are, my sweet little skylark. But, do you know, it strikes me that you are looking rather—what shall I say—rather uneasy to-day?

NORA. Do I?

HELMER. You do, really. Look straight at me.

NORA (*looks at him*). Well?

HELMER (*wagging his finger at her*). Hasn't Miss Sweet-Tooth been breaking rules in town to-day?

NORA. No; what makes you think that?

HELMER. Hasn't she paid a visit to the confectioner's?

NORA. No, I assure you, Torvald—

HELMER. Not been nibbling sweets?

NORA. No, certainly not.

HELMER. Not even taken a bite at a macaroon or two?

NORA. No, Torvald, I assure you really—

HELMER. There, there, of course I was only joking.

NORA (*going to the table on the right*). I should not think of going against your wishes.

HELMER. No, I am sure of that; besides, you gave me your word—(*Going up to her.*) Keep your little Christmas secrets to yourself, my darling. They will all be revealed to-night when the Christmas Tree is lit, no doubt.

NORA. Did you remember to invite Doctor Rank?

HELMER. No. But there is no need; as a matter of course he will come to dinner with us. However, I will ask him when he comes in this morning. I have ordered some good wine. Nora, you can't think how I am looking forward to this evening.

NORA. So am I! And how the children will enjoy themselves, Torvald!

HELMER. It is splendid to feel that one has a perfectly safe appointment, and a big enough income. It's delightful to think of, isn't it?

NORA. It's wonderful!

HELMER. Do you remember last Christmas? For a full three weeks beforehand you shut yourself up every evening till long after midnight, making ornaments for the Christmas Tree, and all the other fine things that were to be a surprise to us. It was the dullest three weeks I ever spent!

NORA. I didn't find it dull.

HELMER (*smiling*). But there was precious little result, Nora.

NORA. Oh, you shouldn't tease me about that again. How could I help the cat's going in and tearing everything to pieces?

HELMER. Of course you couldn't, poor little girl. You had the best of intentions to please us all, and that's the main thing. But it is a good thing that our hard times are over.

NORA. Yes, it is really wonderful.

HELMER. This time I needn't sit here and be dull all alone, and you needn't ruin your dear eyes and your pretty little hands—

NORA (*clapping her hands*). No, Torvald, I needn't any longer, need I! It's wonderfully lovely to hear you say so! (*Taking his arm.*) Now I will tell you how I have been thinking we ought to arrange things, Torvald. As soon as Christmas is over—(*A bell rings in the hall.*) There's the bell. (*She tidies the room a little.*) There's some one at the door. What a nuisance!

HELMER. If it is a caller, remember I am not at home.

MAID (*in the doorway*). A lady to see you, ma'am,—a stranger.

NORA. Ask her to come in.

MAID (*to* HELMER). The doctor came at the same time, sir.

HELMER. Did he go straight into my room?

MAID. Yes, sir.

(HELMER *goes into his room. The* MAID *ushers in* MRS. LINDE, *who is in travelling dress, and shuts the door.*)

MRS. LINDE (*in a dejected and timid voice*). How do you do, Nora?

NORA (*doubtfully*). How do you do—

MRS. LINDE. You don't recognise me, I suppose.

NORA. No, I don't know—yes, to be sure, I seem to— (*Suddenly.*) Yes! Christine! Is it really you?

MRS. LINDE. Yes, it is I.

NORA. Christine! To think of my not recognising you! And yet how could I— (*In a gentle voice.*) How you have altered, Christine!

MRS. LINDE. Yes, I have indeed. In nine, ten long years—

NORA. Is it so long since we met? I suppose it is. The last eight years have been a happy time for me, I can tell you. And so now you have come into the town, and have taken this long journey in winter—that was plucky of you.

MRS. LINDE. I arrived by steamer this morning.

NORA. To have some fun at Christmas-time, of course. How delightful! We will have such fun together! But take off your things. You are not cold, I hope. (*Helps her.*) Now we will sit down by the stove, and be cosy. No, take this arm-chair; I will sit here in the rocking-chair. (*Takes her hands.*) Now you look like your old self again; it was only the first moment—You are a little paler, Christine, and perhaps a little thinner.

MRS. LINDE. And much, much older, Nora.

NORA. Perhaps a little older; very, very little; certainly not much. (*Stops suddenly and speaks seriously.*) What a thoughtless creature I am, chattering away like this. My poor, dear Christine, do forgive me.

MRS. LINDE. What do you mean, Nora?

NORA (*gently*). Poor Christine, you are a widow.

MRS. LINDE. Yes; it is three years ago now.

NORA. Yes, I knew; I saw it in the papers. I assure you, Christine, I meant ever so often to write to you at the time, but I always put it off and something always prevented me.

MRS. LINDE. I quite understand, dear.

NORA. It was very bad of me, Christine. Poor thing, how you must have suffered. And he left you nothing?

MRS. LINDE. No.

NORA. And no children?

MRS. LINDE. No.

NORA. Nothing at all, then.

MRS. LINDE. Not even any sorrow or grief to live upon.

NORA (*looking incredulously at her.*) But, Christine, is that possible?

MRS. LINDE (*smiles sadly and strokes her hair.*) It sometimes happens, Nora.

NORA. So you are quite alone. How dreadfully sad that must be. I have three lovely children. You can't see them just now, for they are out with their nurse. But now you must tell me all about it.

MRS. LINDE. No, no; I want to hear about you.

NORA. No, you must begin. I mustn't be selfish to-day; to-day I must only think of your affairs. But there is one thing I must tell you. Do you know we have just had a great piece of good luck?

MRS. LINDE. No, what is it?

Nora. Just fancy, my husband has been made manager of the Bank!

Mrs. Linde. Your husband? What good luck!

Nora. Yes, tremendous! A barrister's profession is such an uncertain thing, especially if he won't undertake unsavoury cases; and naturally Torvald has never been willing to do that, and I quite agree with him. You may imagine how pleased we are! He is to take up his work in the Bank at the New Year, and then he will have a big salary and lots of commissions. For the future we can live quite differently— we can do just as we like. I feel so relieved and so happy, Christine! It will be splendid to have heaps of money and not need to have any anxiety, won't it?

Mrs. Linde. Yes, anyhow I think it would be delightful to have what one needs.

Nora. No, not only what one needs, but heaps and heaps of money.

Mrs. Linde (smiling). Nora, Nora, haven't you learnt sense yet? In our schooldays you were a great spendthrift.

Nora (laughing). Yes, that is what Torvald says now. (Wags her finger at her.) But "Nora, Nora" is not so silly as you think. We have not been in a position for me to waste money. We have both had to work.

Mrs. Linde. You too?

Nora. Yes; odds and ends, needlework, crotchet-work, embroidery, and that kind of thing. (Dropping her voice.) And other things as well. You know Torvald left his office when we were married? There was no prospect of promotion there, and he had to try and earn more than before. But during the first year he over-worked himself dreadfully. You see, he had to make money every way he could, and he worked early and late; but he couldn't stand it, and fell dreadfully ill, and the doctors said it was necessary for him to go south.

Mrs. Linde. You spent a whole year in Italy, didn't you?

Nora. Yes. It was no easy matter to get away, I can tell you. It was just after Ivar was born; but naturally we had to go. It was a wonderfully beautiful journey, and it saved Torvald's life. But it cost a tremendous lot of money, Christine.

Mrs. Linde. So I should think.

Nora. It cost about two hundred and fifty pounds. That's a lot, isn't it?

Mrs. Linde. Yes, and in emergencies like that it is lucky to have the money.

Nora. I ought to tell you that we had it from papa.

Mrs. Linde. Oh, I see. It was just about that time that he died, wasn't it?

NORA. Yes; and, just think of it, I couldn't go and nurse him. I was expecting little Ivar's birth every day and I had my poor sick Torvald to look after. My dear, kind father— I never saw him again, Christine. That was the saddest time I have known since our marriage.

MRS. LINDE. I know how fond you were of him. And then you went off to Italy?

NORA. Yes; you see we had money then, and the doctors insisted on our going, so we started a month later.

MRS. LINDE. And your husband came back quite well?

NORA. As sound as a bell!

MRS. LINDE. But—the doctor?

NORA. What doctor?

MRS. LINDE. I thought your maid said the gentleman who arrived here just as I did, was the doctor?

NORA. Yes, that was Doctor Rank, but he doesn't come here professionally. He is our greatest friend, and comes in at least once every day. No, Torvald has not had an hour's illness since then, and our children are strong and healthy and so am I. (*Jumps up and claps her hands.*) Christine! Christine! it's good to be alive and happy!—But how horrid of me; I am talking of nothing but my own affairs. (*Sits on a stool near her, and rests her arms on her knees.*) You mustn't be angry with me. Tell me, is it really true that you did not love your husband? Why did you marry him?

MRS. LINDE. My mother was alive then, and was bed-ridden and helpless, and I had to provide for my two younger brothers; so I did not think I was justified in refusing his offer.

NORA. No, perhaps you were quite right. He was rich at that time, then?

MRS. LINDE. I believe he was quite well off. But his business was a precarious one; and, when he died, it all went to pieces and there was nothing left.

NORA. And then?—

MRS. LINDE. Well, I had to turn my hand to anything I could find—first a small shop, then a small school, and so on. The last three years have seemed !ike one long working-day, with no rest. Now it is at an end, Nora. My poor mother needs me no more, for she is gone; and the boys do not need me either; they have got situations and can shift for themselves.

NORA. What a relief you must feel it—

MRS. LINDE. No, indeed; I only feel my life unspeakably empty. No one to live for any more. (*Gets up restlessly.*) That was why I could not stand the life in my little back-water any longer. I hope it may be easier here to find some-thing which will busy me and occupy my thoughts. If only I

could have the good luck to get some regular work—office
work of some kind—

NORA. But, Christine, that is so frightfully tiring, and you
look tired out now. You had far better go away to some
watering-place.

MRS. LINDE (*walking to the window*). I have no father to
give me money for a journey, Nora.

NORA (*rising*). Oh, don't be angry with me.

MRS. LINDE (*going up to her*). It is you that must not be
angry with me, dear. The worst of a position like mine is that
it makes one so bitter. No one to work for, and yet obliged
to be always on the look-out for chances. One must live, and
so one becomes selfish. When you told me of the happy turn
your fortunes have taken—you will hardly believe it—I was
delighted not so much on your account as on my own.

NORA. How do you mean?—Oh, I understand. You mean
that perhaps Torvald could get you something to do.

MRS. LINDE. Yes, that was what I was thinking of.

NORA. He must, Christine. Just leave it to me; I will
broach the subject very cleverly—I will think of something
that will please him very much. It will make me so happy to
be of some use to you.

MRS. LINDE. How kind you are, Nora, to be so anxious to
help me! It is doubly kind in you, for you know so little of
the burdens and troubles of life.

NORA. I—? I know so little of them?

MRS. LINDE (*smiling*). My dear! Small household cares
and that sort of thing!—You are a child, Nora.

NORA (*tosses her head and crosses the stage*). You ought
not to be so superior.

MRS. LINDE. No?

NORA. You are just like the others. They all think that I am
incapable of anything really serious—

MRS. LINDE. Come, come—

NORA. —that I have gone through nothing in this world
of cares.

MRS. LINDE. But, my dear Nora, you have just told me all
your troubles.

NORA. Pooh!—those were trifles. (*Lowering her voice.*) I
have not told you the important thing.

MRS. LINDE. The important thing? What do you mean?

NORA. You look down upon me altogether, Christine—but
you ought not to. You are proud, aren't you, of having
worked so hard and so long for your mother?

MRS. LINDE. Indeed, I don't look down on any one. But it
is true that I am both proud and glad to think that I was

privileged to make the end of my mother's life almost free from care.

NORA. And you are proud to think of what you have done for your brothers.

MRS. LINDE. I think I have the right to be.

NORA. I think so, too. But now, listen to this; I too have something to be proud and glad of.

MRS. LINDE. I have no doubt you have. But what do you refer to?

NORA. Speak low. Suppose Torvald were to hear! He mustn't on any account—no one in the world must know, Christine, except you.

MRS. LINDE. But what is it?

NORA. Come here. (*Pulls her down on the sofa beside her.*) Now I will show you that I too have something to be proud and glad of. It was I who saved Torvald's life.

MRS. LINDE. "Saved"? How?

NORA. I told you about our trip to Italy. Torvald would never have recovered if he had not gone there—

MRS. LINDE. Yes, but your father gave you the necessary funds.

NORA (*smiling*). Yes, that is what Torvald and all the others think, but—

MRS. LINDE. But—

NORA. Papa didn't give us a shilling. It was I who procured the money.

MRS. LINDE. You? All that large sum?

NORA. Two hundred and fifty pounds. What do you think of that?

MRS. LINDE. But, Nora, how could you possibly do it? Did you win a prize in the Lottery?

NORA (*contemptuously*). In the Lottery? There would have been no credit in that.

MRS. LINDE. But where did you get it from, then?

NORA (*humming and smiling with an air of mystery*). Hm, hm! Aha!

MRS. LINDE. Because you couldn't have borrowed it.

NORA. Couldn't I? Why not?

MRS. LINDE. No, a wife cannot borrow without her husband's consent.

NORA (*tossing her head*). Oh, if it is a wife who has any head for business—a wife who has the wit to be a little bit clever—

MRS. LINDE. I don't understand it at all, Nora.

NORA. There is no need you should. I never said I had borrowed the money. I may have got it some other way.

(*Lies back on the sofa.*) Perhaps I got it from some other admirer. When anyone is as attractive as I am—

MRS. LINDE. You are mad creature.

NORA. Now, you know you're full of curiosity, Christine.

MRS. LINDE. Listen to me, Nora dear. Haven't you been a little bit imprudent?

NORA (*sits up straight*). Is it imprudent to save your husband's life?

MRS. LINDE. It seems to me imprudent, without his knowledge, to—

NORA. But it was absolutely necessary that he should not know! My goodness, can't you understand that? It was necessary he should have no idea what a dangerous condition he was in. It was to me that the doctors came and said that his life was in danger, and that the only thing to save him was to live in the south. Do you suppose I didn't try, first of all, to get what I wanted as if it were for myself? I told him how much I should love to travel abroad like other young wives; I tried tears and entreaties with him; I told him that he ought to remember the condition I was in, and that he ought to be kind and indulgent to me; I even hinted that he might raise a loan. That nearly made him angry, Christine. He said I was thoughtless, and that it was his duty as my husband not to indulge me in my whims and caprices—as I believe he called them. Very well, I thought, you must be saved—and that was how I came to devise a way out of the difficulty—

MRS. LINDE. And did your husband never get to know from your father that the money had not come from him?

NORA. No, never. Papa died just at that time. I had meant to let him into the secret and beg him never to reveal it. But he was so ill then—alas, there never was any need to tell him.

MRS. LINDE. And since then have you never told your secret to your husband?

NORA. Good Heavens, no! How could you think so? A man who has such strong opinions about these things! And besides, how painful and humiliating it would be for Torvald, with his manly independence, to know that he owed me anything! It would upset our mutual relations altogether; our beautiful happy home would no longer be what it is now.

MRS. LINDE. Do you mean never to tell him about it?

NORA (*meditatively, and with a half smile*). Yes—some day, perhaps, after many years, when I am no longer as nice-looking as I am now. Don't laugh at me! I mean, of course, when Torvald is no longer as devoted to me as he is now; when my dancing and dressing-up and reciting have palled on him; then it may be a good thing to have something in reserve—(*Breaking off.*) What nonsense! The time will never come. Now, what do you think of my great secret, Christine? Do you still think I am of no use? I can tell you, too, that this affair has caused me a lot of worry. It has been by no means easy for me to meet my engagements punctually. I may tell you that there is something that is called, in business, quarterly interest, and another thing called payment in instalments, and it is always so dreadfully difficult to manage them. I have had to save a little here and there, where I could, you understand. I have not been able to put aside much from my housekeeping money, for Torvald must have a good table. I couldn't let my children be shabbily dressed; I have felt obliged to use up all he gave me for them, the sweet little darlings!

MRS. LINDE. So it has all had to come out of your own necessaries of life, poor Nora?

NORA. Of course. Besides, I was the one responsible for it. Whenever Torvald has given me money for new dresses and such things, I have never spent more than half of it; I have always bought the simplest and cheapest things. Thank Heaven, any clothes look well on me, and so Torvald has never noticed it. But it was often very hard on me, Christine —because it is delightful to be really well dressed, isn't it?

MRS. LINDE. Quite so.

NORA. Well, then I have found other ways of earning money. Last winter I was lucky enough to get a lot of copying to do; so I locked myself up and sat writing every evening until quite late at night. Many a time I was desperately tired; but all the same it was a tremendous pleasure to sit there working and earning money. It was like being a man.

MRS. LINDE. How much have you been able to pay off in that way?

NORA. I can't tell you exactly. You see, it is very difficult to keep an account of a business matter of that kind. I only know that I have paid every penny that I could scrape together. Many a time I was at my wits' end. (*Smiles.*) Then I used to sit here and imagine that a rich old gentleman had fallen in love with me—

MRS. LINDE. What! Who was it?

NORA. Be quiet!—that he had died; and that when his will was opened it contained, written in big letters, the instruction: "The lovely Mrs. Nora Helmer is to have all I possess paid over to her at once in cash."

MRS. LINDE. But, my dear Nora—who could the man be?

NORA. Good gracious, can't you understand? There was no old gentleman at all; it was only something that I used to sit here and imagine, when I couldn't think of any way of procuring money. But it's all the same now; the tiresome old person can stay where he is, as far as I am concerned; I don't care about him or his will either, for I am free from care now. (*Jumps up.*) My goodness, it's delightful to think of, Christine! Free from care! To be able to be free from care, quite free from care; to be able to play and romp with the children; to be able to keep the house beautifully and have everything just as Torvald likes it! And, think of it, soon the spring will come and the big blue sky! Perhaps we shall be able to take a little trip—perhaps I shall see the sea again! Oh, it's a wonderful thing to be alive and be happy. (*A bell is heard in the hall.*)

MRS. LINDE (*rising*). There is the bell; perhaps I had better go.

NORA. No, don't go; no one will come in here; it is sure to be for Torvald.

SERVANT (*at the hall door*). Excuse me, ma'am—there is a gentleman to see the master, and as the doctor is with him—

NORA. Who is it?

KROGSTAD (*at the door*). It is I, Mrs. Helmer. (MRS. LINDE *starts, trembles, and turns to the window.*)

NORA (*takes a step towards him, and speaks in a strained, low voice*). You? What is it? What do you want to see my husband about?

KROGSTAD. Bank business—in a way. I have a small post in the Bank, and I hear your husband is to be our chief now—

NORA. Then it is—

KROGSTAD. Nothing but dry business matters, Mrs. Helmer; absolutely nothing else.

NORA. Be so good as to go into the study, then. (*She bows indifferently to him and shuts the door into the hall; then comes back and makes up the fire in the stove.*)

MRS. LINDE. Nora—who was that man?

NORA. A lawyer, of the name of Krogstad.

MRS. LINDE. Then it really was he.

NORA. Do you know the man?

MRS. LINDE. I used to—many years ago. At one time he was a solicitor's clerk in our town.

NORA. Yes, he was.

MRS. LINDE. He is greatly altered.

NORA. He made a very unhappy marriage.

MRS. LINDE. He is a widower now, isn't he?

NORA. With several children. There now, it is burning up. (*Shuts the door of the stove and moves the rocking-chair aside.*)

MRS. LINDE. They say he carries on various kinds of business.

NORA. Really! Perhaps he does; I don't know anything

about it. But don't let us think of business; it is so tiresome.

DOCTOR RANK (*comes out of* HELMER'S *study. Before he shuts the door he calls to him*). No, my dear fellow, I won't disturb you; I would rather go in to your wife for a little while. (*Shuts the door and sees* MRS. LINDE.) I beg your pardon; I am afraid I am disturbing you too.

NORA. No, not at all. (*Introducing him*). Doctor Rank, Mrs. Linde.

RANK. I have often heard Mrs. Linde's name mentioned here. I think I passed you on the stairs when I arrived, Mrs. Linde?

MRS. LINDE. Yes, I go up very slowly; I can't manage stairs well.

RANK. Ah! some slight internal weakness?

MRS. LINDE. No, the fact is I have been overworking myself.

RANK. Nothing more than that? Then I suppose you have come to town to amuse yourself with our entertainments?

MRS. LINDE. I have come to look for work.

RANK. Is that a good cure for overwork?

MRS. LINDE. One must live, Doctor Rank.

RANK. Yes, the general opinion seems to be that it is necessary.

NORA. Look here, Doctor Rank—you know you want to live.

RANK. Certainly. However wretched I may feel, I want to prolong the agony as long as possible. All my patients are like that. And so are those who are morally diseased; one of them, and a bad case too, is at this very moment with Helmer—

MRS. LINDE (*sadly*). Ah!

NORA. Whom do you mean?

RANK. A lawyer by the name of Krogstad, a fellow you don't know at all. He suffers from a diseased moral character, Mrs. Helmer; but even he began talking of its being highly important that he should live.

NORA. Did he? What did he want to speak to Torvald about?

RANK. I have no idea; I only heard that it was something about the Bank.

NORA. I didn't know this—what's his name—Krogstad had anything to do with the Bank.

RANK. Yes, he has some sort of appointment there. (*To* MRS. LINDE.) I don't know whether you find also in your part of the world that there are certain people who go zealously snuffing about to smell out moral corruption, and, as soon as they have found some, put the person concerned into some lucrative position where they can keep their eye on him. Healthy natures are left out in the cold.

MRS. LINDE. Still I think the sick are those who most need taking care of.

RANK (*shrugging his shoulders*). Yes, there you are. That is the sentiment that is turning Society into a sick-house.

(NORA, *who has been absorbed in her thoughts, breaks out into smothered laughter and claps her hands.*)

RANK. Why do you laugh at that? Have you any notion what Society really is?

NORA. What do I care about tiresome Society? I am laughing at something quite different, something extremely amusing. Tell me, Doctor Rank, are all the people who are employed in the Bank dependent on Torvald now?

RANK. Is that what you find so extremely amusing?

NORA (*smiling and humming*). That's my affair! (*Walking about the room.*) It's perfectly glorious to think that we have —that Torvald has so much power over so many people. (*Takes the packet from her pocket.*) Doctor Rank, what do you say to a macaroon?

RANK. What, macaroons? I thought they were forbidden here.

NORA. Yes, but these are some Christine gave me.

MRS. LINDE. What! I?—

NORA. Oh, well, don't be alarmed! You couldn't know that Torvald had forbidden them. I must tell you that he is afraid they will spoil my teeth. But, bah!—once in a way—That's so, isn't it, Doctor Rank? By your leave! (*Puts a macaroon into his mouth.*) You must have one too, Christine. And I shall have one, just a little one—or at most two. (*Walking about.*) I am tremendously happy. There is just one thing in the world now that I should dearly love to do.

RANK. Well, what is that?

NORA. It's something I should dearly love to say, if Torvald could hear me.

RANK. Well, why can't you say it?

NORA. No, I daren't; it's so shocking.

MRS. LINDE. Shocking?

RANK. Well, I should not advise you to say it. Still, with us you might. What is it you would so much like to say if Torvald could hear you?

NORA. I should just love to say—Well, I'm damned!

RANK. Are you mad?

MRS. LINDE. Nora, dear—!

RANK. Say it, here he is!

NORA (*hiding the packet*). Hush! Hush! Hush! (HELMER *comes out of his room, with his coat over his arm and his hat in his hand.*)

NORA. Well, Torvald dear, have you got rid of him?

HELMER. Yes, he has just gone.

NORA. Let me introduce you—this is Christine, who has come to town.

HELMER. Christine—? Excuse me, but I don't know—

NORA. Mrs. Linde, dear; Christine Linde.

HELMER. Of course. A school friend of my wife's, I presume?

MRS. LINDE. Yes, we have known each other since then.

NORA. And just think, she has taken a long journey in order to see you.

HELMER. What do you mean?

MRS. LINDE. No, really, I—

NORA. Christine is tremendously clever at book-keeping, and she is frightfully anxious to work under some clever man, so as to perfect herself—

HELMER. Very sensible, Mrs. Linde.

NORA. And when she heard you had been appointed manager of the Bank—the news was telegraphed, you know—she travelled here as quick as she could. Torvald, I am sure you will be able to do something for Christine, for my sake, won't you?

HELMER. Well, it is not altogether impossible. I presume you are a widow, Mrs. Linde?

MRS. LINDE. Yes.

HELMER. And have had some experience of book-keeping?

MRS. LINDE. Yes, a fair amount.

HELMER. Ah! well, it's very likely I may be able to find something for you—

NORA (*clapping her hands*). What did I tell you? What did I tell you?

HELMER. You have just come at a fortunate moment, Mrs. Linde.

MRS. LINDE. How am I to thank you?

HELMER. There is no need. (*Puts on his coat.*) But to-day you must excuse me—

RANK. Wait a minute; I will come with you. (*Brings his fur coat from the hall and warms it at the fire.*)

NORA. Don't be long away, Torvald dear.

HELMER. About an hour, not more.

NORA. Are you going too, Christine?

MRS. LINDE (*putting on her cloak*). Yes, I must go and look for a room.

HELMER. Oh, well then, we can walk down the street together.

NORA (*helping her*). What a pity it is we are so short of space here; I am afraid it is impossible for us—

MRS. LINDE. Please don't think of it! Good-bye, Nora dear, and many thanks.

NORA. Good-bye for the present. Of course you will come back this evening. And you too, Dr. Rank. What do you say? If you are well enough? Oh, you must be! Wrap yourself up well. (*They go to the door all talking together. Children's voices are heard on the staircase.*)

NORA. There they are! There they are! (*She runs to open the door. The* NURSE *comes in with the children.*) Come in! Come in! (*Stoops and kisses them.*) Oh, you sweet blessings! Look at them, Christine! Aren't they darlings?

RANK. Don't let us stand here in the draught.

HELMER. Come along, Mrs. Linde; the place will only be bearable for a mother now!

(RANK, HELMER, *and* MRS. LINDE *go downstairs. The* NURSE *comes forward with the children;* NORA *shuts the hall door.*)

NORA. How fresh and well you look! Such red cheeks!— like apples and roses. (*The children all talk at once while she speaks to them.*) Have you had great fun? That's splendid! What, you pulled both Emmy and Bob along on the sledge? —both at once?—that *was* good. You are a clever boy, Ivar. Let me take her for a little, Anne. My sweet little baby doll! (*Takes the baby from the* MAID *and dances it up and down.*) Yes, yes, mother will dance with Bob too. What! Have you been snowballing? I wish I had been there too! No, no, I will take their things off, Anne; please let me do it, it is such fun. Go in now, you look half frozen. There is some hot coffee for you on the stove.

(*The* NURSE *goes into the room on the left.* NORA *takes off the children's things and throws them about, while they all talk to her at once.*)

NORA. Really! Did a big dog run after you? But it didn't bite you? No, dogs don't bite nice little dolly children. You mustn't look at the parcels, Ivar. What are they? Ah, I daresay you would like to know. No, no—it's something nasty! Come, let us have a game! What shall we play at? Hide and Seek? Yes, we'll play Hide and Seek. Bob shall hide first. Must I hide? Very well, I'll hide first. (*She and the children laugh and shout, and romp in and out of the room; at last* NORA *hides under the table, the children rush in and out for her, but do not see her; they hear her smothered laughter, run to*

the table, lift up the cloth and find her. Shouts of laughter.
She crawls forward and pretends to frighten them. Fresh
laughter. Meanwhile there has been a knock at the hall door,
but none of them has noticed it. The door is half opened, and
KROGSTAD *appears. He waits a little; the game goes on.*)

KROGSTAD. Excuse me, Mrs. Helmer.

NORA (*with a stifled cry, turns round and gets up on to*
her knees). Ah! what do you want?

KROGSTAD. Excuse me, the outer door was ajar; I suppose
someone forgot to shut it.

NORA (*rising*). My husband is out, Mr. Krogstad.

KROGSTAD. I know that.

NORA. What do you want here, then?

KROGSTAD. A word with you.

NORA. With me?—(*To the children, gently.*) Go in to
nurse. What? No, the strange man won't do mother any
harm. When he has gone we will have another game. (*She*
takes the children into the room on the left, and shuts the
door after them.) You want to speak to me?

KROGSTAD. Yes, I do.

NORA. To-day? It is not the first of the month yet.

KROGSTAD. No, it is Christmas Eve, and it will depend on
yourself what sort of a Christmas you will spend.

NORA. What do you mean? To-day it is absolutely impossible for me—

KROGSTAD. We won't talk about that till later on. This is
something different. I presume you can give me a moment?

NORA. Yes—yes, I can—although—

KROGSTAD. Good. I was in Olsen's Restaurant and saw
your husband going down the street—

NORA. Yes?

KROGSTAD. With a lady?

NORA. What then?

KROGSTAD. May I make so bold as to ask if it was a Mrs.
Linde?

NORA. It was.

KROGSTAD. Just arrived in town?

NORA. Yes, to-day.

KROGSTAD. She is a great friend of yours, isn't she?

NORA. She is. But I don't see—

KROGSTAD. I knew her too, once upon a time.

NORA. I am aware of that.

KROGSTAD. Are you? So you know all about it; I thought
as much. Then I can ask you, without beating about the
bush—is Mrs. Linde to have an appointment in the Bank?

NORA. What right have you to question me, Mr. Krogstad?
—You, one of my husband's subordinates! But since you ask,

you shall know. Yes, Mrs. Linde *is* to have an appointment. And it was I who pleaded her cause, Mr. Krogstad, let me tell you that.

KROGSTAD. I was right in what I thought, then.

NORA (*walking up and down the stage*). Sometimes one has a tiny bit of influence, I should hope. Because one is a woman, it does not necessarily follow that—. When anyone is in a subordinate position, Mr. Krogstad, they should really be careful to avoid offending anyone who—who—

KROGSTAD. Who has influence?

NORA. Exactly.

KROGSTAD (*changing his tone*). Mrs. Helmer, you will be so good as to use your influence on my behalf.

NORA. What? What do you mean?

KROGSTAD. You will be so kind as to see that I am allowed to keep my subordinate position in the Bank.

NORA. What do you mean by that? Who proposes to take your post away from you?

KROGSTAD. Oh, there is no necessity to keep up the pretence of ignorance. I can quite understand that your friend is not very anxious to expose herself to the chance of rubbing shoulders with me; and I quite understand, too, whom I have to thank for being turned off.

NORA. But I assure you—

KROGSTAD. Very likely; but, to come to the point, the time has come when I should advise you to use your influence to prevent that.

NORA. But, Mr. Krogstad, I *have* no influence.

KROGSTAD. Haven't you? I thought you said yourself just now—

NORA. Naturally I did not mean you to put that construction on it. I! What should make you think I have any influence of that kind with my husband?

KROGSTAD. Oh, I have known your husband from our student days. I don't suppose he is any more unassailable than other husbands.

NORA. If you speak slightingly of my husband, I shall turn you out of the house.

KROGSTAD. You are bold, Mrs. Helmer.

NORA. I am not afraid of you any longer. As soon as the New Year comes, I shall in a very short time be free of the whole thing.

KROGSTAD (*controlling himself*). Listen to me, Mrs. Helmer. If necessary, I am prepared to fight for my small post in the Bank as if I were fighting for my life.

NORA. So it seems.

KROGSTAD. It is not only for the sake of the money; indeed,

that weighs least with me in the matter. There is another reason—well, I may as well tell you. My position is this. I daresay you know, like everybody else, that once, many years ago, I was guilty of an indiscretion.

NORA. I think I have heard something of the kind.

KROGSTAD. The matter never came into court; but every way seemed to be closed to me after that. So I took to the business that you know of. I had to do something; and, honestly, I don't think I've been one of the worst. But now I must cut myself free from all that. My sons are growing up; for their sake I must try and win back as much respect as I can in the town. This post in the Bank was like the first step up for me—and now your husband is going to kick me downstairs again into the mud.

NORA. But you must believe me, Mr. Krogstad; it is not in my power to help you at all.

KROGSTAD. Then it is because you haven't the will; but I have the means to compel you.

NORA. You don't mean that you will tell my husband that I owe you money?

KROGSTAD. Hm!—suppose I were to tell him?

NORA. It would be perfectly infamous of you. (*Sobbing.*) To think of his learning my secret, which has been my joy and pride, in such an ugly, clumsy way—that he should learn it from you! And it would put me in a horribly disagreeable position—

KROGSTAD. Only disagreeable?

NORA (*impetuously*). Well, do it, then!—and it will be the worse for you. My husband will see for himself what a blackguard you are, and you certainly won't keep your post then.

KROGSTAD. I asked you if it was only a disagreeable scene at home that you were afraid of?

NORA. If my husband does get to know of it, of course he will at once pay you what is still owing, and we shall have nothing more to do with you.

KROGSTAD (*coming a step nearer*). Listen to me, Mrs. Helmer. Either you have a very bad memory or you know very little of business. I shall be obliged to remind you of a few details.

NORA. What do you mean?

KROGSTAD. When your husband was ill, you came to me to borrow two hundred and fifty pounds.

NORA. I didn't know anyone else to go to.

KROGSTAD. I promised to get you that amount—

NORA. Yes, and you did so.

KROGSTAD. I promised to get you that amount, on certain conditions. Your mind was so taken up with your husband's illness, and you were so anxious to get the money for your journey, that you seem to have paid no attention to the conditions of our bargain. Therefore it will not be amiss if I remind you of them. Now, I promised to get the money on the security of a bond which I drew up.

NORA. Yes, and which I signed.

KROGSTAD. Good. But below your signature there were a few lines constituting your father a surety for the money; those lines your father should have signed.

NORA. Should? He did sign them.

KROGSTAD. I had left the date blank; that is to say, your father should himself have inserted the date on which he signed the paper. Do you remember that?

NORA. Yes, I think I remember—

KROGSTAD. Then I gave you the bond to send by post to your father. Is that not so?

NORA. Yes.

KROGSTAD. And you naturally did so at once, because five or six days afterwards you brought me the bond with your father's signature. And then I gave you the money.

NORA. Well, haven't I been paying it off regularly?

KROGSTAD. Fairly so, yes. But—to come back to the matter in hand—that must have been a very trying time for you, Mrs. Helmer.

NORA. It was, indeed.

KROGSTAD. Your fathher was very ill, wasn't he?

NORA. He was very near his end.

KROGSTAD. And died soon afterwards?

NORA. Yes.

KROGSTAD. Tell me, Mrs. Helmer, can you by any chance remember what day your father died?—on what day of the month, I mean.

NORA. Papa died on the 29th of September.

KROGSTAD. That is correct; I have ascertained it for myself. And, as that is so, there is a discrepancy (*taking a paper from his pocket*) which I cannot account for.

NORA. What discrepancy? I don't know—

KROGSTAD. The discrepancy consists, Mrs. Helmer, in the fact that your father signed this bond three days after his death.

NORA. What do you mean? I don't understand—

KROGSTAD. Your father died on the 29th of September. But, look here; your father has dated his signature the 2nd of October. It is a discrepancy, isn't it? (NORA *is silent*.) Can you explain it to me? (NORA *is still silent*.) It is a remarkable thing, too, that the words "2nd of October," as well as the year, are not written in your father's handwriting but in one that I think I know. Well, of course it can be explained; your father may have forgotten to date his signature, and someone else may have dated it haphazard before they knew of his death. There is no harm in that. It all depends on the signature of the name; and *that* is genuine, I suppose, Mrs. Helmer? It was your father himself who signed his name here?

NORA (*after a short pause, throws her head up and looks defiantly at him*). No, it was not. It was I that wrote papa's name.

KROGSTAD. Are you aware that is a dangerous confession?

NORA. In what way? You shall have your money soon.

KROGSTAD. Let me ask you a question; why did you not send the paper to your father?

NORA. It was impossible; papa was so ill. If I had asked him for his signature, I should have had to tell him what the money was to be used for; and when he was so ill himself I couldn't tell him that my husband's life was in danger—it was impossible.

KROGSTAD. It would have been better for you if you had given up your trip abroad.

NORA. No, that was impossible. That trip was to save my husband's life; I couldn't give that up.

KROGSTAD. But did it never occur to you that you were committing a fraud on me?

NORA. I couldn't take that into account; I didn't trouble myself about you at all. I couldn't bear you, because you put so many heartless difficulties in my way, although you knew what a dangerous condition my husband was in.

KROGSTAD. Mrs. Helmer, you evidently do not realise clearly what it is that you have been guilty of. But I can assure you that my one false step, which lost me all my reputation, was nothing more or nothing worse than what you have done.

NORA. You? Do you ask me to believe that you were brave enough to run a risk to save your wife's life?

KROGSTAD. The law cares nothing about motives.

NORA. Then it must be a very foolish law.

KROGSTAD. Foolish or not, it is the law by which you will be judged, if I produce this paper in court.

NORA. I don't believe it. Is a daughter not to be allowed to spare her dying father anxiety and care? Is a wife not to be allowed to save her husband's life? I don't know much about law; but I am certain that there must be laws permitting such things as that. Have you no knowledge of such laws—you who are a lawyer? You must be a very poor lawyer, Mr. Krogstad.

KROGSTAD. Maybe. But matters of business—such business as you and I have had together—do you think I don't understand that? Very well. Do as you please. But let me tell you this—if I lose my position a second time, you shall lose yours with me. (*He bows, and goes out through the hall.*)

NORA (*appears buried in thought for a short time, then tosses her head*). Nonsense! Trying to frighten me like that! —I am not so silly as he thinks. (*Begins to busy herself putting the children's things in order.*) And yet—? No, it's impossible! I did it for love's sake.

THE CHILDREN (*in the doorway on the left*). Mother, the stranger man has gone out through the gate.

NORA. Yes, dears, I know. But, don't tell anyone about the stranger man. Do you hear? Not even papa.

CHILDREN. No, mother; but will you come and play again?

NORA. No, no,—not now.

CHILDREN. But, mother, you promised us.

NORA. Yes, but I can't now. Run away in; I have such a lot to do. Run away in, my sweet little darlings. (*She gets them into the room by degrees and shuts the door on them; then sits down on the sofa, takes up a piece of needlework and sews a few stitches, but soon stops.*) No! (*Throws down the work, gets up, goes to the hall door and calls out.*) Helen! bring the Tree in. (*Goes to the table on the left, opens a drawer, and stops again.*) No, no! it is quite impossible!

MAID (*coming in with the Tree*). Where shall I put it, ma'am?

NORA. Here, in the middle of the floor.

MAID. Shall I get you anything else?

NORA. No, thank you. I have all I want.   [*Exit* MAID.

NORA (*begins dressing the tree*). A candle here—and flowers here—. The horrible man! It's all nonsense—there's nothing wrong. The Tree shall be splendid! I will do everything I can think of to please you, Torvald!—I will sing for you, dance for you—(HELMER *comes in with some papers under his arm.*) Oh! are you back already?

HELMER. Yes. Has any one been here?

NORA. Here? No.

HELMER. That is strange. I saw Krogstad going out of the gate.

NORA. Did you? Oh yes, I forgot, Krogstad was here for a moment.

HELMER. Nora, I can see from your manner that he has been here begging you to say a good word for him.

NORA. Yes.

HELMER. And you were to appear to do it of your own

accord; you were to conceal from me the fact of his having been here; didn't he beg that of you too?

NORA. Yes, Torvald, but—

HELMER. Nora, Nora, and you would be a party to that sort of thing? To have any talk with a man like that, and give him any sort of promise? And to tell me a lie into the bargain?

NORA. A lie—?

HELMER. Didn't you tell me no one had been here? (*Shakes his finger at her.*) My little song-bird must never do that again. A song-bird must have a clean beak to chirp with— no false notes! (*Puts his arm around her waist.*) That is so, isn't it? Yes, I am sure it is. (*Lets her go.*) We will say no more about it. (*Sits down by the stove.*) How warm and snug it is here! (*Turns over his papers.*)

NORA (*after a short pause, during which she busies herself with the Christmas Tree.*) Torvald!

HELMER. Yes.

NORA. I am looking forward tremendously to the fancy-dress ball at the Stenborgs' the day after to-morrow.

HELMER. And I am tremendously curious to see what you are going to surprise me with.

NORA. It was very silly of me to want to do that.

HELMER. What do you mean?

NORA. I can't hit upon anything that will do; everything I think of seems so silly and insignificant.

HELMER. Does my little Nora acknowledge that at last?

NORA (*standing behind his chair with her arms on the back of it*). Are you very busy, Torvald?

HELMER. Well—

NORA. What are all those papers?

HELMER. Bank business.

NORA. Already?

HELMER. I have got authority from the retiring manager to undertake the necessary changes in the staff and in the rearrangement of the work; and I must make use of the Christmas week for that, so as to have everything in order for the new year.

NORA. Then that was why this poor Krogstad—

HELMER. Hm!

NORA (*leans against the back of his chair and strokes his hair*). If you hadn't been so busy I should have asked you a tremendously big favour, Torvald.

HELMER. What is that? Tell me.

NORA. There is no one has such good taste as you. And I do so want to look nice at the fancy-dress ball. Torvald, couldn't you take me in hand and decide what I shall go as, and what sort of a dress I shall wear?

HELMER. Aha! so my obstinate little woman is obliged to get someone to come to her rescue?

NORA. Yes, Torvald, I can't get along a bit without your help.

HELMER. Very well, I will think it over, we shall manage to hit upon something.

NORA. That is nice of you. (*Goes to the Christmas Tree. A short pause.*) How pretty the red flowers look——. But, tell me, was it really something very bad that this Krogstad was guilty of?

HELMER. He forged someone's name. Have you any idea what that means?

NORA. Isn't it possible that he was driven to do it by necessity?

HELMER. Yes; or, as in so many cases, by imprudence. I am not so heartless as to condemn a man altogether because of a single false step of that kind.

NORA. No, you wouldn't, would you, Torvald?

HELMER. Many a man has been able to retrieve his character, if he has openly confessed his fault and taken his punishment.

NORA. Punishment—?

HELMER. But Krogstad did nothing of that sort; he got himself out of it by a cunning trick, and that is why he has gone under altogether.

NORA. But do you think it would——?

HELMER. Just think how a guilty man like that has to lie and play the hypocrite with every one, how he has to wear a mask in the presence of those near and dear to him, even before his own wife and children. And about the children—that is the most terrible part of it all, Nora.

NORA. How?

HELMER. Because such an atmosphere of lies infects and poisons the whole life of a home. Each breath the children take in such a house is full of the germs of evil.

NORA (*coming nearer him*). Are you sure of that?

HELMER. My dear, I have often seen it in the course of my life as a lawyer. Almost everyone who has gone to the bad early in life has had a deceitful mother.

NORA. Why do you only say—mother?

HELMER. It seems most commonly to be the mother's influence, though naturally a bad father's would have the same result. Every lawyer is familiar with the fact. This Krogstad, now, has been persistently poisoning his own children with lies and dissimulation; that is why I say he has lost all moral character. (*Holds out his hands to her.*) That is why my sweet little Nora must promise me not to plead his cause. Give me your hand on it. Come, come, what is this? Give me your hand. There now, that's settled. I assure you it would be quite impossible for me to work with him; I literally feel physically ill when I am in the company of such people.

NORA (*takes her hand out of his and goes to the opposite side of the Christmas Tree*). How hot it is in here; and I have such a lot to do.

HELMER (*getting up and putting his papers in order*). Yes, and I must try and read through some of these before dinner; and I must think about your costume, too. And it is just possible I may have something ready in gold paper to hang up on the Tree. (*Puts his hand on her head.*) My precious little singing-bird! (*He goes into his room and shuts the door after him.*)

NORA (*after a pause, whispers*). No, no—it isn't true. It's impossible; it must be impossible.

(*The NURSE opens the door on the left.*)

NURSE. The little ones are begging so hard to be allowed to come in to mamma.

NORA. No, no, no! Don't let them come in to me! You stay with them, Anne.

NURSE. Very well, Ma'am. (*Shuts the door.*)

NORA (*pale with terror*). Deprave my little children? Poison my home? (*A short pause. Then she tosses her head.*) It's not true. It can't possibly be true.

ACT II

(THE SAME SCENE.—*The Christmas Tree is in the corner by the piano, stripped of its ornaments and with burnt-down candle-ends on its dishevelled branches.* NORA'S *cloak and hat are lying on the sofa. She is alone in the room, walking about uneasily. She stops by the sofa and takes up her cloak.*)

NORA (*drops her cloak*). Someone is coming now! (*Goes to the door and listens.*) No—it is no one. Of course, no one will come to-day, Christmas Day—nor to-morrow either. But, perhaps—(*opens the door and looks out*). No, nothing in the letter-box; it is quite empty. (*Comes forward.*) What rubbish! of course he can't be in earnest about it. Such a thing couldn't happen; it is impossible—I have three little children.

(*Enter the* NURSE *from the room on the left, carrying a big cardboard box.*)

NURSE. At last I have found the box with the fancy dress.

NORA. Thanks; put it on the table.

NURSE (*doing so*). But it is very much in want of mending.

NORA. I should like to tear it into a hundred thousand pieces.

NURSE. What an idea! It can easily be put in order—just a little patience.

NORA. Yes, I will go and get Mrs. Linde to come and help me with it.

NURSE. What, out again? In this horrible weather? You will catch cold, ma'am, and make yourself ill.

NORA. Well, worse than that might happen. How are the children?

NURSE. The poor little souls are playing with their Christmas presents, but—

NORA. Do they ask much for me?

NURSE. You see, they are so accustomed to have their mamma with them.

29

Nora. Yes, but, nurse, I shall not be able to be so much with them now as I was before.

Nurse. Oh well, young children easily get accustomed to anything.

Nora. Do you think so? Do you think they would forget their mother if she went away altogether?

Nurse. Good heavens!—went away altogether?

Nora. Nurse, I want you to tell me something I have often wondered about—how could you have the heart to put your own child out among strangers?

Nurse. I was obliged to, if I wanted to be little Nora's nurse.

Nora. Yes, but how could you be willing to do it?

Nurse. What, when I was going to get such a good place by it? A poor girl who has got into trouble should be glad to. Besides, that wicked man didn't do a single thing for me.

Nora. But I suppose your daughter has quite forgotten you.

Nurse. No, indeed she hasn't. She wrote to me when she was confirmed, and when she was married.

Nora (*putting her arms round her neck*). Dear old Anne, you were a good mother to me when I was little.

Nurse. Little Nora, poor dear, had no other mother but me.

Nora. And if my little ones had no other mother, I am sure you would— What nonsense I am talking! (*Opens the box.*) Go in to them. Now I must—. You will see to-morrow how charming I shall look.

Nurse. I am sure there will be no one at the ball so charming as you, ma'am. (*Goes into the room on the left.*)

Nora (*begins to unpack the box, but soon pushes it away from her*). If only I dared go out. If only no one would come. If only I could be sure nothing would happen here in the meantime. Stuff and nonsense! No one will come. Only I mustn't think about it. I will brush my muff. What lovely, lovely gloves! Out of my thoughts, out of my thoughts! One, two, three, four, five, six— (*Screams.*) Ah! there is someone coming—. (*Makes a movement towards the door, but stands irresolute.*)

(*Enter* Mrs. Linde *from the hall, where she has taken off her cloak and hat.*)

Nora. Oh, it's you, Christine. There is no one else out there, is there? How good of you to come!

Mrs. Linde. I heard you were up asking for me.

Nora. Yes, I was passing by. As a matter of fact, it is something you could help me with. Let us sit down here on the sofa. Look here. To-morrow evening there is to be a fancy-dress ball at the Stenborgs', who live above us; and

Torvald wants me to go as a Neapolitan fisher-girl, and dance the Tarantella that I learnt at Capri.

MRS. LINDE. I see; you are going to keep up the character.

NORA. Yes, Torvald wants me to. Look, here is the dress; Torvald had it made for me there, but now it is all so torn, and I haven't any idea—

MRS. LINDE. We will easily put that right. It is only some of the trimming come unsewn here and there. Needle and thread? Now then, that's all we want.

NORA. It *is* nice of you.

MRS. LINDE (*sewing*). So you are going to be dressed up to-morrow, Nora. I will tell you what—I shall come in for a moment and see you in your fine feathers. But I have completely forgotten to thank you for a delightful evening yesterday.

NORA (*gets up, and crosses the stage*). Well, I don't think yesterday was as pleasant as usual. You ought to have come to town a little earlier, Christine. Certainly Torvald does understand how to make a house dainty and attractive.

MRS. LINDE. And so do you, it seems to me; you are not your father's daughter for nothing. But tell me, is Doctor Rank always as depressed as he was yesterday?

NORA. No; yesterday it was very noticeable. I must tell you that he suffers from a very dangerous disease. He has consumption of the spine, poor creature. His father was a horrible man who committed all sorts of excesses; and that is why his son was sickly from childhood, do you understand?

MRS. LINDE (*dropping her sewing*). But, my dearest Nora, how do you know anything about such things?

NORA (*walking about*). Pooh! When you have three children, you get visits now and then from—from married women, who know something of medical matters, and they talk about one thing and another.

MRS. LINDE (*goes on sewing. A short silence*). Does Doctor Rank come here every day?

NORA. Every day regularly. He is Torvald's most intimate friend, and a great friend of mine too. He is just like one of the family.

MRS. LINDE. But tell me this—is he perfectly sincere? I mean, isn't he the kind of man that is very anxious to make himself agreeable?

NORA. Not in the least. What makes you think that?

MRS. LINDE. When you introduced him to me yesterday, he declared he had often heard my name mentioned in this house; but afterwards I noticed that your husband hadn't the slightest idea who I was. So how could Doctor Rank—?

NORA. That is quite right, Christine. Torvald is so absurdly fond of me that he wants me absolutely to himself, as he says. At first he used to seem almost jealous if I mentioned any of the dear folk at home, so naturally I gave up doing so. But I often talk about such things with Doctor Rank, because he likes hearing about them.

MRS. LINDE. Listen to me, Nora. You are still very like a child in many things, and I am older than you in many ways and have a little more experience. Let me tell you this—you ought to make an end of it with Doctor Rank.

NORA. What ought I to make an end of?

MRS. LINDE. Of two things, I think. Yesterday you talked some nonsense about a rich admirer who was to leave you money—

NORA. An admirer who doesn't exist, unfortunately! But what then?

MRS. LINDE. Is Doctor Rank a man of means?

NORA. Yes, he is.

MRS. LINDE. And has no one to provide for?

NORA. No, no one; but—

MRS. LINDE. And comes here every day?

NORA. Yes, I told you so.

MRS. LINDE. But how can this well-bred man be so tactless?

NORA. I don't understand you at all.

MRS. LINDE. Don't prevaricate, Nora. Do you suppose I don't know who lent you the two hundred and fifty pounds?

NORA. Are you out of your senses? How can you think of such a thing! A friend of ours, who comes here every day! Do you realise what a horribly painful position that would be?

MRS. LINDE. Then it really isn't he?

NORA. No, certainly not. It would never have entered into my head for a moment. Besides, he had no money to lend then; he came into his money afterwards.

MRS. LINDE. Well, I think that was lucky for you, my dear Nora.

NORA. No, it would never have come into my head to ask Doctor Rank. Although I am quite sure that if I had asked him—

MRS. LINDE. But of course you won't.

NORA. Of course not. I have no reason to think it could possibly be necessary. But I am quite sure that if I told Doctor Rank—

MRS. LINDE. Behind your husband's back?

NORA. I must make an end of it with the other one, and that will be behind his back too. I *must* make an end of it with him.

MRS. LINDE. Yes, that is what I told you yesterday, but—

Nora (*walking up and down*). A man can put a thing like that straight much easier than a woman—

Mrs. Linde. One's husband, yes.

Nora. Nonsense! (*Standing still.*) When you pay off a debt you get your bond back, don't you?

Mrs. Linde. Yes, as a matter of course.

Nora. And can tear it into a hundred thousand pieces, and burn it up—the nasty dirty paper!

Mrs. Linde (*looks hard at her, lays down her sewing and gets up slowly*). Nora, you are concealing something from me.

Nora. Do I look as if I were?

Mrs. Linde. Something has happened to you since yesterday morning. Nora, what is it?

Nora (*going nearer to her*). Christine! (*Listens.*) Hush! there's Torvald come home. Do you mind going in to the children for the present? Torvald can't bear to see dress-making going on. Let Anne help you.

Mrs. Linde (*gathering some of the things together*). Certainly—but I am not going away from here till we have had it out with one another. (*She goes into the room on the left, as* Helmer *comes in from the hall.*)

Nora (*going up to* Helmer). I have wanted you so much, Torvald dear.

Helmer. Was that the dressmaker?

Nora. No, it was Christine; she is helping me to put my dress in order. You will see I shall look quite smart.

Helmer. Wasn't that a happy thought of mine, now?

Nora. Splendid! But don't you think it is nice of me, too, to do as you wish?

Helmer. Nice?—because you do as your husband wishes? Well, well, you little rogue, I am sure you did not mean it in that way. But I am not going to disturb you; you will want to be trying on your dress, I expect.

Nora. I suppose you are going to work.

Helmer. Yes. (*Shows her a bundle of papers.*) Look at that. I have just been into the bank. (*Turns to go into his room.*)

Nora. Torvald.

Helmer. Yes.

Nora. If your little squirrel were to ask you for something very, very prettily—?

Helmer. What then?

Nora. Would you do it?

Helmer. I should like to hear what it is, first.

Nora. Your squirrel would run about and do all her tricks if you would be nice, and do what she wants.

Helmer. Speak plainly.

NORA. Your skylark would chirp about in every room, with her song rising and falling—

HELMER. Well, my skylark does that anyhow.

NORA. I would play the fairy and dance for you in the moonlight, Torvald.

HELMER. Nora—you surely don't mean that request you made to me this morning?

NORA (*going near him*). Yes, Torvald, I beg you so earnestly—

HELMER. Have you really the courage to open up that question again?

NORA. Yes, dear, you *must* do as I ask; you *must* let Krogstad keep his post in the bank.

HELMER. My dear Nora, it is his post that I have arranged Mrs. Linde shall have.

NORA. Yes, you have been awfully kind about that; but you could just as well dismiss some other clerk instead of Krogstad.

HELMER. This is simply incredible obstinacy! Because you chose to give him a thoughtless promise that you would speak for him, I am expected to—

NORA. That isn't the reason, Torvald. It is for your own sake. This fellow writes in the most scurrilous newspapers; you have told me so yourself. He can do you an unspeakable amount of harm. I am frightened to death of him—

HELMER. Ah, I understand; it is recollections of the past that scare you.

NORA. What do you mean?

HELMER. Naturally you are thinking of your father.

NORA. Yes—yes, of course. Just recall to your mind what these malicious creatures wrote in the papers about papa, and how horribly they slandered him. I believe they would have procured his dismissal if the Department had not sent you over to inquire into it, and if you had not been so kindly disposed and helpful to him.

HELMER. My little Nora, there is an important difference between your father and me. Your father's reputation as a public official was not above suspicion. Mine is, and I hope it will continue to be so, as long as I hold my office.

NORA. You never can tell what mischief these men may contrive. We ought to be so well off, so snug and happy here in our peaceful home, and have no cares—you and I and the children, Torvald! That is why I beg you so earnestly—

HELMER. And it is just by interceding for him that you make it impossible for me to keep him. It is already known at the Bank that I mean to dismiss Krogstad. Is it to get about now that the new manager has changed his mind at his wife's bidding—

NORA. And what if it did?

HELMER. Of course!—if only this obstinate little person can get her way! Do you suppose I am going to make myself ridiculous before my whole staff, to let people think that I am a man to be swayed by all sorts of outside influence? I should very soon feel the consequences of it, I can tell you! And besides, there is one thing that makes it quite impossible for me to have Krogstad in the Bank as long as I am manager.

NORA. Whatever is that?

HELMER. His moral failings I might perhaps have over-looked, if necessary—

NORA. Yes, you could—couldn't you?

HELMER. And I hear he is a good worker, too. But I knew him when we were boys. It was one of those rash friendships that so often prove an incubus in after life. I may as well tell you plainly, we were once on very intimate terms with one another. But this tactless fellow lays no restraint on himself when other people are present. On the contrary, he thinks it gives him the right to adopt a familiar tone with me, and every minute it is "I say, Helmer, old fellow!" and that sort of thing. I assure you it is extremely painful to me. He would make my position in the Bank intolerable.

NORA. Torvald, I don't believe you mean that.

HELMER. Don't you? Why not?

NORA. Because it is such a narrow-minded way of looking at things.

HELMER. What are you saying? Narrow-minded? Do you think I am narrow-minded?

NORA. No, just the opposite, dear—and it is exactly for that reason.

HELMER. It's the same thing. You say my point of view is narrow-minded, so I must be so too. Narrow-minded! Very well—I must put an end to this. (*Goes to the hall door and calls.*) Helen!

NORA. What are you going to do?

HELMER (*looking among his papers*). Settle it. (*Enter* MAID.) Look here; take this letter and go downstairs with it at once. Find a messenger and tell him to deliver it, and be quick. The address is on it, and here is the money.

MAID. Very well, sir. (*Exit with the letter.*)

HELMER (*putting his papers together*). Now then, little Miss Obstinate.

NORA (*breathlessly*). Torvald—what was that letter?

HELMER. Krogstad's dismissal.

NORA. Call her back, Torvald! There is still time. Oh Torvald, call her back! Do it for my sake—for your own sake—for the children's sake! Do you hear me, Torvald? Call her back! You don't know what that letter can bring upon us.

HELMER. It's too late.

NORA. Yes, it's too late.

HELMER. My dear Nora, I can forgive the anxiety you are in, although really it is an insult to me. It is, indeed. Isn't it an insult to think that I should be afraid of a starving quill-driver's vengeance? But I forgive you nevertheless, because it is such eloquent witness to your great love for me. (*Takes her in his arms.*) And that is as it should be, my own darling Nora. Come what will, you may be sure I shall have both courage and strength if they be needed. You will see I am man enough to take everything upon myself.

NORA (*in a horror-stricken voice*). What do you mean by that?

HELMER. Everything, I say—

NORA (*recovering herself*). You will never have to do that.

HELMER. That's right. Well, we will share it, Nora, as man and wife should. That is how it shall be. (*Caressing her.*) Are you content now? There! there!—not these frightened dove's eyes! The whole thing is only the wildest fancy!—Now, you must go and play through the Tarantella and practise with your tambourine. I shall go into the inner office and shut the door, and I shall hear nothing; you can make as much noise as you please. (*Turns back at the door.*) And when Rank comes, tell him where he will find me. (*Nods to her, takes his papers and goes into his room, and shuts the door after him.*)

NORA (*bewildered with anxiety, stands as if rooted to the spot, and whispers*). He was capable of doing it. He will do it. He will do it in spite of everything.—No, not that! Never, never! Anything rather than that! Oh, for some help, some way out of it! (*The door-bell rings.*) Doctor Rank! Anything rather than that—anything, whatever it is! (*She puts her hands over her face, pulls herself together, goes to the door and opens it.* RANK *is standing without, hanging up his coat. During the following dialogue it begins to grow dark.*)

NORA. Good-day, Doctor Rank. I knew your ring. But you mustn't go in to Torvald now; I think he is busy with something.

RANK. And you?

NORA (*brings him in and shuts the door after him*). Oh, you know very well I always have time for you.

RANK. Thank you. I shall make use of as much of it as I can.

NORA. What do you mean by that? As much of it as you can?

RANK. Well, does that alarm you?

NORA. It was such a strange way of putting it. Is anything likely to happen?

RANK. Nothing but what I have long been prepared for. But I certainly didn't expect it to happen so soon.

NORA (*gripping him by the arm*). What have you found out? Doctor Rank, you must tell me.

RANK (*sitting down by the stove*). It is all up with me. And it can't be helped.

NORA (*with a sigh of relief*). Is it about yourself?

RANK. Who else? It is no use lying to one's self. I am the most wretched of all my patients, Mrs. Helmer. Lately I have been taking stock of my internal economy. Bankrupt! Probably within a month I shall lie rotting in the churchyard.

NORA. What an ugly thing to say!

RANK. The thing itself is cursedly ugly, and the worst of it is that I shall have to face so much more that is ugly before that. I shall only make one more examination of myself; when I have done that, I shall know pretty certainly when it will be that the horrors of dissolution will begin. There is something I want to tell you. Helmer's refined nature gives him an unconquerable disgust at everything that is ugly; I won't have him in my sick-room.

NORA. Oh, but, Doctor Rank—

RANK. I won't have him there. Not on any account. I bar my door to him. As soon as I am quite certain that the worst has come, I shall send you my card with a black cross on it, and then you will know that the loathsome end has begun.

NORA. You are quite absurd to-day. And I wanted you so much to be in a really good humour.

RANK. With death stalking beside me?—To have to pay this penalty for another man's sin! Is there any justice in that? And in every single family, in one way or another, some such inexorable retribution is being exacted—

NORA (*putting her hands over her ears*). Rubbish! Do talk of something cheerful.

RANK. Oh, it's a mere laughing matter, the whole thing. My poor innocent spine has to suffer for my father's youthful amusements.

NORA (*sitting at the table on the left*). I suppose you mean that he was too partial to asparagus and pâté de foie gras, don't you?

RANK. Yes, and to truffles.

NORA. Truffles, yes. And oysters too, I suppose?

RANK. Oysters, of course, that goes without saying.

NORA. And heaps of port and champagne. It is sad that all these nice things should take their revenge on our bones.

RANK. Especially that they should revenge themselves on the unlucky bones of those who have not had the satisfaction of enjoying them.

NORA. Yes, that's the saddest part of it all.

RANK (*with a searching look at her*). Hm!—

NORA (*after a short pause*). Why did you smile?

RANK. No, it was you that laughed.

NORA. No, it was you that smiled, Doctor Rank!

RANK (*rising*). You are a greater rascal than I thought.

NORA. I am in a silly mood to-day.

RANK. So it seems.

NORA (*putting her hands on his shoulders*). Dear, dear Doctor Rank, death mustn't take you away from Torvald and me.

RANK. It is a loss you would easily recover from. Those who are gone are soon forgotten.

NORA (*looking at him anxiously*). Do you believe that?

RANK. People form new ties, and then—

NORA. Who will form new ties?

RANK. Both you and Helmer, when I am gone. You yourself are already on the high road to it, I think. What did that Mrs. Linde want here last night?

NORA. Oho!—you don't mean to say you are jealous of poor Christine?

RANK. Yes, I am. She will be my successor in this house. When I am done for, this woman will—

NORA. Hush! don't speak so loud. She is in that room.

RANK. To-day again. There, you see.

NORA. She has only come to sew my dress for me. Bless my soul, how unreasonable you are! (*Sits down on the sofa.*) Be nice now, Doctor Rank, and to-morrow you will see how beautifully I shall dance, and you can imagine I am doing it all for you—and for Torvald too, of course. (*Takes various things out of the box.*) Doctor Rank, come and sit down here, and I will show you something.

RANK (*sitting down*). What is it?

NORA. Just look at those!

RANK. Silk stockings.

NORA. Flesh-coloured. Aren't they lovely? It is so dark here now, but to-morrow—. No, no, no! you must only look at the feet. Oh well, you may have leave to look at the legs too.

RANK. Hm!—

NORA. Why are you looking so critical? Don't you think they will fit me?

RANK. I have no means of forming an opinion about that.

NORA (*looks at him for a moment*). For shame! (*Hits him lightly on the ear with the stockings.*) That's to punish you. (*Folds them up again.*)

RANK. And what other nice things am I to be allowed to see?

NORA. Not a single thing more, for being so naughty. (*She looks among the things, humming to herself.*)

RANK (*after a short silence*). When I am sitting here, talking to you as intimately as this, I cannot imagine for a moment what would have become of me if I had never come into this house.

NORA (*smiling*). I believe you do feel thoroughly at home with us.

RANK (*in a lower voice, looking straight in front of him*). And to be obliged to leave it all—

NORA. Nonsense, you are not going to leave it.

RANK (*as before*). And not be able to leave behind one the slightest token of one's gratitude, scarcely even a fleeting regret—nothing but an empty place which the first comer can fill as well as any other.

NORA. And if I asked you now for a—? No!

RANK. For what?

NORA. For a big proof of your friendship—

RANK. Yes, yes!

NORA. I mean a tremendously big favour—

RANK. Would you really make me so happy for once?

NORA. Ah, but you don't know what it is yet.

RANK. No—but tell me.

NORA. I really can't, Doctor Rank. It is something out of all reason; it means advice, and help, and a favour—

RANK. The bigger a thing it is the better. I can't conceive what it is you mean. Do tell me. Haven't I your confidence?

NORA. More than any one else. I know you are my truest and best friend, and so I will tell you what it is. Well, Doctor Rank, it is something you must help me to prevent. You know how devotedly, how inexpressibly deeply Torvald loves me; he would never for a moment hesitate to give his life for me.

RANK (*leaning towards her*). Nora—do you think he is the only one—?

NORA (*with a slight start*). The only one—?

RANK. The only one who would gladly give his life for your sake.

NORA (*sadly*). Is that it?

RANK. I was determined you should know it before I went away, and there will never be a better opportunity than this. Now you know it, Nora. And now you know, too, that you can trust me as you would trust no one else.

Nora (*rises, deliberately and quietly.*) Let me pass.

Rank (*makes room for her to pass him, but sits still*). Nora!

Nora (*at the hall door*). Helen, bring in the lamp. (*Goes over to the stove.*) Dear Doctor Rank, that was really horrid of you.

Rank. To have loved you as much as any one else does? Was that horrid?

Nora. No, but to go and tell me so. There was really no need—

Rank. What do you mean? Did you know—? (MAID *enters with lamp, puts it down on the table, and goes out.*) Nora —Mrs. Helmer—tell me, had you any idea of this?

Nora. Oh, how do I know whether I had or whether I hadn't? I really can't tell you— To think you could be so clumsy, Doctor Rank! We were getting on so nicely.

Rank. Well, at all events you know now that you can command me, body and soul. So won't you speak out?

Nora (*looking at him*). After what happened?

Rank. I beg you to let me know what it is.

Nora. I can't tell you anything now.

Rank. Yes, yes. You mustn't punish me in that way. Let me have permission to do for you whatever a man may do.

Nora. You can do nothing for me now. Besides, I really don't need any help at all. You will find that the whole thing is merely fancy on my part. It really is so—of course it is! (*Sits down in the rocking-chair, and looks at him with a smile.*) You are a nice sort of man, Doctor Rank!—don't you feel ashamed of yourself, now the lamp has come?

Rank. Not a bit. But perhaps I had better go—for ever?

Nora. No, indeed, you shall not. Of course you must come here just as before. You know very well Torvald can't do without you.

Rank. Yes, but you?

Nora. Oh, I am always tremendously pleased when you come.

Rank. It is just that, that put me on the wrong track. You are a riddle to me. I have often thought that you would almost as soon be in my company as in Helmer's.

Nora. Yes—you see there are some people one loves best, and others whom one would almost always rather have as companions.

Rank. Yes, there is something in that.

Nora. When I was at home, of course I loved papa best. But I always thought it tremendous fun if I could steal down into the maids' room, because they never moralised at all, and talked to each other about such entertaining things.

RANK. I see—it is *their* place I have taken.

NORA (*jumping up and going to him*). Oh, dear, nice Doctor Rank, I never meant that at all. But surely you can understand that being with Torvald is a little like being with papa—

(*Enter* MAID *from the hall.*)

MAID. If you please, ma'am. (*Whispers and hands her a card.*)

NORA (*glancing at the card*). Oh! (*Puts it in her pocket.*)

RANK. Is there anything wrong?

NORA. No, no, not in the least. It is only something—it is my new dress—

RANK. What? Your dress is lying there.

NORA. Oh, yes, that one; but this is another. I ordered it. Torvald mustn't know about it—

RANK. Oho! Then that was the great secret.

NORA. Of course. Just go in to him; he is sitting in the inner room. Keep him as long as—

RANK. Make your mind easy; I won't let him escape. (*Goes into* HELMER'S *room.*)

NORA (*to the* MAID). And he is standing waiting in the kitchen?

MAID. Yes; he came up the back stairs.

NORA. But didn't you tell him no one was in?

MAID. Yes, but it was no good.

NORA. He won't go away?

MAID. No; he says he won't until he has seen you, ma'am.

NORA. Well, let him come in—but quietly. Helen, you mustn't say anything about it to any one. It is a surprise for my husband.

MAID. Yes, ma'am, I quite understand. (*Exit.*)

NORA. This dreadful thing is going to happen! It will happen in spite of me! No, no, no, it can't happen—it shan't happen! (*She bolts the door of* HELMER'S *room. The* MAID *opens the hall door for* KROGSTAD *and shuts it after him. He is wearing a fur coat, high boots and a fur cap.*)

NORA (*advancing towards him*). Speak low—my husband is at home.

KROGSTAD. No matter about that.

NORA. What do you want of me?

KROGSTAD. An explanation of something.

NORA. Make haste then. What is it?

KROGSTAD. You know, I suppose, that I have got my dismissal.

NORA. I couldn't prevent it, Mr. Krogstad. I fought as hard as I could on your side, but it was no good.

KROGSTAD. Does your husband love you so little, then?

He knows what I can expose you to, and yet he ventures—

NORA. How can you suppose that he has any knowledge of the sort?

KROGSTAD. I didn't suppose so at all. It would not be the least like our dear Torvald Helmer to show so much courage—

NORA. Mr. Krogstad, a little respect for my husband, please.

KROGSTAD. Certainly—all the respect he deserves. But since you have kept the matter so carefully to yourself, I make bold to suppose that you have a little clearer idea, than you had yesterday, of what it actually is that you have done?

NORA. More than you could ever teach me.

KROGSTAD. Yes, such a bad lawyer as I am.

NORA. What is it you want of me?

KROGSTAD. Only to see how you were, Mrs. Helmer. I have been thinking about you all day long. A mere cashier, a quill-driver, a—well, a man like me—even if he has a little of what is called feeling, you know.

NORA. Show it, then; think of my little children.

KROGSTAD. Have you and your husband thought of mine? But never mind about that. I only wanted to tell you that you need not take this matter too seriously. In the first place there will be no accusation made on my part.

NORA. No, of course not; I was sure of that.

KROGSTAD. The whole thing can be arranged amicably; there is no reason why anyone should know anything about it. It will remain a secret between us three.

NORA. My husband must never get to know anything about it.

KROGSTAD. How will you be able to prevent it? Am I to understand that you can pay the balance that is owing?

NORA. No, not just at present.

KROGSTAD. Or perhaps that you have some expedient for raising the money soon?

NORA. No expedient that I mean to make use of.

KROGSTAD. Well, in any case, it would have been of no use to you now. If you stood there with ever so much money in your hand, I would never part with your bond.

NORA. Tell me what purpose you mean to put it to.

KROGSTAD. I shall only preserve it—keep it in my possession. No one who is not concerned in the matter shall have the slightest hint of it. So that if the thought of it has driven you to any desperate resolution—

NORA. It has.

KROGSTAD. If you had put it in your mind to run away from your home—

NORA. I had.

KROGSTAD. Or even something worse—

NORA. How could you know that?

KROGSTAD. Give up the idea.

NORA. How did you know I had thought of *that*?

KROGSTAD. Most of us think of that at first. I did, too—but I hadn't the courage.

NORA (*faintly*). No more had I.

KROGSTAD (*in a tone of relief*). No, that's it, isn't it—you hadn't the courage either?

NORA. No, I haven't—I haven't.

KROGSTAD. Besides, it would have been a great piece of folly. Once the first storm at home is over—. I have a letter for your husband in my pocket.

NORA. Telling him everything?

KROGSTAD. In as lenient a manner as I possibly could.

NORA (*quickly*). He mustn't get the letter. Tear it up. I will find some means of getting money.

KROGSTAD. Excuse me, Mrs. Helmer, but I think I told you just now—

NORA. I am not speaking of what I owe you. Tell me what sum you are asking my husband for, and I will get the money.

KROGSTAD. I am not asking your husband for a penny.

NORA. What do you want, then?

KROGSTAD. I will tell you. I want to rehabilitate myself, Mrs. Helmer; I want to get on; and in that your husband must help me. For the last year and a half I have not had a hand in anything dishonourable, and all that time I have been struggling in most restricted circumstances. I was content to work my way up step by step. Now I am turned out, and I am not going to be satisfied with merely being taken into favour again. I want to get on, I tell you. I want to get into the Bank again, in a higher position. Your husband must make a place for me—

NORA. That he will never do!

KROGSTAD. He will; I know him; he dare not protest. And as soon as I am in there again with him, then you will see! Within a year I shall be the manager's right hand. It will be Nils Krogstad and not Torvald Helmer who manages the Bank.

NORA. That's a thing you will never see!

KROGSTAD. Do you mean that you will—?

NORA. I have courage enough for it now.

KROGSTAD. Oh, you can't frighten me. A fine, spoilt lady like you—

NORA. You will see, you will see.

KROGSTAD. Under the ice, perhaps? Down into the cold,

coal-black water? And then, in the spring, to float up to the surface, all horrible and unrecognisable, with your hair fallen out—

NORA. You can't frighten me.

KROGSTAD. Nor you me. People don't do such things, Mrs. Helmer. Besides, what use would it be? I should have him completely in my power all the same.

NORA. Afterwards? When I am no longer—

KROGSTAD. Have you forgotten that it is I who have the keeping of your reputation? (NORA *stands speechlessly looking at him.*) Well, now, I have warned you. Do not do anything foolish. When Helmer has had my letter, I shall expect a message from him. And be sure you remember that it is your husband himself who has forced me into such ways as this again. I will never forgive him for that. Good-bye, Mrs. Helmer. (*Exit through the hall.*)

NORA (*goes to the hall door, opens it slightly and listens.*) He is going. He is not putting the letter in the box. Oh no, no! that's impossible! (*Opens the door by degrees.*) What is that? He is standing outside. He is not going downstairs. Is he hesitating? Can he—? (*A letter drops into the box; then* KROGSTAD'S *footsteps are heard, till they die away as he goes downstairs.* NORA *utters a stifled cry, and runs across the room to the table by the sofa. A short pause.*)

NORA. In the letter-box. (*Steals across to the hall door.*) There it lies—Torvald, Torvald, there is no hope for us now!

(MRS. LINDE *comes in from the room on the left, carrying the dress.*)

MRS. LINDE. There, I can't see anything more to mend now. Would you like to try it on—?

NORA (*in a hoarse whisper*). Christine, come here.

MRS. LINDE (*throwing the dress down on the sofa*). What is the matter with you? You look so agitated!

NORA. Come here. Do you see that letter? There, look— you can see it through the glass in the letter-box.

MRS. LINDE. Yes, I see it.

NORA. That letter is from Krogstad.

MRS. LINDE. Nora—it was Krogstad who lent you the money!

NORA. Yes, and now Torvald will know all about it.

MRS. LINDE. Believe me, Nora, that's the best thing for both of you.

NORA. You don't know all. I forged a name.

MRS. LINDE. Good heavens—!

NORA. I only want to say this to you, Christine—you must be my witness.

MRS. LINDE. Your witness? What do you mean? What am I to—?

NORA. If I should go out of my mind—and it might easily happen—

MRS. LINDE. Nora!

NORA. Or if anything else should happen to me—anything, for instance, that might prevent my being here—

MRS. LINDE. Nora! Nora! you are quite out of your mind.

NORA. And if it should happen that there were some one who wanted to take all the responsibility, all the blame, you understand—

MRS. LINDE. Yes, yes—but how can you suppose—?

NORA. Then you must be my witness, that it is not true, Christine. I am not out of my mind at all! I am in my right senses now, and I tell you no one else has known anything about it; I, and I alone, did the whole thing. Remember that.

MRS. LINDE. I will, indeed. But I don't understand all this.

NORA. How should you understand it? A wonderful thing is going to happen!

MRS. LINDE. A wonderful thing?

NORA. Yes, a wonderful thing!—But it is so terrible, Christine; it *mustn't* happen, not for all the world.

MRS. LINDE. I will go at once and see Krogstad.

NORA. Don't go to him; he will do you some harm.

MRS. LINDE. There was a time when he would gladly do anything for my sake.

NORA. He?

MRS. LINDE. Where does he live?

NORA. How should I know—? Yes (*feeling in her pocket*), here is his card. But the letter, the letter—!

HELMER (*calls from his room, knocking at the door*). Nora!

NORA (*cries out anxiously*). Oh, what's that? What do you want?

HELMER. Don't be so frightened. We are not coming in; you have locked the door. Are you trying on your dress?

NORA. Yes, that's it. I look so nice, Torvald.

MRS. LINDE (*who has read the card*). I see he lives at the corner here.

NORA. Yes, but it's no use. It is hopeless. The letter is lying there in the box.

MRS. LINDE. And your husband keeps the key?

NORA. Yes, always.

MRS. LINDE. Krogstad must ask for his letter back unread, he must find some pretence—

NORA. But it is just at this time that Torvald generally—

MRS. LINDE. You must delay him. Go in to him in the meantime. I will come back as soon as I can. (*She goes out hurriedly through the hall door.*)

NORA (*goes to* HELMER'S *door, opens it and peeps in*). Torvald!

HELMER (*from the inner room*). Well? May I venture at last to come into my own room again? Come along, Rank, now you will see— (*Halting in the doorway.*) But what is this?

NORA. What is what, dear?

HELMER. Rank led me to expect a splendid transformation.

RANK (*in the doorway*). I understood so, but evidently I was mistaken.

NORA. Yes, nobody is to have the chance of admiring me in my dress until to-morrow.

HELMER. But, my dear Nora, you look so worn out. Have you been practising too much?

NORA. No, I have not practised at all.

HELMER. But you will need to—

NORA. Yes, indeed I shall, Torvald. But I can't get on a bit without you to help me; I have absolutely forgotten the whole thing.

HELMER. Oh, we will soon work it up again.

NORA. Yes, help me, Torvald. Promise that you will! I am so nervous about it—all the people—. You must give yourself up to me entirely this evening. Not the tiniest bit of business —you mustn't even take a pen in your hand. Will you promise, Torvald dear?

HELMER. I promise. This evening I will be wholly and absolutely at your service, you helpless little mortal. Ah, by the way, first of all I will just— (*Goes towards the hall door.*)

NORA. What are you going to do there?

HELMER. Only see if any letters have come.

NORA. No, no! don't do that, Torvald!

HELMER. Why not?

NORA. Torvald, please don't. There is nothing there.

HELMER. Well, let me look. (*Turns to go to the letter-box.* NORA, *at the piano, plays the first bars of the Tarantella.* HELMER *stops in the doorway.*) Aha!

NORA. I can't dance to-morrow if I don't practise with you.

HELMER (*going up to her*). Are you really so afraid of it, dear?

NORA. Yes, so dreadfully afraid of it. Let me practise at once; there is time now, before we go to dinner. Sit down and play for me, Torvald dear; criticise me, and correct me as you play.

HELMER. With great pleasure, if you wish me to. (*Sits down at the piano.*)

NORA (*takes out of the box a tambourine and a long variegated shawl. She hastily drapes the shawl round her. Then she springs to the front of the stage and calls out*). Now play for me! I am going to dance!

(HELMER *plays and* NORA *dances.* RANK *stands by the piano behind* HELMER, *and looks on.*)

HELMER (*as he plays*). Slower, slower!

NORA. I can't do it any other way.

HELMER. Not so violently, Nora!

NORA. This is the way.

HELMER (*stops playing*). No, no—that is not a bit right.

NORA (*laughing and swinging the tambourine*). Didn't I tell you so?

RANK. Let me play for her.

HELMER (*getting up*). Yes, do. I can correct her better then.

(RANK *sits down at the piano and plays.* NORA *dances more and more wildly.* HELMER *has taken up a position beside the stove, and during her dance gives her frequent instructions. She does not seem to hear him; her hair comes down and falls over her shoulders; she pays no attention to it, but goes on dancing. Enter* MRS. LINDE.)

MRS. LINDE (*standing as if spell-bound in the doorway.*) Oh!—

NORA (*as she dances*). Such fun, Christine!

HELMER. My dear darling Nora, you are dancing as if your life depended on it.

NORA. So it does.

HELMER. Stop, Rank; this is sheer madness. Stop, I tell you! (RANK *stops playing, and* NORA *suddenly stands still.* HELMER *goes up to her.*) I could never have believed it. You have forgotten everything I taught you.

NORA (*throwing away the tambourine*). There, you see.

HELMER. You will want a lot of coaching.

NORA. Yes, you see how much I need it. You must coach me up to the last minute. Promise me that, Torvald!

HELMER. You can depend on me.

NORA. You must not think of anything but me, either to-day or to-morrow; you mustn't open a single letter—not even open the letter-box—

HELMER. Ah, you are still afraid of that fellow—

NORA. Yes, indeed I am.

HELMER. Nora, I can tell from your looks that there is a letter from him lying there.

NORA. I don't know; I think there is; but you must not read anything of that kind now. Nothing horrid must come between us till this is all over.

RANK (*whispers to* HELMER). You mustn't contradict her.

HELMER (*taking her in his arms*). The child shall have her way. But to-morrow night, after you have danced—

NORA. Then you will be free. (*The* MAID *appears in the doorway to the right.*)

MAID. Dinner is served, ma'am.

NORA. We will have champagne, Helen.

MAID. Very good, ma'am.   [*Exit.*

HELMER. Hullo!—are we going to have a banquet?

NORA. Yes, a champagne banquet till the small hours. (*Calls out.*) And a few macaroons, Helen—lots, just for once!

HELMER. Come, come, don't be so wild and nervous. Be my own little skylark, as you used.

NORA. Yes, dear, I will. But go in now and you too, Doctor Rank. Christine, you must help me to do up my hair.

RANK (*whispers to* HELMER *as they go out*). I suppose there is nothing—she is not expecting anything?

HELMER. Far from it, my dear fellow; it is simply nothing more than this childish nervousness I was telling you of. (*They go into the right-hand room.*)

NORA. Well!

MRS. LINDE. Gone out of town.

NORA. I could tell from your face.

MRS. LINDE. He is coming home to-morrow evening. I wrote a note for him.

NORA. You should have let it alone; you must prevent nothing. After all, it is splendid to be waiting for a wonderful thing to happen.

MRS. LINDE. What is it that you are waiting for?

NORA. Oh, you wouldn't understand. Go in to them, I will come in a moment. (MRS. LINDE *goes into the dining-room.* NORA *stands still for a little while, as if to compose herself. Then she looks at her watch.*) Five o'clock. Seven hours till midnight; and then four-and-twenty hours till the next midnight. Then the Tarantella will be over. Twenty-four and seven? Thirty-one hours to live.

HELMER (*from the doorway on the right*). Where's my little skylark?

NORA (*going to him with her arms outstretched*). Here she is!

ACT III

(THE SAME SCENE.—*The table has been placed in the middle of the stage, with chairs round it. A lamp is burning on the table. The door into the hall stands open. Dance music is heard in the room above.* MRS. LINDE *is sitting at the table idly turning over the leaves of a book; she tries to read, but does not seem able to collect her thoughts. Every now and then she listens intently for a sound at the outer door.*)

MRS. LINDE (*looking at her watch*). Not yet—and the time is nearly up. If only he does not—. (*Listens again.*) Ah, there he is. (*Goes into the hall and opens the outer door carefully. Light footsteps are heard on the stairs. She whispers.*) Come in. There is no one here.

KROGSTAD (*in the doorway*). I found a note from you at home. What does this mean?

MRS. LINDE. It is absolutely necessary that I should have a talk with you.

KROGSTAD. Really? And is it absolutely necessary that it should be here?

MRS. LINDE. It is impossible where I live; there is no private entrance to my rooms. Come in; we are quite alone. The maid is asleep, and the Helmers are at the dance upstairs.

KROGSTAD (*coming into the room*). Are the Helmers really at a dance to-night?

MRS. LINDE. Yes, why not?

KROGSTAD. Certainly—why not?

MRS. LINDE. Now, Nils, let us have a talk.

KROGSTAD. Can we two have anything to talk about?

MRS. LINDE. We have a great deal to talk about.

KROGSTAD. I shouldn't have thought so.

MRS. LINDE. No, you have never properly understood me.

KROGSTAD. Was there anything else to understand except what was obvious to all the world—a heartless woman jilts a man when a more lucrative chance turns up?

MRS. LINDE. Do you believe I am as absolutely heartless as all that? And do you believe that I did it with a light heart?

KROGSTAD. Didn't you?

MRS. LINDE. Nils, did you really think that?

KROGSTAD. If it were as you say, why did you write to me as you did at the time?

MRS. LINDE. I could do nothing else. As I had to break with you, it was my duty also to put an end to all that you felt for me.

KROGSTAD (*wringing his hands*). So that was it. And all this—only for the sake of money!

MRS. LINDE. You must not forget that I had a helpless mother and two little brothers. We couldn't wait for you, Nils; your prospects seemed hopeless then.

KROGSTAD. That may be so, but you had no right to throw me over for anyone else's sake.

MRS. LINDE. Indeed I don't know. Many a time did I ask myself if I had the right to do it.

KROGSTAD (*more gently*). When I lost you, it was as if all the solid ground went from under my feet. Look at me now— I am a shipwrecked man clinging to a bit of wreckage.

MRS. LINDE. But help may be near.

KROGSTAD. It *was* near; but then you came and stood in my way.

MRS. LINDE. Unintentionally, Nils. It was only to-day that I learnt it was your place I was going to take in the Bank.

KROGSTAD. I believe you, if you say so. But now that you know it, are you not going to give it up to me?

MRS. LINDE. No, because that would not benefit you in the least.

KROGSTAD. Oh, benefit, benefit—I would have done it whether or no.

MRS. LINDE. I have learnt to act prudently. Life, and hard, bitter necessity have taught me that.

KROGSTAD. And life has taught me not to believe in fine speeches.

MRS. LINDE. Then life has taught you something very reasonable. But deeds you must believe in?

KROGSTAD. What do you mean by that?

MRS. LINDE. You said you were like a shipwrecked man clinging to some wreckage.

KROGSTAD. I had good reason to say so.

MRS. LINDE. Well, I am like a shipwrecked woman clinging to some wreckage—no one to mourn for, no one to care for.

KROGSTAD. It was your own choice.

MRS. LINDE. There was no other choice—then.

KROGSTAD. Well, what now?

MRS. LINDE. Nils, how would it be if we two shipwrecked people could join forces?

KROGSTAD. What are you saying?

MRS. LINDE. Two on the same piece of wreckage would stand a better chance than each on their own.

KROGSTAD. Christine!

MRS. LINDE. What do you suppose brought me to town?

KROGSTAD. Do you mean that you gave me a thought?

MRS. LINDE. I could not endure life without work. All my life, as long as I can remember, I have worked, and it has been my greatest and only pleasure. But now I am quite alone in the world—my life is so dreadfully empty and I feel so forsaken. There is not the least pleasure in working for one's self. Nils, give me someone and something to work for.

KROGSTAD. I don't trust that. It is nothing but a woman's overstrained sense of generosity that prompts you to make such an offer of yourself.

MRS. LINDE. Have you ever noticed anything of the sort in me?

KROGSTAD. Could you really do it? Tell me—do you know all about my past life?

MRS. LINDE. Yes.

KROGSTAD. And do you know what they think of me here?

MRS. LINDE. You seemed to me to imply that with me you might have been quite another man.

KROGSTAD. I am certain of it.

MRS. LINDE. Is it too late now?

KROGSTAD. Christine, are you saying this deliberately? Yes, I am sure you are. I see it in your face. Have you really the courage, then—?

MRS. LINDE. I want to be a mother to someone, and your children need a mother. We two need each other. Nils, I have faith in your real character—I can dare anything together with you.

KROGSTAD (*grasps her hands*). Thanks, thanks, Christine! Now I shall find a way to clear myself in the eyes of the world. Ah, but I forgot—

MRS. LINDE (*listening*). Hush! The Tarantella! Go, go!

KROGSTAD. Why? What is it?

MRS. LINDE. Do you hear them up there? When that is over, we may expect them back.

KROGSTAD. Yes, yes—I will go. But it is all no use. Of course you are not aware what steps I have taken in the matter of the Helmers.

MRS. LINDE. Yes, I know all about that.

KROGSTAD. And in spite of that have you the courage to—?

MRS. LINDE. I understand very well to what lengths a man like you might be driven by despair.

KROGSTAD. If I could only undo what I have done!

MRS. LINDE. You cannot. Your letter is lying in the letter-box now.

KROGSTAD. Are you sure of that?

MRS. LINDE. Quite sure, but—

KROGSTAD (*with a searching look at her*). Is that what it all means?—that you want to save your friend at any cost? Tell me frankly. Is that it?

MRS. LINDE. Nils, a woman who has once sold herself for another's sake, doesn't do it a second time.

KROGSTAD. I will ask for my letter back.

MRS. LINDE. No, no.

KROGSTAD. Yes, of course I will. I will wait here till Helmer comes; I will tell him he must give me my letter back—that it only concerns my dismissal—that he is not to read it—

MRS. LINDE. No, Nils, you must not recall your letter.

KROGSTAD. But, tell me, wasn't it for that very purpose that you asked me to meet you here?

MRS. LINDE. In my first moment of fright, it was. But twenty-four hours have elapsed since then, and in that time I have witnessed incredible things in this house. Helmer must know all about it. This unhappy secret must be disclosed; they must have a complete understanding between them, which is impossible with all this concealment and falsehood going on.

KROGSTAD. Very well, if you will take the responsibility. But there is one thing I can do in any case, and I shall do it at once.

MRS. LINDE (*listening*). You must be quick and go! The dance is over; we are not safe a moment longer.

KROGSTAD. I will wait for you below.

MRS. LINDE. Yes, do. You must see me back to my door.

KROGSTAD. I have never had such an amazing piece of good fortune in my life! (*Goes out through the outer door. The door between the room and the hall remains open.*)

MRS. LINDE (*tidying up the room and laying her hat and cloak ready*). What a difference! what a difference! Some one to work for and live for—a home to bring comfort into. That I will do, indeed. I wish they would be quick and come —(*Listens.*) Ah, there they are now. I must put on my things. (*Takes up her hat and cloak.* HELMER'S *and* NORA'S *voices are heard outside; a key is turned, and* HELMER *brings* NORA *almost by force into the hall. She is in an Italian costume*

*with a large black shawl round her; he is in evening dress,
and a black domino which is flying open.*)

NORA (*hanging back in the doorway, and struggling with
him*). No, no, no!—don't take me in. I want to go upstairs
again; I don't want to leave so early.

HELMER. But, my dearest Nora—

NORA. Please, Torvald dear—please, *please*—only an hour
more.

HELMER. Not a single minute, my sweet Nora. You know
that was our agreement. Come along into the room; you are
catching cold standing there. (*He brings her gently into the
room, in spite of her resistance.*)

MRS. LINDE. Good-evening.

NORA. Christine!

HELMER. You here, so late, Mrs. Linde?

MRS. LINDE. Yes, you must excuse me; I was so anxious to
see Nora in her dress.

NORA. Have you been sitting here waiting for me?

MRS. LINDE. Yes, unfortunately I came too late, you had
already gone upstairs; and I thought I couldn't go away again
without having seen you.

HELMER (*taking off* NORA's *shawl*). Yes, take a good look
at her. I think she is worth looking at. Isn't she charming,
Mrs. Linde?

MRS. LINDE. Yes, indeed she is.

HELMER. Doesn't she look remarkably pretty? Everyone
thought so at the dance. But she is terribly self-willed, this
sweet little person. What are we to do with her? You will
hardly believe that I had almost to bring her away by force.

NORA. Torvald, you will repent not having let me stay,
even if it were only for half an hour.

HELMER. Listen to her, Mrs. Linde! She had danced her
Tarantella, and it had been a tremendous success, as it de-
served—although possibly the performance was a trifle too
realistic—a little more so, I mean, than was strictly com-
patible with the limitations of art. But never mind about that!
The chief thing is, she had made a success—she had made a
tremendous success. Do you think I was going to let her
remain there after that, and spoil the effect? No, indeed! I
took my charming little Capri maiden—my capricious little
Capri maiden, I should say—on my arm; took one quick turn
round the room; a curtsey on either side, and, as they say in
novels, the beautiful apparition disappeared. An exit ought
always to be effective, Mrs. Linde; but that is what I cannot
make Nora understand. Pooh! this room is hot. (*Throws his
domino on a chair, and opens the door of his room.*) Hullo!

it's all dark in here. Oh, of course—excuse me—. (*He goes in, and lights some candles.*)

NORA (*in a hurried and breathless whisper.*) Well?

MRS. LINDE (*in a low voice*). I have had a talk with him.

NORA. Yes, and—

MRS. LINDE. Nora, you must tell your husband all about ti.

NORA (*in an expressionless voice*). I knew it.

MRS. LINDE. You have nothing to be afraid of as far as Krogstad is concerned; but you must tell him.

NORA. I won't tell him.

MRS. LINDE. Then the letter will.

NORA. Thank you, Christine. Now I know what I must do. Hush—!

HELMER (*coming in again*). Well, Mrs. Linde, have you admired her?

MRS. LINDE. Yes, and now I will say good-night.

HELMER. What, already? Is this yours, this knitting?

MRS. LINDE (*taking it*). Yes, thank you, I had very nearly forgotten it.

HELMER. So you knit?

MRS. LINDE. Of course.

HELMER. Do you know, you ought to embroider.

MRS. LINDE. Really? Why?

HELMER. Yes, it's far more becoming. Let me show you. You hold the embroidery thus in your left hand, and use the needle with the right—like this—with a long, easy sweep. Do you see?

MRS. LINDE. Yes, perhaps—

HELMER. But in the case of knitting—that can never be anything but ungraceful; look here—the arms close together, the knitting-needles going up and down—it has a sort of Chinese effect—. That was really excellent champagne they gave us.

MRS. LINDE. Well,—good-night, Nora, and don't be self-willed any more.

HELMER. That's right, Mrs. Linde.

MRS. LINDE. Good-night, Mr. Helmer.

HELMER (*accompanying her to the door*). Good-night, good-night. I hope you will get home all right. I should be very happy to—but you haven't any great distance to go. Good-night, good-night. (*She goes out; he shuts the door after her, and comes in again.*) Ah!—at last we have got rid of her. She is a frightful bore, that woman.

NORA. Aren't you very tired, Torvald?

HELMER. No, not in the least.

NORA. Nor sleepy?

HELMER. Not a bit. On the contrary, I feel extraordinarily lively. And you?—you really look both tired and sleepy.

NORA. Yes, I am very tired. I want to go to sleep at once.

HELMER. There, you see it was quite right of me not to let you stay there any longer.

NORA. Everything you do is quite right, Torvald.

HELMER (*kissing her on the forehead*). Now my little skylark is speaking reasonably. Did you notice what good spirits Rank was in this evening?

NORA. Really? Was he? I didn't speak to him at all.

HELMER. And I very little, but I have not for a long time seen him in such good form. (*Looks for a while at her and then goes nearer to her.*) It is delightful to be at home by ourselves again, to be all alone with you—you fascinating, charming little darling!

NORA. Don't look at me like that, Torvald.

HELMER. Why shouldn't I look at my dearest treasure? —at all the beauty that is mine, all my very own?

NORA (*going to the other side of the table*). You mustn't say things like that to me to-night.

HELMER (*following her*). You have still got the Tarantella in your blood, I see. And it makes you more captivating than ever. Listen—the guests are beginning to go now. (*In a lower voice.*) Nora—soon the whole house will be quiet.

NORA. Yes, I hope so.

HELMER. Yes, my own darling Nora. Do you know, when I am out at a party with you like this, why I speak so little to you, keep away from you, and only send a stolen glance in your direction now and then?—do you know why I do that? It is because I make believe to myself that we are secretly in love, and you are my secretly promised bride, and that no one suspects there is anything between us.

NORA. Yes, yes—I know very well your thoughts are with me all the time.

HELMER. And when we are leaving, and I am putting the shawl over your beautiful young shoulders—on your lovely neck—then I imagine that you are my young bride and that we have just come from the wedding, and I am bringing you for the first time into our home—to be alone with you for the first time—quite alone with my shy little darling! All this evening I have longed for nothing but you. When I watched the seductive figures of the Tarantella, my blood was on fire; I could endure it no longer, and that was why I brought you down so early—

NORA. Go away, Torvald! You must let me go. I won't—

HELMER. What's that? You're joking, my little Nora! You

won't—you won't? Am I not your husband—? (*A knock is heard at the outer door.*)

NORA (*starting*). Did you hear—?

HELMER (*going into the hall*). Who is it?

RANK (*outside*). It is I. May I come in for a moment?

HELMER (*in a fretful whisper*). Oh, what does he want now? (*Aloud.*) Wait a minute! (*Unlocks the door.*) Come, that's kind of you not to pass by our door.

RANK. I thought I heard your voice, and felt as if I should like to look in. (*With a swift glance round.*) Ah, yes!—these dear familiar rooms. You are very happy and cosy in here, you two.

HELMER. It seems to me that you looked after yourself pretty well upstairs too.

RANK. Excellently. Why shouldn't I? Why shouldn't one enjoy everything in this world?—at any rate as much as one can, and as long as one can. The wine was capital—

HELMER. Especially the champagne.

RANK. So you noticed that too? It is almost incredible how much I managed to put away!

NORA. Torvald drank a great deal of champagne to-night too.

RANK. Did he?

NORA. Yes, and he is always in such good spirits afterwards.

RANK. Well, why should one not enjoy a merry evening after a well-spent day?

HELMER. Well spent? I am afraid I can't take credit for that.

RANK (*slapping him on the back*). But I can, you know!

NORA. Doctor Rank, you must have been occupied with some scientific investigation to-day.

RANK. Exactly.

HELMER. Just listen!—little Nora talking about scientific investigations!

NORA. And may I congratulate you on the result?

RANK. Indeed you may.

NORA. Was it favourable, then?

RANK. The best possible, for both doctor and patient—certainty.

NORA (*quickly and searchingly*). Certainty?

RANK. Absolute certainty. So wasn't I entitled to make a merry evening of it after that?

NORA. Yes, you certainly were, Doctor Rank.

HELMER. I think so too, so long as you don't have to pay for it in the morning.

RANK. Oh well, one can't have anything in this life without paying for it.

NORA. Doctor Rank—are you fond of fancy-dress balls?

RANK. Yes, if there is a fine lot of pretty costumes.

NORA. Tell me—what shall we two wear at the next?

HELMER. Little featherbrain!—are you thinking of the next already?

RANK. We two? Yes, I can tell you. You shall go as a good fairy—

HELMER. Yes, but what do you suggest as an appropriate costume for that?

RANK. Let your wife go dressed just as she is in everyday life.

HELMER. That was really very prettily turned. But can't you tell us what you will be?

RANK. Yes, my dear friend, I have quite made up my mind about that.

HELMER. Well?

RANK. At the next fancy-dress ball I shall be invisible.

HELMER. That's a good joke!

RANK. There is a big black hat—have you never heard of hats that make you invisible? If you put one on, no one can see you.

HELMER (*suppressing a smile*). Yes, you are quite right.

RANK. But I am clean forgetting what I came for. Helmer, give me a cigar—one of the dark Havanas.

HELMER. With the greatest pleasure. (*Offers him his case.*)

RANK (*takes a cigar and cuts off the end*). Thanks.

NORA (*striking a match*). Let me give you a light.

RANK. Thank you. (*She holds the match for him to light his cigar.*) And now good-bye!

HELMER. Good-bye, good-bye, dear old man!

NORA. Sleep well, Doctor Rank.

RANK. Thank you for that wish.

NORA. Wish me the same.

RANK. You? Well, if you want me to sleep well! And thanks for the light. (*He nods to them both and goes out.*)

HELMER (*in a subdued voice*). He has drunk more than he ought.

NORA (*absently*). Maybe. (HELMER *takes a bunch of keys out of his pocket and goes into the hall.*) Torvald! what are you going to do there?

HELMER. Empty the letter-box; it is quite full; there will be no room to put the newspaper in to-morrow morning.

NORA. Are you going to work to-night?

HELMER. You know quite well I'm not. What is this? Some-one has been at the lock.

NORA. At the lock—?

HELMER. Yes, someone has. What can it mean? I should

never have thought the maid—. Here is a broken hairpin. Nora, it is one of yours.

NORA (*quickly*). Then it must have been the children—

HELMER. Then you must get them out of those ways. There, at last I have got it open. (*Takes out the contents of the letter-box, and calls to the kitchen.*) Helen!—Helen, put out the light over the front door. (*Goes back into the room and shuts the door into the hall. He holds out his hand full of letters.*) Look at that—look what a heap of them there are. (*Turning them over.*) What on earth is that?

NORA (*at the window*). The letter—No! Torvald, no!

HELMER. Two cards—of Rank's.

NORA. Of Doctor Rank's?

HELMER (*looking at them*). Doctor Rank. They were on the top. He must have put them in when he went out.

NORA. Is there anything written on them?

HELMER. There is a black cross over the name. Look there —what an uncomfortable idea! It looks as if he were announcing his own death.

NORA. It is just what he is doing.

HELMER. What? Do you know anything about it? Has he said anything to you?

NORA. Yes. He told me that when the cards came it would be his leave-taking from us. He means to shut himself up and die.

HELMER. My poor old friend! Certainly I knew we should not have him very long with us. But so soon! And so he hides himself away like a wounded animal.

NORA. If it has to happen, it is best it should be without a word—don't you think so, Torvald?

HELMER (*walking up and down*). He had so grown into our lives. I can't think of him as having gone out of them. He, with his sufferings and his loneliness, was like a cloudy background to our sunlit happiness. Well, perhaps it is best so. For him, anyway. (*Standing still.*) And perhaps for us too, Nora. We two are thrown quite upon each other now. (*Puts his arms round her.*) My darling wife, I don't feel as if I could hold you tight enough. Do you know, Nora, I have often wished that you might be threatened by some great danger, so that I might risk my life's blood, and everything, for your sake.

NORA (*disengages herself, and says firmly and decidedly*). Now you must read your letters, Torvald.

HELMER. No, no; not to-night. I want to be with you, my darling wife.

NORA. With the thought of your friend's death—

HELMER. You are right, it has affected us both. Something

ugly has come between us—the thought of the horrors of death. We must try and rid our minds of that. Until then— we will each go to our own room.

NORA (*hanging on his neck*). Good-night, Torvald—Good-night!

HELMER (*kissing her on the forehead*). Good-night, my little singing-bird. Sleep sound, Nora. Now I will read my letters through. (*He takes his letters and goes into his room, shutting the door after him.*)

NORA (*gropes distractedly about, seizes* HELMER's *domino, throws it round her, while she says in quick, hoarse, spasmodic whispers*). Never to see him again. Never! Never! (*Puts her shawl over her head.*) Never to see my children again either—never again. Never! Never!—Ah! the icy, black water—the unfathomable depths—If only it were over! He has got it now—now he is reading it. Good-bye, Torvald and my children! (*She is about to rush out through the hall, when* HELMER *opens his door hurriedly and stands with an open letter in his hand.*)

HELMER. Nora!

NORA. Ah!—

HELMER. What is this? Do you know what is in this letter?

NORA. Yes, I know. Let me go! Let me get out!

HELMER (*holding her back*). Where are you going?

NORA (*trying to get free*). You shan't save me, Torvald!

HELMER (*reeling*). True? Is this true, that I read here? Horrible! No, no—it is impossible that it can be true.

NORA. It is true. I have loved you above everything else in the world.

HELMER. Oh, don't let us have any silly excuses.

NORA (*taking a step towards him*). Torvald—!

HELMER. Miserable creature—what have you done?

NORA. Let me go. You shall not suffer for my sake. You shall not take it upon yourself.

HELMER. No tragedy airs, please. (*Locks the hall door.*) Here you shall stay and give me an explanation. Do you understand what you have done? Answer me! Do you understand what you have done?

NORA (*looks steadily at him and says with a growing look of coldness in her face*). Yes, now I am beginning to understand thoroughly.

HELMER (*walking about the room*). What a horrible awakening! All these eight years—she who was my joy and pride—a hypocrite, a liar—worse, worse—a criminal! The unutterable ugliness of it all!—For shame! For shame! (*NORA is silent and looks steadily at him. He stops in front of her.*) I ought to have suspected that something of the sort would happen. I ought to have foreseen it. All your father's want of principle—be silent!—all your father's want of principle has come out in you. No religion, no morality, no sense of duty —. How I am punished for having winked at what he did! I did it for your sake, and this is how you repay me.

NORA. Yes, that's just it.

HELMER. Now you have destroyed all my happiness. You have ruined all my future. It is horrible to think of! I am in the power of an unscrupulous man; he can do what he likes with me, ask anything he likes of me, give me any orders he pleases—I dare not refuse. And I must sink to such miserable depths because of a thoughtless woman!

NORA. When I am out of the way, you will be free.

HELMER. No fine speeches, please. Your father had always plenty of those ready, too. What good would it be to me if you were out of the way, as you say? Not the slightest. He can make the affair known everywhere; and if he does, I may be falsely suspected of having been a party to your criminal action. Very likely people will think I was behind it all—that it was I who prompted you! And I have to thank you for all this—you whom I have cherished during the whole of our married life. Do you understand now what it is you have done for me?

NORA (coldly and quietly). Yes.

HELMER. It is so incredible that I can't take it in. But we must come to some understanding. Take off that shawl. Take it off, I tell you. I must try and appease him some way or another. The matter must be hushed up at any cost. And as for you and me, it must appear as if everything between us were just as before—but naturally only in the eyes of the world. You will still remain in my house, that is a matter of course. But I shall not allow you to bring up the children; I dare not trust them to you. To think that I should be obliged to say so to one whom I have loved so dearly, and whom I still—. No, that is all over. From this moment happiness is not the question; all that concerns us is to save the remains, the fragments, the appearance—

(A ring is heard at the front-door bell.)

HELMER (with a start). What is that? So late! Can the worst—? Can he—? Hide yourself, Nora. Say you are ill.

(NORA stands motionless. HELMER goes and unlocks the hall door.)

MAID (half-dressed, comes to the door). A letter for the mistress.

HELMER. Give it to me. (Takes the letter, and shuts the door.) Yes, it is from him. You shall not have it; I will read it myself.

NORA. Yes, read it.

HELMER (*standing by the lamp*). I scarcely have the courage to do it. It may mean ruin for both of us. No, I must know. (*Tears open the letter, runs his eye over a few lines, looks at a paper enclosed, and gives a shout of joy.*) Nora! (*She looks at him questioningly.*) Nora!—No, I must read it once again—. Yes, it is true! I am saved! Nora, I am saved!

NORA. And I?

HELMER. You too, of course; we are both saved, both you and I. Look, he sends you your bond back. He says he regrets and repents—that a happy change in his life—never mind what he says! We are saved, Nora! No one can do anything to you. Oh, Nora, Nora!—no, first I must destroy these hateful things. Let me see—. (*Takes a look at the bond.*) No, no, I won't look at it. The whole thing shall be nothing but a bad dream to me. (*Tears up the bond and both letters, throws them all into the stove, and watches them burn.*) There—now it doesn't exist any longer. He says that since Christmas Eve you—. These must have been three dreadful days for you, Nora.

NORA. I have fought a hard fight these three days.

HELMER. And suffered agonies, and seen no way out but—. No, we won't call any of the horrors to mind. We will only shout with joy, and keep saying, "It's all over! It's all over!" Listen to me, Nora. You don't seem to realise that it is all over. What is this?—such a cold, set face! My poor little Nora, I quite understand; you don't feel as if you could believe that I have forgiven you. But it is true, Nora, I swear it; I have forgiven you everything. I know that what you did, you did out of love for me.

NORA. That is true.

HELMER. You have loved me as a wife ought to love her husband. Only you had not sufficient knowledge to judge of the means you used. But do you suppose you are any the less dear to me, because you don't understand how to act on your own responsibility? No, no; only lean on me; I will advise you and direct you. I should not be a man if this womanly helplessness did not just give you a double attractiveness in my eyes. You must not think any more about the hard things I said in my first moment of consternation, when I thought everything was going to overwhelm me. I have forgiven you, Nora; I swear to you I have forgiven you.

NORA. Thank you for your forgiveness. (*She goes out through the door to the right.*)

HELMER. No, don't go—. (*Looks in.*) What are you doing in there?

NORA (*from within*). Taking off my fancy dress.

HELMER (*standing at the open door*). Yes, do. Try and calm yourself, and make your mind easy again, my frightened little singing-bird. Be at rest, and feel secure; I have broad wings to shelter you under. (*Walks up and down by the door.*) How warm and cosy our home is, Nora. Here is shelter for you; here I will protect you like a hunted dove that I have saved from a hawk's claws; I will bring peace to your poor beating heart. It will come, little by little, Nora, believe me. To-morrow morning you will look upon it all quite differently; soon everything will be just as it was before. Very soon you won't need me to assure you that I have forgiven you; you will yourself feel the certainty that I have done so. Can you suppose I should ever think of such a thing as repudiating you, or even reproaching you? You have no idea what a true man's heart is like, Nora. There is something so indescribably sweet and satisfying, to a man, in the knowledge that he has forgiven his wife—forgiven her freely, and with all his heart. It seems as if that had made her, as it were, doubly his own; he has given her a new life, so to speak; and she has in a way become both wife and child to him. So you shall be for me after this, my little scared, helpless darling. Have no anxiety about anything, Nora; only be frank and open with me, and I will serve as will and conscience both to you—. What is this? Not gone to bed? Have you changed your things?

NORA (*in everyday dress*). Yes, Torvald, I have changed my things now.

HELMER. But what for?—so late as this.

NORA. I shall not sleep to-night.

HELMER. But, my dear Nora—

NORA (*looking at her watch*). It is not so very late. Sit down here, Torvald. You and I have much to say to one another. (*She sits down at one side of the table.*)

HELMER. Nora—what is this?—this cold, set face?

NORA. Sit down. It will take some time; I have a lot to talk over with you.

HELMER (*sits down at the opposite side of the table*). You alarm me, Nora!—and I don't understand you.

NORA. No, that is just it. You don't understand me, and I have never understood you either—before to-night. No, you mustn't interrupt me. You must simply listen to what I say. Torvald, this is a settling of accounts.

HELMER. What do you mean by that?

NORA (*after a short silence*). Isn't there one thing that strikes you as strange in our sitting here like this?

HELMER. What is that?

NORA. We have been married now eight years. Does it not

occur to you that this is the first time we two, you and I, husband and wife, have had a serious conversation?

HELMER. What do you mean by serious?

NORA. In all these eight years—longer than that—from the very beginning of our acquaintance, we have never exchanged a word on any serious subject.

HELMER. Was it likely that I would be continually and for ever telling you about worries that you could not help me to bear?

NORA. I am not speaking about business matters. I say that we have never sat down in earnest together to try and get at the bottom of anything.

HELMER. But, dearest Nora, would it have been any good to you?

NORA. That is just it; you have never understood me. I have been greatly wronged, Torvald—first by papa and then by you.

HELMER. What! By us two—by us two, who have loved you better than anyone else in the world?

NORA (*shaking her head*). You have never loved me. You have only thought it pleasant to be in love with me.

HELMER. Nora, what do I hear you saying?

NORA. It is perfectly true, Torvald. When I was at home with papa, he told me his opinion about everything, and so I had the same opinions; and if I differed from him I concealed the fact, because he would not have liked it. He called me his doll-child, and he played with me just as I used to play with my dolls. And when I came to live with you—

HELMER. What sort of an expression is that to use about our marriage?

NORA (*undisturbed*). I mean that I was simply transferred from papa's hands into yours. You arranged everything according to your own taste, and so I got the same tastes as you—or else I pretended to, I am really not quite sure which —I think sometimes the one and sometimes the other. When I look back on it, it seems to me as if I had been living here like a poor woman—just from hand to mouth. I have existed merely to perform tricks for you, Torvald. But you would have it so. You and papa have committed a great sin against me. It is your fault that I have made nothing of my life.

HELMER. How unreasonable and how ungrateful you are, Nora! Have you not been happy here?

NORA. No, I have never been happy. I thought I was, but it has never really been so.

HELMER. Not—not happy!

NORA. No, only merry. And you have always been so kind

to me. But our home has been nothing but a playroom. I have been your doll-wife, just as at home I was papa's doll-child; and here the children have been my dolls. I thought it great fun when you played with me, just as they thought it great fun when I played with them. That is what our marriage has been, Torvald.

HELMER. There is some truth in what you say—exaggerated and strained as your view of it is. But for the future it shall be different. Playtime shall be over, and lesson-time shall begin.

NORA. Whose lessons? Mine, or the children's?

HELMER. Both yours and the children's, my darling Nora.

NORA. Alas, Torvald, you are not the man to educate me into being a proper wife for you.

HELMER. And you can say that!

NORA. And I—how am I fitted to bring up the children?

HELMER. Nora!

NORA. Didn't you say so yourself a little while ago—that you dare not trust me to bring them up?

HELMER. In a moment of anger! Why do you pay any heed to that?

NORA. Indeed, you were perfectly right. I am not fit for the task. There is another task I must undertake first. I must try and educate myself—you are not the man to help me in that. I must do that for myself. And that is why I am going to leave you now.

HELMER (springing up). What do you say?

NORA. I must stand quite alone, if I am to understand myself and everything about me. It is for that reason that I cannot remain with you any longer.

IIELMER. Nora, Nora!

NORA. I am going away from here now, at once. I am sure Christine will take me in for the night—

HELMER. You are out of your mind! I won't allow it! I forbid you!

NORA. It is no use forbidding me anything any longer. I will take with me what belongs to myself. I will take nothing from you, either now or later.

HELMER. What sort of madness is this!

NORA. To-morrow I shall go home—I mean, to my old home. It will be easiest for me to find something to do there.

HELMER. You blind, foolish woman!

NORA. I must try and get some sense, Torvald.

HELMER. To desert your home, your husband and your children! And you don't consider what people will say!

NORA. I cannot consider that at all. I only know that it is necessary for me.

HELMER. It's shocking. This is how you would neglect your most sacred duties.

NORA. What do you consider my most sacred duties?

HELMER. Do I need to tell you that? Are they not your duties to your husband and your children?

NORA. I have other duties just as sacred.

HELMER. That you have not. What duties could those be?

NORA. Duties to myself.

HELMER. Before all else, you are a wife and a mother.

NORA. I don't believe that any longer. I believe that before all else I am a reasonable human being, just as you are—or, at all events, that I must try and become one. I know quite well, Torvald, that most people would think you right, and that views of that kind are to be found in books; but I can no longer content myself with what most people say, or with what is found in books. I must think over things for myself and get to understand them.

HELMER. Can you not understand your place in your own home? Have you not a reliable guide in such matters as that?—have you no religion?

NORA. I am afraid, Torvald, I do not exactly know what religion is.

HELMER. What are you saying?

NORA. I know nothing but what the clergyman said, when I went to be confirmed. He told us that religion was this, and that, and the other. When I am away from all this, and am alone, I will look into that matter too. I will see if what the clergyman said is true, or at all events if it is true for me.

HELMER. This is unheard of in a girl of your age! But if religion cannot lead you aright, let me try and awaken your conscience. I suppose you have some moral sense? Or—answer me—am I to think you have none?

NORA. I assure you, Torvald, that is not an easy question to answer. I really don't know. The thing perplexes me altogether. I only know that you and I look at it in quite a different light. I am learning, too, that the law is quite another thing from what I supposed; but I find it impossible to convince myself that the law is right. According to it a woman has no right to spare her old dying father, or to save her husband's life. I can't believe that.

HELMER. You talk like a child. You don't understand the conditions of the world in which you live.

NORA. No, I don't. But now I am going to try. I am going to see if I can make out who is right, the world or I.

HELMER. You are ill, Nora; you are delirious; I almost think you are out of your mind.

NORA. I have never felt my mind so clear and certain as to-night.

HELMER. And is it with a clear and certain mind that you forsake your husband and your children?

NORA. Yes, it is.

HELMER. Then there is only one possible explanation.

NORA. What is that?

HELMER. You do not love me any more.

NORA. No, that is just it.

HELMER. Nora!—and you can say that?

NORA. It gives me great pain, Torvald, for you have always been so kind to me, but I cannot help it. I do not love you any more.

HELMER (*regaining his composure*). Is that a clear and certain conviction too?

NORA. Yes, absolutely clear and certain. That is the reason why I will not stay here any longer.

HELMER. And can you tell me what I have done to forfeit your love?

NORA. Yes, indeed I can. It was to-night, when the wonderful thing did not happen; then I saw you were not the man I had thought you.

HELMER. Explain yourself better. I don't understand you.

NORA. I have waited so patiently for eight years; for, goodness knows, I knew very well that wonderful things don't happen every day. Then this horrible misfortune came upon me; and then I felt quite certain that the wonderful thing was going to happen at last. When Krogstad's letter was lying out there, never for a moment did I imagine that you would consent to accept this man's conditions. I was so absolutely certain that you would say to him: Publish the thing to the whole world. And when that was done—

HELMER. Yes, what then?—when I had exposed my wife to shame and disgrace?

NORA. When that was done, I was so absolutely certain, you would come forward and take everything upon yourself, and say: I am the guilty one.

HELMER. Nora—!

NORA. You mean that I would never have accepted such a sacrifice on your part? No, of course not. But what would my assurances have been worth against yours? That was the wonderful thing which I hoped for and feared; and it was to prevent that, that I wanted to kill myself.

HELMER. I would gladly work night and day for you, Nora —bear sorrow and want for your sake. But no man would sacrifice his honour for the one he loves.

NORA. It is a thing hundreds of thousands of women have done.

HELMER. Oh, you think and talk like a heedless child.

NORA. Maybe. But you neither think nor talk like the man I could bind myself to. As soon as your fear was over—and it was not fear for what threatened me, but for what might happen to you—when the whole thing was past, as far as you were concerned it was exactly as if nothing at all had happened. Exactly as before, I was your little skylark, your doll, which you would in future treat with doubly gentle care, because it was so brittle and fragile. (*Getting up.*) Torvald—it was then it dawned upon me that for eight years I had been living here with a strange man, and had borne him three children—. Oh, I can't bear to think of it! I could tear myself into little bits!

HELMER (*sadly*). I see, I see. An abyss has opened between us—there is no denying it. But, Nora, would it not be possible to fill it up?

NORA. As I am now, I am no wife for you.

HELMER. I have it in me to become a different man.

NORA. Perhaps—if your doll is taken away from you.

HELMER. But to part!—to part from you! No, no, Nora, I can't understand that idea.

NORA (*going out to the right*). That makes it all the more certain that it must be done. (*She comes back with her cloak and hat and a small bag which she puts on a chair by the table.*)

HELMER. Nora, Nora, not now! Wait till to-morrow.

NORA (*putting on her cloak*). I cannot spend the night in a strange man's room.

HELMER. But can't we live here like brother and sister—?

NORA (*putting on her hat*). You know very well that would not last long. (*Puts the shawl around her.*) Good-bye, Torvald. I won't see the little ones. I know they are in better hands than mine. As I am now, I can be of no use to them.

HELMER. But some day, Nora—some day?

NORA. How can I tell? I have no idea what is going to become of me.

HELMER. But you are my wife, whatever becomes of you.

NORA. Listen, Torvald. I have heard that when a wife deserts her husband's house, as I am doing now, he is legally freed from all obligations towards her. In any case I set you free from all your obligations. You are not to feel yourself bound in the slightest way, any more than I shall. There must be perfect freedom on both sides. See, here is your ring back. Give me mine.

NORA. It is a thing hundreds of thousands of women have done.

HELMER. Oh, you think and talk like a heedless child.

NORA. Maybe. But you neither think nor talk like the man I could bind myself to. As soon as your fear was over—and it was not fear for what threatened me, but for what might happen to you—when the whole thing was past, as far as you were concerned it was exactly as if nothing at all had happened. Exactly as before, I was your little skylark, your doll, which you would in future treat with doubly gentle care, because it was so brittle and fragile. (*Getting up.*) Torvald—it was then it dawned upon me that for eight years I had been living here with a strange man, and had borne him three children—. Oh, I can't bear to think of it! I could tear myself into little bits!

HELMER (*sadly*). I see, I see. An abyss has opened between us—there is no denying it. But, Nora, would it not be possible to fill it up?

NORA. As I am now, I am no wife for you.

HELMER. I have it in me to become a different man.

NORA. Perhaps—if your doll is taken away from you.

HELMER. But to part!—to part from you! No, no, Nora, I can't understand that idea.

NORA (*going out to the right*). That makes it all the more certain that it must be done. (*She comes back with her cloak and hat and a small bag which she puts on a chair by the table.*)

HELMER. Nora, Nora, not now! Wait till to-morrow.

NORA (*putting on her cloak*). I cannot spend the night in a strange man's room.

HELMER. But can't we live here like brother and sister—?

NORA (*putting on her hat*). You know very well that would not last long. (*Puts the shawl around her.*) Good-bye, Torvald. I won't see the little ones. I know they are in better hands than mine. As I am now, I can be of no use to them.

HELMER. But some day, Nora—some day?

NORA. How can I tell? I have no idea what is going to become of me.

HELMER. But you are my wife, whatever becomes of you.

NORA. Listen, Torvald. I have heard that when a wife deserts her husband's house, as I am doing now, he is legally freed from all obligations towards her. In any case I set you free from all your obligations. You are not to feel yourself bound in the slightest way, any more than I shall. There must be perfect freedom on both sides. See, here is your ring back. Give me mine.

HELMER. That too?

NORA. That too.

HELMER. Here it is.

NORA. That's right. Now it is all over. I have put the keys here. The maids know all about everything in the house—better than I do. To-morrow, after I have left her, Christine will come here and pack my own things that I brought with me from home. I will have them sent after me.

HELMER. All over! All over!—Nora, shall you never think of me again?

NORA. I know I shall often think of you and the children and this house.

HELMER. May I write to you, Nora?

NORA. No—never. You must not do that.

HELMER. But at least let me send you—

NORA. Nothing—nothing—

HELMER. Let me help you if you are in want.

NORA. No. I can receive nothing from a stranger.

HELMER. Nor—can I never be anything more than a stranger to you?

NORA (*taking her bag*). Ah, Torvald, the most wonderful thing of all would have to happen.

HELMER. Tell me what that would be!

NORA. Both you and I would have to be so changed that—. Oh, Torvald, I don't believe any longer in wonderful things happening.

HELMER. But I will believe in it. Tell me! So changed that—?

NORA. That our life together would be a real wedlock. Good-bye. (*She goes out through the hall.*)

HELMER (*sinks down on a chair at the door and buries his face in his hands*). Nora! Nora! (*Looks round, and rises.*) Empty. She is gone. (*A hope flashes across his mind.*) The most wonderful thing of all—?

(*The sound of a door shutting is heard from below.*)

NORA. It is a thing hundreds of thousands of women have done.

HELMER. Oh, you think and talk like a heedless child.

NORA. Maybe. But you neither think nor talk like the man I could bind myself to. As soon as your fear was over—and it was not fear for what threatened me, but for what might happen to you—when the whole thing was past, as far as you were concerned it was exactly as if nothing at all had happened. Exactly as before, I was your little skylark, your doll, which you would in future treat with doubly gentle care, because it was so brittle and fragile. (*Getting up.*) Torvald—it was then it dawned upon me that for eight years I had been living here with a strange man, and had borne him three children—. Oh, I can't bear to think of it! I could tear myself into little bits!

HELMER (*sadly*). I see, I see. An abyss has opened between us—there is no denying it. But, Nora, would it not be possible to fill it up?

NORA. As I am now, I am no wife for you.

HELMER. I have it in me to become a different man.

NORA. Perhaps—if your doll is taken away from you.

HELMER. But to part!—to part from you! No, no, Nora, I can't understand that idea.

NORA (*going out to the right*). That makes it all the more certain that it must be done. (*She comes back with her cloak and hat and a small bag which she puts on a chair by the table.*)

HELMER. Nora, Nora, not now! Wait till to-morrow.

NORA (*putting on her cloak*). I cannot spend the night in a strange man's room.

HELMER. But can't we live here like brother and sister—?

NORA (*putting on her hat*). You know very well that would not last long. (*Puts the shawl around her.*) Good-bye, Torvald. I won't see the little ones. I know they are in better hands than mine. As I am now, I can be of no use to them.

HELMER. But some day, Nora—some day?

NORA. How can I tell? I have no idea what is going to become of me.

HELMER. But you are my wife, whatever becomes of you.

NORA. Listen, Torvald. I have heard that when a wife deserts her husband's house, as I am doing now, he is legally freed from all obligations towards her. In any case I set you free from all your obligations. You are not to feel yourself bound in the slightest way, any more than I shall. There must be perfect freedom on both sides. See, here is your ring back. Give me mine.

Ghosts

A DOMESTIC DRAMA IN THREE ACTS

With the publication of *Ghosts,* Ibsen announced himself to the world as an author not to be deterred by conventional reticence in assessing the moral health of his society. In daring to bring the theme of venereal disease into the theatre, he violated one of the major unwritten taboos of the nineteenth century. Predictably, puritanical critics responded with outrage to Ibsen's discreet references to Oswald's inherited disease. In their single-minded anger, however, they overlooked the most challenging aspect of Ibsen's drama.

As the smoke of controversy cleared in the twentieth century, it became increasingly apparent that Ibsen's real target was an entire way of life dedicated to provincial and puritanical repressiveness. The basic source of Mrs. Alving's misfortunes is not venereal disease, but the Victorian upbringing which caused her to drive her spirited young husband outside their marriage to search for "the joy of life." Her effort to conceal the failure of her marriage and the mistakes of her past by building an orphanage to the memory of her husband only marks the beginning of an inexorable chain of painful revelations which underline the defects of the Puritan tradition. As the play proceeds, Ibsen forces Mrs. Alving to condone the possibility of an incestuous love affair between her ailing husband and his own half-sister, Regina. Later, Ibsen compels Mrs. Alving to face her own son's horrifying demand that she do away with him.

Despite its controversial theme, *Ghosts* is an intricate work of art rather than a naturalistic or clinical "slice of life." Ibsen's retrospective method of exposition recalls the dramatic construction of Greek tragedy, and one can only marvel at his ability to relate present events to incidents from the past.

In his use of irony, Ibsen is not the least bit deterred by coincidences and contrivances. He makes Oswald pursue Regina just as her father had pursued her mother. He rewards Mrs. Alving's virtuous return to her husband at the request of her pastor with the birth of a syphilitic son. He replaces the Nordic weather with sunshine just as Oswald loses his mind. When, because of the carelessness of a drunken carpenter, the orphanage has burned down completely just before it is to be hypocritically dedicated to the memory of Mrs.

Alving's philandering husband, Ibsen has the carpenter himself propose to build a tavern in a red-light district and dedicate it to the memory of Mr. Alving. In a final irony, Ibsen makes the Pastor, himself, who was partly responsible for the loss of the orphan asylum, the patron of a bordello. This web of irony, in which Ibsen ensnares both victims and enforcers of conventional morality, is the most devastating aspect of his play.

DRAMATIS PERSONÆ

Mrs. Alving (a widow).
Oswald Alving (her son, an artist).
Manders (the Pastor of the parish).
Engstrand (a carpenter).
Regina Engstrand (his daughter, in Mrs. Alving's service).

(The action takes place at Mrs. Alving's house on one of the larger fjords of western Norway.)

ACT I

(SCENE.—*A large room looking upon a garden. A door in the left-hand wall, and two in the right. In the middle of the room, a round table with chairs set about it, and books, magazines and newspapers upon it. In the foreground on the left, a window, by which is a small sofa with a work-table in front of it. At the back the room opens into a conservatory rather smaller than the room. From the right-hand side of this a door leads to the garden. Through the large panes of glass that form the outer wall of the conservatory, a gloomy fjord landscape can be discerned, half obscured by steady rain.*

ENGSTRAND *is standing close up to the garden door. His left leg is slightly deformed, and he wears a boot with a clump of wood under the sole.* REGINA, *with an empty garden-syringe in her hand, is trying to prevent his coming in.*)

REGINA (*below her breath*). What is it you want? Stay where you are. The rain is dripping off you.

ENGSTRAND. God's good rain, my girl.

REGINA. The Devil's own rain, that's what it is!

ENGSTRAND. Lord, how you talk, Regina. (*Takes a few limping steps forward.*) What I wanted to tell you was this—

REGINA. Don't clump about like that, stupid! The young master is lying asleep upstairs.

ENGSTRAND. Asleep still? In the middle of the day?

REGINA. Well, it's no business of yours.

ENGSTRAND. I was out on the spree last night—

REGINA. I don't doubt it.

ENGSTRAND. Yes, we are poor weak mortals, my girl—

REGINA. We are indeed.

ENGSTRAND. —and the temptations of the world are manifold, you know—but, for all that, here I was at my work at half-past five this morning.

REGINA. Yes, yes, but make yourself scarce now. I am not going to stand here as if I had a *rendez-vous* with you.

71

ENGSTRAND. As if you had a what?

REGINA. I am not going to have any one find you here; so now you know, and you can go.

ENGSTRAND (*coming a few steps nearer*). Not a bit of it! Not before we have had a little chat. This afternoon I shall have finished my job down at the school house, and I shall be off home to town by to-night's boat.

REGINA (*mutters*). Pleasant journey to you!

ENGSTRAND. Thanks, my girl. To-morrow is the opening of the Orphanage, and I expect there will be a fine kick-up here and plenty of good strong drink, don't you know. And no one shall say of Jacob Engstrand that he can't hold off when temptation comes in his way.

REGINA. Oho!

ENGSTRAND. Yes, because there will be a lot of fine folk here to-morrow. Parson Manders is expected from town, too.

REGINA. What is more, he's coming to-day.

ENGSTRAND. There you are! And I'm going to be precious careful he doesn't have anything to say against me, do you see?

REGINA. Oh, that's your game, is it?

ENGSTRAND. What do you mean?

REGINA (*with a significant look at him*). What is it you want to humbug Mr. Manders out of, this time?

ENGSTRAND. Sh! Sh! Are you crazy? Do you suppose *I* would want to humbug Mr. Manders? No, no—Mr. Manders has always been too kind a friend for me to do that. But what I wanted to talk to you about, was my going back home to-night.

REGINA. The sooner you go, the better I shall be pleased.

ENGSTRAND. Yes, only I want to take you with me, Regina.

REGINA (*open-mouthed*). You want to take me—? What did you say?

ENGSTRAND. I want to take you home with me, I said.

REGINA (*contemptuously*). You will never get me home with you.

ENGSTRAND. Ah, we shall see about that.

REGINA. Yes, you can be quite certain we *shall* see about that. I, who have been brought up by a lady like Mrs. Alving? —I, who have been treated almost as if I were her own child?—do you suppose I am going home with *you?*—to such a house as yours? Not likely!

ENGSTRAND. What the devil do you mean? Are you setting yourself up against your father, you hussy?

REGINA (*mutters, without looking at him.*) You have often told me I was none of yours.

ENGSTRAND. Bah!—why do you want to pay any attention to that?

REGINA. Haven't you many and many a time abused me and called me a—? For shame!

ENGSTRAND. I'll swear I never used such an ugly word.

REGINA. Oh, it doesn't matter what word you used.

ENGSTRAND. Besides, that was only when I was a bit fuddled —hm! Temptations are manifold in this world, Regina.

REGINA. Ugh!

ENGSTRAND. And it was when your mother was in a nasty temper. I had to find some way of getting my knife into her, my girl. She was always so precious genteel. (*Mimicking her.*) "Let go, Jacob! Let me be! Please to remember that I was three years with the Alvings at Rosenvold, and they were people who went to Court!" (*Laughs*). Bless my soul, she never could forget that Captain Alving got a Court appointment while she was in service here.

REGINA. Poor mother—you worried her into her grave pretty soon.

ENGSTRAND (*shrugging his shoulders*). Of course, of course; I have got to take the blame for everything.

REGINA (*beneath her breath, as she turns away*). Ugh— that leg, too!

ENGSTRAND. What are you saying, my girl?

REGINA. *Pied de mouton.*

ENGSTRAND. Is that English?

REGINA. Yes.

ENGSTRAND. You have had a good education out here, and no mistake; and it may stand you in good stead now, Regina.

REGINA (*after a short silence*). And what was it you wanted me to come to town for?

ENGSTRAND. Need you ask why a father wants his only child? Ain't I a poor lonely widower?

REGINA. Oh, don't come to me with that tale. Why do you want me to go?

ENGSTRAND. Well, I must tell you I am thinking of taking up a new line now.

REGINA (*whistles*). You have tried that so often—but it has always proved a fool's errand.

ENGSTRAND. Ah, but this time you will just see, Regina! Strike me dead if—

REGINA (*stamping her foot*). Stop swearing!

ENGSTRAND. Sh! Sh!—you're quite right, my girl, quite right! What I wanted to say was only this, that I have put by a tidy penny out of what I have made by working at this new Orphanage up here.

REGINA. Have you? All the better for you.

ENGSTRAND. What is there for a man to spend his money on, out here in the country?

REGINA. Well, what then?

ENGSTRAND. Well, you see, I thought of putting the money into something that would pay. I thought of some kind of an eating-house for seafaring folk—

REGINA. Heavens!

ENGSTRAND. Oh, a high-class eating-house, of course,—not a pigsty for common sailors. Damn it, no; it would be a place ships' captains and first mates would come to; really good sort of people, you know.

REGINA. And what should I—?

ENGSTRAND. You would help there. But only to make a show, you know. You wouldn't find it hard work, I can promise you, my girl. You should do exactly as you liked.

REGINA. Oh, yes, quite so!

ENGSTRAND. But we must have some women in the house; that is as clear as daylight. Because in the evening we must make the place a little attractive—some singing and dancing, and that sort of thing. Remember they are seafolk—wayfarers on the waters of life! (*Coming nearer to her.*) Now don't be a fool and stand in your own way, Regina. What good are you going to do here? Will this education, that your mistress has paid for, be of any use? You are to look after the children in the new Home, I hear. Is that the sort of work for you? Are you so frightfully anxious to go and wear out your health and strength for the sake of these dirty brats?

REGINA. No, if things were to go as I want them to, then—. Well, it may happen; who knows? It may happen!

ENGSTRAND. What may happen?

REGINA. Never you mind. Is it much that you have put by, up here?

ENGSTRAND. Taking it all round, I should say about forty or fifty pounds.

REGINA. That's not so bad.

ENGSTRAND. It's enough to make a start with, my girl.

REGINA. Don't you mean to give me any of the money?

ENGSTRAND. No, I'm hanged if I do.

REGINA. Don't you mean to send me as much as a dress-length of stuff, just for once?

ENGSTRAND. Come and live in the town with me and you shall have plenty of dresses.

REGINA. Pooh!—I can get that much for myself, if I have a mind to.

ENGSTRAND. But it's far better to have a father's guiding hand, Regina. Just now I can get a nice house in Little Harbour Street. They don't want much money down for it—and we could make it like a sort of seamen's home, don't you know.

REGINA. But I have no intention of living with you! I have nothing whatever to do with you. So now, be off!

ENGSTRAND. You wouldn't be living with me long, my girl. No such luck—not if you knew how to play your cards. Such a fine wench as you have grown this last year or two—

REGINA. Well—?

ENGSTRAND. It wouldn't be very long before some first mate came along—or perhaps a captain.

REGINA. I don't mean to marry a man of that sort. Sailors have no *savoir-vivre*.

ENGSTRAND. What haven't they got?

REGINA. I know what sailors are, I tell you. They aren't the sort of people to marry.

ENGSTRAND. Well, don't bother about marrying them. You can make it pay just as well. (*More confidentially.*) That fellow—the Englishman—the one with the yacht—he gave seventy pounds, he did; and she wasn't a bit prettier than you.

REGINA (*advancing towards him*). Get out!

ENGSTRAND (*stepping back*). Here! here!—you're not going to hit me, I suppose?

REGINA. Yes! If you talk like that of mother, I will hit you. Get out, I tell you! (*Pushes him up to the garden door.*) And don't bang the doors. Young Mr. Alving—

ENGSTRAND. Is asleep—I know. It's funny how anxious you are about young Mr. Alving. (*In a lower tone.*) Oho! is it possible that it is *he* that—?

REGINA. Get out, and be quick about it! Your wits are wandering, my good man. No, don't go that way; Mr. Manders is just coming along. Be off down the kitchen stairs.

ENGSTRAND (*moving towards the right*). Yes, yes—all right. But have a bit of a chat with him that's coming along. He's the chap to tell you what a child owes to its father. For I am your father, anyway, you know. I can prove it by the Register. (*He goes out through the farther door which REGINA has opened. She shuts it after him, looks hastily at herself in the mirror, fans herself with her handkerchief and sets her collar straight; then busies herself with the flowers. MANDERS enters the conservatory through the garden door. He wears an overcoat, carries an umbrella, and has a small travelling-bag slung over his shoulder on a strap.*)

MANDERS. Good morning, Miss Engstrand.

REGINA (*turning round with a look of pleased surprise*). Oh, Mr. Manders, good morning. The boat is in, then?

MANDERS. Just in. (*Comes into the room.*) It is most tiresome, this rain every day.

REGINA (*following him in*). It's a splendid rain for the farmers, Mr. Manders.

MANDERS. Yes, you are quite right. We town-folk think so little about that. (*Begins to take off his overcoat.*)

REGINA. Oh, let me help you. That's it. Why, how wet it is! I will hang it up in the hall. Give me your umbrella, too; I will leave it open, so that it will dry.

(*She goes out with the things by the farther door on the right.* MANDERS *lays his bag and his hat down on a chair.* REGINA *re-enters.*)

MANDERS. Ah, it's very pleasant to get indoors. Well, is everything going on well here?

REGINA. Yes, thanks.

MANDERS. Properly busy, though, I expect, getting ready for to-morrow?

REGINA. Oh, yes, there is plenty to do.

MANDERS. And Mrs. Alving is at home, I hope?

REGINA. Yes, she is. She has just gone upstairs to take the young master his chocolate.

MANDERS. Tell me—I heard down at the pier that Oswald had come back.

REGINA. Yes, he came the day before yesterday. We didn't expect him till to-day.

MANDERS. Strong and well, I hope?

REGINA. Yes, thank you, well enough. But dreadfully tired after his journey. He came straight from Paris without a stop —I mean, he came all the way without breaking his journey. I fancy he is having a sleep now, so we must talk a little bit more quietly, if you don't mind.

MANDERS. All right, we will be very quiet.

REGINA (*while she moves an armchair up to the table*). Please sit down, Mr. Manders, and make yourself at home. (*He sits down; she puts a footstool under his feet.*) There! Is that comfortable?

MANDERS. Thank you, thank you. That is most comfortable. (*Looks at her.*) I'll tell you what, Miss Engstrand, I certainly think you have grown up since I saw you last.

REGINA. Do you think so? Mrs. Alving says, too, that I have developed.

MANDERS. Developed? Well, perhaps a little—just suitably. (*A short pause.*)

REGINA. Shall I tell Mrs. Alving you are here?

MANDERS. Thanks, there is no hurry, my dear child.— Now tell me, Regina, my dear, how has your father been getting on here?

REGINA. Thank you, Mr. Manders, he is getting on pretty well.

MANDERS. He came to see me, the last time he was in town.

REGINA. Did he? He is always so glad when he can have a chat with you.

MANDERS. And I suppose you have seen him pretty regularly every day?

REGINA. I? Oh, yes, I do—whenever I have time, that is to say.

MANDERS. Your father has not a very strong character, Miss Engstrand. He sadly needs a guiding hand.

REGINA. Yes, I can quite believe that.

MANDERS. He needs someone with him that he can cling to, someone whose judgment he can rely on. He acknowledged that freely himself, the last time he came up to see me.

REGINA. Yes, he has said something of the same sort to me. But I don't know whether Mrs. Alving could do without me—most of all just now, when we have the new Orphanage to see about. And I should be dreadfully unwilling to leave Mrs. Alving, too; she has always been so good to me.

MANDERS. But a daughter's duty, my good child—. Naturally we should have to get your mistress' consent first.

REGINA. Still I don't know whether it would be quite the thing, at my age, to keep house for a single man.

MANDERS. What! ! My dear Miss Engstrand, it is your own father we are speaking of!

REGINA. Yes, I dare say, but still—. Now, if it were in a good house and with a real gentleman—

MANDERS. But, my dear Regina—

REGINA. —one whom I could feel an affection for, and really feel in the position of a daughter to—

MANDERS. Come, come—my dear good child—

REGINA. I should like very much to live in town. Out here it is terribly lonely; and you know yourself, Mr. Manders, what it is to be alone in the world. And, though I say it, I really am both capable and willing. Don't you know any place that would be suitable for me, Mr. Manders?

MANDERS. I? No, indeed I don't.

REGINA. But, dear Mr. Manders—at any rate don't forget me, in case—

MANDERS (*getting up*). No, I won't forget you, Miss Engstrand.

REGINA. Because, if I—

MANDERS. Perhaps you will be so kind as to let Mrs. Alving know I am here?

REGINA. I will fetch her at once, Mr. Manders. (*Goes out to the left.* MANDERS *walks up and down the room once or twice, stands for a moment at the farther end of the room with his hands behind his back and looks out into the garden.*

*Then he comes back to the table, takes up a book and looks
at the title page, gives a start, and looks at some of the others.*)

MANDERS. Hm!—Really!

(MRS. ALVING *comes in by the door on the left. She is
followed by* REGINA, *who goes out again at once through
the nearer door on the right.*)

MRS. ALVING (*holding out her hand*). I am very glad to
see you, Mr. Manders.

MANDERS. How do you do, Mrs. Alving. Here I am, as I
promised.

MRS. ALVING. Always punctual!

MANDERS. Indeed, I was hard put to it to get away. What
with vestry meetings and committees—

MRS. ALVING. It was all the kinder of you to come in such
good time; we can settle our business before dinner. But where
is your luggage?

MANDERS (*quickly*). My things are down at the village
shop. I am going to sleep there to-night.

MRS. ALVING (*repressing a smile*). Can't I really persuade
you to stay the night here this time?

MANDERS. No, no; many thanks all the same; I will put up
there, as usual. It is so handy for getting on board the boat
again.

MRS. ALVING. Of course you shall do as you please. But
it seems to me quite another thing, now we are two old
people—

MANDERS. Ha! ha! You will have your joke! And it's
natural you should be in high spirits to-day—first of all there
is the great event to-morrow, and also you have got Oswald
home.

MRS. ALVING. Yes, am I not a lucky woman! It is more
than two years since he was home last, and he has promised
to stay the whole winter with me.

MANDERS. Has he, really? That is very nice and filial of
him; because there must be many more attractions in his life
in Rome or in Paris, I should think.

MRS. ALVING. Yes, but he has his mother here, you see.
Bless the dear boy, he has got a corner in his heart for his
mother still.

MANDERS. Oh, it would be very sad if absence and pre-
occupation with such a thing as Art were to dull the natural
affections.

MRS. ALVING. It would, indeed. But there is no fear of that
with him, I am glad to say. I am quite curious to see if you
recognise him again. He will be down directly; he is just lying
down for a little on the sofa upstairs. But do sit down, my
dear friend.

MANDERS. Thank you. You are sure I am not disturbing you?

MRS. ALVING. Of course not. (*She sits down at the table.*)

MANDERS. Good. Then I will show you—. (*He goes to the chair where his bag is lying and takes a packet of papers from it; then sits down at the opposite side of the table and looks for a clear space to put the papers down.*) Now first of all, here is—(*breaks off*). Tell me, Mrs. Alving, what are these books doing here?

MRS. ALVING. These books? I am reading them.

MANDERS. Do you read this sort of thing?

MRS. ALVING. Certainly I do.

MANDERS. Do you feel any the better or the happier for reading books of this kind?

MRS. ALVING. I think it makes me, as it were, more self-reliant.

MANDERS. That is remarkable. But why?

MRS. ALVING. Well, they give me an explanation or a confirmation of lots of different ideas that have come into my own mind. But what surprises me, Mr. Manders, is that, properly speaking, there is nothing at all new in these books. There is nothing more in them than what most people think and believe. The only thing is, that most people either take no account of it or won't admit it to themselves.

MANDERS. But, good heavens, do you seriously think that most people—?

MRS. ALVING. Yes, indeed, I do.

MANDERS. But not here in the country at any rate? Not here amongst people like ourselves?

MRS. ALVING. Yes, amongst people like ourselves too.

MANDERS. Well, really, I must say—!

MRS. ALVING. But what is the particular objection that you have to these books?

MANDERS. What objection? You surely don't suppose that I take any particular interest in such productions?

MRS. ALVING. In fact, you don't know anything about what you are denouncing?

MANDERS. I have read quite enough about these books to disapprove of them.

MRS. ALVING. Yes, but your own opinion—

MANDERS. My dear Mrs. Alving, there are many occasions in life when one has to rely on the opinion of others. That is the way in this world, and it is quite right that it should be so. What would become of society, otherwise?

MRS. ALVING. Well, you may be right.

MANDERS. Apart from that, naturally I don't deny that literature of this kind may have a considerable attraction. And

I cannot blame you, either, for wishing to make yourself acquainted with the intellectual tendencies which I am told are at work in the wider world in which you have allowed your son to wander for so long. But—

MRS. ALVING. But—?

MANDERS (*lowering his voice*). But one doesn't talk about it, Mrs. Alving. One certainly is not called upon to account to every one for what one reads or thinks in the privacy of one's own room.

MRS. ALVING. Certainly not. I quite agree with you.

MANDERS. Just think of the consideration you owe to this Orphanage, which you decided to build at a time when your thoughts on such subjects were very different from what they are now—as far as I am able to judge.

MRS. ALVING. Yes, I freely admit that. But it was about the Orphanage—

MANDERS. It was about the Orphanage we were going to talk; quite so. Well—walk warily, dear Mrs. Alving! And now let us turn to the business in hand. (*Opens an envelope and takes out some papers.*) You see these?

MRS. ALVING. The deeds?

MANDERS. Yes, the whole lot—and everything in order. I can tell you it has been no easy matter to get them in time. I had positively to put pressure on the authorities; they are almost painfully conscientious when it is a question of settling property. But here they are at last. (*Turns over the papers.*) Here is the deed of conveyance of that part of the Rosenvold estate known as the Solvik property, together with the buildings newly erected thereon—the school, the masters' houses and the chapel. And here is the legal sanction for the statutes of the institution. Here, you see—(*reads*) "Statutes for the Captain Alving Orphanage."

MRS. ALVING (*after a long look at the papers*). That seems all in order.

MANDERS. I thought "Captain" was the better title to use, rather than your husband's Court title of "Chamberlain." "Captain" seems less ostentatious.

MRS. ALVING. Yes, yes; just as you think best.

MANDERS. And here is the certificate for the investment of the capital in the bank, the interest being earmarked for the current expenses of the Orphanage.

MRS. ALVING. Many thanks; but I think it will be most convenient if you will kindly take charge of them.

MANDERS. With pleasure. I think it will be best to leave the money in the bank for the present. The interest it not very high, it is true; four per cent at six months' call. Later on, if we can find some good mortgage—or course it must be a first mortgage and on unexceptionable security—we can consider the matter further.

MRS. ALVING. Yes, yes, my dear Mr. Manders, you know best about all that.

MANDERS. I will keep my eye on it, anyway. But there is one thing in connection with it that I have often meant to ask you about.

MRS. ALVING. What is that?

MANDERS. Shall we insure the buildings, or not?

MRS. ALVING. Of course we must insure them.

MANDERS. Ah, but wait a moment, dear lady. Let us look into the matter a little more closely.

MRS. ALVING. Everything of mine is insured—the house and its contents, my livestock—everything.

MANDERS. Naturally. They are your own property. I do exactly the same, of course. But this, you see, is quite a different case. The Orphanage is, so to speak, dedicated to higher uses.

MRS. ALVING. Certainly, but—

MANDERS. As far as I am personally concerned, I can conscientiously say that I don't see the smallest objection to our insuring ourselves against all risks.

MRS. ALVING. That is exactly what I think.

MANDERS. But what about the opinion of the people hereabouts?

MRS. ALVING. Their opinion—?

MANDERS. Is there any considerable body of opinion here —opinion of some account, I mean—that might take exception to it?

MRS. ALVING. What, exactly, do you mean by opinion of some account?

MANDERS. Well, I was thinking particularly of persons of such independent and influential position that one could hardly refuse to attach weight to their opinion.

MRS. ALVING. There are a certain number of such people here, who might perhaps take exception to it if we—

MANDERS. That's just it, you see. In town there are lots of them. All my fellow-clergymen's congregations, for instance! It would be so extremely easy for them to interpret it as meaning that neither you nor I had a proper reliance on Divine protection.

MRS. ALVING. But as far as you are concerned, my dear friend, you have at all events the consciousness that—

MANDERS. Yes I know, I know; my own mind is quite easy about it, it is true. But we should not be able to prevent a wrong and injurious interpretation of our action. And that sort of thing, moreover, might very easily end in exercising a hampering influence on the work of the Orphanage.

MRS. ALVING. Oh, well, if that is likely to be the effect of it—

MANDERS. Nor can I entirely overlook the difficult—indeed, I may say, painful—position I might possibly be placed in. In the best circles in town the matter of this Orphanage is attracting a great deal of attention. Indeed the Orphanage is to some extent built for the benefit of the town too, and it is to be hoped that it may result in the lowering of our poor-rate by a considerable amount. But as I have been your adviser in the matter and have taken charge of the business side of it, I should be afraid that it would be I that spiteful persons would attack first of all—

MRS. ALVING. Yes, you ought not to expose yourself to that.

MANDERS. Not to mention the attacks that would undoubtedly be made upon me in certain newspapers and reviews—

MRS. ALVING. Say no more about it, dear Mr. Manders; that quite decides it.

MANDERS. Then you don't wish it to be insured?

MRS. ALVING. No, we will give up the idea.

MANDERS (leaning back in his chair). But suppose, now, that some accident happened?—one can never tell—would you be prepared to make good the damage?

MRS. ALVING. No; I tell you quite plainly I would not do so under any circumstances.

MANDERS. Still, you know, Mrs. Alving—after all, it is a serious responsibility that we are taking upon ourselves.

MRS. ALVING. But do you think we can do otherwise?

MANDERS. No, that's just it. We really can't do otherwise. We ought not to expose ourselves to a mistaken judgment; and we have no right to do anything that will scandalise the community.

MRS. ALVING. You ought not to, as a clergyman, at any rate.

MANDERS. And, what is more, I certainly think that we may count upon our enterprise being attended by good fortune—indeed, that it will be under a special protection.

MRS. ALVING. Let us hope so, Mr. Manders.

MANDERS. Then we will leave it alone?

MRS. ALVING. Certainly.

MANDERS. Very good. As you wish. (Makes a note.) No insurance, then.

MRS. ALVING. It's a funny thing that you should just have happened to speak about that to-day—

MANDERS. I have often meant to ask you about it—

MRS. ALVING. —because yesterday we very nearly had a fire up there.

MANDERS. Do you mean it!

MRS. ALVING. Oh, as a matter of fact it was nothing of any consequence. Some shavings in the carpenter's shop caught fire.

MANDERS. Where Engstrand works?

MRS. ALVING. Yes. They say he is often so careless with matches.

MANDERS. He has so many things on his mind, poor fellow —so many anxieties. Heaven be thanked, I am told he is really making an effort to live a blameless life.

MRS. ALVING. Really? Who told you so?

MANDERS. He assured me himself that it is so. He's a good workman, too.

MRS. ALVING. Oh, yes, when he is sober.

MANDERS. Ah, that sad weakness of his! But the pain in his poor leg often drives him to it, he tells me. The last time he was in town, I was really quite touched by him. He came to my house and thanked me so gratefully for getting him work here, where he could have the chance of being with Regina.

MRS. ALVING. He doesn't see very much of her.

MANDERS. But he assured me that he saw her every day.

MRS. ALVING. Oh well, perhaps he does.

MANDERS. He feels so strongly that he needs some one who can keep a hold on him when temptations assail him. That is the most winning thing about Jacob Engstrand; he comes to one like a helpless child and accuses himself and confesses his frailty. The last time he came and had a talk with me—. Suppose now, Mrs. Alving, that it were really a necessity of his existence to have Regina at home with him again—

MRS. ALVING (*standing up suddenly*). Regina!

MANDERS. —you ought not to set yourself against him.

MRS. ALVING. Indeed, I set myself very definitely against that. And, besides, you know Regina is to have a post in the Orphanage.

MANDERS. But consider, after all he is her father—

MRS. ALVING. I know best what sort of a father he has been to her. No, she shall never go to him with my consent.

MANDERS (*getting up*). My dear lady, don't judge so hastily. It is very sad how you misjudge poor Engstrand. One would really think you were afraid—

MRS. ALVING (*more calmly*). That is not the question. I have taken Regina into my charge, and in my charge she remains. (*Listens.*) Hush, dear Mr. Manders, don't say any

more about it. (*Her face brightens with pleasure.*) Listen!
Oswald is coming downstairs. We will only think about him
now.

OSWALD ALVING, *in a light overcoat, hat in hand and smoking a big meerschaum pipe, comes in by the door on the
left.*)

OSWALD (*standing in the doorway*). Oh, I beg your pardon,
I thought you were in the office. (*Comes in.*) Good morning,
Mr. Manders.

MANDERS (*staring at him*). Well! It's most extraordinary—

MRS. ALVING. Yes, what do you think of him, Mr. Manders?

MANDERS. I—I— no, can it possibly be—?

OSWALD. Yes, it really is the prodigal son, Mr. Manders,

MANDERS. Oh, my dear young friend—

OSWALD. Well, the son come home, then.

MRS. ALVING. Oswald is thinking of the time when you
were so opposed to the idea of his being a painter.

MANDERS. We are only fallible, and many steps seem to us
hazardous at first, that afterwards—(*grasps his hand*). Welcome, welcome! Really, my dear Oswald—may I still call you
Oswald?

OSWALD. What else would you think of calling me?

MANDERS. Thank you. What I mean, my dear Oswald, is
that you must not imagine that I have any unqualified disapproval of the artist's life. I admit that there are many who,
even in that career, can keep the inner man free from harm.

OSWALD. Let us hope so.

MRS. ALVING (*beaming with pleasure*). I know one who
has kept both the inner and the outer man free from harm.
Just take a look at him, Mr. Manders.

OSWALD (*walks across the room*). Yes, yes, mother dear,
of course.

MANDERS. Undoubtedly—no one can deny it. And I hear
you have begun to make a name for yourself. I have often
seen mention of you in the papers—and extremely favourable
mention, too. Although, I must admit, latterly I have not
seen your name so often.

OSWALD (*going towards the conservatory*). I haven't done
so much painting just lately.

MRS. ALVING. An artist must take a rest sometimes, like
other people.

MANDERS. Of course, of course. At those times the artist is
preparing and strengthening himself for a greater effort.

OSWALD. Yes. Mother, will dinner soon be ready?

MRS. ALVING. In half an hour. He has a fine appetite, thank
goodness.

MANDERS. And a liking for tobacco too.

OSWALD. I found father's pipe in the room upstairs, and—

MANDERS. Ah, that is what it was!

MRS. ALVING. What?

MANDERS. When Oswald came in at that door with the pipe in his mouth, I thought for the moment it was his father in the flesh.

OSWALD. Really?

MRS. ALVING. How can you say so! Oswald takes after me.

MANDERS. Yes, but there is an expression about the corners of his mouth—something about the lips—that reminds me so exactly of Mr. Alving—especially when he smokes.

MRS. ALVING. I don't think so at all. To my mind, Oswald has much more of a clergyman's mouth.

MANDERS. Well, yes—a good many of my colleagues in the church have a similar expression.

MRS. ALVING. But put your pipe down, my dear boy. I don't allow any smoking in here.

OSWALD (*puts down his pipe*). All right, I only wanted to try it, because I smoked it once when I was a child.

MRS. ALVING. You?

OSWALD. Yes; it was when I was quite a little chap. And I can remember going upstairs to father's room one evening when he was in very good spirits.

MRS. ALVING. Oh, you can't remember anything about those days.

OSWALD. Yes, I remember plainly that he took me on his knee and let me smoke his pipe. "Smoke, my boy," he said, "have a good smoke, boy!" And I smoked as hard as I could, until I felt I was turning quite pale and the perspiration was standing in great drops on my forehead. Then he laughed—such a hearty laugh—

MANDERS. It was an extremely odd thing to do.

MRS. ALVING. Dear Mr. Manders, Oswald only dreamt it.

OSWALD. No indeed, mother, it was no dream. Because—don't you remember—you came into the room and carried me off to the nursery, where I was sick, and I saw that you were crying. Did father often play such tricks?

MANDERS. In his young days he was full of fun—

OSWALD. And, for all that, he did so much with his life—so much that was good and useful, I mean—short as his life was.

MANDERS. Yes, my dear Oswald Alving, you have inherited the name of a man who undoubtedly was both energetic and worthy. Let us hope it will be a spur to your energies—

OSWALD. It ought to be, certainly.

MANDERS. In any case it was nice of you to come home for the day that is to honour his memory.

OSWALD. I could do no less for my father.

MRS. ALVING. And to let me keep him so long here—that's the nicest part of what he has done.

MANDERS. Yes, I hear you are going to spend the winter at home.

OSWALD. I am here for an indefinite time, Mr. Manders. —Oh, it's good to be at home again!

MRS. ALVING (*beaming*). Yes, isn't it?

MANDERS (*looking sympathetically at him*). You went out into the world very young, my dear Oswald.

OSWALD. I did. Sometimes I wonder if I wasn't too young.

MRS. ALVING. Not a bit of it. It is the best thing for an active boy, and especially for an only child. It's a pity when they are kept at home with their parents and get spoilt.

MANDERS. That is a very debatable question, Mrs. Alving. A child's own home is, and always must be, his proper place.

OSWALD. There I agree entirely with Mr. Manders.

MANDERS. Take the case of your own son. Oh yes, we can talk about it before him. What has the result been in his case? He is six or seven and twenty, and has never yet had the opportunity of learning what a well-regulated home means.

OSWALD. Excuse me, Mr. Manders, you are quite wrong there.

MANDERS. Indeed? I imagined that your life abroad had practically been spent entirely in artistic circles.

OSWALD. So it has.

MANDERS. And chiefly amongst the younger artists.

OSWALD. Certainly.

MANDERS. But I imagined that those gentry, as a rule, had not the means necessary for family life and the support of a home.

OSWALD. There are a considerable number of them who have not the means to marry, Mr. Manders.

MANDERS. That is exactly my point.

OSWALD. But they can have a home of their own, all the same; a good many of them have. And they are very well-regulated and very comfortable homes, too.

(MRS. ALVING, *who has listened to him attentively, nods assent, but says nothing.*)

MANDERS. Oh, but I am not talking of bachelor establishments. By a home I mean family life—the life a man lives with his wife and children.

OSWALD. Exactly, or with his children and his children's mother.

MANDERS (*starts and clasps his hands*). Good heavens!

OSWALD. What is the matter?

MANDERS. Lives with—with—his children's mother!

OSWALD. Well, would you rather he should repudiate his children's mother?

MANDERS. Then what you are speaking of are those unprincipled conditions known as irregular unions!

OSWALD. I have never noticed anything particularly unprincipled about these people's lives.

MANDERS. But do you mean to say that it is possible for a man of any sort of bringing up, and a young woman, to reconcile themselves to such a way of living—and to make no secret of it, either!

OSWALD. What else are they to do? A poor artist, and a poor girl—it costs a good deal to get married. What else are they to do?

MANDERS. What are they to do? Well, Mr. Alving, I will tell you what they ought to do. They ought to keep away from each other from the very beginning—that is what they ought to do!

OSWALD. That advice wouldn't have much effect upon hot-blooded young folk who are in love.

MRS. ALVING. No, indeed it wouldn't.

MANDERS (*persistently*). And to think that the authorities tolerate such things! That they are allowed to go on, openly! (*Turns to* MRS. ALVING.) Had I so little reason, then, to be sadly concerned about your son? In circles where open immorality is rampant—where, one may say, it is honoured—

OSWALD. Let me tell you this, Mr. Manders. I have been a constant Sunday guest at one or two of these "irregular" households—

MANDERS. On Sunday, too!

OSWALD. Yes, that is the day of leisure. But never have I heard one objectionable word there, still less have I ever seen anything that could be called immoral. No; but do you know when and where I *have* met with immorality in artists' circles?

MANDERS. No, thank heaven, I don't!

OSWALD. Well, then, I shall have the pleasure of telling you. I have met with it when some one or other of your model husbands and fathers have come out there to have a bit of a look round on their own account, and have done the artists the honour of looking them up in their humble quarters. Then we had a chance of learning something, I can tell you. These gentlemen were able to instruct us about places and things that we had never so much as dreamt of.

MANDERS. What? Do you want me to believe that honourable men when they get away from home will—

OSWALD. Have you never, when these same honourable

men come home again, heard them deliver themselves on the subject of the prevalence of immorality abroad?

MANDERS. Yes, of course, but—

MRS. ALVING. I have heard them, too.

OSWALD. Well, you can take their word for it, unhesitatingly. Some of them are experts in the matter. (*Putting his hands to his head.*) To think that the glorious freedom of the beautiful life over there should be so besmirched!

MRS. ALVING. You mustn't get too heated, Oswald; you gain nothing by that.

OSWALD. No, you are quite right, mother. Besides, it isn't good for me. It's because I am so infernally tired, you know. I will go out and take a turn before dinner. I beg your pardon, Mr. Manders. It is impossible for you to realise the feeling; but it takes me that way. (*Goes out by the farther door on the right.*)

MRS. ALVING. My poor boy!

MANDERS. You may well say so. This is what it has brought him to! (MRS. ALVING *looks at him, but does not speak.*) He called himself the prodigal son. It's only too true, alas—only too true! (MRS. ALVING *looks steadily at him.*) And what do you say to all this?

MRS. ALVING. I say that Oswald was right in every single word he said.

MANDERS. Right? Right? To hold such principles as that?

MRS. ALVING. In my loneliness here I have come to just the same opinions as he, Mr. Manders. But I have never presumed to venture upon such topics in conversation. Now there is no need; my boy shall speak for me.

MANDERS. You deserve the deepest pity, Mrs. Alving. It is my duty to say an earnest word to you. It is no longer your business man and adviser, no longer your old friend and your dead husband's old friend, that stands before you now. It is your priest that stands before you, just as he did once at the most critical moment of your life.

MRS. ALVING. And what is it that my priest has to say to me?

MANDERS. First of all I must stir your memory. The moment is well chosen. To-morrow is the tenth anniversary of your husband's death; to-morrow the memorial to the departed will be unveiled; to-morrow I shall speak to the whole assembly that will be met together. But to-day I want to speak to you alone.

MRS. ALVING. Very well, Mr. Manders, speak!

MANDERS. Have you forgotten that after barely a year of married life you were standing at the very edge of a precipice?

—that you forsook your house and home?—that you ran away from your husband—yes, Mrs. Alving, ran away, ran away—and refused to return to him in spite of his requests and entreaties?

MRS. ALVING. Have you forgotten how unspeakably unhappy I was during that first year?

MANDERS. To crave for happiness in this world is simply to be possessed by a spirit of revolt. What right have we to happiness? No! we must do our duty, Mrs. Alving. And your duty was to cleave to the man you had chosen and to whom you were bound by a sacred bond.

MRS. ALVING. You know quite well what sort of a life my husband was living at that time—what excesses he was guilty of.

MANDERS. I know only too well what rumour used to say of him; and I should be the last person to approve of his conduct as a young man, supposing that rumour spoke the truth. But it is not a wife's part to be her husband's judge. You should have considered it your bounden duty humbly to have borne the cross that a higher will had laid upon you. But, instead of that, you rebelliously cast off your cross, you deserted the man whose stumbling footsteps you should have supported, you did what was bound to imperil your good name and reputation, and came very near to imperilling the reputation of others into the bargain.

MRS. ALVING. Of others? Of one other, you mean.

MANDERS. It was the height of imprudence, your seeking refuge with me.

MRS. ALVING. With our priest? With our intimate friend?

MANDERS. All the more on that account. You should thank God that I possessed the necessary strength of mind—that I was able to turn you from your outrageous intention, and that it was vouchsafed to me to succeed in leading you back into the path of duty and back to your lawful husband.

MRS. ALVING. Yes, Mr. Manders, that certainly was your doing.

MANDERS. I was but the humble instrument of a higher power. And is it not true that my having been able to bring you again under the yoke of duty and obedience sowed the seeds of a rich blessing on all the rest of your life? Did things not turn out as I foretold to you? Did not your husband turn from straying in the wrong path, as a man should? Did he not, after that, live a life of love and good report with you all his days? Did he not become a benefactor to the neighbourhood? Did he not so raise you up to his level, so that by degrees you became his fellow-worker in all his undertakings

—and a noble fellow-worker, too, I know, Mrs. Alving; that praise I will give you.—But now I come to the second serious false step in your life.

MRS. ALVING. What do you mean?

MANDERS. Just as once you forsook your duty as a wife, so, since then, you have forsaken your duty as a mother.

MRS. ALVING. Oh—!

MANDERS. You have been overmastered all your life by a disastrous spirit of wilfulness. All your impulses have led you towards what is undisciplined and lawless. You have never been willing to submit to any restraint. Anything in life that has seemed irksome to you, you have thrown aside recklessly and unscrupulously, as if it were a burden that you were free to rid yourself of if you would. It did not please you to be a wife any longer, and so you left your husband. Your duties as a mother were irksome to you, so you sent your child away among strangers.

MRS. ALVING. Yes, that is true; I did that.

MANDERS. And that is why you have become a stranger to him.

MRS. ALVING. No, no, I am not that!

MANDERS. You are; you must be. And what sort of a son is it that you have got back? Think over it seriously, Mrs. Alving. You erred grievously in your husband's case—you acknowledge as much, by erecting this memorial to him. Now you are bound to acknowledge how much you have erred in your son's case; possibly there may still be time to reclaim him from the paths of wickedness. Turn over a new leaf, and set yourself to reform what there may still be that is capable of reformation in him. Because (*with uplifted forefinger*) in very truth, Mrs. Alving, you are a guilty mother!—That is what I have thought it my duty to say to you.

(*A short silence.*)

MRS. ALVING (*speaking slowly and with self-control*). You have had your say, Mr. Manders, and to-morrow you will be making a public speech in memory of my husband. I shall not speak to-morrow. But now I wish to speak to you for a little, just as you have been speaking to me.

MANDERS. By all means; no doubt you wish to bring forward some excuses for your behaviour—

MRS. ALVING. No. I only want to tell you something.

MANDERS. Well?

MRS. ALVING. In all that you said just now about me and my husband, and about our life together after you had, as you put it, led me back into the path of duty—there was nothing that you knew at first hand. From that moment you never again set foot in our house—you, who had been our daily companion before that.

MANDERS. Remember that you and your husband moved out of town immediately afterwards.

MRS. ALVING. Yes, and you never once came out here to see us in my husband's lifetime. It was only the business in connection with the Orphanage that obliged you to come and see me.

MANDERS (*in a low and uncertain voice*). Helen—if that is a reproach, I can only beg you to consider—

MRS. ALVING. —the respect you owed to your calling?— yes. All the more as I was a wife who had tried to run away from her husband. One can never be too careful to have nothing to do with such reckless women.

MANDERS. My dear—Mrs. Alving, you are exaggerating dreadfully—

MRS. ALVING. Yes, yes,—very well. What I mean is this, that when you condemn my conduct as a wife you have nothing more to go upon than ordinary public opinion.

MANDERS. I admit it. What then?

MRS. ALVING. Well—now, Mr. Manders, now I am going to tell you the truth. I had sworn to myself that you should know it one day—you, and you only!

MANDERS. And what may the truth be?

MRS. ALVING. The truth is this, that my husband died just as great a profligate as he had been all his life.

MANDERS (*feeling for a chair*). What are you saying?

MRS. ALVING. After nineteen years of married life, just as profligate—in his desires at all events—as he was before you married us.

MANDERS. And can you talk of his youthful indiscretions— his irregularities—his excesses, if you like—as a profligate life!

MRS. ALVING. That was what the doctor who attended him called it.

MANDERS. I don't understand what you mean.

MRS. ALVING. It is not necessary you should.

MANDERS. It makes my brain reel. To think that your marriage—all the years of wedded life you spent with your husband—were nothing but a hidden abyss of misery.

MRS. ALVING. That and nothing else. Now you know.

MANDERS. This—this bewilders me. I can't understand it! I can't grasp it! How in the world was it possible—? How could such a state of things remain concealed?

MRS. ALVING. That was just what I had to fight for incessantly, day after day. When Oswald was born, I thought

I saw a slight improvement. But it didn't last long. And after that I had to fight doubly hard—fight a desperate fight so that no one should know what sort of a man my child's father was. You know quite well what an attractive manner he had; it seemed as if people could believe nothing but good of him. He was one of those men whose mode of life seems to have no effect upon their reputations. But at last, Mr. Manders—you must hear this too—at last something happened more abominable than everything else.

MANDERS. More abominable than what you have told me!

MRS. ALVING. I had borne with it all, though I knew only too well what he indulged in in secret, when he was out of the house. But when it came to the point of the scandal coming within our four walls—

MANDERS. Can you mean it! Here?

MRS. ALVING. Yes, here, in our own home. It was in there (*pointing to the nearer door on the right*) in the dining-room that I got the first hint of it. I had something to do in there and the door was standing ajar. I heard our maid come up from the garden with water for the flowers in the conservatory.

MANDERS. Well—?

MRS. ALVING. Shortly afterwards I heard my husband come in too. I heard him say something to her in a low voice. And then I heard—(*with a short laugh*)—oh, it rings in my ears still, with its mixture of what was heartbreaking and what was so ridiculous—I heard my own servant whisper: "Let me go, Mr. Alving! Let me be!"

MANDERS. What unseemly levity on his part! But surely nothing more than levity, Mrs. Alving, believe me.

MRS. ALVING. I soon knew what to believe. My husband had his will of the girl—and that intimacy had consequences, Mr. Manders.

MANDERS (*as if turned to stone*). And all that in this house! In this house!

MRS. ALVING. I have suffered a good deal in this house. To keep him at home in the evening—and at night—I have had to play the part of boon companion in his secret drinking-bouts in his room up there. I have had to sit there alone with him, have had to hobnob and drink with him, have had to listen to his ribald senseless talk, have had to fight with brute force to get him to bed—

MANDERS (*trembling*). And you were able to endure all this!

MRS. ALVING. I had my little boy, and endured it for his sake. But when the crowning insult came—when my own servant—then I made up my mind that there should be an end of it. I took the upper hand in the house, absolutely—both with him and all the others. I had a weapon to use against him, you see; he didn't dare to speak. It was then that Oswald was sent away. He was about seven then, and was beginning to notice things and ask questions as children will. I could endure all that, my friend. It seemed to me that the child would be poisoned if he breathed the air of this polluted house. That was why I sent him away. And now you understand, too, why he never set foot here as long as his father was alive. No one knows what it meant to me.

MANDERS. You have indeed had a pitiable experience.

MRS. ALVING. I could never have gone through with it, if I had not had my work. Indeed, I can boast that I have worked. All the increase in the value of the property, all the improvements, all the useful arrangements that my husband got the honour and glory of—do you suppose that he troubled himself about any of them? He, who used to lie the whole day on the sofa reading old Official Lists! No, you may as well know that too. It was I that kept him up to the mark when he had his lucid intervals; it was I that had to bear the whole burden of it when he began his excesses again or took to whining about his miserable condition.

MANDERS. And this is the man you are building a memorial to!

MRS. ALVING. There you see the power of an uneasy conscience.

MANDERS. An uneasy conscience? What do you mean?

MRS. ALVING. I had always before me the fear that it was impossible that the truth should not come out and be believed. That is why the Orphanage is to exist, to silence all rumours and clear away all doubt.

MANDERS. You certainly have not fallen short of the mark in that, Mrs. Alving.

MRS. ALVING. I had another very good reason. I did not wish Oswald, my own son, to inherit a penny that belonged to his father.

MANDERS. Then it is with Mr. Alving's property—

MRS. ALVING. Yes. The sums of money that, year after year, I have given towards this Orphanage, make up the amount of property—I have reckoned it carefully—which in the old days made Lieutenant Alving a catch.

MANDERS. I understand.

MRS. ALVING. That was my purchase money. I don't wish it to pass into Oswald's hands. My son shall have everything from me, I am determined.

(OSWALD *comes in by the farther door on the right. He has left his hat and coat outside.*)

MRS. ALVING. Back again, my own dear boy?

OSWALD. Yes, what can one do outside in this everlasting rain? I hear dinner is nearly ready. That's good!

(REGINA *comes in from the dining-room, carrying a parcel.*)

REGINA. This parcel has come for you, ma'am. (*Gives it to her.*)

MRS. ALVING (*glancing at* MANDERS). The ode to be sung to-morrow, I expect.

MANDERS. Hm—!

REGINA. And dinner is ready.

MRS. ALVING. Good. We will come in a moment. I will just —(*begins to open the parcel*).

REGINA (*to* OSWALD). Will you drink white or red wine, sir?

OSWALD. Both, Miss Engstrand.

REGINA. *Bien*—very good, Mr. Alving. (*Goes into the dining-room.*)

OSWALD. I may as well help you to uncork it—. (*Follows her into the dining-room, leaving the door ajar after him.*)

MRS. ALVING. Yes, I thought so. Here is the ode, Mr. Manders.

MANDERS (*clasping his hands*). How shall I ever have the courage to-morrow to speak the address that—

MRS. ALVING. Oh, you will get through it.

MANDERS (*in a low voice, fearing to be heard in the dining-room*). Yes, we must raise no suspicions.

MRS. ALVING (*quietly but firmly*). No; and then this long dreadful comedy will be at an end. After to-morrow, I shall feel as if my dead husband had never lived in this house. There will be no one else here then but my boy and his mother.

(*From the dining-room is heard the noise of a chair falling; then* REGINA's *voice is heard in a loud whisper:* Oswald! Are you mad? Let me go!)

MRS. ALVING (*starting in horror*). Oh—!

(*She stares wildly at the half-open door.* OSWALD *is heard coughing and humming, then the sound of a bottle being uncorked.*)

MANDERS (*in an agitated manner*). What's the matter? What is it, Mrs. Alving?

MRS. ALVING (*hoarsely*). Ghosts. The couple in the conservatory—over again.

MANDERS. What are you saying! Regina—? Is *she*—?

MRS. ALVING. Yes. Come. Not a word!

(*Grips* MANDERS *by the arm and walks unsteadily with him into the dining-room.*)

ACT II

(*The same scene. The landscape is still obscured by mist.* MANDERS *and* MRS. ALVING *come in from the dining-room.*)

MRS. ALVING (*calls into the dining-room from the doorway*). Aren't you coming in here, Oswald?

OSWALD. No, thanks; I think I will go out for a bit.

MRS. ALVING. Yes, do; the weather is clearing a little. (*She shuts the dining-room door, then goes to the hall door and calls.*) Regina!

REGINA (*from without*). Yes, ma'am?

MRS. ALVING. Go down into the laundry and help with the garlands.

REGINA. Yes, ma'am.

(MRS. ALVING *satisfies herself that she has gone, then shuts the door.*)

MANDERS. I suppose he can't hear us?

MRS. ALVING. Not when the door is shut. Besides, he is going out.

MANDERS. I am still quite bewildered. I don't know how I managed to swallow a mouthful of your excellent dinner.

MRS. ALVING (*walking up and down, and trying to control her agitation*). Nor I. But what are we to do?

MANDERS. Yes, what are we to do? Upon my word I don't know; I am so completely unaccustomed to things of this kind.

MRS. ALVING. I am convinced that nothing serious has happened yet.

MANDERS. Heaven forbid! But it is most unseemly behaviour, for all that.

MRS. ALVING. It is nothing more than a foolish jest of Oswald's, you may be sure.

MANDERS. Well, of course, as I said, I am quite inexperienced in such matters; but it certainly seems to me—

MRS. ALVING. Out of the house she shall go—and at once. That part of it is as clear as daylight—

95

MANDERS. Yes, that is quite clear.

MRS. ALVING. But where is she to go? We should not be justified in—

MANDERS. Where to? Home to her father, of course.

MRS. ALVING. To whom, did you say?

MANDERS. To her—. No, of course Engstrand isn't—. But, great heavens, Mrs. Alving, how is such a thing possible? You surely may have been mistaken, in spite of everything.

MRS. ALVING. There was no chance of mistake, more's the pity. Joanna was obliged to confess it to me—and my husband couldn't deny it. So there was nothing else to do but to hush it up.

MANDERS. No, that was the only thing to do.

MRS. ALVING. The girl was sent away at once, and was given a tolerably liberal sum to hold her tongue. She looked after the rest herself when she got to town. She renewed an old acquaintance with the carpenter Engstrand; gave him a hint, I suppose, of how much money she had got, and told him some fairy tale about a foreigner who had been here in his yacht in the summer. So she and Engstrand were married in a great hurry. Why, you married them yourself!

MANDERS. I can't understand it—. I remember clearly Engstrand's coming to arrange about the marriage. He was full of contrition, and accused himself bitterly for the light conduct he and his fiancée had been guilty of.

MRS. ALVING. Of course he had to take the blame on himself.

MANDERS. But the deceitfulness of it! And with me, too! I positively would not have believed it of Jacob Engstrand. I shall most certainly give him a serious talking to.—And the immorality of such a marriage! Simply for the sake of the money—! What sum was it that the girl had?

MRS. ALVING. It was seventy pounds.

MANDERS. Just think of it—for a paltry seventy pounds to let yourself be bound in marriage to a fallen woman!

MRS. ALVING. What about myself, then?—I let myself be bound in marriage to a fallen man.

MANDERS. Heaven forgive you! what are you saying? A fallen man?

MRS. ALVING. Do you suppose my husband was any purer, when I went with him to the altar, than Joanna was when Engstrand agreed to marry her?

MANDERS. The two cases are as different as day from night—

MRS. ALVING. Not so very different, after all. It is true there was a great difference in the price paid, between a paltry seventy pounds and a whole fortune.

MANDERS. How can you compare such totally different things! I presume you consulted your own heart—and your relations.

MRS. ALVING (*looking away from him*). I thought you understood where what you call my heart had strayed to at that time.

MANDERS (*in a constrained voice*). If I had understood anything of the kind, I would not have been a daily guest in your husband's house.

MRS. ALVING. Well, at any rate this much is certain, that I didn't consult myself in the matter at all.

MANDERS. Still you consulted those nearest to you, as was only right—your mother, your two aunts.

MRS. ALVING. Yes, that is true. The three of them settled the whole matter for me. It seems incredible to me now, how clearly they made out that it would be sheer folly to reject such an offer. If my mother could only see what all that fine prospect has led to!

MANDERS. No one can be responsible for the result of it. Anyway there is this to be said, that the match was made in complete conformity with law and order.

MRS. ALVING (*going to the window*). Oh, law and order! I often think it is that that is at the bottom of all the misery in the world.

MANDERS. Mrs. Alving, it is very wicked of you to say that.

MRS. ALVING. That may be so; but I don't attach importance to those obligations and considerations any longer. I cannot! I must struggle for my freedom.

MANDERS. What do you mean?

MRS. ALVING (*tapping on the window panes*). I ought never to have concealed what sort of a life my husband led. But I had not the courage to do otherwise then—for my own sake, either. I was too much of a coward.

MANDERS. A coward?

MRS. ALVING. If others had known anything of what happened, they would have said: "Poor man, it is natural enough that he should go astray, when he has a wife that has run away from him."

MANDERS. They would have had a certain amount of justification for saying so.

MRS. ALVING (*looking fixedly at him*). If I had been the woman I ought, I would have taken Oswald into my confidence and said to him: "Listen, my son, your father was a dissolute man"—

MANDERS. Miserable woman—

MRS. ALVING. —and I would have told him all I have told you, from beginning to end.

MANDERS. I am almost shocked at you, Mrs. Alving.

MRS. ALVING. I know. I know quite well! I am shocked at myself when I think of it. (*Comes away from the window.*) I am coward enough for that.

MANDERS. Can you call it cowardice that you simply did your duty! Have you forgotten that a child should love and honour his father and mother?

MRS. ALVING. Don't let us talk in such general terms. Suppose we say: "Ought Oswald to love and honour Mr. Alving?"

MANDERS. You are a mother—isn't there a voice in your heart that forbids you to shatter your son's ideals?

MRS. ALVING. And what about the truth?

MANDERS. What about his ideals?

MRS. ALVING. Oh—ideals, ideals! If only I were not such a coward as I am!

MANDERS. Do not spurn ideals, Mrs. Alving—they have a way of avenging themselves cruelly. Take Oswald's own case, now. He hasn't many ideals, more's the pity. But this much I have seen, that his father is something of an ideal to him.

MRS. ALVING. You are right there.

MANDERS. And his conception of his father is what you inspired and encouraged by your letters.

MRS. ALVING. Yes, I was swayed by duty and consideration for others; that was why I lied to my son, year in and year out. Oh, what a coward—what a coward I have been!

MANDERS. You have built up a happy illusion in your son's mind, Mrs. Alving—and that is a thing you certainly ought not to undervalue.

MRS. ALVING. Ah, who knows if that is such a desirable thing after all!—But anyway I don't intend to put up with any goings on with Regina. I am not going to let him get the poor girl into trouble.

MANDERS. Good heavens, no—that would be a frightful thing!

MRS. ALVING. If only I knew whether he meant it seriously, and whether it would mean happiness for him—

MANDERS. In what way? I don't understand.

MRS. ALVING. But that is impossible; Regina is not equal to it, unfortunately.

MANDERS. I don't understand. What do you mean?

MRS. ALVING. If I were not such a miserable coward, I would say to him: "Marry her, or make any arrangements you like with her—only let there be no deceit in the matter."

MANDERS. Heaven forgive you! Are you actually suggesting anything so abominable, so unheard of, as a marriage between them!

MRS. ALVING. Unheard of, do you call it? Tell me honestly, Mr. Manders, don't you suppose there are plenty of married couples out here in the country that are just as nearly related as they are?

MANDERS. I am sure I don't understand you.

MRS. ALVING. Indeed you do.

MANDERS. I suppose you are thinking of cases where possibly—. It is only too true, unfortunately, that family life is not always as stainless as it should be. But as for the sort of thing you hint at—well, it's impossible to tell, at all events with any certainty. Here, on the other hand—for you, a mother, to be willing to allow your—

MRS. ALVING. But I am not willing to allow it. I would not allow it for anything in the world; that is just what I was saying.

MANDERS. No, because you are a coward, as you put it. But, supposing you were not a coward—! Great heavens—such a revolting union!

MRS. ALVING. Well, for the matter of that, we are all descended from a union of that description, so we are told. And who was it that was responsible for this state of things, Mr. Manders?

MANDERS. I can't discuss such questions with you, Mrs. Alving; you are by no means in the right frame of mind for that. But for you to dare to say that it is cowardly of you—!

MRS. ALVING. I will tell you what I mean by that. I am frightened and timid, because I am obsessed by the presence of ghosts that I never can get rid of.

MANDERS. The presence of what?

MRS. ALVING. Ghosts. When I heard Regina and Oswald in there, it was just like seeing ghosts before my eyes. I am half inclined to think we are all ghosts, Mr. Manders. It is not only what we have inherited from our fathers and mothers that exists again in us, but all sorts of old dead ideas and all kinds of old dead beliefs and things of that kind. They are not actually alive in us; but there they are dormant, all the same, and we can never be rid of them. Whenever I take up a newspaper and read it, I fancy I see ghosts creeping between the lines. There must be ghosts all over the world. They must be as countless as the grains of the sands, it seems to be. And we are so miserably afraid of the light, all of us.

MANDERS. Ah!—there we have the outcome of your reading. Fine fruit it has borne—this abominable, subversive, free-thinking literature!

MRS. ALVING. You are wrong there, my friend. You are the one who made me begin to think; and I owe you my best thanks for it.

MANDERS. I!

MRS. ALVING. Yes, by forcing me to submit to what you called my duty and my obligations; by praising as right and just what my whole soul revolted against, as it would against something abominable. That was what led me to examine your teachings critically. I only wanted to unravel one point in them; but as soon as I had got that unravelled, the whole fabric came to pieces. And then I realised that it was only machine-made.

MANDERS (*softly, and with emotion*). Is that all I accomplished by the hardest struggle of my life?

MRS. ALVING. Call it rather the most ignominious defeat of your life.

MANDERS. It was the greatest victory of my life, Helen; victory over myself.

MRS. ALVING. It was a wrong done to both of us.

MANDERS. A wrong?—wrong for me to entreat you as a wife to go back to your lawful husband, when you came to me half distracted and crying: "Here I am, take me!" Was that a wrong?

MRS. ALVING. I think it was.

MANDERS. We two do not understand one another.

MRS. ALVING. Not now, at all events.

MANDERS. Never—even in my most secret thoughts—have I for a moment regarded you as anything but the wife of another.

MRS. ALVING. Do you believe what you say?

MANDERS. Helen—!

MRS. ALVING. One so easily forgets one's own feelings.

MANDERS. Not I. I am the same as I always was.

MRS. ALVING. Yes, yes—don't let us talk any more about the old days. You are buried up to your eyes now in committees and all sorts of business; and I am here, fighting with ghosts both without and within me.

MANDERS. I can at all events help you to get the better of those without you. After all that I have been horrified to hear from you to-day, I cannot conscientiously allow a young defenceless girl to remain in your house.

MRS. ALVING. Don't you think it would be best if we could get her settled?—by some suitable marriage, I mean.

MANDERS. Undoubtedly. I think, in any case, it would have been desirable for her. Regina is at an age now that—well, I don't know much about these things, but—

MRS. ALVING. Regina developed very early.

MANDERS. Yes, didn't she. I fancy I remember thinking she was remarkably well developed, bodily, at the time I prepared her for Confirmation. But, for the time being, she must in any case go home. Under her father's care—no, but of course Engstrand is not—. To think that he, of all men, could so conceal the truth from me!

(*A knock is heard at the hall door.*)

MRS. ALVING. Who can that be? Come in!

(ENGSTRAND, *dressed in his Sunday clothes, appears in the doorway.*)

ENGSTRAND. I humbly beg pardon, but—

MANDERS. Aha! Hm!—

MRS. ALVING. Oh, it's you, Engstrand!

ENGSTRAND. There were none of the maids about, so I took the great liberty of knocking.

MRS. ALVING. That's all right. Come in. Do you want to speak to me?

ENGSTRAND (*coming in*). No, thank you very much, ma'am. It was Mr. Manders I wanted to speak to for a moment.

MANDERS (*walking up and down*). Hm!—do you. You want to speak to me, do you?

ENGSTRAND. Yes, sir, I wanted so very much to—

MANDERS (*stopping in front of him.*) Well, may I ask what it is you want?

ENGSTRAND. It's this way, Mr. Manders. We are being paid off now. And many thanks to you, Mrs. Alving. And now the work is quite finished, I thought it would be so nice and suitable if all of us, who have worked so honestly together all this time, were to finish up with a few prayers this evening.

MANDERS. Prayers? Up at the Orphanage?

ENGSTRAND. Yes, sir, but if it isn't agreeable to you, then—

MANDERS. Oh, certainly—but—hm!—

ENGSTRAND. I have made a practice of saying a few prayers there myself each evening—

MRS. ALVING. Have you?

ENGSTRAND. Yes, ma'am, now and then—just as a little edification, so to speak. But I am only a poor common man, and haven't rightly the gift, alas—and so I thought that as Mr. Manders happened to be here, perhaps—

MANDERS. Look here, Engstrand. First of all I must ask you a question. Are you in a proper frame of mind for such a thing? Is your conscience free and untroubled?

ENGSTRAND. Heaven have mercy on me a sinner! My conscience isn't worth our speaking about, Mr. Manders.

MANDERS. But it is just what we must speak about. What do you say to my question?

ENGSTRAND. My conscience? Well—it's uneasy sometimes, of course.

MANDERS. Ah, you admit that at all events. Now will you tell me, without any concealment—what is your relationship to Regina?

MRS. ALVING (*hastily*). Mr. Manders!

MANDERS (*calming her*).—Leave it to me!

ENGSTRAND. With Regina? Good Lord, how you frightened me! (*Looks at* MRS. ALVING.) There is nothing wrong with Regina, is there?

MANDERS. Let us hope not. What I want to know is, what is your relationship to her? You pass as her father, don't you?

ENGSTRAND (*unsteadily*). Well—hm!—you know, sir, what happened between me and my poor Joanna.

MANDERS. No more distortion of the truth! Your late wife made a full confession to Mrs. Alving, before she left her service.

ENGSTRAND. What!—do you mean to say—? Did she do that after all?

MANDERS. You see it has all come out, Engstrand.

ENGSTRAND. Do you mean to say that she, who gave me her promise and solemn oath—

MANDERS. Did she take an oath?

ENGSTRAND. Well, no—she only gave me her word, but as seriously as a woman could.

MANDERS. And all these years you have been hiding the truth from me—from me, who have had such complete and absolute faith in you.

ENGSTRAND. I am sorry to say I have, sir.

MANDERS. Did I deserve that from you, Engstrand? Haven't I been always ready to help you in word and deed as far as lay in my power? Answer me! Is it not so?

ENGSTRAND. Indeed there's many a time I should have been very badly off without you, sir.

MANDERS. And this is the way you repay me—by causing me to make false entries in the church registers, and afterwards keeping back from me for years the information which you owed it both to me and to your sense of the truth to divulge. Your conduct has been absolutely inexcusable, Engstrand, and from today everything is at an end between us.

ENGSTRAND (*with a sigh*). Yes, I can see that's what it means.

MANDERS. Yes, because how can you possibly justify what you did?

ENGSTRAND. Was the poor girl to go and increase her load of shame by talking about it? Just suppose, sir, for a moment that your reverence was in the same predicament as my poor Joanna—

MANDERS. I!

ENGSTRAND. Good Lord, sir, I don't mean the same predicament. I mean, suppose there were something your reverence were ashamed of in the eyes of the world, so to speak. We men oughtn't to judge a poor woman too hardly, Mr. Manders.

MANDERS. But I am not doing so at all. It is you I am blaming.

ENGSTRAND. Will your reverence grant me leave to ask you a small question?

MANDERS. Ask away.

ENGSTRAND. Shouldn't you say it was right for a man to raise up the fallen?

MANDERS. Of course it is.

ENGSTRAND. And isn't a man bound to keep his word of honour?

MANDERS. Certainly he is; but—

ENGSTRAND. At the time when Joanna had her misfortune with this Englishman—or maybe he was an American or a Russian, as they call 'em—well, sir, then she came to town. Poor thing, she had refused me once or twice before; she only had eyes for good-looking men in those days, and I had this crooked leg then. Your reverence will remember how I had ventured up into a dancing-saloon where seafaring men were revelling in drunkenness and intoxication, as they say. And when I tried to exhort them to turn from their evil ways—

MRS. ALVING (*coughs from the window*). Ahem!

MANDERS. I know, Engstrand, I know—the rough brutes threw you downstairs. You have told me about that incident before. The affliction to your leg is a credit to you.

ENGSTRAND. I don't want to claim credit for it, your reverence. But what I wanted to tell you was that she came then and confided in me with tears and gnashing of teeth. I can tell you, sir, it went to my heart to hear her.

MANDERS. Did it, indeed, Engstrand? Well, what then?

ENGSTRAND. Well, then I said to her: "The American is roaming about on the high seas, he is. And you, Joanna," I said, "you have committed a sin and are a fallen woman. But here stands Jacob Engstrand," I said, "on two strong legs"— of course that was only speaking in a kind of metaphor, as it were, your reverence.

MANDERS. I quite understand. Go on.

ENGSTRAND. Well, sir, that was how I rescued her and made her my lawful wife, so that no one should know how recklessly she had carried on with the stranger.

MANDERS. That was all very kindly done. The only thing I cannot justify was your bringing yourself to accept the money—

ENGSTRAND. Money? I? Not a farthing.

MANDERS (to MRS. ALVING, in a questioning tone). But—

ENGSTRAND. Ah, yes!—wait a bit; I remember now. Joanna did have a trifle of money, you are quite right. But I didn't want to know anything about that. "Fie," I said, "on the mammon of unrighteousness, it's the price of your sin; as for this tainted gold"—or notes, or whatever it was—"we will throw it back in the American's face," I said. But he had gone away and disappeared on the stormy seas, your reverence.

MANDERS. Was that how it was, my good fellow?

ENGSTRAND. It was, sir. So then Joanna and I decided that the money should go towards the child's bringing-up, and that's what became of it; and I can give a faithful account of every single penny of it.

MANDERS. This alters the complexion of the affair very considerably.

ENGSTRAND. That's how it was, your reverence. And I make bold to say that I have been a good father to Regina—as far as was in my power—for I am a poor erring mortal, alas!

MANDERS. There, there, my dear Engstrand—

ENGSTRAND. Yes, I do make bold to say that I brought up the child, and made my poor Joanna a loving and careful husband, as the Bible says we ought. But it never occurred to me to go to your reverence and claim credit for it or boast about it because I had done one good deed in this world. No; when Jacob Engstrand does a thing like that, he holds his tongue about it. Unfortunately it doesn't often happen, I know that only too well. And whenever I do come to see your reverence, I never seem to have anything but trouble and wickedness to talk about. Because, as I said just now—and I say it again—conscience can be very hard on us sometimes.

MANDERS. Give me your hand, Jacob Engstrand.

ENGSTRAND. Oh, sir, I don't like—

MANDERS. No nonsense. (Grasps his hand.) That's it!

ENGSTRAND. And may I make bold humbly to beg your reverence's pardon—

MANDERS. You? On the contrary it is for me to beg your pardon—

ENGSTRAND. Oh no, sir.

MANDERS. Yes, certainly it is, and I do it with my whole heart. Forgive me for having so much misjudged you. And I assure you that if I can do anything for you to prove my sincere regret and my goodwill towards you—

ENGSTRAND. Do you mean it, sir?

MANDERS. It would give me the greatest pleasure.

ENGSTRAND. As a matter of fact, sir, you could do it now. I am thinking of using the honest money I have put away out of my wages up here, in establishing a sort of Sailors' Home in the town.

MRS. ALVING. You?

ENGSTRAND. Yes, to be a sort of Refuge, as it were. There are such manifold temptations lying in wait for sailor men when they are roaming about on shore. But my idea is that in this house of mine they should have a sort of parental care looking after them.

MANDERS. What do you say to that, Mrs. Alving!

ENGSTRAND. I haven't much to begin such a work with, I know; but Heaven might prosper it, and if I found any helping hand stretched out to me, then—

MANDERS. Quite so; we will talk over the matter further. Your project attracts me enormously. But in the meantime go back to the Orphanage and put everything tidy and light the lights, so that the occasion may seem a little solemn. And then we will spend a little edifying time together, my dear Engstrand, for now I am sure you are in a suitable frame of mind.

ENGSTRAND. I believe I am, sir, truly. Good-bye, then, Mrs. Alving, and thank you for all your kindness; and take good care of Regina for me. (*Wipes a tear from his eye.*) Poor Joanna's child—it is an extraordinary thing, but she seems to have grown into my life and to hold me by the heartstrings. That's how I feel about it, truly. (*Bows, and goes out.*)

MANDERS. Now, then, what do you think of him, Mrs. Alving! That was quite another explanation that he gave us.

MRS. ALVING. It was, indeed.

MANDERS. There, you see how exceedingly careful we ought to be in condemning our fellow-men. But at the same time it gives one genuine pleasure to find that one was mistaken. Don't you think so?

MRS. ALVING. What I think is that you are, and always will remain, a big baby, Mr. Manders.

MANDERS. I?

MRS. ALVING (*laying her hands on his shoulders*). And I think that I should like very much to give you a good hug.

MANDERS (*drawing back hastily*). No, no, good gracious! What an idea!

MRS. ALVING (*with a smile*). Oh, you needn't be afraid of me.

MANDERS (*standing by the table*). You choose such an extravagant way of expressing yourself sometimes. Now I must get these papers together and put them in my bag.

(*Does so.*) That's it. And now good-bye, for the present. Keep your eyes open when Oswald comes back. I will come back and see you again presently.

(*He takes his hat and goes out by the hall door.* MRS. ALVING *sighs, glances out of the window, puts one or two things tidy in the room and turns to go into the dining-room. She stops in the doorway with a stifled cry.*)

MRS. ALVING. Oswald, are you still sitting at table!

OSWALD (*from the dining-room*). I am only finishing my cigar.

MRS. ALVING. I thought you had gone out for a little turn.

OSWALD (*from within the room*). In weather like this? (*A glass is heard clinking.* MRS. ALVING *leaves the door open and sits down with her knitting on the couch by the window.*) Wasn't that Mr. Manders that went out just now?

MRS. ALVING. Yes, he has gone over to the Orphanage.

OSWALD. Oh. (*The clink of a bottle on a glass is heard again.*)

MRS. ALVING (*with an uneasy expression*). Oswald, dear, you should be careful with that liqueur. It is strong.

OSWALD. It's a good protective against the damp.

MRS. ALVING. Wouldn't you rather come in here?

OSWALD. You know you don't like smoking in there.

MRS. ALVING. You may smoke a cigar in here, certainly.

OSWALD. All right; I will come in, then. Just one drop more. There! (*Comes in, smoking a cigar, and shuts the door after him. A short silence.*) Where has the parson gone?

MRS. ALVING. I told you he had gone over to the Orphanage.

OSWALD. Oh, so you did.

MRS. ALVING. You shouldn't sit so long at table, Oswald.

OSWALD (*holding his cigar behind his back*). But it's so nice and cosy, mother dear. (*Caresses her with one hand.*) Think what it means to me—to have come home; to sit at my mother's own table, in my mother's own room, and to enjoy the charming meals she gives me.

MRS. ALVING. My dear, dear boy!

OSWALD (*a little impatiently, as he walks up and down smoking*). And what else is there for me to do here? I have no occupation——

MRS. ALVING. No occupation?

OSWALD. Not in this ghastly weather, when there isn't a blink of sunshine all day long. (*Walks up and down the floor.*) Not to be able to work, it's——!

MRS. ALVING. I don't believe you were wise to come home.

OSWALD. Yes, mother; I had to.

MRS. ALVING. Because I would ten times rather give up the

happiness of having you with me, sooner than that you should—

OSWALD (*standing still by the table*). Tell me, mother— is it really such a great happiness for you to have me at home?

MRS. ALVING. Can you ask?

OSWALD (*crumpling up a newspaper*). I should have thought it would have been pretty much the same to you whether I were here or away.

MRS. ALVING. Have you the heart to say that to your mother, Oswald?

OSWALD. But you have been quite happy living without me so far.

MRS. ALVING. Yes, I have lived without you—that is true.

(*A silence. The dusk falls by degrees. OSWALD walks restlessly up and down. He has laid aside his cigar.*)

OSWALD (*stopping beside MRS. ALVING*). Mother, may I sit on the couch beside you?

MRS. ALVING. Of course, my dear boy.

OSWALD (*sitting down*). Now I must tell you something mother.

MRS. ALVING (*anxiously*). What?

OSWALD (*staring in front of him*). I can't bear it any longer.

MRS. ALVING. Bear what? What do you mean?

OSWALD (*as before*). I couldn't bring myself to write to you about it; and since I have been at home—

MRS. ALVING (*catching him by the arm*). Oswald, what is it?

OSWALD. Both yesterday and to-day I have tried to push my thoughts away from me—to free myself from them. But I can't.

MRS. ALVING (*getting up*). You must speak plainly, Oswald!

OSWALD (*drawing her down to her seat again*). Sit still, and I will try and tell you. I have made a great deal of the fatigue I felt after my journey—

MRS. ALVING. Well, what of that?

OSWALD. But that isn't what is the matter. It is no ordinary fatigue—

MRS. ALVING (*trying to get up*). You are not ill, Oswald!

OSWALD (*pulling her down again*). Sit still, mother. Do take it quietly. I am not exactly ill—not ill in the usual sense. (*Takes his head in his hands.*) Mother, it's my mind that has broken down—gone to pieces—I shall never be able to work any more! (*Buries his face in his hands and throws himself at her knees in an outburst of sobs.*)

MRS. ALVING (*pale and trembling*). Oswald! Look at me! No, no, it isn't true!

OSWALD (*looking up with a distracted expression*). Never to be able to work any more! Never—never! A living death! Mother, can you imagine anything so horrible!

MRS. ALVING. My poor unhappy boy! How has this terrible thing happened?

OSWALD (*sitting up again*). That is just what I cannot possibly understand. I have never lived recklessly, in any sense. You must believe that of me, mother! I have never done that.

MRS. ALVING. I haven't a doubt of it, Oswald.

OSWALD. And yet this comes upon me all the same!—this terrible disaster!

MRS. ALVING. Oh, but it will all come right again, my dear precious boy. It is nothing but overwork. Believe me, that is so.

OSWALD (*dully*). I thought so too, at first; but it isn't so.

MRS. ALVING. Tell me all about it.

OSWALD. Yes, I will.

MRS. ALVING. When did you first feel anything?

OSWALD. It was just after I had been home last time and had got back to Paris. I began to feel the most violent pains in my head—mostly at the back, I think. It was as if a tight band of iron was pressing on me from my neck upwards.

MRS. ALVING. And then?

OSWALD. At first I thought it was nothing but the headaches I always used to be so much troubled with while I was growing.

MRS. ALVING. Yes, yes—

OSWALD. But it wasn't; I soon saw that. I couldn't work any longer. I would try and start some big new picture; but it seemed as if all my faculties had forsaken me, as if all my strength were paralysed. I couldn't manage to collect my thoughts; my head seemed to swim—everything went round and round. It was a horrible feeling! As last I sent for a doctor —and from him I learnt the truth.

MRS. ALVING. In what way, do you mean?

OSWALD. He was one of the best doctors there. He made me describe what I felt, and then he began to ask me a whole heap of questions which seemed to me to have nothing to do with the matter. I couldn't see what he was driving at—

MRS. ALVING. Well?

OSWALD. At last he said: "You have had the canker of disease in you practically from your birth"—the actual word he used was *"vermoulu."*

MRS. ALVING (*anxiously*). What did he mean by that?

OSWALD. I couldn't understand, either—and I asked him

for a clearer explanation. And then the old cynic said—
(*clenching his fist.*) Oh!—

MRS. ALVING. What did he say?

OSWALD. He said: "The sins of the fathers are visited on
the children."

MRS. ALVING (*getting up slowly*). The sins of the fathers—.

OSWALD. I nearly struck him in the face—

MRS. ALVING (*walking across the room*). The sins of the
fathers—!

OSWALD (*smiling sadly*). Yes, just imagine! Naturally I
assured him that what he thought was impossible. But do you
think he paid any heed to me? No, he persisted in his opinion;
and it was only when I got out your letters and translated to
him all the passages that referred to my father—

MRS. ALVING. Well, and then?

OSWALD. Well, then of course he had to admit that he was
on the wrong tack; and then I learnt the truth—the incom-
prehensible truth! I ought to have had nothing to do with the
joyous happy life I had lived with my comrades. It had been
too much for my strength. So it was my own fault!

MRS. ALVING. No, no, Oswald! Don't believe that!

OSWALD. There was no other explanation of it possible, he
said. That is the most horrible part of it. My whole life
incurably ruined—just because of my own imprudence. All
that I wanted to do in the world—not to dare to think of it
any more—not to be *able* to think of it! Oh! if only I could
live my life over again—if only I could undo what I have
done! (*Throws himself on his face on the couch.* MRS. ALVING
*wrings her hands, and walks up and down silently fighting with
herself.*)

OSWALD (*looks up after a while, raising himself on his
elbows*). If only it had been something I had inherited—
something I could not help. But, instead of that, to have
disgracefully, stupidly, thoughtlessly thrown away one's happiness, one's health, everything in the world—one's future, one's
life—

MRS. ALVING. No, no, my darling boy; that is impossible!
(*Bending over him.*) Things are not so desperate as you think.

OSWALD. Ah, you don't know—. (*Springs up.*) And to
think, mother, that I should bring all this sorrow upon you!
Many a time I have almost wished and hoped that you really
did not care so very much for me.

MRS. ALVING. I, Oswald? My only son! All that I have in
the world! The only thing I care about!

OSWALD (*taking hold of her hands and kissing them*). Yes,
yes, I know that is so. When I am at home I know that is

true. And that is one of the hardest parts of it to me. But now you know all about it; and now we won't talk any more about it to-day. I can't stand thinking about it long at a time. (*Walks across the room.*) Let me have something to drink, mother!

MRS. ALVING. To drink? What do you want?

OSWALD. Oh, anything you like. I suppose you have got some punch in the house.

MRS. ALVING. Yes, but my dear Oswald—!

OSWALD. Don't tell me I mustn't, mother. Do be nice! I must have something to drown these gnawing thoughts. (*Goes into the conservatory.*) And how—how gloomy it is here! (MRS. ALVING *rings the bell.*) And this incessant rain. It may go on week after week—a whole month. Never a ray of sunshine. I don't remember ever having seen the sun shine once when I have been at home.

MRS. ALVING. Oswald—you are thinking of going away from me!

OSWALD. Hm!—(*sighs deeply*). I am not thinking about anything. I *can't* think about anything! (*In a low voice.*) I have to let that alone.

RÉGINA (*coming from the dining-room*). Did you ring, ma'am?

MRS. ALVING. Yes, let us have the lamp in.

REGINA. In a moment, ma'am; it is all ready lit. (*Goes out.*)

MRS. ALVING (*going up to* OSWALD). Oswald, don't keep anything back from me.

OSWALD. I don't mother. (*Goes to the table.*) It seems to me I have told you a good lot.

(REGINA *brings the lamp and puts it upon the table.*)

MRS. ALVING. Regina, you might bring us a small bottle of champagne.

REGINA. Yes, ma'am. (*Goes out.*)

OSWALD (*taking hold of his mother's face*). That's right. I knew my mother wouldn't let her son go thirsty.

MRS. ALVING. My poor dear boy, how could I refuse you anything now?

OSWALD (*eagerly*). Is that true, mother? Do you mean it?

MRS. ALVING. Mean what?

OSWALD. That you couldn't deny me anything?

MRS. ALVING. My dear Oswald—

OSWALD. Hush!

(REGINA *brings in a tray with a small bottle of champagne and two glasses, which she puts on the table.*)

REGINA. Shall I open the bottle?

OSWALD. No, thank you, I will do it.

(REGINA *goes out.*)

MRS. ALVING (*sitting down at the table*). What did you mean, when you asked if I could refuse you nothing?

OSWALD (*busy opening the bottle*). Let us have a glass first—or two.

(*He draws the cork, fills one glass and is going to fill the other.*)

MRS. ALVING (*holding her hand over the second glass*). No, thanks—not for me.

OSWALD. Oh, well, for me then! (*He empties his glass, fills it again and empties it; then sits down at the table.*)

MRS. ALVING (*expectantly*). Now, tell me.

OSWALD (*without looking at her*). Tell me this; I thought you and Mr. Manders seemed so strange—so quiet—at dinner.

MRS. ALVING. Did you notice that?

OSWALD. Yes. Ahem! (*After a short pause.*) Tell me— what do you think of Regina?

MRS. ALVING. What do I think of her?

OSWALD. Yes, isn't she splendid!

MRS. ALVING. Dear Oswald, you don't know her as well as I do—

OSWALD. What of that?

MRS. ALVING. Regina was too long at home, unfortunately. I ought to have taken her under my charge sooner.

OSWALD. Yes, but isn't she splendid to look at, mother? (*Fills his glass.*)

MRS. ALVING. Regina has many serious faults—

OSWALD. Yes, but what of that? (*Drinks.*)

MRS. ALVING. But I am fond of her, all the same; and I have made myself responsible for her. I wouldn't for the world she should come to any harm.

OSWALD (*jumping up*). Mother, Regina is my only hope of salvation!

MRS. ALVING (*getting up*). What do you mean?

OSWALD. I can't go on bearing all this agony of mind alone.

MRS. ALVING. Haven't you your mother to help you to bear it?

OSWALD. Yes, I thought so; that was why I came home to you. But it is no use; I see that it isn't. I cannot spend my life here.

MRS. ALVING. Oswald!

OSWALD. I must live a different sort of life, mother; so I shall have to go away from you. I don't want you watching it.

MRS. ALVING. My unhappy boy! But, Oswald, as long as you are ill like this—

OSWALD. If it was only a matter of feeling ill, I would

stay with you, mother. You are the best friend I have in the world.

MRS. ALVING. Yes, I am that, Oswald, am I not?

OSWALD (*walking restlessly about*). But all this torment —the regret, the remorse—and the deadly fear. Oh—this horrible fear!

MRS. ALVING (*following him*). Fear? Fear of what? What do you mean?

OSWALD. Oh, don't ask me any more about it. I don't know what it is. I can't put it into words. (MRS. ALVING *crosses the room and rings the bell.*) What do you want?

MRS. ALVING. I want my boy to be happy, that's what I want. He mustn't brood over anything. (*To* REGINA, *who has come to the door.*) More champagne—a large bottle.

OSWALD. Mother!

MRS. ALVING. Do you think we country people don't know how to live?

OSWALD. Isn't she splendid to look at! What a figure! And the picture of health!

MRS. ALVING (*sitting down at the table*). Sit down, Oswald, and let us have a quiet talk.

OSWALD (*sitting down*). You don't know, mother, that I owe Regina a little reparation.

MRS. ALVING. You!

OSWALD. Oh, it was only a little thoughtlessness—call it what you like. Something quite innocent, anyway. The last time I was home—

MRS. ALVING. Yes?

OSWALD. —she used often to ask me questions about Paris, and I told her one thing and another about the life there. And I remember saying one day: "Wouldn't you like to go there yourself?"

MRS. ALVING. Well?

OSWALD. I saw her blush, and she said: "Yes, I should like to very much." "All right," I said, "I daresay it might be managed"—or something of that sort.

MRS. ALVING. And then?

OSWALD. I naturally had forgotten all about it; but the day before yesterday I happened to ask her if she was glad I was to be so long at home—

MRS. ALVING. Well?

OSWALD. —and she looked so queerly at me, and asked: "But what is to become of my trip to Paris?"

MRS. ALVING. Her trip!

OSWALD. And then I got it out of her that she had taken the thing seriously, and had been thinking about me all the time, and had set herself to learn French—

MRS. ALVING. So that was why—

OSWALD. Mother—when I saw this fine, splendid, handsome girl standing there in front of me—I had never paid any attention to her before then—but now, when she stood there as if with open arms ready for me to take her to myself—

MRS. ALVING. Oswald!

OSWALD. —then I realised that my salvation lay in her, for I saw the joy of life in her.

MRS. ALVING (*starting back*). The joy of life—? Is there salvation in that?

REGINA (*coming in from the dining-room with a bottle of champagne*). Excuse me for being so long; but I had to go to the cellar. (*Puts the bottle down on the table.*)

OSWALD. Bring another glass, too.

REGINA (*looking at him in astonishment*). The mistress's glass is there, sir.

OSWALD. Yes, but fetch one for yourself, Regina. (REGINA *starts, and gives a quick shy glance at* MRS. ALVING.) Well?

REGINA (*in a low and hesitating voice*). Do you wish me to, ma'am?

MRS. ALVING. Fetch the glass, Regina. (REGINA *goes into the dining-room.*)

OSWALD (*looking after her*). Have you noticed how well she walks?—so firmly and confidently!

MRS. ALVING. It cannot be, Oswald.

OSWALD. It is settled. You must see that. It is no use forbidding it. (REGINA *comes in with a glass, which she holds in her hand.*) Sit down, Regina. (REGINA *looks questioningly at* MRS. ALVING.)

MRS. ALVING. Sit down. (REGINA *sits down on a chair near the dining-room door, still holding the glass in her hand.*) Oswald, what was it you were saying about the joy of life?

OSWALD. Ah, mother—the joy of life! You don't know very much about that at home here. I shall never realise it here.

MRS. ALVING. Not even when you are with me?

OSWALD. Never at home. But you can't understand that.

MRS. ALVING. Yes, indeed I almost think I do understand you—now.

OSWALD. That—and the joy of work. They are really the same thing at bottom. But you don't know anything about that either.

MRS. ALVING. Perhaps you are right. Tell me some more about it, Oswald.

OSWALD. Well, all I mean is that here people are brought up to believe that work is a curse and a punishment for sin, and that life is a state of wretchedness and that the sooner we can get out of it the better.

MRS. ALVING. A vale of tears, yes. And we quite conscientiously make it so.

OSWALD. But the people over there will have none of that. There is no one there who really believes doctrines of that kind any longer. Over there the mere fact of being alive is thought to be a matter for exultant happiness. Mother, have you noticed that everything I have painted has turned upon the joy of life?—always upon the joy of life, unfailingly. There is light there, and sunshine, and a holiday feeling—and people's faces beaming with happiness. That is why I am afraid to stay at home here with you.

MRS. ALVING. Afraid? What are you afraid of here, with with me?

OSWALD. I am afraid that all these feelings that are so strong in me would degenerate into something ugly here.

MRS. ALVING (*looking steadily at him*). Do you think that is what would happen?

OSWALD. I am certain it would. Even if one lived the same life at home here, as over there—it would never really be the same life.

MRS. ALVING (*who has listened anxiously to him, gets up with a thoughtful expression and says:*) Now I see clearly how it all happened.

OSWALD. What do you see?

MRS. ALVING. I see it now for the first time. And now I can speak.

OSWALD (*getting up*). Mother, I don't understand you.

REGINA (*who has got up also*). Perhaps I had better go.

MRS. ALVING. No, stay here. Now I can speak. Now, my son, you shall know the whole truth. Oswald! Regina!

OSWALD. Hush!—here is the parson—

(MANDERS *comes in by the hall door.*)

MANDERS. Well, my friends, we have been spending an edifying time over there.

OSWALD. So have we.

MANDERS. Engstrand must have help with his Sailors' Home. Regina must go home with him and give him her assistance.

REGINA. No, thank you, Mr. Manders.

MANDERS (*perceiving her for the first time*). What—? You in here?—and with a wineglass in your hand!

REGINA (*putting down the glass hastily*). I beg your pardon—!

OSWALD. Regina is going away with me, Mr. Manders.

MANDERS. Going away! With you!

OSWALD. Yes, as my wife—if she insists on that.

MANDERS. But, good heavens—!

REGINA. It is not my fault, Mr. Manders.

OSWALD. Or else she stays here if I stay.

REGINA (*involuntarily*). Here!

MANDERS. I am amazed at you, Mrs. Alving.

MRS. ALVING. Neither of those things will happen, for now I can speak openly.

MANDERS. But you won't do that! No, no, no!

MRS. ALVING. Yes, I can and I will. And without destroying any one's ideals.

OSWALD. Mother, what is it that is being concealed from me?

REGINA (*listening*). Mrs. Alving! Listen! They are shouting outside.

(*Goes into the conservatory and looks out.*)

OSWALD (*going to the window on the left*). What can be the matter? Where does that glare come from?

REGINA (*calls out*). The Orphanage is on fire!

MRS. ALVING (*going to the window*). On fire?

MANDERS. On fire? Impossible. I was there just a moment ago.

OSWALD. Where is my hat? Oh, never mind that. Father's Orphanage—!

(*Runs out through the garden door.*)

MRS. ALVING. My shawl, Regina! The whole place is in flames.

MANDERS. How terrible! Mrs. Alving, That fire is a judgment on this house of sin!

MRS. ALVING. Quite so. Come, Regina.

(*She and REGINA hurry out.*)

MANDERS (*clasping his hands*). And no insurance!

(*Follows them out.*)

ACT III

(*The same scene. All the doors are standing open. The lamp is still burning on the table. It is dark outside, except for a faint glimmer of light seen through the windows at the back.* MRS. ALVING, *with a shawl over her head, is standing in the conservatory, looking out.* REGINA, *also wrapped in a shawl, is standing a little behind her.*)

MRS. ALVING. Everything burnt—down to the ground.

REGINA. It is burning still in the basement.

MRS. ALVING. I can't think why Oswald doesn't come back. There is no chance of saving anything.

REGINA. Shall I go and take his hat to him?

MRS. ALVING. Hasn't he even got his hat?

REGINA (*pointing to the hall*). No, there it is, hanging up.

MRS. ALVING. Never mind. He is sure to come back soon. I will go and see what he is doing. (*Goes out by the garden door.* MANDERS *comes in from the hall.*)

MANDERS. Isn't Mrs. Alving here?

REGINA. She has just this moment gone down into the garden.

MANDERS. I have never spent such a terrible night in my life.

REGINA. Isn't it a shocking misfortune, sir!

MANDERS. Oh, don't speak about it. I scarcely dare to think about it.

REGINA. But how can it have happened?

MANDERS. Don't ask me, Miss Engstrand! How should I know! Are you going to suggest too—? Isn't it enough that your father—?

REGINA. What has he done?

MANDERS. He has nearly driven me crazy.

ENGSTRAND (*coming in from the hall*). Mr. Manders—!

MANDERS (*turning round with a start*). Have you even followed me here!

116

ENGSTRAND. Yes, God help us all—! Great heavens! What a dreadful thing, your reverence!

MANDERS (*walking up and down*). Oh dear, oh dear!

REGINA. What do you mean?

ENGSTRAND. Our little prayer-meeting was the cause of it all, don't you see? (*Aside, to* REGINA.) Now we've got the old fool, my girl. (*Aloud.*) And to think it is my fault that Mr. Manders should be the cause of such a thing!

MANDERS. I assure you, Engstrand—

ENGSTRAND. But there was no one else carrying a light there except you, sir.

MANDERS (*standing still*). Yes, so you say. But I have no clear recollection of having had a light in my hand.

ENGSTRAND. But I saw quite distinctly your reverence take a candle and snuff it with your fingers and throw away the burning bit of wick among the shavings.

MANDERS. Did you see that?

ENGSTRAND. Yes, distinctly.

MANDERS. I can't understand it at all. It is never my habit to snuff a candle with my fingers.

ENGSTRAND. Yes, it wasn't like you to do that, sir. But who would have thought it could be such a dangerous thing to do?

MANDERS (*walking restlessly backwards and forwards*). Oh, don't ask me!

ENGSTRAND (*following him about*). And you hadn't insured it either, had you, sir?

MANDERS. No, no, no; you heard me say so.

ENGSTRAND. You hadn't insured it—and then went and set light to the whole place! Good Lord, what bad luck!

MANDERS (*wiping the perspiration from his forehead*). You may well say so, Engstrand.

ENGSTRAND. And that it should happen to a charitable institution that would have been of service both to the town and the country, so to speak! The newspapers won't be very kind to your reverence, I expect.

MANDERS. No, that is just what I am thinking of. It is almost the worst part of the whole thing. The spiteful attacks and accusations—it is horrible to think of!

MRS. ALVING (*coming in from the garden*). I can't get him away from the fire.

MANDERS. Oh, there you are, Mrs. Alving.

MRS. ALVING. You will escape having to make your inaugural address now, at all events, Mr. Manders.

MANDERS. Oh, I would so gladly have—

MRS. ALVING (*in a dull voice*). It is just as well it has happened. This Orphanage would never have come to any good.

MANDERS. Don't you think so?

MRS. ALVING. Do you?

MANDERS. But it is none the less an extraordinary piece of ill luck.

MRS. ALVING. We will discuss it simply as a business matter.—Are you waiting for Mr. Manders, Engstrand?

ENGSTRAND (*at the hall door*). Yes, I am.

MRS. ALVING. Sit down then, while you are waiting.

ENGSTRAND. Thank you, I would rather stand.

MRS. ALVING (*to* MANDERS). I suppose you are going by the boat?

MANDERS. Yes. It goes in about an hour.

MRS. ALVING. Please take all the documents back with you. I don't want to hear another word about the matter. I have something else to think about now—

MANDERS. Mrs. Alving—

MRS. ALVING. Later on I will send you a power of attorney to deal with it exactly as you please.

MANDERS. I shall be most happy to undertake that. I am afraid the original intention of the bequest will have to be entirely altered now.

MRS. ALVING. Of course.

MANDERS. Provisionally, I should suggest this way of disposing of it. Make over the Solvik property to the parish. The land is undoubtedly not without a certain value; it will always be useful for some purpose or another. And as for the interest on the remaining capital that is on deposit in the bank, possibly I might make suitable use of that in support of some undertaking that promises to be of use to the town.

MRS. ALVING. Do exactly as you please. The whole thing is a matter of indifference to me now.

ENGSTRAND. You will think of my Sailors' Home, Mr. Manders?

MANDERS. Yes, certainly, that is a suggestion. But we must consider the matter carefully.

ENGSTRAND (*aside*). Consider!—devil take it! Oh Lord.

MANDERS (*sighing*). And unfortunately I can't tell how much longer I may have anything to do with the matter—whether public opinion may not force me to retire from it altogether. That depends entirely upon the result of the enquiry into the cause of the fire.

MRS. ALVING. What do you say?

MANDERS. And one cannot in any way reckon upon the result beforehand.

ENGSTRAND (*going nearer to him*). Yes, indeed one can; because here stand I, Jacob Engstrand.

MANDERS. Quite so, but—

ENGSTRAND (*lowering his voice*). And Jacob Engstrand isn't the man to desert a worthy benefactor in the hour of need, as the saying is.

MANDERS. Yes, but, my dear fellow—how—?

ENGSTRAND. You might say Jacob Engstrand is an angel of salvation, so to speak, your reverence.

MANDERS. No, no, I couldn't possibly accept that.

ENGSTRAND. That's how it will be, all the same. I know some one who has taken the blame for some one else on his shoulders before now, I do.

MANDERS. Jacob! (*Grasps his hand.*) You are one in a thousand! You shall have assistance in the matter of your Sailors' Home, you may rely upon that.

(ENGSTRAND *tries to thank him, but is prevented by emotion.*)

MANDERS (*hanging his wallet over his shoulder*). Now we must be off. We will travel together.

ENGSTRAND (*by the dining-room, says aside to* REGINA). Come with me, you hussy! You shall be as cosy as the yolk in an egg!

REGINA (*tossing her head*). *Merci!*

(*She goes out into the hall and brings back* MANDERS' *luggage.*)

MANDERS. Good-bye, Mrs. Alving! And may the spirit of order and of what is lawful speedily enter into this house.

MRS. ALVING. Good-bye, Mr. Manders.

(*She goes into the conservatory, as she sees* OSWALD *coming in by the garden door.*)

ENGSTRAND (*as he and* REGINA *are helping* MANDERS *on with his coat*). Good-bye, my child. And if anything should happen to you, you know where Jacob Engstrand is to be found. (*Lowering his voice.*) Little Harbour Street, ahem—! (*To* MRS. ALVING *and* OSWALD.) And my house for poor seafaring men shall be called the "Alving Home," it shall. And, if I can carry out my own ideas about it, I shall make bold to hope that it may be worthy of bearing the late Mr. Alving's name.

MANDERS (*at the door*). Ahem—ahem! Come along, my dear Engstrand. Good-bye—good-bye!

(*He and* ENGSTRAND *go out by the hall door.*)

OSWALD (*going to the table*). What house was he speaking about?

MRS. ALVING. I believe it is some sort of a Home that he and Mr. Manders want to start.

OSWALD. It will be burnt up just like this one.

MRS. ALVING. What makes you think that?

OSWALD. Everything will be burnt up; nothing will be left that is in memory of my father. Here am I being burnt up, too.

(REGINA *looks at him in alarm.*)

MRS. ALVING. Oswald! You should not have stayed so long over there, my poor boy.

OSWALD (*sitting down at the table*). I almost believe you are right.

MRS. ALVING. Let me dry your face, Oswald; you are all wet. (*Wipes his face with her handkerchief.*)

OSWALD (*looking straight before him, with no expression in his eyes*). Thank you, mother.

MRS. ALVING. And aren't you tired, Oswald? Don't you want to go to sleep?

OSWALD (*uneasily*). No, no—not to sleep! I never sleep; I only pretend to. (*Gloomily.*) That will come soon enough.

MRS. ALVING (*looking at him anxiously*). Anyhow you are really ill, my darling boy.

REGINA (*intently*). Is Mr. Alving ill?

OSWALD (*impatiently*). And do shut all the doors! This deadly fear—

MRS. ALVING. Shut the doors, Regina. (REGINA *shuts the doors and remains standing by the hall door.* MRS. ALVING *takes off her shawl;* REGINA *does the same.* MRS. ALVING *draws up a chair near to* OSWALD'S *and sits down beside him.*) That's it! Now I will sit beside you—

OSWALD. Yes, do. And Regina must stay in here too. Regina must always be near me. You must give me a helping hand, you know, Regina. Won't you do that?

REGINA. I don't understand—

MRS. ALVING. A helping hand?

OSWALD. Yes—when there is need for it.

MRS. ALVING. Oswald, have you not your mother to give you a helping hand?

OSWALD. You? (*Smiles.*) No, mother, you will never give me the kind of helping hand I mean. (*Laughs grimly.*) You! Ha, ha! (*Looks gravely at her.*) After all, you have the best right. (*Impetuously.*) Why don't you call me by my Christian name, Regina? Why don't you say Oswald?

REGINA (*in a low voice*). I did not think Mrs. Alving would like it.

MRS. ALVING. It will not be long before you have the right to do it. Sit down here now beside us, too. (REGINA *sits down quietly and hesitatingly at the other side of the table.*) And now, my poor tortured boy, I am going to take the burden off your mind —

OSWALD. You, mother?

Mrs. ALVING. —all that you call remorse and regret and self-reproach.

OSWALD. And you think you can do that?

Mrs. ALVING. Yes, now I can, Oswald. A little while ago you were talking about the joy of life, and what you said seemed to shed a new light upon everything in my whole life.

OSWALD (*shaking his head*). I don't in the least understand what you mean.

Mrs. ALVING. You should have known your father in his young days in the army. He was full of the joy of life, I can tell you.

OSWALD. Yes, I know.

Mrs. ALVING. It gave me a holiday feeling only to look at him, full of irrepressible energy and exuberant spirits.

OSWALD. What then?

Mrs. ALVING. Well, then this boy, full of the joy of life—for he was just like a boy, then—had to make his home in a second-rate town which had none of the joy of life to offer him, but only dissipations. He had to come out here and live an aimless life; he had only an official post. He had no work worth devoting his whole mind to; he had nothing more than official routine to attend to. He had not a single companion capable of appreciating what the joy of life meant; nothing but idlers and tipplers—

OSWALD. Mother—!

Mrs. ALVING. And so the inevitable happened!

OSWALD. What was the inevitable?

Mrs. ALVING. You said yourself this evening what would happen in your case if you stayed at home.

OSWALD. Do you mean by that, that father—?

Mrs. ALVING. Your poor father never found any outlet for the overmastering joy of life that was in him. And I brought no holiday spirit into his home, either.

OSWALD. You didn't, either?

Mrs. ALVING. I had been taught about duty, and the sort of thing that I believed in so long here. Everything seemed to turn upon duty—my duty, or his duty—and I am afraid I made your poor father's home unbearable to him, Oswald.

OSWALD. Why did you never say anything about it to me in your letters?

Mrs. ALVING. I never looked at it as a thing I could speak of to you, who were his son.

OSWALD. What way did you look at it, then?

Mrs. ALVING. I only saw the one fact, that your father was a lost man before ever you were born.

OSWALD (*in a choking voice*). Ah—! (*He gets up and goes to the window.*)

MRS. ALVING. And then I had the one thought in my mind, day and night, that Regina in fact has as good a right in this house—as my own boy had.

OSWALD (*turns round suddenly*). Regina—?

REGINA (*gets up and asks in choking tones*). I—?

MRS. ALVING. Yes, now you both know it.

OSWALD. Regina!

REGINA (*to herself*). So mother was one of that sort too.

MRS. ALVING. Your mother had many good qualities, Regina.

REGINA. Yes, but she was one of that sort too, all the same. I have even thought so myself, sometimes, but—. Then, if you please, Mrs. Alving, may I have permission to leave at once?

MRS. ALVING. Do you really wish to, Regina?

REGINA. Yes, indeed, I certainly wish to.

MRS. ALVING. Of course you shall do as you like, but—

OSWALD (*going up to* REGINA). Leave now? This is your home.

REGINA. *Merci*, Mr. Alving—oh, of course, I may say Oswald now, but that is not the way I thought it would become allowable.

MRS. ALVING. Regina, I have not been open with you—

REGINA. No, I can't say you have! If I had known Oswald was ill—. And now that there can never be anything serious between us—. No, I really can't stay here in the country and wear myself out looking after invalids.

OSWALD. Not even for the sake of one who has so near a claim on you?

REGINA. No, indeed I can't. A poor girl must make some use of her youth, otherwise she may easily find herself out in the cold before she knows where she is. And I have got the joy of life in me too, Mrs. Alving!

MRS. ALVING. Yes, unfortunately; but don't throw yourself away, Regina.

REGINA. Oh, what's going to happen will happen. If Oswald takes after his father, it is just as likely I take after my mother, I expect.—May I ask, Mrs. Alving, whether Mr. Manders knows this about me?

MRS. ALVING. Mr. Manders knows everything.

REGINA (*putting on her shawl*). Oh, well then, the best thing I can do is to get away by the boat as soon as I can. Mr. Manders is such a nice gentleman to deal with; and it certainly seems to me that I have just as much right to some of that money as he—as that horrid carpenter.

MRS. ALVING. You are quite welcome to it, Regina.

REGINA (*looking at her fixedly*). You might as well have brought me up like a gentleman's daughter; it would have been more suitable. (*Tosses her head.*) Oh, well—never mind! (*With a bitter glance at the unopened bottle.*) I daresay some day I shall be drinking champagne with gentlefolk, after all.

MRS. ALVING. If ever you need a home, Regina, come to me.

REGINA. No, thank you, Mrs. Alving. Mr. Manders takes an interest in me, I know. And if things should go very badly with me, I know one house at any rate where I shall feel at home.

MRS. ALVING. Where is that?

REGINA. In the "Alving Home."

MRS. ALVING. Regina—I can see quite well—you are going to your ruin!

REGINA. Pooh!—good-bye.

(*She bows to them and goes out through the hall.*)

OSWALD (*standing by the window and looking out*). Has she gone?

MRS. ALVING. Yes.

OSWALD (*muttering to himself*). I think it's all wrong.

MRS. ALVING (*going up to him from behind and putting her hands on his shoulders*). Oswald, my dear boy—has it been a great shock to you?

OSWALD (*turning his face towards her*). All this about father, do you mean?

MRS. ALVING. Yes, about your unhappy father. I am so afraid it may have been too much for you.

OSWALD. What makes you think that? Naturally it has taken me entirely by surprise; but, after all, I don't know that it matters much to me.

MRS. ALVING (*drawing back her hands*). Doesn't matter!— that your father's life was such a terrible failure!

OSWALD. Of course I can feel sympathy for him, just as I would for anyone else, but—

MRS. ALVING. No more than that! For your own father!

OSWALD (*impatiently*). Father—father! I never knew anything of my father. I don't remember anything else about him except that he once made me sick.

MRS. ALVING. It is dreadful to think of!—But surely a child should feel some affection for his father, whatever happens?

OSWALD. When the child has nothing to thank his father for? When he has never known him? Do you really cling to that antiquated superstition—you, who are so broad-minded in other things?

MRS. ALVING. You call it nothing but a superstition!

OSWALD. Yes, and you can see that for yourself quite well, mother. It is one of those beliefs that are put into circulation in the world, and—

MRS. ALVING. Ghosts of beliefs!

OSWALD (*walking across the room*). Yes, you might call them ghosts.

MRS. ALVING (*with an outburst of feeling*). Oswald—then you don't love me either!

OSWALD. You I know, at any rate—

MRS. ALVING. You know me, yes; but is that all?

OSWALD. And I know how fond you are of me, and I ought to be grateful to you for that. Besides, you can be so tremendously useful to me, now that I am ill.

MRS. ALVING. Yes, can't I, Oswald! I could almost bless your illness, as it has driven you home to me. For I see quite well that you are not my very own yet; you must be won.

OSWALD (*impatiently*). Yes, yes, yes; all that is just a way of talking. You must remember I am a sick man, mother. I can't concern myself much with anyone else; I have enough to do, thinking about myself.

MRS. ALVING (*gently*). I will be very good and patient.

OSWALD. And cheerful too, mother!

MRS. ALVING. Yes, my dear boy, you are quite right. (*Goes up to him.*) Now have I taken away all your remorse and self-approach?

OSWALD. Yes, you have done that. But who will take away the fear?

MRS. ALVING. The fear?

OSWALD (*crossing the room*). Regina would have done it for one kind word.

MRS. ALVING. I don't understand you. What fear do you mean—and what has Regina to do with it?

OSWALD. Is it very late, mother?

MRS. ALVING. It is early morning. (*Looks out through the conservatory windows.*) The dawn is breaking already on the heights. And the sky is clear, Oswald. In a little while you will see the sun.

OSWALD. I am glad of that. After all, there may be many things yet for me to be glad of and to live for—

MRS. ALVING. I should hope so!

OSWALD. Even if I am not able to work—

MRS. ALVING. You will soon find you are able to work again now, my dear boy. You have no longer all those painful depressing thoughts to brood over.

OSWALD. No, it is a good thing that you have been able to rid me of those fancies. If only, now, I could overcome this one thing—. (*Sits down on the couch.*) Let us have a little chat, mother.

MRS. ALVING. Yes, let us. (*Pushes an armchair near to the couch and sits down beside him.*)

OSWALD. The sun is rising—and you know all about it; so I don't feel the fear any longer.

MRS. ALVING. I know all about what?

OSWALD (*without listening to her*). Mother, isn't it the case that you said this evening there was nothing in the world you would not do for me if I asked you?

MRS. ALVING. Yes, certainly I said so.

OSWALD. And will you be as good as your word, mother?

MRS. ALVING. You may rely upon that, my own dear boy. I have nothing else to live for, but you.

OSWALD. Yes, yes; well, listen to me, mother. You are very strong-minded, I know. I want you to sit quite quiet when you hear what I am going to tell you.

MRS. ALVING. But what is this dreadful thing—?

OSWALD. You mustn't scream. Do you hear? Will you promise me that? We are going to sit and talk it over quite quietly. Will you promise me that, mother?

MRS. ALVING. Yes, yes, I promise—only tell me what it is.

OSWALD. Well, then, you must know that this fatigue of mine—and my not being able to think about my work—all that is not really the illness itself—

MRS. ALVING. What is the illness itself?

OSWALD. What I am suffering from is hereditary; it— (*touches his forehead, and speaks very quietly*)—it lies here.

MRS. ALVING (*almost speechless*). Oswald! No—no!

OSWALD. Don't scream; I can't stand it. Yes, I tell you, it lies here, waiting. And any time, any moment, it may break out.

MRS. ALVING. How horrible—!

OSWALD. Do keep quiet. That is the state I am in—

MRS. ALVING (*springing up*). It isn't true, Oswald! It is impossible! It can't be that!

OSWALD. I had one attack while I was abroad. It passed off quickly. But when I learnt the condition I had been in, then this dreadful haunting fear took possession of me.

MRS. ALVING. That was the fear, then—

OSWALD. Yes, it is so indescribably horrible, you know. If only it had been an ordinary mortal disease—. I am not so much afraid of dying; though, of course, I should like to live as long as I can.

MRS. ALVING. Yes, yes, Oswald, you must!

OSWALD. But this is so appallingly horrible. To become like a helpless child again—to have to be fed, to have to be—. Oh, it's unspeakable!

MRS. ALVING. My child has his mother to tend him.

OSWALD (*jumping up*). No, never; that is just what I won't endure! I dare not think what it would mean to linger on like

that for years—to get old and grey like that. And you might
die before I did. (*Sits down in* MRS. ALVING's *chair*.) Because it doesn't necessarily have a fatal end quickly, the
doctor said. He called it a kind of softening of the brain—or
something of that sort. (*Smiles mournfully*.) I think that
expression sounds so nice. It always makes me think of
cherry-coloured velvet curtains—something that is soft to
stroke.

MRS. ALVING (*with a scream*). Oswald!

OSWALD (*jumps up and walks about the room*). And now
you have taken Regina from me! If I had only had her. She
would have given me a helping hand, I know.

MRS. ALVING (*going up to him*). What do you mean, my
darling boy? Is there any help in the world I would not be
willing to give you?

OSWALD. When I had recovered from the attack I had
abroad, the doctor told me that when it recurred—and it will
recur—there would be no more hope.

MRS. ALVING. And he was a heartless enough to—

OSWALD. I insisted on knowing. I told him I had arrangements to make—. (*Smiles cunningly*.) And so I had. (*Takes
a small box from his inner breast-pocket*.) Mother, do you
see this?

MRS. ALVING. What is it?

OSWALD. Morphia powders.

MRS. ALVING (*looking at him in terror*). Oswald—my boy!

OSWALD. I have twelve of them saved up—

MRS. ALVING (*snatching at it*). Give me the box, Oswald!

OSWALD. Not yet, mother. (*Puts it back in his pocket*.)

MRS. ALVING. I shall never get over this!

OSWALD. You must. If I had had Regina here now, I would
have told her quietly how things stand with me—and asked
her to give me this last helping hand. She would have helped
me, I am certain.

MRS. ALVING. Never!

OSWALD. If this horrible thing had come upon me and she
had seen me lying helpless, like a baby, past help, past saving, past hope—with no chance of recovering—

MRS. ALVING. Never in the world would Regina have
done it.

OSWALD. Regina would have done it. Regina was so splendidly light-hearted. And she would very soon have tired of
looking after an invalid like me.

MRS. ALVING. Then thank heaven Regina is not here!

OSWALD. Well, now you have got to give me that helping
hand, mother.

MRS. ALVING (*with a loud scream*). I!

OSWALD. Who has a better right than you?

MRS. ALVING. I! Your mother!

OSWALD. Just for that reason.

MRS. ALVING. I, who gave you your life!

OSWALD. I never asked you for life. And what kind of a life was it that you gave me? I don't want it! You shall take it back!

MRS. ALVING. Help! Help! (*Runs into the hall.*)

OSWALD (*following her*). Don't leave me! Where are you going?

MRS. ALVING (*in the hall*). To fetch the doctor to you, Oswald! Let me out!

OSWALD (*going into the hall*). You shan't go out. And no one shall come in. (*Turns the key in the lock.*)

MRS. ALVING (*coming in again*). Oswald! Oswald!—my child!

OSWALD (*following her*). Have you a mother's heart—and can bear to see me suffering this unspeakable terror?

MRS. ALVING (*controlling herself, after a moment's silence*). There is my hand on it.

OSWALD. Will you—?

MRS. ALVING. If it becomes necessary. But it shan't become necessary. No, no—it is impossible it should!

OSWALD. Let us hope so. And let us live together as long as we can. Thank you, mother.

(*He sits down in the armchair, which* MRS. ALVING *had moved beside the couch. Day is breaking; the lamp is still burning on the table.*)

MRS. ALVING (*coming cautiously nearer*). Do you feel calmer now?

OSWALD. Yes.

MRS. ALVING (*bending over him*). It has only been a dreadful fancy of yours, Oswald. Nothing but fancy. All this upset has been bad for you. But now you will get some rest, at home with your own mother, my darling boy. You shall have everything you want, just as you did when you were a little child.—There, now. The attack is over. You see how easily it passed off! I knew it would.—And look, Oswald, what a lovely day we are going to have? Brilliant sunshine. Now you will be able to see your home properly. (*She goes to the table and puts out the lamp. It is sunrise. The glaciers and peaks in the distance are seen bathed in bright morning light.*)

OSWALD (*who has been sitting motionless in the armchair, with his back to the scene outside, suddenly says:*) Mother, give me the sun.

MRS. ALVING (*standing at the table, and looking at him in amazement*). What do you say?

OSWALD (*repeats in a dull, toneless voice*). The sun—the sun.

MRS. ALVING (*going up to him*). Oswald, what is the matter with you? (OSWALD *seems to shrink up in the chair; all his muscles relax; his face loses its expression, and his eyes stare stupidly.* MRS. ALVING *is trembling with terror.*) What is it! (*Screams.*) Oswald! What is the matter with you! (*Throws herself on her knees beside him and shakes him.*) Oswald! Oswald! Look at me! Don't you know me!

OSWALD (*in an expressionless voice, as before*). The sun—the sun.

MRS. ALVING (*jumps up despairingly, beats her head with her hands, and screams*). I can't bear it! (*Whispers as though paralysed with fear.*) I can't bear it! Never! (*Suddenly.*) Where has he got it? (*Passes her hand quickly over his coat.*) Here! (*Draws back a little way and cries:*) No, no, no!— Yes!—no, no! (*She stands a few steps from him, her hands thrust into her hair, and stares at him in speechless terror.*)

OSWALD (*sitting motionless, as before*). The sun—the sun.

An Enemy of the People
A PLAY IN FIVE ACTS

Ibsen responded to the abuse that had been hurled at him for *Ghosts* by writing one of his most popular and least complicated plays, *An Enemy of the People.* Its hero's ringing statements that "the minority is always right" and that "the strongest man in the world is he who stands most alone," reveal Ibsen's own rage at the cowardly reception given *Ghosts* by the supposedly enlightened Scandinavian press. But though Ibsen used the play to vent his spleen against vested interests and their opportunistic minions in the professions and the intelligentsia, he did not lose his sense of humanity, or his command of characterization. The human contradictions of at least a dozen major characters are developed in the play.

Ibsen's view seems to have been that a mixture of wisdom and folly was to be found among the best of men. Even his admiration for his embattled hero's sentiments is qualified by mordant awareness of the complexity of human motivations and a comic appreciation of Stockmann's boyish naiveté and boisterous overconfidence. Stockmann's opponents are not represented as unmitigated rascals but as fallible human beings who heed the call of self-interest under a variety of social influences and pressures. Toward all these individuals, Ibsen manifests consideration as well as the severity of an acute social and moral critic. Only for the unthinking and easily manipulated masses does he exhibit contempt and mistrust. For the then disenchanted Ibsen, as for his hero Dr. Stockmann, "the majority is always wrong."

An Enemy of the People continues to interest modern audiences because of its satiric vigor as well as the ease with which progressives can apply its substance to the fight against conservatism and vested interest. How much loss of texture and insight is entailed in such a simplistic view of the play was made clear when Arthur Miller, in 1950, adapted it for the New York stage and turned it into a directly moralizing drama. He presented the play simply as the heroic struggle of a noble man against the ignoble leaders of a community. As such it was capable of arousing an audience concerned with the growing intolerance of political criticism in the United States during the McCarthy period, but Miller's version did so at the expense of Ibsen's complex moral vision. Ibsen's Dr. Stockmann, animated by "temperamental pugnacity, an active feeling of personal jealousy and an extremely good opinion of himself," is a decidedly more complicated stage character than any one-dimensional idealist could possibly be.

DRAMATIS PERSONÆ

Dr. Thomas Stockmann, Medical Officer of the Municipal Baths.
Mrs. Stockmann, his wife.
Petra, their daughter, a teacher.
Ejlif
Morten } their sons (aged 13 and 10 respectively).
Peter Stockmann, the Doctor's elder brother; Mayor of the Town and Chief Constable, Chairman of the Baths' Committee, etc., etc.
Morten, Kiil, a tanner (Mrs. Stockmann's adoptive father).
Hovstad, editor of the "People's Messenger."
Billing, sub-editor.
Captain Horster.
Aslaksen, a printer.
Men of various conditions and occupations, some few women, and a troop of schoolboys—the audience at a public meeting.

(*The action takes place in a coast town in southern Norway.*)

ACT I

(SCENE.—DR. STOCKMANN'S *sitting-room. It is evening.
The room is plainly but neatly appointed and furnished. In
the right-hand wall are two doors; the farther leads out to the
hall, the nearer to the doctor's study. In the left-hand wall,
opposite the door leading to the hall, is a door leading to the
other rooms occupied by the family. In the middle of the same
wall stands the stove, and, further forward, a couch with a
looking-glass hanging over it and an oval table in front of it.
On the table, a lighted lamp, with a lampshade. At the back
of the room, an open door leads to the dining-room. BILLING
is seen sitting at the dining table, on which a lamp is burning.
He has a napkin tucked under his chin, and MRS. STOCKMANN
is standing by the table handing him a large plate-full of roast
beef. The other places at the table are empty, and the table
somewhat in disorder, a meal having evidently recently been
finished.*)

MRS. STOCKMANN. You see, if you come an hour late, Mr.
Billing, you have to put up with cold meat.

BILLING (*as he eats*). It is uncommonly good, thank you
—remarkably good.

MRS. STOCKMANN. My husband makes such a point of
having his meals punctually, you know—

BILLING. That doesn't affect me a bit. Indeed, I almost
think I enjoy a meal all the better when I can sit down and
eat all by myself and undisturbed.

MRS. STOCKMANN. Oh well, as long as you are enjoying
it—. (*Turns to the hall door, listening.*) I expect that is Mr.
Hovstad coming too.

BILLING. Very likely.

(PETER STOCKMANN *comes in. He wears an overcoat and
his official hat, and carries a stick.*)

PETER STOCKMANN. Good evening, Katherine.

131

MRS. STOCKMANN (*coming forward into the sitting-room*). Ah, good evening—is it you? How good of you to come up and see us!

PETER STOCKMANN. I happened to be passing, and so— (*looks into the dining-room*). But you have company with you, I see.

MRS. STOCKMANN (*a little embarrassed*). Oh, no—it was quite by chance he came in. (*Hurriedly.*) Won't you come in and have something, too?

PETER STOCKMANN. I! No, thank you. Good gracious— hot meat at night! Not with my digestion.

MRS. STOCKMANN. Oh, but just once in a way—

PETER STOCKMANN. No, no, my dear lady; I stick to my tea and bread and butter. It is much more wholesome in the long run—and a little more economical, too.

MRS. STOCKMANN (*smiling*). Now you mustn't think that Thomas and I are spendthrifts.

PETER STOCKMANN. Not you, my dear; I would never think that of you. (*Points to the Doctor's study.*) Is he not at home?

MRS. STOCKMANN. No, he went for a little turn after supper—he and the boys.

PETER STOCKMANN. I doubt if that is a wise thing to do. (*Listens.*) I fancy I hear him coming now.

MRS. STOCKMANN. No, I don't think it is he. (*A knock is heard at the door.*) Come in! (HOVSTAD *comes in from the hall.*) Oh, it is you, Mr. Hovstad!

HOVSTAD. Yes, I hope you will forgive me, but I was delayed at the printers. Good evening, Mr. Mayor.

PETER STOCKMANN (*bowing a little distantly*). Good evening. You have come on business, no doubt.

HOVSTAD. Partly. It's about an article for the paper.

PETER STOCKMANN. So I imagined. I hear my brother has become a prolific contributor to the "People's Messenger."

HOVSTAD. Yes, he is good enough to write in the "People's Messenger" when he has any home truths to tell.

MRS. STOCKMANN (*to* HOVSTAD). But won't you—? (*Points to the dining-room.*)

PETER STOCKMANN. Quite so, quite so. I don't blame him in the least, as a writer, for addressing himself to the quarters where he will find the readiest sympathy. And, besides that, I personally have no reason to bear any ill will to your paper, Mr. Hovstad.

HOVSTAD. I quite agree with you.

PETER STOCKMANN. Taking one thing with another, there is an excellent spirit of toleration in the town—an admirable municipal spirit. And it all springs from the fact of our having a great common interest to unite us—an interest that is in an equally high degree the concern of every right-minded citizen—

HOVSTAD. The Baths, yes.

PETER STOCKMANN. Exactly—our fine, new, handsome Baths. Mark my words, Mr. Hovstad—the Baths will become the focus of our municipal life! Not a doubt of it!

MRS. STOCKMANN. That is just what Thomas says.

PETER STOCKMANN. Think how extraordinarily the place has developed within the last year or two! Money has been flowing in, and there is some life and some business doing in the town. Houses and landed property are rising in value every day.

HOVSTAD. And unemployment is diminishing.

PETER STOCKMANN. Yes, that is another thing. The burden of the poor rates has been lightened, to the great relief of the propertied classes; and that relief will be even greater if only we get a really good summer this year, and lots of visitors— plenty of invalids, who will make the Baths talked about.

HOVSTAD. And there is a good prospect of that, I hear.

PETER STOCKMANN. It looks very promising. Enquiries about apartments and that sort of thing are reaching us every day.

HOVSTAD. Well, the doctor's article will come in very suitably.

PETER STOCKMANN. Has he been writing something just lately?

HOVSTAD. This is something he wrote in the winter; a recommendation of the Baths—an account of the excellent sanitary conditions here. But I held the article over, temporarily.

PETER STOCKMANN. Ah,—some little difficulty about it, I suppose?

HOVSTAD. No, not at all; I thought it would be better to wait till the spring, because it is just at this time that people begin to think seriously about their summer quarters.

PETER STOCKMANN. Quite right; you were perfectly right, Mr. Hovstad.

HOVSTAD. Yes, Thomas is really indefatigable when it is a question of the Baths.

PETER STOCKMANN. Well—remember, he is the Medical Officer to the Baths.

HOVSTAD. Yes, and what is more, they owe their existence to him.

PETER STOCKMANN. To him? Indeed! It is true I have heard from time to time that some people are of that opinion. At the same time I must say I imagined that I took a modest part in the enterprise.

MRS. STOCKMANN. Yes, that is what Thomas is always saying.

HOVSTAD. But who denies it, Mr. Stockmann? You set the thing going and made a practical concern of it; we all know that. I only meant that the idea of it came first from the doctor.

PETER STOCKMANN. Oh, ideas—yes! My brother has had plenty of them in his time—unfortunately. But when it is a question of putting an idea into practical shape, you have to apply to a man of different mettle, Mr. Hovstad. And I certainly should have thought that in this house at least—

MRS. STOCKMANN. My dear Peter—

HOVSTAD. How can you think that—?

MRS. STOCKMANN. Won't you go in and have something, Mr. Hovstad? My husband is sure to be back directly.

HOVSTAD. Thank you, perhaps just a morsel. (*Goes into the dining-room.*)

PETER STOCKMANN (*lowering his voice a little*). It is a curious thing that these farmers' sons never seem to lose their want of tact.

MRS. STOCKMANN. Surely it is not worth bothering about! Cannot you and Thomas share the credit as brothers?

PETER STOCKMANN. I should have thought so; but apparently some people are not satisfied with a share.

MRS. STOCKMANN. What nonsense! You and Thomas get on so capitally together. (*Listens.*) There he is at last, I think. (*Goes out and opens the door leading to the hall.*)

DR. STOCKMANN (*laughing and talking outside*). Look here—here is another guest for you, Katherine. Isn't that jolly! Come in, Captain Horster; hang your coat upon this peg. Ah, you don't wear an overcoat. Just think, Katherine; I met him in the street and could hardly persuade him to come up! (CAPTAIN HORSTER *comes into the room and greets* MRS. STOCKMANN. *He is followed by* DR. STOCKMANN.) Come along in, boys. They are ravenously hungry again, you know. Come along, Captain Horster; you must have a slice of beef. (*Pushes* HORSTER *into the dining-room.* EJLIF *and* MORTEN *go in after them.*)

MRS. STOCKMANN. But, Thomas, don't you see—?

DR. STOCKMANN (*turning in the doorway*). Oh, is it you, Peter? (*Shakes hands with him.*) Now that is very delightful.

PETER STOCKMANN. Unfortunately I must go in a moment—

DR. STOCKMANN. Rubbish! There is some toddy just coming in. You haven't forgotten the toddy, Katherine?

MRS. STOCKMANN. Of course not; the water is boiling now. (*Goes into the dining-room.*)

PETER STOCKMANN. Toddy too!

DR. STOCKMANN. Yes, sit down and we will have it comfortably.

PETER STOCKMANN. Thanks, I never care about an evening's drinking.

DR. STOCKMANN. But this isn't an evening's drinking.

PETER STOCKMANN. It seems to me—. (*Looks towards the dining-room.*) It is extraordinary how they can put away all that food.

DR. STOCKMANN (*rubbing his hands*). Yes, isn't it splendid to see young people eat? They have always got an appetite, you know! That's as it should be. Lots of food—to build up their strength! They are the people who are going to stir up the fermenting forces of the future, Peter.

PETER STOCKMANN. May I ask what they will find here to "stir up," as you put it?

DR. STOCKMANN. Ah, you must ask the young people that —when the times comes. We shan't be able to see it, of course. That stands to reason—two old fogies, like us—

PETER STOCKMANN. Really, really! I must say that is an extremely odd expression to—

DR. STOCKMANN. Oh, you mustn't take me too literally, Peter. I am so heartily happy and contented, you know. I think it is such an extraordinary piece of good fortune to be in the middle of all this growing, germinating life. It is a splendid time to live in! It is as if a whole new world were being created around one.

PETER STOCKMANN. Do you really think so?

DR. STOCKMANN. Ah, naturally you can't appreciate it as keenly as I. You have lived all your life in these surroundings, and your impressions have got blunted. But I, who have been buried all these years in my little corner up north, almost without ever seeing a stranger who might bring new ideas with him—well, in my case it has just the same effect as if I had been transported into the middle of a crowded city.

PETER STOCKMANN. Oh, a city—!

DR. STOCKMANN. I know, I know; it is all cramped enough here, compared with many other places. But there is life here —there is promise—there are innumerable things to work for and fight for; and that is the main thing. (*Calls.*) Katherine, hasn't the postman been here?

MRS. STOCKMANN (*from the dining-room*). No.

DR. STOCKMANN. And then to be comfortably off, Peter! That is something one learns to value, when one has been on the brink of starvation, as we have.

PETER STOCKMANN. Oh, surely—

DR. STOCKMANN. Indeed I can assure you we have often

been very hard put to it, up there. And now to be able to live like a lord! To-day, for instance, we had roast beef for dinner—and, what is more, for supper too. Won't you come and have a little bit? Or let me show it you, at any rate? Come here—

PETER STOCKMANN. No, no—not for worlds!

DR. STOCKMANN. Well, but just come here then. Do you see, we have got a table-cover?

PETER STOCKMANN. Yes, I noticed it.

DR. STOCKMANN. And we have got a lamp-shade too. Do you see? All out of Katherine's savings! It makes the room so cosy. Don't you think so? Just stand here for a moment—no, no, not there—just here, that's it! Look now, when you get the light on it altogether—I really think it looks very nice, doesn't it?

PETER STOCKMANN. Oh, if you can afford luxuries of this kind—

DR. STOCKMANN. Yes, I can afford it now. Katherine tells me I earn almost as much as we spend.

PETER STOCKMANN. Almost—yes!

DR. STOCKMANN. But a scientific man must live in a little bit of style. I am quite sure an ordinary civil servant spends more in a year than I do.

PETER STOCKMANN. I daresay. A civil servant—a man in a well-paid position—

DR. STOCKMANN. Well, any ordinary merchant, then! A man in that position spends two or three times as much as—

PETER STOCKMANN. It just depends on circumstances.

DR. STOCKMANN. At all events I assure you I don't waste money unprofitably. But I can't find it in my heart to deny myself the pleasure of entertaining my friends. I need that sort of thing, you know. I have lived for so long shut out of it all, that it is a necessity of life to me to mix with young, eager, ambitious men, men of liberal and active minds; and that describes every one of those fellows who are enjoying their supper in there. I wish you knew more of Hovstad—

PETER STOCKMANN. By the way, Hovstad was telling me he was going to print another article of yours.

DR. STOCKMANN. An article of mine?

PETER STOCKMANN. Yes, about the Baths. An article you wrote in the winter.

DR. STOCKMANN. Oh, that one! No, I don't intend that to appear just for the present.

PETER STOCKMANN. Why not? It seems to me that this would be the most opportune moment.

DR. STOCKMANN. Yes, very likely—under normal conditions. (*Crosses the room.*)

PETER STOCKMANN (*following him with his eyes*). Is there anything abnormal about the present conditions?

DR. STOCKMANN (*standing still*). To tell you the truth, Peter, I can't say just at this moment—at all events not to-night. There may be much that is very abnormal about the present conditions—and it is possible there may be nothing abnormal about them at all. It is quite possible it may be merely my imagination.

PETER STOCKMANN. I must say it all sounds most mysterious. Is there something going on that I am to be kept in ignorance of? I should have imagined that I, as Chairman of the governing body of the Baths——

DR. STOCKMANN. And I should have imagined that I——. Oh, come, don't let us fly out at one another, Peter.

PETER STOCKMANN. Heaven forbid! I am not in the habit of flying out at people, as you call it. But I am entitled to request most emphatically that all arrangements shall be made in a business-like manner, through the proper channels, and shall be dealt with by the legally constituted authorities. I can allow no going behind our backs by any roundabout means.

DR. STOCKMANN. Have I ever at any time tried to go behind your backs!

PETER STOCKMANN. You have an ingrained tendency to take your own way, at all events; and that is almost equally inadmissible in a well ordered community. The individual ought undoubtedly to acquiesce in subordinating himself to the community—or, to speak more accurately, to the authorities who have the care of the community's welfare.

DR. STOCKMANN. Very likely. But what the deuce has all this got to do with me?

PETER STOCKMANN. That is exactly what you never appear to be willing to learn, my dear Thomas. But, mark my words, some day you will have to suffer for it—sooner or later. Now I have told you. Good-bye.

DR. STOCKMANN. Have you taken leave of your senses? You are on the wrong scent altogether.

PETER STOCKMANN. I am not usually that. You must excuse me now if I—(*calls into the dining-room*). Good night, Katherine. Good night, gentlemen. (*Goes out.*)

MRS. STOCKMANN (*coming from the dining-room*). Has he gone?

DR. STOCKMANN. Yes, and in such a bad temper.

MRS. STOCKMANN. But, dear Thomas, what have you been doing to him again?

DR. STOCKMANN. Nothing at all. And, anyhow, he can't oblige me to make my report before the proper time.

MRS. STOCKMANN. What have you got to make a report to him about?

DR. STOCKMANN. Hm! Leave that to me, Katherine.—It is an extraordinary thing that the postman doesn't come.

(HOVSTAD, BILLING *and* HORSTER *have got up from the table and come into the sitting-room.* EJLIF *and* MORTEN *come in after them.*)

BILLING (*stretching himself*). Ah!—one feels a new man after a meal like that.

HOVSTAD. The mayor wasn't in a very sweet temper tonight, then.

DR. STOCKMANN. It is his stomach; he has a wretched digestion.

HOVSTAD. I rather think it was us two of the "People's Messenger" that he couldn't digest.

MRS. STOCKMANN. I thought you came out of it pretty well with him.

HOVSTAD. Oh yes; but it isn't anything more than a sort of truce.

BILLING. That is just what it is! That word sums up the situation.

DR. STOCKMANN. We must remember that Peter is a lonely man, poor chap. He has no home comforts of any kind; nothing but everlasting business. And all that infernal weak tea wash that he pours into himself! Now then, my boys, bring chairs up to the table. Aren't we going to have that toddy, Katherine?

MRS. STOCKMANN (*going into the dining-room*). I am just getting it.

DR. STOCKMANN. Sit down here on the couch beside me, Captain Horster. We so seldom see you——. Please sit down, my friends. (*They sit down at the table.* MRS. STOCKMANN *brings a tray, with a spirit-lamp, glasses, bottles, etc., upon it.*)

MRS. STOCKMANN. There you are! This is arrack, and this is rum, and this one is the brandy. Now every one must help themselves.

DR. STOCKMANN (*taking a glass*). We will. (*They all mix themselves some toddy.*) And let us have the cigars. Ejlif, you know where the box is. And you, Morten, can fetch my pipe. (*The two boys go into the room on the right.*) I have a suspicion that Ejlif pockets a cigar now and then!—but I take no notice of it. (*Calls out.*) And my smoking-cap too, Morten. Katherine, you can tell him where I left it. Ah, he has got it. (*The boys bring the various things.*) Now, my friends. I stick to my pipe, you know. This one has seen plenty of bad weather with me up north. (*Touches glasses with them.*)

Your good health! Ah, it is good to be sitting snug and warm here.

MRS. STOCKMANN (*who sits knitting*). Do you sail soon, Captain Horster?

HORSTER. I expect to be ready to sail next week.

MRS. STOCKMANN. I suppose you are going to America?

HORSTER. Yes, that is the plan.

MRS. STOCKMANN. Then you won't be able to take part in the coming election.

HORSTER. Is there going to be an election?

BILLING. Didn't you know?

HORSTER. No, I don't mix myself up with those things.

BILLING. But do you not take an interest in public affairs?

HORSTER. No, I don't know anything about politics.

BILLING. All the same, one ought to vote, at any rate.

HORSTER. Even if one doesn't know anything about what is going on?

BILLING. Doesn't know! What do you mean by that? A community is like a ship; every one ought to be prepared to take the helm.

HORSTER. May be that is all very well on shore; but on board ship it wouldn't work.

HOVSTAD. It is astonishing how little most sailors care about what goes on on shore.

BILLING. Very extraordinary.

DR. STOCKMANN. Sailors are like birds of passage; they feel equally at home in any latitude. And that is only an additional reason for our being all the more keen, Hovstad. Is there to be anything of public interest in tomorrow's "Messenger"?

HOVSTAD. Nothing about municipal affairs. But the day after to-morrow I was thinking of printing your article—

DR. STOCKMANN. Ah, devil take it—my article! Look here, that must wait a bit.

HOVSTAD. Really? We had just got convenient space for it, and I thought it was just the opportune moment—

DR. STOCKMANN. Yes, yes, very likely you are right; but it must wait all the same. I will explain to you later. (PETRA *comes in from the hall, in hat and cloak and with a bundle of exercise books under her arm*.)

PETRA. Good evening.

DR. STOCKMANN. Good evening, Petra; come along.

(*Mutual greetings;* PETRA *takes off her things and puts them down on a chair by the door*.)

PETRA. And you have all been sitting here enjoying yourselves, while I have been out slaving!

DR. STOCKMANN. Well, come and enjoy yourself too!

BILLING. May I mix a glass for you?

PETRA (*coming to the table*). Thanks, I would rather do it; you always mix it too strong. But I forgot, father—I have a letter for you. (*Goes to the chair where she has laid her things.*)

DR. STOCKMANN. A letter? From whom?

PETRA (*looking in her coat pocket*). The postman gave it to me just as I was going out—

DR. STOCKMANN (*getting up and going to her*). And you only give to me now!

PETRA. I really had not time to run up again. There it is!

DR. STOCKMANN (*seizing the letter*). Let's see, let's see, child! (*Looks at the address.*) Yes, that's all right!

MRS. STOCKMANN. Is it the one you have been expecting so anxiously, Thomas?

DR. STOCKMANN. Yes, it is. I must go to my room now and—. Where shall I get a light, Katherine? Is there no lamp in my room again?

MRS. STOCKMANN. Yes, your lamp is all ready lit on your desk.

DR. STOCKMANN. Good, good. Excuse me for a moment—. (*Goes into his study.*)

PETRA. What do you suppose it is, mother?

MRS. STOCKMANN. I don't know; for the last day or two he has always been asking if the postman has not been.

BILLING. Probably some country patient.

PETRA. Poor old dad!—he will overwork himself soon. (*Mixes a glass for herself.*) There, that will taste good!

HOVSTAD. Have you been teaching in the evening school again to-day?

PETRA (*sipping from her glass*). Two hours.

BILLING. And four hours of school in the morning—

PETRA. Five hours.

MRS. STOCKMANN. And you have still got exercises to correct, I see.

PETRA. A whole heap, yes.

HORSTER. You are pretty full up with work too, it seems to me.

PETRA. Yes—but that is good. One is so delightfully tired after it.

BILLING. Do you like that?

PETRA. Yes, because one sleeps so well then.

MORTEN. You must be dreadfully wicked, Petra.

PETRA. Wicked?

MORTEN. Yes, because you work so much. Mr. Rörlund says work is a punishment for our sins.

EJLIF. Pooh, what a duffer you are, to believe a thing like that!

MRS. STOCKMANN. Come, come, Ejlif!

BILLING (*laughing*). That's capital!

HOVSTAD. Don't you want to work as hard as that, Morten?

MORTEN. No, indeed I don't.

HOVSTAD. What do you want to be, then?

MORTEN. I should like best to be a Viking.

EJLIF. You would have to be a pagan then.

MORTEN. Well, I could become a pagan, couldn't I?

BILLING. I agree with you, Morten! My sentiments, exactly.

MRS. STOCKMANN (*signalling to him*). I am sure that is not true, Mr. Billing.

BILLING. Yes, I swear it is! I am a pagan, and I am proud of it. Believe me, before long we shall all be pagans.

MORTEN. And then shall be allowed to do anything we like?

BILLING. Well, you see, Morten—.

MRS. STOCKMANN. You must go to your room now, boys; I am sure you have some lessons to learn for to-morrow.

EJLIF. I should like so much to stay a little longer—

MRS. STOCKMANN. No, no; away you go, both of you. (*The boys say good night and go into the room on the left.*)

HOVSTAD. Do you really think it can do the boys any harm to hear such things?

MRS. STOCKMANN. I don't know; but I don't like it.

PETRA. But you know, mother, I think you really are wrong about it.

MRS. STOCKMANN. Maybe, but I don't like it—not in our own home.

PETRA. There is so much falsehood both at home and at school. At home one must not speak, and at school we have to stand and tell lies to the children.

HORSTER. Tell lies?

PETRA. Yes, don't you suppose we have to teach them all sorts of things that we don't believe?

BILLING. That is perfectly true.

PETRA. If only I had the means I would start a school of my own, and it would be conducted on very different lines.

BILLING. Oh, bother the means—!

HORSTER. Well if you are thinking of that, Miss Stockmann, I shall be delighted to provide you with a schoolroom. The great big old house my father left me is standing almost empty; there is an immense dining-room downstairs—

PETRA (*laughing*). Thank you very much; but I am afraid nothing will come of it.

HOVSTAD. No, Miss Petra is much more likely to take to

journalism, I expect. By the way, have you had time to do anything with that English story you promised to translate for us?

PETRA. No, not yet; but you shall have it in good time.

(DR. STOCKMANN *comes in from his room with an open letter in his hand.*)

DR. STOCKMANN (*waving the letter*). Well, now the town will have something new to talk about, I can tell you!

BILLING. Something new?

MRS. STOCKMANN. What is this?

DR. STOCKMANN. A great discovery, Katherine.

HOVSTAD. Really?

MRS. STOCKMANN. A discovery of yours?

DR. STOCKMANN. A discovery of mine. (*Walks up and down.*) Just let them come saying, as usual, that it is all fancy and a crazy man's imagination! But they will be careful what they say this time, I can tell you!

PETRA. But, father, tell us what it is.

DR. STOCKMANN. Yes, yes—only give me time, and you shall know all about it. If only I had Peter here now! It just shows how we men can go about forming our judgments, when in reality we are as blind as any moles—

HOVSTAD. What are you driving at, Doctor?

DR. STOCKMANN (*standing still by the table*). Isn't it the universal opinion that our town is a healthy spot?

HOVSTAD. Certainly.

DR. STOCKMANN. Quite an unusually healthy spot, in fact —a place that deserves to be recommended in the warmest possible manner either for invalids or for people who are well—

MRS. STOCKMANN. Yes, but my dear Thomas—

DR. STOCKMANN. And we have been recommending it and praising it—I have written and written, both in the "Messenger" and in pamphlets—

HOVSTAD. Well, what then?

DR. STOCKMANN. And the Baths—we have called them the "main artery of the town's life-blood," the "nerve-centre of our town," and the devil knows what else—

BILLING. "The town's pulsating heart" was the expression I once used on an important occasion—

DR. STOCKMANN. Quite so. Well, do you know what they really are, these great, splendid, much praised Baths, that have cost so much money—do you know what they are?

HOVSTAD. No, what are they?

MRS. STOCKMANN. Yes, what are they?

DR. STOCKMANN. The whole place is a pesthouse!

PETRA. The Baths, father?

MRS. STOCKMANN (*at the same time*). Our Baths!

HOVSTAD. But, Doctor—

BILLING. Absolutely incredible!

DR. STOCKMANN. The whole Bath establishment is a whited, poisoned sepulchre, I tell you—the gravest danger to the public health! All the nastiness up at Mölledal, all that stinking filth, is infecting the water in the conduit-pipes leading to the reservoir; and the same cursed, filthy poison oozes out on the shore too—

HORSTER. Where the bathing-place is?

DR. STOCKMANN. Just there.

HOVSTAD. How do you come to be so certain of all this, Doctor?

DR. STOCKMANN. I have investigated the matter most conscientiously. For a long time past I have suspected something of the kind. Last year we had some very strange cases of illness among the visitors—typhoid cases, and cases of gastric fever—

MRS. STOCKMANN. Yes, that is quite true.

DR. STOCKMANN. At the time, we supposed the visitors had been infected before they came; but later on, in the winter, I began to have a different opinion; and so I set myself to examine the water, as well as I could.

MRS. STOCKMANN. Then that is what you have been so busy with?

DR. STOCKMANN. Indeed I have been busy, Katherine. But here I had none of the necessary scientific apparatus; so I sent samples, both of the drinking-water and of the sea-water, up to the University, to have an accurate analysis made by a chemist.

HOVSTAD. And have you got that?

DR. STOCKMANN (*showing him the letter*). Here it is! It proves the presence of decomposing organic matter in the water—it is full of infusoria. The water is absolutely dangerous to use, either internally or externally.

MRS. STOCKMANN. What a mercy you discovered it in time.

DR. STOCKMANN. You may well say so.

HOVSTAD. And what do you propose to do now, Doctor?

DR. STOCKMANN. To see the matter put right—naturally.

HOVSTAD. Can that be done?

DR. STOCKMANN. It must be done. Otherwise the Baths will be absolutely useless and wasted. But we need not anticipate that; I have a very clear idea what we shall have to do.

MRS. STOCKMANN. But why have you kept this all so secret, dear?

DR. STOCKMANN. Do you suppose I was going to run about the town gossiping about it, before I had absolute proof? No, thank you. I am not such a fool.

PETRA. Still, you might have told us—

DR. STOCKMANN. Not a living soul. But to-morrow you may run around to the old Badger—

MRS. STOCKMANN. Oh, Thomas! Thomas!

DR. STOCKMANN. Well, to your grandfather, then. The old boy will have something to be astonished at! I know he thinks I am cracked—and there are lots of other people think so too, I have noticed. But now these good folks shall see—they shall just see—! (*Walks about, rubbing his hands.*) There will be a nice upset in the town, Katherine; you can't imagine what it will be. All the conduit-pipes will have to be relaid.

HOVSTAD (*getting up*). All the conduit-pipes—?

DR. STOCKMANN. Yes, of course. The intake is too low down; it will have to be lifted to a position much higher up.

PETRA. Then you were right after all.

DR. STOCKMANN. Ah, you remember, Petra—I wrote opposing the plans before the work was begun. But at that time no one would listen to me. Well, I am going to let them have it, now! Of course I have prepared a report for the Baths Committee; I have had it ready for a week, and was only waiting for this to come. (*Shows the letter.*) Now it shall go off at once. (*Goes into his room and comes back with some papers.*) Look at that! Four closely written sheets!—and the letter shall go with them. Give me a bit of paper, Katherine —something to wrap them up in. That will do! Now give it to—to—(*stamps his foot*)—what the deuce is her name?— give it to the maid, and tell her to take it at once to the Mayor.

(MRS. STOCKMANN *takes the packet and goes out through the dining-room.*)

PETRA. What do you think uncle Peter will say, father?

DR. STOCKMANN. What is there for him to say? I should think he would be very glad that such an important truth has been brought to light.

HOVSTAD. Will you let me print a short note about your discovery in the "Messenger"?

DR. STOCKMANN. I shall be very much obliged if you will.

HOVSTAD. It is very desirable that the public should be informed of it without delay.

DR. STOCKMANN. Certainly.

MRS. STOCKMANN (*coming back*). She has just gone with it.

BILLING. Upon my soul, Doctor, you are going to be the foremost man in the town!

DR. STOCKMANN (*walking about happily*). Nonsense! As a

matter of fact I have done nothing more than my duty. I have only made a lucky find—that's all. Still, all the same—

BILLING. Hovstad, don't you think the town ought to give Dr. Stockmann some sort of testimonial?

HOVSTAD. I will suggest it, anyway.

BILLING. And I will speak to Aslaksen about it.

DR. STOCKMANN. No, my good friends, don't let us have any of that nonsense. I won't hear of anything of the kind. And if the Baths Committee should think of voting me an increase of salary, I will not accept it. Do you hear, Katherine?—I won't accept it.

MRS. STOCKMANN. You are quite right, Thomas.

PETRA (*lifting her glass*). Your health, father!

HOVSTAD and BILLING. Your health, Doctor! Good health!

HORSTER (*touches glasses with* DR. STOCKMANN). I hope it will bring you nothing but good luck.

DR. STOCKMANN. Thank you, thank you, my dear fellows! I feel tremendously happy! It is a splendid thing for a man to be able to feel that he has done a service to his native town and to his fellow-citizens. Hurrah, Katherine! (*He puts his arms round her and whirls her round and round, while she protests with laughing cries. They all laugh, clap their hands, and cheer the* DOCTOR. *The boys put their heads in at the door to see what is going on.*)

ACT II

(SCENE—*The same. The door into the dining-room is shut. It is morning.* MRS. STOCKMANN, *with a sealed letter in her hand, comes in from the dining-room, goes to the door of the* DOCTOR'S *study, and peeps in.*)

MRS. STOCKMANN. Are you in, Thomas?

DR. STOCKMANN (*from within his room*). Yes, I have just come in. (*Comes into the room.*) What is it?

MRS. STOCKMANN. A letter from your brother.

DR. STOCKMANN. Aha, let us see! (*Opens the letter and reads:*) "I return herewith the manuscript you sent me"— (*reads on in a low murmur*) Hm!—

MRS. STOCKMANN. What does he say?

DR. STOCKMANN (*putting the papers in his pocket*). Oh, he only writes that he will come up here himself about midday.

MRS. STOCKMANN. Well, try and remember to be at home this time.

DR. STOCKMANN. That will be all right; I have got through all my morning visits.

MRS. STOCKMANN. I am extremely curious to know how he takes it.

DR. STOCKMANN. You will see he won't like it's having been I, and not he, that made the discovery.

MRS. STOCKMANN. Aren't you a little nervous about that?

DR. STOCKMANN. Oh, he really will be pleased enough, you know. But, at the same time, Peter is so confoundedly afraid of anyone's doing any service to the town except himself.

MRS. STOCKMANN. I will tell you what, Thomas—you should be good natured, and share the credit of this with him. Couldn't you make out that it was he who set you on the scent of this discovery?

146

Dr. Stockmann. I am quite willing. If only I can get the thing set right. I—

(Morten Kiil *puts his head in through the door leading from the hall, looks round in an enquiring manner, and chuckles.*)

Morten Kiil (*slyly*). Is it—is it true?

Mrs. Stockmann (*going to the door*). Father!—is it you?

Dr. Stockmann. Ah, Mr. Kiil—good morning, good morning!

Mrs. Stockmann. But come along in.

Morten Kiil. If it is true, I will; if not, I am off.

Dr. Stockmann. If what is true?

Morten Kiil. This tale about the water supply. Is it true?

Dr. Stockmann. Certainly it is true. But how did you come to hear it?

Morten Kiil (*coming in*). Petra ran in on her way to the school—

Dr. Stockmann. Did she?

Morten Kiil. Yes; and she declares that—. I thought she was only making a fool of me, but it isn't like Petra to do that.

Dr. Stockmann. Of course not. How could you imagine such a thing!

Morten Kiil. Oh well, it is better never to trust anybody; you may find you have been made a fool of before you know where you are. But it is really true, all the same?

Dr. Stockmann. You can depend upon it that it is true. Won't you sit down? (*Settles him on the couch.*) Isn't it a real bit of luck for the town—

Morten Kiil (*suppressing his laughter*). A bit of luck for the town?

Dr. Stockmann. Yes, that I made the discovery in good time.

Morten Kiil (*as before*). Yes, yes, yes!—But I should never have thought you the sort of man to pull your own brother's leg like this!

Dr. Stockmann. Pull his leg!

Mrs. Stockmann. Really, father dear—

Morten Kiil (*resting his hands and his chin on the handle of his stick and winking slyly at the* Doctor). Let me see, what was the story? Some kind of beast that had got into the water-pipes, wasn't it?

Dr. Stockmann. Infusoria—yes.

Morten Kiil. And a lot of these beasts had got in, according to Petra—a tremendous lot.

Dr. Stockmann. Certainly; hundreds of thousands of them, probably.

MORTEN KIIL. But no one can see them—isn't that so?

DR. STOCKMANN. Yes; you can't see them.

MORTEN KIIL (*with a quiet chuckle*). Damme—it's the finest story I have ever heard!

DR. STOCKMANN. What do you mean?

MORTEN KIIL. But you will never get the Mayor to believe a thing like that.

DR. STOCKMANN. We shall see.

MORTEN KIIL. Do you think he will be fool enough to—?

DR. STOCKMANN. I hope the whole town will be fools enough.

MORTEN KIIL. The whole town! Well, it wouldn't be a bad thing. It would just serve them right, and teach them a lesson. They think themselves so much cleverer than we old fellows. They hounded me out of the council; they did, I tell you—they hounded me out. Now they shall pay for it. You pull their legs too, Thomas!

DR. STOCKMANN. Really, I—

MORTEN KIIL. You pull their legs! (*Gets up.*) If you can work it so that the Mayor and his friends all swallow the same bait, I will give ten pounds to a charity—like a shot!

DR. STOCKMANN. That is very kind of you.

MORTEN KIIL. Yes, I haven't got much money to throw away, I can tell you; but if you can work this, I will give five pounds to a charity at Christmas.

(HOVSTAD *comes in by the hall door.*)

HOVSTAD. Good morning! (*Stops.*) Oh, I beg your pardon—

DR. STOCKMANN. Not at all; come in.

MORTEN KIIL (*with another chuckle*). Oho!—is he in this too?

HOVSTAD. What do you mean?

DR. STOCKMANN. Certainly he is.

MORTEN KIIL. I might have known it! It must get into the papers. You know how to do it, Thomas! Set your wits to work. Now I must go.

DR. STOCKMANN. Won't you stay a little while?

MORTEN KIIL. No, I must be off now. You keep up this game for all it is worth; you won't repent it, I'm damned if you will!

(*He goes out;* MRS. STOCKMANN *follows him into the hall.*)

DR. STOCKMANN (*laughing*). Just imagine—the old chap doesn't believe a word of all this about the water supply.

HOVSTAD. Oh that was it, then?

DR. STOCKMANN. Yes, that was what we were talking about. Perhaps it is the same thing that brings you here?

HOVSTAD. Yes, it is. Can you spare me a few minutes, Doctor?

DR. STOCKMANN. As long as you like, my dear fellow.

HOVSTAD. Have you heard from the Mayor yet?

DR. STOCKMANN. Not yet. He is coming here later.

HOVSTAD. I have given the matter a great deal of thought since last night.

DR. STOCKMANN. Well?

HOVSTAD. From your point of view, as a doctor and a man of science, this affair of the water-supply is an isolated matter. I mean, you do not realise that it involves a great many other things.

DR. STOCKMANN. How, do you mean?—Let us sit down, my dear fellow. No, sit here on the couch. (HOVSTAD sits down on the couch, DR. STOCKMANN on a chair on the other side of the table.) Now then. You mean that—?

HOVSTAD. You said yesterday that the pollution of the water was due to impurities in the soil.

DR. STOCKMANN. Yes, unquestionably it is due to that poisonous morass up at Mölledal.

HOVSTAD. Begging your pardon, doctor, I fancy it is due to quite another morass altogether.

DR. STOCKMANN. What morass?

HOVSTAD. The morass that the whole life of our town is built on and is rotting in.

DR. STOCKMANN. What the deuce are you driving at, Hovstad?

HOVSTAD. The whole of the town's interests have, little by little, got into the hands of a pack of officials.

DR. STOCKMANN. Oh, come!—they are not all officials.

HOVSTAD. No, but those that are not officials are at any rate the officials' friends and adherents; it is the wealthy folk, the old families in the town, that have got us entirely in their hands.

DR. STOCKMANN. Yes, but after all they are men of ability and knowledge.

HOVSTAD. Did they show any ability or knowledge when they laid the conduit-pipes where they are now?

DR. STOCKMANN. No, of course that was a great piece of stupidity on their part. But that is going to be set right now.

HOVSTAD. Do you think that will be all such plain sailing?

DR. STOCKMANN. Plain sailing or no, it has got to be done, anyway.

HOVSTAD. Yes, provided the press takes up the question.

DR. STOCKMANN. I don't think that will be necessary, my dear fellow, I am certain my brother—

HOVSTAD. Excuse me, doctor; I feel bound to tell you I am inclined to take the matter up.

DR. STOCKMANN. In the paper?

HOVSTAD. Yes, When I took over the "People's Messenger" my idea was to break up this ring of self-opinionated old fossils who had got hold of all the influence.

DR. STOCKMANN. But you know you told me yourself what the result had been; you nearly ruined your paper.

HOVSTAD. Yes, at the time we were obliged to climb down a peg or two, it is quite true; because there was a danger of the whole project of the Baths coming to nothing if they failed us. But now the scheme has been carried through, and we can dispense with these grand gentlemen.

DR. STOCKMANN. Dispense with them, yes; but we owe them a great debt of gratitude.

HOVSTAD. That shall be recognised ungrudgingly. But a journalist of my democratic tendencies cannot let such an opportunity as this slip. The bubble of official infallibility must be pricked. This superstition must be destroyed, like any other.

DR. STOCKMANN. I am whole-heartedly with you in that, Mr. Hovstad; if it is a superstition, away with it!

HOVSTAD. I should be very reluctant to bring the Mayor into it, because he is your brother. But I am sure you will agree with me that truth should be the first consideration.

DR. STOCKMANN. That goes without saying. (*With sudden emphasis.*) Yes, but—but—

HOVSTAD. You must not misjudge me. I am neither more self-interested nor more ambitious than most men.

DR. STOCKMANN. My dear fellow—who suggests anything of that kind?

HOVSTAD. I am of humble origin, as you know; and that has given me opportunities of knowing what is the most crying need in the humbler ranks of life. It is that they should be allowed some part in the direction of public affairs, Doctor. That is what will develop their faculties and intelligence and self respect—

DR. STOCKMANN. I quite appreciate that.

HOVSTAD. Yes—and in my opinion a journalist incurs a heavy responsibility if he neglects a favourable opportunity of emancipating the masses—the humble and oppressed. I know well enough that in exalted circles I shall be called an agitator, and all that sort of thing; but they may call what they like. If only my conscience doesn't reproach me, then—

DR. STOCKMANN. Quite right! Quite right, Mr. Hovstad. But all the same—devil take it! (*A knock is heard at the door.*) Come in!

(ASLAKSEN *appears at the door. He is poorly but decently dressed, in black, with a slightly crumpled white neck-cloth; he wears gloves and has a felt hat in his hand.*)

ASLAKSEN (*bowing*). Excuse my taking the liberty, Doctor—

DR. STOCKMANN (*getting up*). Ah, it is you, Aslaksen!

ASLAKSEN. Yes, Doctor.

HOVSTAD (*standing up*). Is it me you want, Aslaksen?

ASLAKSEN. No; I didn't know I should find you here. No, it was the Doctor I—

DR. STOCKMANN. I am quite at your service. What is it?

ASLAKSEN. Is what I heard from Mr. Billing true, sir—that you mean to improve our water-supply?

DR. STOCKMANN. Yes, for the Baths.

ASLAKSEN. Quite so, I understand. Well, I have come to say that I will back that up by every means in my power.

HOVSTAD (*to the* DOCTOR). You see!

DR. STOCKMANN. I shall be very grateful to you, but—

ASLAKSEN. Because it may be no bad thing to have us small tradesmen at your back. We form, as it were, a compact majority in the town—if we choose. And it is always a good thing to have the majority with you, Doctor.

DR. STOCKMANN. This is undeniably true; but I confess I don't see why such unusual precautions should be necessary in this case. It seems to me that such a plain, straightforward thing—

ASLAKSEN. Oh, it may be very desirable, all the same. I know our local authorities so well; officials are not generally very ready to act on proposals that come from other people. That is why I think it would not be at all amiss if we made a little demonstration.

HOVSTAD. That's right.

DR. STOCKMANN. Demonstration, did you say? What on earth are you going to make a demonstration about?

ASLAKSEN. We shall proceed with the greatest moderation, Doctor. Moderation is always my aim; it is the greatest virtue in a citizen—at least, I think so.

DR. STOCKMANN. It is well known to be a characteristic of yours, Mr. Aslaksen.

ASLAKSEN. Yes, I think I may pride myself on that. And this matter of the water-supply is of the greatest importance to us small tradesmen. The Baths promise to be a regular gold-mine for the town. We shall all make our living out of them, especially those of us who are householders. That is why we will back up the project as strongly as possible. And as I am at present Chairman of the Householders' Association—

DR. STOCKMANN. Yes——?

ASLAKSEN. And, what is more, local secretary of the Temperance Society——you know, sir, I suppose, that I am a worker in the temperance cause?

DR. STOCKMANN. Of course, of course.

ASLAKSEN. Well, you can understand that I come into contact with a great many people. And as I have the reputation of a temperate and law-abiding citizen——like yourself, Doctor——I have a certain influence in the town, a little bit of power, if I may be allowed to say so.

DR. STOCKMANN. I know that quite well, Mr. Aslaksen.

ASLAKSEN. So you see it would be an easy matter for me to set on foot some testimonial, if necessary.

DR. STOCKMANN. A testimonial?

ASLAKSEN. Yes, some kind of an address of thanks from the townsmen for your share in a matter of such importance to the community. I need scarcely say that it would have to be drawn up with the greatest regard to moderation, so as not to offend the authorities——who, after all, have the reins in their hands. If we pay strict attention to that, no one can take it amiss, I should think!

HOVSTAD. Well, and even supposing they didn't like it——

ASLAKSEN. No, no, no; there must be no discourtesy to the authorities, Mr. Hovstad. It is no use falling foul of those upon whom our welfare so closely depends. I have done that in my time, and no good ever comes of it. But no one can take exception to a reasonable and frank expression of a citizen's views.

DR. STOCKMANN (shaking him by the hand). I can't tell you, dear Mr. Aslaksen, how extremely pleased I am to find such hearty support among my fellow-citizens. I am delighted ——delighted! Now, you will take a small glass of sherry, eh?

ASLAKSEN. No, thank you; I never drink alcohol of that kind.

DR. STOCKMANN. Well, what do you say to a glass of beer, then?

ASLAKSEN. Nor that either, thank you, Doctor. I never drink anything as early as this. I am going into town now to talk this over with one or two householders, and prepare the ground.

DR. STOCKMANN. It is tremendously kind of you, Mr. Aslaksen; but I really cannot understand the necessity for all these precautions. It seems to me that the thing should go of itself.

ASLAKSEN. The authorities are somewhat slow to move, Doctor. Far be it from me to seem to blame them——

Hovstad. We are going to stir them up in the paper to-morrow, Aslaksen.

Aslaksen. But not violently, I trust, Mr. Hovstad. Proceed with moderation, or you will do nothing with them. You may take my advice; I have gathered my experience in the school of life. Well, I must say good-bye, Doctor. You know now that we small tradesmen are at your back at all events, like a solid wall. You have the compact majority on your side, Doctor.

Dr. Stockmann. I am very much obliged, dear Mr. Aslaksen. (*Shakes hands with him.*) Good-bye, good-bye.

Aslaksen. Are you going my way, towards the printing-office, Mr. Hovstad?

Hovstad. I will come later; I have something to settle up first.

Aslaksen. Very well. (*Bows and goes out;* Stockmann *follows him into the hall.*)

Hovstad (*as* Stockmann *comes in again*). Well, what do you think of that, Doctor? Don't you think it is high time we stirred a little life into all this slackness and vacillation and cowardice?

Dr. Stockmann. Are you referring to Aslaksen?

Hovstad. Yes, I am. He is one of those who are flounder-ing in a bog—decent enough fellow though he may be, other-wise. And most of the people here are in just the same case—see-sawing and edging first to one side and then to the other, so overcome with caution and scruple that they never dare to take any decided step.

Dr. Stockmann. Yes, but Aslaksen seemed to me so thoroughly well-intentioned.

Hovstad. There is one thing I esteem higher than that; and that is for a man to be self-reliant and sure of himself.

Dr. Stockmann. I think you are perfectly right there.

Hovstad. That is why I want to seize this opportunity, and try if I cannot manage to put a little virility into these well-intentioned people for once. The idol of Authority must be shattered in this town. This gross and inexcusable blunder about the water-supply must be brought home to the mind of every municipal voter.

Dr. Stockmann. Very well; if you are of opinion that it is for the good of the community, so be it. But not until I have had a talk with my brother.

Hovstad. Anyway, I will get a leading article ready; and if the Mayor refuses to take the matter up—

Dr. Stockmann. How can you suppose such a thing pos-sible?

HOVSTAD. It is conceivable. And in that case—

DR. STOCKMANN. In that case I promise you—. Look here, in that case you may print my report—every word of it.

HOVSTAD. May I? Have I your word for it?

DR. STOCKMANN (*giving him the MS.*). Here it is; take it with you. It can do no harm for you to read it through, and you can give it back to me later on.

HOVSTAD. Good, good! That is what I will do. And now good-bye, Doctor.

DR. STOCKMANN. Good-bye, good-bye. You will see everything will run quite smoothly, Mr. Hovstad—quite smoothly.

HOVSTAD. Hm!—we shall see. (*Bows and goes out.*)

DR. STOCKMANN (*opens the dining-room door and looks in*). Katherine! Oh, you are back, Petra?

PETRA (*coming in*). Yes, I have just come from the school.

MRS. STOCKMANN (*coming in*). Has he not been here yet?

DR. STOCKMANN. Peter? No. But I have had a long talk with Hovstad. He is quite excited about my discovery. I find it has a much wider bearing than I at first imagined. And he has put his paper at my disposal if necessity should arise.

MRS. STOCKMANN. Do you think it will?

DR. STOCKMANN. Not for a moment. But at all events it makes me feel proud to know that I have the liberal-minded independent press on my side. Yes, and—just imagine—I have had a visit from the Chairman of the Householders' Association!

MRS. STOCKMANN. Oh! What did he want?

DR. STOCKMANN. To offer me his support too. They will support me in a body if it should be necessary. Katherine—do you know what I have got behind me?

MRS. STOCKMANN. Behind you? No, what have you got behind you?

DR. STOCKMANN. The compact majority.

MRS. STOCKMANN. Really? Is that a good thing for you Thomas?

DR. STOCKMANN. I should think it was a good thing. (*Walks up and down rubbing his hands.*) By Jove, it's a fine thing to feel this bond of brotherhood between oneself and one's fellow citizens!

PETRA. And to be able to do so much that is good and useful, father!

DR. STOCKMANN. And for one's own native town into the bargain, my child!

MRS. STOCKMANN. That was a ring at the bell.

DR. STOCKMANN. It must be he, then. (*A knock is heard at the door.*) Come in!

PETER STOCKMANN (*comes in from the hall*). Good morning.

DR. STOCKMANN. Glad to see you, Peter!

MRS. STOCKMANN. Good morning, Peter. How are you?

PETER STOCKMANN. So so, thank you. (*To* DR. STOCKMANN.) I received from you yesterday, after office hours, a report dealing with the condition of the water at the Baths.

DR. STOCKMANN. Yes. Have you read it?

PETER STOCKMANN. Yes, I have.

DR. STOCKMANN. And what have you to say to it?

PETER STOCKMANN (*with a sidelong glance*). Hm!—

MRS. STOCKMANN. Come along, Petra. (*She and* PETRA *go into the room on the left.*)

PETER STOCKMANN (*after a pause*). Was it necessary to make all these investigations behind my back?

DR. STOCKMANN. Yes, because until I was absolutely certain about it—

PETER STOCKMANN. Then you mean that you are absolutely certain now?

DR. STOCKMANN. Surely you are convinced of that.

PETER STOCKMANN. Is it your intention to bring this document before the Baths Committee as a sort of official communication?

DR. STOCKMANN. Certainly. Something must be done in the matter—and that quickly.

PETER STOCKMANN. As usual, you employ violent expressions in your report. You say, amongst other things, that what we offer visitors in our Baths is a permanent supply of poison.

DR. STOCKMANN. Well, can you describe it any other way, Peter? Just think—water that is poisonous, whether you drink it or bathe in it! And this we offer to the poor sick folk who come to us trustfully and pay us at an exorbitant rate to be made well again!

PETER STOCKMANN. And your reasoning leads you to this conclusion, that we must build a sewer to draw off the alleged impurities from Mölledal and must relay the water-conduits.

DR. STOCKMANN. Yes. Do you see any other way out of it? I don't.

PETER STOCKMANN. I made a pretext this morning to go and see the town engineer, and, as if only half seriously, broached the subject of these proposals as a thing we might perhaps have to take under consideration some time later on.

DR. STOCKMANN. Some time later on!

PETER STOCKMANN. He smiled at what he considered to be my extravagance, naturally. Have you taken the trouble to consider what your proposed alterations would cost? Accord-

ing to the information I obtained, the expenses would probably mount up to fifteen or twenty thousand pounds.

DR. STOCKMANN. Would it cost so much?

PETER STOCKMANN. Yes; and the worst part of it would be
that the work would take at least two years.

DR. STOCKMANN. Two years? Two whole years?

PETER STOCKMANN. At least. And what are we to do with
the Baths in the meantime? Close them? Indeed we should be
obliged to. And do you suppose any one would come near
the place after it had got about that the water was dangerous?

DR. STOCKMANN. Yes but, Peter, that is what it is.

PETER STOCKMANN. And all this at this juncture—just as
the Baths are beginning to be known. There are other towns
in the neighbourhood with qualifications to attract visitors
for bathing purposes. Don't you suppose they would immediately strain every nerve to divert the entire stream of
strangers to themselves? Unquestionably they would; and then
where should we be? We should probably have to abandon
the whole thing, which has cost us so much money—and then
you would have ruined your native town.

DR. STOCKMANN. I—should have ruined—!

PETER STOCKMANN. It is simply and solely through the
Baths that the town has before it any future worth mention-
ing. You know that just as well as I.

DR. STOCKMANN. But what do you think ought to be done,
then?

PETER STOCKMANN. Your report has not convinced me that
the condition of the water at the Baths is as bad as you
represent it to be.

DR. STOCKMANN. I tell you it is even worse!—or at all
events it will be in summer, when the warm weather comes.

PETER STOCKMANN. As I said, I believe you exaggerate
the matter considerably. A capable physician ought to know
what measures to take—he ought to be capable of preventing
injurious influences or of remedying them if they become
obviously persistent.

DR. STOCKMANN. Well? What more?

PETER STOCKMANN. The water supply for the Baths is now
an established fact, and in consequence must be treated as
such. But probably the Committee, at its discretion, will not
be disinclined to consider the question of how far it might
be possible to introduce certain improvements consistently
with a reasonable expenditure.

DR. STOCKMANN. And do you suppose that I will have
anything to do with such a piece of trickery as that?

PETER STOCKMANN. Trickery! !

DR. STOCKMANN. Yes, it would be a trick—a fraud, a lie, a downright crime towards the public, towards the whole community!

PETER STOCKMANN. I have not, as I remarked before, been able to convince myself that there is actually any imminent danger.

DR. STOCKMANN. You have! It is impossible that you should not be convinced. I know I have represented the facts absolutely truthfully and fairly. And you know it very well, Peter, only you won't acknowledge it. It was owing to your action that both the Baths and the water-conduits were built where they are; and that is what you won't acknowledge—that damnable blunder of yours. Pooh!—do you suppose I don't see through you?

PETER STOCKMANN. And even if that were true? If I perhaps guard my reputation somewhat anxiously, it is in the best interests of the town. Without moral authority I am powerless to direct public affairs as seems, to my judgment, to be best for the common good. And on that account—and for various other reasons too—it appears to me to be a matter of importance that your report should not be delivered to the Committee. In the interests of the public, you must withhold it. Then, later on, I will raise the question and we will do our best, privately; but nothing of this unfortunate affair—not a single word of it—must come to the ears of the public.

DR. STOCKMANN. I am afraid you will not be able to prevent that now, my dear Peter.

PETER STOCKMANN. It must and shall be prevented.

DR. STOCKMANN. It is no use, I tell you. There are too many people that know about it.

PETER STOCKMANN. That know about it? Who? Surely you don't mean those fellows on the "People's Messenger"?

DR. STOCKMANN. Yes, they know. The liberal-minded independent press is going to see that you do your duty.

PETER STOCKMANN (after a short pause). You are an extraordinarily independent man, Thomas. Have you given no thought to the consequences this may have for yourself?

DR. STOCKMANN. Consequences?—for me?

PETER STOCKMANN. For you and yours, yes.

DR. STOCKMANN. What the deuce do you mean?

PETER STOCKMANN. I believe I have always behaved in a brotherly way to you—have always been ready to oblige or to help you?

DR. STOCKMANN. Yes, you have, and I am grateful to you for it.

PETER STOCKMANN. There is no need. Indeed, to some

extent I was forced to do so—for my own sake. I always hoped that, if I helped to improve your financial position, I should be able to keep some check on you.

DR. STOCKMANN. What! ! Then it was only for your own sake—!

PETER STOCKMANN. Up to a certain point, yes. It is painful for a man in an official position to have his nearest relative compromising himself time after time.

DR. STOCKMANN. And do you consider that I do that?

PETER STOCKMANN. Yes, unfortunately, you do, without even being aware of it. You have a restless, pugnacious, rebellious disposition. And then there is that disastrous propensity of yours to want to write about every sort of possible and impossible thing. The moment an idea comes into your head, you must needs go and write a newspaper article or a whole pamphlet about it.

DR. STOCKMANN. Well, but is it not the duty of a citizen to let the public share in any new ideas he may have?

PETER STOCKMANN. Oh, the public doesn't require any new ideas. The public is best served by the good, old-established ideas it already has.

DR. STOCKMANN. And that is your honest opinion?

PETER STOCKMANN. Yes, and for once I must talk frankly to you. Hitherto I have tried to avoid doing so, because I know how irritable you are; but now I must tell you the truth, Thomas. You have no conception what an amount of harm you do yourself by your impetuosity. You complain of the authorities, you even complain of the government— you are always pulling them to pieces; you insist that you have been neglected and persecuted. But what else can such a cantankerous man as you expect?

DR. STOCKMANN. What next! Cantankerous, am I?

PETER STOCKMANN. Yes, Thomas, you are an extremely cantankerous man to work with—I know that to my cost. You disregard everything that you ought to have consideration for. You seem completely to forget that it is me you have to thank for your appointment here as medical officer to the Baths—

DR. STOCKMANN. I was entitled to it as a matter of course!— I and nobody else! I was the first person to see that the town could be made into a flourishing watering-place, and I was the only one who saw it at that time. I had to fight single-handed in support of the idea for many years; and I wrote and wrote—

PETER STOCKMANN. Undoubtedly. But things were not ripe for the scheme then—though, of course, you could not judge of that in your out-of-the-way corner up north. But as soon as the opportune moment came I—and the others—took the matter into our hands—

DR. STOCKMANN. Yes, and made this mess of all my beautiful plan. It is pretty obvious now what clever fellows you were!

PETER STOCKMANN. To my mind the whole thing only seems to mean that you are seeking another outlet for your combativeness. You want to pick a quarrel with your superiors —an old habit of yours. You cannot put up with any authority over you. You look askance at anyone who occupies a superior official position; you regard him as a personal enemy, and then any stick is good enough to beat him with. But now I have called your attention to the fact that the town's interests are at stake—and, incidentally, my own too. And therefore I must tell you, Thomas, that you will find me inexorable with regard to what I am about to require you to do.

DR. STOCKMANN. And what is that?

PETER STOCKMANN. As you have been so indiscreet as to speak of this delicate matter to outsiders, despite the fact that you ought to have treated it as entirely official and confidential, it is obviously impossible to hush it up now. All sorts of rumours will get about directly, and everybody who has a grudge against us will take care to embellish these rumours. So it will be necessary for you to refute them publicly.

DR. STOCKMANN. I! How? I don't understand.

PETER STOCKMANN. What we shall expect is that, after making further investigations, you will come to the conclusion that the matter is not by any means as dangerous or as critical as you imagined in the first instance.

DR. STOCKMANN. Oho!—so that is what you expect!

PETER STOCKMANN. And, what is more, we shall expect you to make public profession of your confidence in the Committee and in their readiness to consider fully and conscientiously what steps may be necessary to remedy any possible defects.

DR. STOCKMANN. But you will never be able to do that by patching and tinkering at it—never! Take my word for it, Peter; I mean what I say, as deliberately and emphatically as possible.

PETER STOCKMANN. As an officer under the Committee, you have no right to any individual opinion.

DR. STOCKMANN (amazed). No right?

PETER STOCKMANN. In your official capacity, no. As a private person, it is quite another matter. But as a subordinate member of the staff of the Baths, you have no right to express any opinion which runs contrary to that of your superiors.

DR. STOCKMANN. This is too much! I, a doctor, a man of science, have no right to—!

PETER STOCKMANN. The matter in hand is not simply a scientific one. It is a complicated matter, and has its economic as well as its technical side.

DR. STOCKMANN. I don't care what it is! I intend to be free to express my opinion on any subject under the sun.

PETER STOCKMANN. As you please—but not on any subject concerning the Baths. That we forbid.

DR. STOCKMANN (*shouting*). You forbid—! You! A pack of—

PETER STOCKMANN. *I* forbid it—I, your chief; and if I forbid it, you have to obey.

DR. STOCKMANN (*controlling himself*). Peter—if you were not my brother—

PETRA (*throwing open the door*). Father, you shan't stand this!

MRS. STOCKMANN (*coming in after her*). Petra, Petra!

PETER STOCKMANN. Oh, so you have been eavesdropping.

MRS. STOCKMANN. You were talking so loud, we couldn't help—

PETRA. Yes, I was listening.

PETER STOCKMANN. Well, after all, I am very glad—

DR. STOCKMANN (*going up to him*). You were saying something about forbidding and obeying?

PETER STOCKMANN. You obliged me to take that tone with you.

DR. STOCKMANN. And so I am to give myself the lie, publicly?

PETER STOCKMANN. We consider it absolutely necessary that you should make some such public statement as I have asked for.

DR. STOCKMANN. And if I do not—obey?

PETER STOCKMANN. Then we shall publish a statement ourselves to reassure the public.

DR. STOCKMANN. Very well; but in that case I shall use my pen against you. I stick to what I have said; I will show that I am right and that you are wrong. And what will you do then?

PETER STOCKMANN. Then I shall not be able to prevent your being dismissed.

DR. STOCKMANN. What—?

PETRA. Father—dismissed!

MRS. STOCKMANN. Dismissed!

PETER STOCKMANN. Dismissed from the staff of the Baths. I shall be obliged to propose that you shall immediately be given notice, and shall not be allowed any further participation in the Baths' affairs.

DR. STOCKMANN. You would dare to do that!

PETER STOCKMANN. It is you that are playing the daring game.

PETRA. Uncle, that is a shameful way to treat a man like father!

MRS. STOCKMANN. Do hold your tongue, Petra!

PETER STOCKMANN (*looking at* PETRA). Oh, so we volunteer our opinions already, do we? Of course. (*To* MRS. STOCKMANN.) Katherine, I imagine you are the most sensible person in this house. Use any influence you may have over your husband, and make him see what this will entail for his family as well as—

DR. STOCKMANN. My family is my own concern and nobody else's!

PETER STOCKMANN. —for his own family, as I was saying, as well as for the town he lives in.

DR. STOCKMANN. It is I who have the real good of the town at heart! I want to lay bare the defects that sooner or later must come to the light of day. I will show whether I love my native town.

PETER STOCKMANN. You, who in your blind obstinacy want to cut off the most important source of the town's welfare?

DR. STOCKMANN. The source is poisoned, man! Are you mad? We are making our living by retailing filth and corruption! The whole of our flourishing municipal life derives its sustenance from a lie!

PETER STOCKMANN. All imagination—or something even worse. The man who can throw out such offensive insinuations about his native town must be an enemy to our community.

DR. STOCKMANN (*going up to him*). Do you dare to—!

MRS. STOCKMANN (*throwing herself between them*). Thomas!

PETRA (*catching her father by the arm*). Don't lose your temper, father!

PETER STOCKMANN. I will not expose myself to violence. Now you have had a warning; so reflect on what you owe to yourself and your family. Good-bye. (*Goes out.*)

DR. STOCKMANN (*walking up and down*). Am I to put up with such treatment as this? In my own house, Katherine! What do you think of that!

MRS. STOCKMANN. Indeed it is both shameful and absurd, Thomas—

PETRA. If only I could give uncle a piece of my mind—

DR. STOCKMANN. It is my own fault. I ought to have flown out at him long ago!—shown my teeth!—bitten! To hear him call me an enemy to our community! Me! I shall not take that lying down, upon my soul!

MRS. STOCKMANN. But, dear Thomas, your brother has power on his side—

DR. STOCKMANN. Yes, but I have right on mine, I tell you.

MRS. STOCKMANN. Oh yes, right—right. What is the use of having right on your side if you have not got might?

PETRA. Oh, mother!—how can you say such a thing!

DR. STOCKMANN. Do you imagine that in a free country it is no use having right on your side? You are absurd, Katherine. Besides, haven't I got the liberal-minded independent press to lead the way, and the compact majority behind me? That is might enough, I should think!

MRS. STOCKMANN. But, good heavens, Thomas, you don't mean to—?

DR. STOCKMANN. Don't mean to what?

MRS. STOCKMANN. To set yourself up in opposition to your brother.

DR. STOCKMANN. In God's name, what else do you suppose I should do but take my stand on right and truth?

PETRA. Yes, I was just going to say that.

MRS. STOCKMANN. But it won't do you any earthly good. If they won't do it, they won't.

DR. STOCKMANN. Oho, Katherine! Just give me time, and you will see how I will carry the war into their camp.

MRS. STOCKMANN. Yes, you carry the war into their camp, and you get your dismissal—that is what you will do.

DR. STOCKMANN. In any case I shall have done my duty towards the public—towards the community. I, who am called its enemy!

MRS. STOCKMANN. But towards your family, Thomas? Towards your own home! Do you think that is doing your duty towards those you have to provide for?

PETRA. Ah, don't think always first of us, mother.

MRS. STOCKMANN. Oh, it is easy for you to talk; you are able to shift for yourself, if need be. But remember the boys, Thomas; and think a little too of yourself, and of me—

DR. STOCKMANN. I think you are out of your senses, Katherine! If I were to be such a miserable coward as to go on my knees to Peter and his damned crew, do you suppose I should ever know an hour's peace of mind all my life afterwards?

MRS. STOCKMANN. I don't know anything about that; but God preserve us from the peace of mind we shall have, all the same, if you go on defying him! You will find yourself again without the means of subsistence, with no income to count upon. I should think we had had enough of that in the old days. Remember that, Thomas; think what that means.

DR. STOCKMANN (*collecting himself with a struggle and clenching his fists*). And this is what this slavery can bring upon a free, honourable man! Isn't it horrible, Katherine?

MRS. STOCKMANN. Yes, it is sinful to treat you so, it is perfectly true. But, good heavens, one has to put up with so much injustice in this world.—There are the boys, Thomas! Look at them! What is to become of them? Oh, no, you can never have the heart—. (EJLIF *and* MORTEN *have come in while she was speaking, with their school books in their hands.*)

DR. STOCKMANN. The boys—! (*Recovers himself suddenly.*) No, even if the whole world goes to pieces, I will never bow my neck to this yoke! (*Goes towards his room.*)

MRS. STOCKMANN (*following him*). Thomas—what are you going to do!

DR. STOCKMANN (*at his door*). I mean to have the right to look my sons in the face when they are grown men. (*Goes into his room.*)

MRS. STOCKMANN (*bursting into tears*). God help us all!

PETRA. Father is splendid! He will not give in.

(*The boys look on in amazement;* PETRA *signs to them not to speak.*)

ACT III

(SCENE.—*The editorial office of the "People's Messenger."
The entrance door is on the left-hand side of the back wall;
on the right-hand side is another door with glass panels
through which the printing-room can be seen. Another door
in the right-hand wall. In the middle of the room is a large
table covered with papers, newspapers and books. In the
foreground on the left a window, before which stands a desk
and a high stool. There are a couple of easy chairs by the
table, and other chairs standing along the wall. The room is
dingy and uncomfortable; the furniture is old, the chairs
stained and torn. In the printing-room the compositors are
seen at work, and a printer is working a hand-press.* HOVSTAD
is sitting at the desk, writing. BILLING *comes in from the right
with* DR. STOCKMANN'S *manuscript in his hand.*)

BILLING. Well, I must say!

HOVSTAD (*still writing*). Have you read it through?

BILLING (*laying the MS. on the desk*). Yes, indeed I have.

HOVSTAD. Don't you think the Doctor hits them pretty
hard?

BILLING. Hard? Bless my soul, he's crushing! Every word
falls like—how shall I put it?—like the blow of a sledge-
hammer.

HOVSTAD. Yes, but they are not the people to throw up the
sponge at the first blow.

BILLING. That is true; and for that reason we must strike
blow upon blow until the whole of this aristocracy tumbles to
pieces. As I sat there reading this, I almost seemed to see a
revolution in being.

HOVSTAD (*turning round*). Hush!—Speak so that Aslaksen
cannot hear you.

BILLING (*lowering his voice*). Aslaksen is a chicken-hearted
chap, a coward; there is nothing of the man in him. But this

164

time you will insist on your own way, won't you? You will put the Doctor's article in?

HOVSTAD. Yes, and if the Mayor doesn't like it—

BILLING. That will be the devil of a nuisance.

HOVSTAD. Well, fortunately we can turn the situation to good account, whatever happens. If the Mayor will not fall in with the Doctor's project, he will have all the small tradesmen down on him—the whole of the Householders' Association and the rest of them. And if he does fall in with it, he will fall out with the whole crowd of large shareholders in the Baths, who up to now have been his most valuable supporters—

BILLING. Yes, because they will certainly have to fork out a pretty penny—

HOVSTAD. Yes, you may be sure they will. And in this way the ring will be broken up, you see, and then in every issue of the paper we will enlighten the public on the Mayor's incapability on one point and another, and make it clear that all the positions of trust in the town, the whole control of municipal affairs, ought to be put in the hands of the Liberals.

BILLING. That is perfectly true! I see it coming—I see it coming; we are on the threshold of a revolution!

(*A knock it heard at the door.*)

HOVSTAD. Hush! (*Calls out.*) Come in! (DR. STOCKMANN *comes in by the street door.* HOVSTAD *goes to meet him.*) Ah, it is you, Doctor! Well?

DR. STOCKMANN. You may set to work and print it, Mr. Hovstad!

HOVSTAD. Has it come to that, then?

BILLING. Hurrah!

DR. STOCKMANN. Yes, print away. Undoubtedly it has come to that. Now they must take what they get. There is going to be a fight in the town, Mr. Billing!

BILLING. War to the knife, I hope! We will get our knives to their throats, Doctor!

DR. STOCKMANN. This article is only a beginning. I have already got four or five more sketched out in my head. Where is Aslaksen?

BILLING (*calls into the printing-room*). Aslaksen, just come here for a minute!

HOVSTAD. Four or five more articles, did you say? On the same subject?

DR. STOCKMANN. No—far from it, my dear fellow. No, they are about quite another matter. But they all spring from the question of the water-supply and the drainage. One thing leads to another, you know. It is like beginning to pull down an old house, exactly.

BILLING. Upon my soul, it's true; you find you are not done till you have pulled all the old rubbish down.

ASLAKSEN (*coming in*). Pulled down? You are not thinking of pulling down the Baths surely, Doctor?

HOVSTAD. Far from it, don't be afraid.

DR. STOCKMANN. No, we meant something quite different. Well, what do you think of my article, Mr. Hovstad?

HOVSTAD. I think it is simply a masterpiece—

DR. STOCKMANN. Do you really think so? Well, I am very pleased, very pleased.

HOVSTAD. It is so clear and intelligible. One need have no special knowledge to understand the bearing of it. You will have every enlightened man on your side.

ASLAKSEN. And every prudent man too, I hope?

BILLING. The prudent and the imprudent—almost the whole town.

ASLAKSEN. In that case we may venture to print it.

DR. STOCKMANN. I should think so!

HOVSTAD. We will put it in to-morrow morning.

DR. STOCKMANN. Of course—you must not lose a single day. What I wanted to ask you, Mr. Aslaksen, was if you would supervise the printing of it yourself.

ASLAKSEN. With pleasure.

DR. STOCKMANN. Take care of it as if it were a treasure! No misprints—every word is important. I will look in again a little later; perhaps you will be able to let me see a proof. I can't tell you how eager I am to see it in print, and see it burst upon the public—

BILLING. Burst upon them—yes, like a flash of lightning!

DR. STOCKMANN. —and to have it submitted to the judgment of my intelligent fellow-townsmen. You cannot imagine what I have gone through to-day. I have been threatened first with one thing and then with another; they have tried to rob me of my most elementary rights as a man—

BILLING. What! Your rights as a man!

DR. STOCKMANN. —they have tried to degrade me, to make a coward of me, to force me to put personal interests before my most sacred convictions—

BILLING. That is too much—I'm damned if it isn't.

HOVSTAD. Oh, you mustn't be surprised at anything from that quarter.

DR. STOCKMANN. Well, they will get the worst of it with me; they may assure themselves of that. I shall consider the "People's Messenger" my sheet-anchor now, and every single day I will bombard them with one article after another, like bomb-shells—

ASLAKSEN. Yes, but—

BILLING. Hurrah!—it is war, it is war!

DR. STOCKMANN. I shall smite them to the ground—I shall crush them—I shall break down all their defences, before the eyes of the honest public! That is what I shall do!

ASLAKSEN. Yes, but in moderation, Doctor—proceed with moderation—

BILLING. Not a bit of it, not a bit of it! Don't spare the dynamite!

DR. STOCKMANN. Because it is not merely a question of water-supply and drains now, you know. No—it is the whole of our social life that we have got to purify and disinfect—

BILLING. Spoken like a deliverer!

DR. STOCKMANN. All the incapables must be turned out, you understand—and that in every walk of life! Endless vistas have opened themselves to my mind's eye to-day. I cannot see it all quite clearly yet, but I shall in time. Young and vigorous standard-bearers—those are what we need and must seek, my friends; we must have new men in command at all our outposts.

BILLING. Hear, hear!

DR. STOCKMANN. We only need to stand by one another, and it will all be perfectly easy. The revolution will be launched like a ship that runs smoothly off the stocks. Don't you think so?

HOVSTAD. For my part I think we have now a prospect of getting the municipal authority into the hands where it should lie.

ASLAKSEN. And if only we proceed with moderation, I cannot imagine that there will be any risk.

DR. STOCKMANN. Who the devil cares whether there is any risk or not! What I am doing, I am doing in the name of truth and for the sake of my conscience.

HOVSTAD. You are a man who deserves to be supported, Doctor.

ASLAKSEN. Yes, there is no denying that the Doctor is a true friend to the town—a real friend to the community, that he is.

BILLING. Take my word for it, Aslaksen, Dr. Stockmann is a friend of the people.

ASLAKSEN. I fancy the Householders' Association will make use of that expression before long.

DR. STOCKMANN (affected, grasps their hands). Thank you, thank you, my dear staunch friends. It is very refreshing to me to hear you say that; my brother called me something quite different. By Jove, he shall have it back, with interest! But now I must be off to see a poor devil—. I will come back, as I said. Keep a very careful eye on the manuscript, Aslaksen, and don't for worlds leave out any of my notes of exclamation! Rather put one or two more in! Capital, capital! Well, good-bye for the present—good-bye, good-bye!

(*They show him to the door, and bow him out.*)

HOVSTAD. He may prove an invaluably useful man to us.

ASLAKSEN. Yes, so long as he confines himself to this matter of the Baths. But if he goes farther afield, I don't think it would be advisable to follow him.

HOVSTAD. Hm!—that all depends—

BILLING. You are so infernally timid, Aslaksen!

ASLAKSEN. Timid? Yes, when it is a question of the local authorities, I am timid, Mr. Billing; it is a lesson I have learnt in the school of experience, let me tell you. But try me in higher politics, in matters that concern the government itself, and then see if I am timid.

BILLING. No, you aren't, I admit. But this is simply contradicting yourself.

ASLAKSEN. I am a man with a conscience, and that is the whole matter. If you attack the government, you don't do the community any harm, anyway; those fellows pay no attention to attacks, you see—they go on just as they are, in spite of them. But *local* authorities are different; they *can* be turned out, and then perhaps you may get an ignorant lot into office who may do irreparable harm to the householders and everybody else.

HOVSTAD. But what of the education of citizens by self government—don't you attach any importance to that?

ASLAKSEN. When a man has interests of his own to protect, he cannot think of everything, Mr. Hovstad.

HOVSTAD. Then I hope I shall never have interests of my own to protect!

BILLING. Hear, hear!

ASLAKSEN (*with a smile*). Hm! (*Points to the desk.*) Mr. Sheriff Stensgaard was your predecessor at that editorial desk.

BILLING (*spitting*). Bah! That turncoat.

HOVSTAD. I am not a weathercock—and never will be.

ASLAKSEN. A politician should never be too certain of anything, Mr. Hovstad. And as for you, Mr. Billing, I should think it is time for you to be taking in a reef or two in your sails, seeing that you are applying for the post of secretary to the Bench.

BILLING. I—!

HOVSTAD. Are you, Billing?

BILLING. Well, yes—but you must clearly understand I am only doing it to annoy the bigwigs.

ASLAKSEN. Anyhow, it is no business of mine. But if I am to be accused of timidity and of inconsistency in my principles, this is what I want to point out: my political past is an open book. I have never changed, except perhaps to become a little more moderate, you see. My heart is still with the people; but I don't deny that my reason has a certain bias towards the authorities—the local ones, I mean. (*Goes into the printing-room.*)

BILLING. Oughtn't we to try and get rid of him, Hovstad?

HOVSTAD. Do you know anyone else who will advance the money for our paper and printing bill?

BILLING. It is an infernal nuisance that we don't possess some capital to trade on.

HOVSTAD (*sitting down at his desk*). Yes, if we only had that, then—

BILLING. Suppose you were to apply to Dr. Stockmann?

HOVSTAD (*turning over some papers*). What is the use? He has got nothing.

BILLING. No, but he has got a warm man in the background, old Morten Kiil—"the Badger," as they call him.

HOVSTAD (*writing*). Are you so sure *he* has got anything?

BILLING. Good Lord, of course he has! And some of it must come to the Stockmanns. Most probably he will do something for the children, at all events.

HOVSTAD (*turning half round*). Are you counting on that?

BILLING. Counting on it? Of course I am not counting on anything.

HOVSTAD. That is right. And I should not count on the secretaryship to the Bench either, if I were you; for I can assure you—you won't get it.

BILLING. Do you think I am not quite aware of that? My object is precisely *not* to get it. A slight of that kind stimulates a man's fighting power—it is like getting a supply of fresh bile—and I am sure one needs that badly enough in a hole-and-corner place like this, where it is so seldom anything happens to stir one up.

HOVSTAD (*writing*). Quite so, quite so.

BILLING. Ah, I shall be heard of yet!—Now I shall go and write the appeal to the Householders' Association. (*Goes into the room on the right.*)

HOVSTAD (*sitting at his desk, biting his penholder, says slowly*). Hm!—that's it, is it. (*A knock is heard.*) Come in! (*PETRA comes in by the outer door. HOVSTAD gets up.*) What, you!—here?

PETRA. Yes, you must forgive me—

HOVSTAD (*pulling a chair forward*). Won't you sit down?

PETRA. No, thank you; I must go again in a moment.

HOVSTAD. Have you come with a message from your father, by any chance?

PETRA. No, I have come on my own account. (*Takes a book out of her coat pocket.*) Here is the English story.

HOVSTAD. Why have you brought it back?

PETRA. Because I am not going to translate it.

HOVSTAD. But you promised me faithfully—

PETRA. Yes, but then I had not read it. I don't suppose you have read it either?

HOVSTAD. No, you know quite well I don't understand English; but—

PETRA. Quite so. That is why I wanted to tell you that you must find something else. (*Lays the book on the table.*) You can't use this for the "People's Messenger."

HOVSTAD. Why not?

PETRA. Because it conflicts with all your opinions.

HOVSTAD. Oh, for that matter—

PETRA. You don't understand me. The burden of this story is that there is a supernatural power that looks after the so-called good people in this world and makes everything happen for the best in their case—while all the so-called bad people are punished.

HOVSTAD. Well, but that is all right. That is just what our readers want.

PETRA. And are you going to be the one to give it to them? For myself, I do not believe a word of it. You know quite well that things do not happen so in reality.

HOVSTAD. You are perfectly right; but an editor cannot always act as he would prefer. He is often obliged to bow to the wishes of the public in unimportant matters. Politics are the most important thing in life—for a newspaper, anyway; and if I want to carry my public with me on the path that leads to liberty and progress, I must not frighten them away. If they find a moral tale of this sort in the serial at the bottom of the page, they will be all the more ready to read what is printed above it; they feel more secure, as it were.

PETRA. For shame! You would never go and set a snare like that for your readers; you are not a spider!

HOVSTAD (*smiling*). Thank you for having such a good opinion of me. No; as a matter of fact that is Billing's idea and not mine.

PETRA. Billing's!

HOVSTAD. Yes; anyway he propounded that theory here one day. And it is Billing who is so anxious to have that story in the paper; I don't know anything about the book.

PETRA. But how can Billing, with his emancipated views—

HOVSTAD. Oh, Billing is a many-sided man. He is applying for the post of secretary to the Bench, too, I hear.

PETRA. I don't believe it, Mr. Hovstad. How could he possibly bring himself to do such a thing?

HOVSTAD. Ah, you must ask him that.

PETRA. I should never have thought it of him.

HOVSTAD (*looking more closely at her*). No? Does it really surprise you so much?

PETRA. Yes. Or perhaps not altogether. Really, I don't quite know—

HOVSTAD. We journalists are not much worth, Miss Stockmann.

PETRA. Do you really mean that?

HOVSTAD. I think so sometimes.

PETRA. Yes, in the ordinary affairs of everyday life, perhaps; I can understand that. But now, when you have taken a weighty matter in hand—

HOVSTAD. This matter of your father's, you mean?

PETRA. Exactly. It seems to me that now you must feel you are a man worth more than most.

HOVSTAD. Yes, to-day I do feel something of that sort.

PETRA. Of course you do, don't you? It is a splendid vocation you have chosen—to smooth the way for the march of unappreciated truths, and new and courageous lines of thought. If it were nothing more than because you stand fearlessly in the open and take up the cause of an injured man—

HOVSTAD. Especially when that injured man is—ahem!—I don't rightly know how to—

PETRA. When that man is so upright and so honest, you mean?

HOVSTAD (*more gently*). Especially when he is your father, I meant.

PETRA (*suddenly checked*). *That?*

HOVSTAD. Yes, Petra—Miss Petra.

PETRA. Is it *that*, that is first and foremost with you? Not the matter itself? Not the truth?—not my father's big generous heart?

HOVSTAD. Certainly—of course—that too.

PETRA. No, thank you; you have betrayed yourself, Mr. Hovstad, and now I shall never trust you again in anything.

HOVSTAD. Can you really take it so amiss in me that it is mostly for your sake—?

PETRA. What I am angry with you for, is for not having been honest with my father. You talked to him as if the truth and the good of the community were what lay nearest to your heart. You have made fools of both my father and me. You are not the man you made yourself out to be. And that I shall never forgive you—never!

HOVSTAD. You ought not to speak so bitterly, Miss Petra —least of all now.

PETRA. Why not now, especially?

HOVSTAD. Because your father cannot do without my help.

PETRA (*looking him up and down*). Are you that sort of man too? For shame!

HOVSTAD. No, no, I am not. This came upon me so unexpectedly—you must believe that.

PETRA. I know what to believe. Good-bye.

ASLAKSEN (*coming from the printing-room, hurriedly and with an air of mystery*). Damnation, Hovstad!—(*Sees* PETRA.) Oh, this is awkward—

PETRA. There is the book; you must give it to some one else. (*Goes towards the door.*)

HOVSTAD (*following her*). But, Miss Stockmann—

PETRA. Good-bye. (*Goes out.*)

ASLAKSEN. I say—Mr. Hovstad—

HOVSTAD. Well, well!—what is it?

ASLAKSEN. The Mayor is outside in the printing-room.

HOVSTAD. The Mayor, did you say?

ASLAKSEN. Yes, he wants to speak to you. He came in by the back door—didn't want to be seen, you understand.

HOVSTAD. What can he want? Wait a bit—I will go myself. (*Goes to the door of the printing-room, opens it, bows and invites* PETER STOCKMANN *in.*) Just see, Aslaksen, that no one—

ASLAKSEN. Quite so. (*Goes into the printing-room.*)

PETER STOCKMANN. You did not expect to see me here, Mr. Hovstad?

HOVSTAD. No, I confess I did not.

PETER STOCKMANN (*looking round*). You are very snug in here—very nice indeed.

HOVSTAD. Oh—

PETER STOCKMANN. And here I come, without any notice, to take up your time!

HOVSTAD. By all means, Mr. Mayor. I am at your service. But let me relieve you of your— (*takes* STOCKMANN'S *hat and stick and puts them on a chair*). Won't you sit down?

PETER STOCKMANN (*sitting down by the table*). Thank you. (HOVSTAD *sits down.*) I have had an extremely annoying experience to-day, Mr. Hovstad.

HOVSTAD. Really? Ah well, I expect with all the various business you have to attend to—

PETER STOCKMANN. The Medical Officer of the Baths is responsible for what happened to-day.

HOVSTAD. Indeed? The Doctor?

PETER STOCKMANN. He has addressed a kind of report to

the Baths Committee on the subject of certain supposed defects in the Baths.

HOVSTAD. Has he indeed?

PETER STOCKMANN. Yes—has he not told you? I thought he said—

HOVSTAD. Ah, yes—it is true he did mention something about—

ASLAKSEN (*coming from the printing-room*). I ought to have that copy—

HOVSTAD (*angrily*). Ahem!—there it is on the desk.

ASLAKSEN (*taking it*). Right.

PETER STOCKMANN. But look there—that is the thing I was speaking of!

ASLAKSEN. Yes, that is the Doctor's article, Mr. Mayor.

HOVSTAD. Oh, is *that* what you were speaking about?

PETER STOCKMANN. Yes, that is it. What do you think of it?

HOVSTAD. Oh, I am only a layman—and I have only taken a very cursory glance at it.

PETER STOCKMANN. But you are going to print it?

HOVSTAD. I cannot very well refuse a distinguished man—

ASLAKSEN. I have nothing to do with editing the paper, Mr. Mayor—

PETER STOCKMANN. I understand.

ASLAKSEN. I merely print what is put into my hands.

PETER STOCKMANN. Quite so.

ASLAKSEN. And so I must— (*moves off towards the printing-room*).

PETER STOCKMANN. No, wait a moment, Mr. Aslaksen. You will allow me, Mr. Hovstad?

HOVSTAD. If you please, Mr. Mayor.

PETER STOCKMANN. You are a discreet and thoughtful man, Mr. Aslaksen.

ASLAKSEN. I am delighted to hear you think so, sir.

PETER STOCKMANN. And a man of very considerable influence.

ASLAKSEN. Chiefly among the small tradesmen, sir.

PETER STOCKMANN. The small tax-payers are the majority —here as everywhere else.

ASLAKSEN. That is true.

PETER STOCKMANN. And I have no doubt you know the general trend of opinion among them, don't you?

ASLAKSEN. Yes I think I may say I do, Mr. Mayor.

PETER STOCKMANN. Yes. Well, since there is such a praise-worthy spirit of self-sacrifice among the less wealthy citizens of our town—

ASLAKSEN. What?

HOVSTAD. Self-sacrifice?

PETER STOCKMANN. It is pleasing evidence of a public-spirited feeling, extremely pleasing evidence. I might almost say I hardly expected it. But you have a closer knowledge of public opinion than I.

ASLAKSEN. But, Mr. Mayor—

PETER STOCKMANN. And indeed it is no small sacrifice that the town is going to make.

HOVSTAD. The town?

ASLAKSEN. But I don't understand. Is it the Baths—?

PETER STOCKMANN. At a provisional estimate, the alterations that the Medical Officer asserts to be desirable will cost somewhere about twenty thousand pounds.

ASLAKSEN. That is a lot of money, but—

PETER STOCKMANN. Of course it will be necessary to raise a municipal loan.

HOVSTAD (*getting up*). Surely you never mean that the town must pay—?

ASLAKSEN. Do you mean that it must come out of the municipal funds?—out of the ill-filled pockets of the small tradesmen?

PETER STOCKMANN. Well, my dear Mr. Aslaksen, where else is the money to come from?

ASLAKSEN. The gentlemen who own the Baths ought to provide that.

PETER STOCKMANN. The proprietors of the Baths are not in a position to incur any further expense.

ASLAKSEN. Is that absolutely certain, Mr. Mayor.

PETER STOCKMANN. I have satisfied myself that it is so. If the town wants these very extensive alterations, it will have to pay for them.

ASLAKSEN. But, damn it all—I beg your pardon—this is quite another matter, Mr. Hovstad!

HOVSTAD. It is, indeed.

PETER STOCKMANN. The most fatal part of it is that we shall be obliged to shut the Baths for a couple of years.

HOVSTAD. Shut them? Shut them altogether?

ASLAKSEN. For two years?

PETER STOCKMANN. Yes, the work will take as long as that —at least.

ASLAKSEN. I'm damned if we will stand that, Mr. Mayor! What are we householders to live upon in the meantime?

PETER STOCKMANN. Unfortunately that is an extremely difficult question to answer, Mr. Aslaksen. But what would you have us do? Do you suppose we shall have a single visitor in the town, if we go about proclaiming that our water is polluted, that we are living over a plague spot, that the entire town—

ASLAKSEN. And the whole thing is merely imagination?

PETER STOCKMANN. With the best will in the world, I have not been able to come to any other conclusion.

ASLAKSEN. Well then I must say it is absolutely unjustifiable of Dr. Stockmann—I beg your pardon, Mr. Mayor—

PETER STOCKMANN. What you say is lamentably true, Mr. Aslaksen. My brother has unfortunately always been a headstrong man.

ASLAKSEN. After this, do you mean to give him your support, Mr. Hovstad?

HOVSTAD. Can you suppose for a moment that I—?

PETER STOCKMANN. I have drawn up a short *résumé* of the situation as it appears from a reasonable man's point of view. In it I have indicated how certain possible defects might suitably be remedied without out-running the resources of the Baths Committee.

HOVSTAD. Have you got it with you, Mr. Mayor.

PETER STOCKMANN (*fumbling in his pocket*). Yes, I brought it with me in case you should—

ASLAKSEN. Good Lord, there he is!

PETER STOCKMANN. Who? My brother?

HOVSTAD. Where? Where?

ASLAKSEN. He has just gone through the printing-room.

PETER STOCKMANN. How unlucky! I don't want to meet him here, and I had still several things to speak to you about.

HOVSTAD (*pointing to the door on the right*). Go in there for the present.

PETER STOCKMANN. But—?

HOVSTAD. You will only find Billing in there.

ASLAKSEN. Quick, quick, Mr. Mayor—he is just coming.

PETER STOCKMANN. Yes, very well; but see that you get rid of him quickly. (*Goes out through the door on the right, which* ASLAKSEN *opens for him and shuts after him.*)

HOVSTAD. Pretend to be doing something, Aslaksen. (*Sits down and writes.* ASLAKSEN *begins foraging among a heap of newspapers that are lying on a chair.*)

DR. STOCKMANN (*coming in from the printing-room*). Here I am again. (*Puts down his hat and stick.*)

HOVSTAD (*writing*). Already, Doctor? Hurry up with what we were speaking about, Aslaksen. We are very pressed for time to-day.

DR. STOCKMANN (*to* ASLAKSEN). No proof for me to see yet, I hear.

ASLAKSEN (*without turning round*). You couldn't expect it yet, Doctor.

DR. STOCKMANN. No, no; but I am impatient, as you can

understand. I shall not know a moment's peace of mind till I
see it in print.

HOVSTAD. Hm!—It will take a good while yet, won't it,
Aslaksen?

ASLAKSEN. Yes, I am almost afraid it will.

DR. STOCKMANN. All right, my dear friends; I will come
back. I do not mind coming back twice if necessary. A matter
of such great importance—the welfare of the town at stake—
it is no time to shirk trouble. (*Is just going, but stops and
comes back.*) Look here—there is one thing more I want to
speak to you about.

HOVSTAD. Excuse me, but could it not wait till some other
time?

DR. STOCKMANN. I can tell you in half a dozen words. It is
only this. When my article is read to-morrow and it is realised
that I have been quietly working the whole winter for the
welfare of the town—

HOVSTAD. Yes but, Doctor—

DR. STOCKMANN. I know what you are going to say. You
don't see how on earth it was any more than my duty—my
obvious duty as a citizen. Of course it wasn't; I know that as
well as you. But my fellow citizens, you know—! Good Lord,
think of all the good souls who think so highly of me—!

ASLAKSEN. Yes, our townsfolk have had a very high
opinion of you so far, Doctor.

DR. STOCKMANN. Yes, and that is just why I am afraid
they—. Well, this is the point; when this reaches them, especially the poorer classes, and sounds in their ears like a sum-
mons to take the town's affairs into their own hands for the
future—

HOVSTAD (*getting up*). Ahem! Doctor, I won't conceal
from you the fact—

DR. STOCKMANN. Ah!—I knew there was something in the
wind! But I won't hear a word of it. If anything of that sort
is being set on foot—

HOVSTAD. Of what sort?

DR. STOCKMANN. Well, whatever it is—whether it is a
demonstration in my honour, or a banquet, or a subscription
list for some presentation to me—whatever it is, you most
promise me solemnly and faithfully to put a stop to it. You
too, Mr. Aslaksen; do you understand?

HOVSTAD. You must forgive me, Doctor, but sooner or later
we must tell you the plain truth—

(*He is interrupted by the entrance of* MRS. STOCKMANN,
who comes in from the street door.)

MRS. STOCKMANN (*seeing her husband*). Just as I thought!

HOVSTAD (*going towards her*). You too, Mrs. Stockmann?

DR. STOCKMANN. What on earth do *you* want here, Katherine?

MRS. STOCKMANN. I should think you know very well what I want.

HOVSTAD. Won't you sit down? Or perhaps—

MRS. STOCKMANN. No, thank you; don't trouble. And you must not be offended at my coming to fetch my husband; I am the mother of three children, you know.

DR. STOCKMANN. Nonsense!—we know all about that.

MRS. STOCKMANN. Well, one would not give you credit for much thought for your wife and children to-day; if you had had that, you would not have gone and dragged us all into misfortune.

DR. STOCKMANN. Are you out of your senses, Katherine! Because a man has a wife and children, is he not to be allowed to proclaim the truth—is he not to be allowed to be an actively useful citizen—is he not to be allowed to do a service to his native town!

MRS. STOCKMANN. Yes, Thomas—in reason.

ASLAKSEN. Just what I say. Moderation in everything.

MRS. STOCKMANN. And that is why you wrong us, Mr. Hovstad, in enticing my husband away from his home and making a dupe of him in all this.

HOVSTAD. I certainly am making a dupe of no one—

DR. STOCKMANN. Making a dupe of me! Do you suppose *I* should allow myself to be duped!

MRS. STOCKMANN. It is just what you do. I know quite well you have more brains than anyone in the town, but you are extremely easily duped, Thomas. (*To Hovstad.*) Please to realise that he loses his post at the Baths if you print what he has written—

ASLAKSEN. What!

HOVSTAD. Look here, Doctor—

DR. STOCKMANN (*laughing*). Ha—ha!—just let them try! No, no—they will take good care not to. I have got the compact majority behind me, let me tell you!

MRS. STOCKMANN. Yes, that is just the worst of it—your having any such horrid thing behind you.

DR. STOCKMANN. Rubbish, Katherine!—Go home and look after your house and leave me to look after the community. How can you be so afraid, when I am so confident and happy? (*Walks up and down, rubbing his hands.*) Truth and the People will win the fight, you may be certain! I see the whole of the broad-minded middle class marching like a victorious army—! (*Stops beside a chair.*) What the deuce is that lying there?

ASLAKSEN. Good Lord!

HOVSTAD. Ahem!

DR. STOCKMANN. Here we have the topmost pinnacle of authority! (*Takes the Mayor's official hat carefully between his finger-tips and holds it up in the air.*)

MRS. STOCKMANN. The Mayor's hat!

DR. STOCKMANN. And here is the staff of office too. How in the name of all that's wonderful—?

HOVSTAD. Well, you see—

DR. STOCKMANN. Oh, I understand. He has been here trying to talk you over. Ha—ha!—he made rather a mistake there! And as soon as he caught sight of me in the printing-room—. (*Bursts out laughing.*) Did he run away, Mr. Aslaksen?

ASLAKSEN (*hurriedly*). Yes, he ran away, Doctor.

DR. STOCKMANN. Ran away without his stick or his—. Fiddlesticks! Peter doesn't run away and leave his belongings behind him. But what the deuce have you done with him? Ah!—in there, of course. Now you shall see, Katherine!

MRS. STOCKMANN. Thomas—please don't—!

ASLAKSEN. Don't be rash, Doctor.

(DR. STOCKMANN *has put on the Mayor's hat and taken his stick in his hand. He goes up to the door, opens it, and stands with his hand to his hat at the salute.* PETER STOCKMANN *comes in, red with anger.* BILLING *follows him.*)

PETER STOCKMANN. What does this tomfoolery mean?

DR. STOCKMANN. Be respectful, my good Peter. I am the chief authority in the town now. (*Walks up and down.*)

MRS. STOCKMANN (*almost in tears*). Really, Thomas!

PETER STOCKMANN (*following him about*). Give me my hat and stick.

DR. STOCKMANN (*in the same tone as before*). If you are chief constable, let me tell you that I am the Mayor—I am the master of the whole town, please understand!

PETER STOCKMANN. Take off my hat, I tell you. Remember it is part of an official uniform.

DR. STOCKMANN. Pooh! Do you think the newly awakened lion-hearted people are going to be frightened by an official hat? There is going to be a revolution in the town to-morrow, let me tell you. You thought you could turn me out; but now I shall turn you out—turn you out of all your various offices. Do you think I cannot? Listen to me. I have triumphant social forces behind me. Hovstad and Billing will thunder in the "People's Messenger," and Aslaksen will take the field at the head of the whole Householders' Association—

ASLAKSEN. That I won't, Doctor.

DR. STOCKMANN. Of course you will—

PETER STOCKMANN. Ah!—may I ask then if Mr. Hovstad intends to join this agitation.

HOVSTAD. No, Mr. Mayor.

ASLAKSEN. No, Mr. Hovstad is not such a fool as to go and ruin his paper and himself for the sake of an imaginary grievance.

DR. STOCKMANN (*looking round him*). What does this mean?

HOVSTAD. You have represented your case in a false light, Doctor, and therefore I am unable to give you my support.

BILLING. And after what the Mayor was so kind as to tell me just now, I—

DR. STOCKMANN. A false light! Leave that part of it to me. Only print my article; I am quite capable of defending it.

HOVSTAD. I am not going to print it. I cannot and will not and dare not print it.

DR. STOCKMANN. You dare not? What nonsense!—you are the editor; and an editor controls his paper, I suppose!

ASLAKSEN. No, it is the subscribers, Doctor.

PETER STOCKMANN. Fortunately, yes.

ASLAKSEN. It is public opinion—the enlightened public— householders and people of that kind; they control the newspapers.

DR. STOCKMANN (*composedly*). And I have all these influences against me?

ASLAKSEN. Yes, you have. It would mean the absolute ruin of the community if your article were to appear.

DR. STOCKMANN. Indeed.

PETER STOCKMANN. My hat and stick, if you please. (DR. STOCKMANN *takes off the hat and lays it on the table with the stick.* PETER STOCKMANN *takes them up.*) Your authority as mayor has come to an untimely end.

DR. STOCKMANN. We have not got to the end yet. (*To* HOVSTAD.) Then it is quite impossible for you to print my article in the "People's Messenger"?

HOVSTAD. Quite impossible—out of regard for your family as well.

MRS. STOCKMANN. You need not concern yourself about his family, thank you, Mr. Hovstad.

PETER STOCKMANN (*taking a paper from his pocket*). It will be sufficient, for the guidance of the public, if this appears. It is an official statement. May I trouble you?

HOVSTAD (*taking the paper*). Certainly; I will see that it is printed.

DR. STOCKMANN. But not mine. Do you imagine that you can silence me and stifle the truth! You will not find it so easy as you suppose. Mr. Aslaksen, kindly take my manuscript at once and print it as a pamphlet—at my expense. I will have four hundred copies—no, five—six hundred.

ASLAKSEN. If you offered me its weight in gold, I could not lend my press for any such purpose, Doctor. It would be flying in the face of public opinion. You will not get it printed anywhere in the town.

DR. STOCKMANN. Then give it back to me.

HOVSTAD (*giving him the MS.*). Here it is.

DR. STOCKMANN (*taking his hat and stick*). It shall be made public all the same. I will read it out at a mass meeting of the townspeople. All my fellow-citizens shall hear the voice of truth!

PETER STOCKMANN. You will not find any public body in the town that will give you the use of their hall for such a purpose.

ASLAKSEN. Not a single one, I am certain.

BILLING. No, I'm damned if you will find one.

MRS. STOCKMANN. But this is too shameful! Why should every one turn against you like that?

DR. STOCKMANN (*angrily*). I will tell you why. It is because all the men in this town are old women—like you; they all think of nothing but their families, and never of the community.

MRS. STOCKMANN (*putting her arm into his*). Then I will show them that an—an old woman can be a man for once. I am going to stand by you, Thomas!

DR. STOCKMANN. Bravely said, Katherine! It shall be made public—as I am a living soul! If I can't hire a hall, I shall hire a drum, and parade the town with it and read it at every street-corner.

PETER STOCKMANN. You are surely not such an arrant fool as that!

DR. STOCKMANN. Yes, I am.

ASLAKSEN. You won't find a single man in the whole town to go with you.

BILLING. No, I'm damned if you will.

MRS. STOCKMANN. Don't give in, Thomas. I will tell the boys to go with you.

DR. STOCKMANN. That is a splendid idea!

MRS. STOCKMANN. Morten will be delighted; and Ejlif will do whatever he does.

DR. STOCKMANN. Yes, and Petra!—and you too, Katherine!

MRS. STOCKMANN. No, I won't do that; but I will stand at the window and watch you, that's what I will do.

DR. STOCKMANN (*puts his arms round her and kisses her*). Thank you, my dear! Now you and I are going to try a fall, my fine gentlemen! I am going to see whether a pack of cowards can succeed in gagging a patriot who wants to purify society! (*He and his wife go out by the street door.*)

PETER STOCKMANN (*shaking his head seriously*). Now he has sent *her* out of her senses, too.

ACT IV

(SCENE.—*A big old-fashioned room in* CAPTAIN HORSTER'S *house. At the back folding-doors, which are standing open, lead to an ante-room. Three windows in the left-hand wall. In the middle of the opposite wall a platform has been erected. On this is a small table with two candles, a water-bottle and glass, and a bell. The room is lit by lamps placed between the windows. In the foreground on the left there is a table with candles and a chair. To the right is a door and some chairs standing near it. The room is nearly filled with a crowd of townspeople of all sorts, a few women and schoolboys being amongst them. People are still streaming in from the back, and the room is soon filled.*)

1ST CITIZEN (*meeting another*). Hullo, Lamstad! You here too?

2ND CITIZEN. I go to every public meeting, I do.

3RD CITIZEN. Brought your whistle too, I expect!

2ND CITIZEN. I should think so. Haven't you?

3RD CITIZEN. Rather! And old Evensen said he was going to bring a cow-horn, he did.

2ND CITIZEN. Good old Evensen! (*Laughter among the crowd.*)

4TH CITIZEN (*coming up to them*). I say, tell me what is going on here to-night.

2ND CITIZEN. Dr. Stockmann is going to deliver an address attacking the Mayor.

4TH CITIZEN. But the Mayor is his brother.

1ST CITIZEN. That doesn't matter; Dr. Stockmann's not the chap to be afraid.

3RD CITIZEN. But he is in the wrong; it said so in the "People's Messenger."

2ND CITIZEN. Yes, I expect he must be in the wrong this time, because neither the Householders' Association nor the Citizens' Club would lend him their hall for his meeting.

182

1ST CITIZEN. He couldn't even get the loan of the hall at the Baths.

2ND CITIZEN. No, I should think not.

A MAN IN ANOTHER PART OF THE CROWD. I say—who are we to back up in this?

ANOTHER MAN, BESIDE HIM. Watch Aslaksen, and do as he does.

BILLING (*pushing his way through the crowd, with a writing-case under his arm*). Excuse me, gentlemen— do you mind letting me through? I am reporting for the "People's Messenger." Thank you very much! (*He sits down at the table on the left.*)

A WORKMAN. Who was that?

SECOND WORKMAN. Don't you know him? It's Billing, who writes for Aslaksen's paper.

(CAPTAIN HORSTER *brings in* MRS. STOCKMANN *and* PETRA *through the door on the right.* EJLIF *and* MORTEN *follow them in.*)

HORSTER. I thought you might all sit here; you can slip out easily from here, if things get too lively.

MRS. STOCKMANN. Do you think there will be a disturbance?

HORSTER. One can never tell—with such a crowd. But sit down, and don't be uneasy.

MRS. STOCKMANN (*sitting down*). It was extremely kind of you to offer my husband the room.

HORSTER. Well, if nobody else would—

PETRA (*who has sat down beside her mother*). And it was a plucky thing to do, Captain Horster.

HORSTER. Oh, it is not such a great matter as all that.

(HOVSTAD *and* ASLAKSEN *make their way through the crowd.*)

ASLAKSEN (*going up to* HORSTER). Has the Doctor not come yet?

HORSTER. He is waiting in the next room. (*Movement in the crowd by the door at the back.*)

HOVSTAD. Look—here comes the Mayor!

BILLING. Yes, I'm damned if he hasn't come after all!

(PETER STOCKMANN *makes his way gradually through the crowd, bows courteously, and takes up a position by the wall on the left. Shortly afterwards* DR. STOCKMANN *comes in by the right-hand door. He is dressed in a black frock-coat, with a white tie. There is a little feeble applause, which is hushed down. Silence is obtained.*)

DR. STOCKMANN (*in an undertone*). How do you feel, Katherine?

MRS. STOCKMANN. All right, thank you. (*Lowering her voice.*) Be sure not to lose your temper, Thomas.

DR. STOCKMANN. Oh, I know how to control myself. (*Looks at his watch, steps on to the platform, and bows.*) It is a quarter past—so I will begin. (*Takes his MS. out of his pocket.*)

ASLAKSEN. I think we ought to elect a chairman first.

DR. STOCKMANN. No, it is quite unnecessary.

SOME OF THE CROWD. Yes—yes!

PETER STOCKMANN. I certainly think too that we ought to have a chairman.

DR. STOCKMANN. But I have called this meeting to deliver a lecture, Peter.

PETER STOCKMANN. Dr. Stockmann's lecture may possibly lead to a considerable conflict of opinion.

VOICES IN THE CROWD. A chairman! A chairman!

HOVSTAD. The general wish of the meeting seems to be that a chairman should be elected.

DR. STOCKMANN (*restraining himself*). Very well—let the meeting have its way.

ASLAKSEN. Will the Mayor be good enough to undertake the task?

THREE MEN (*clapping their hands*). Bravo! Bravo!

PETER STOCKMANN. For various reasons, which you will easily understand, I must beg to be excused. But fortunately we have amongst us a man who I think will be acceptable to you all. I refer to the President of the Householders' Association, Mr. Aslaksen!

SEVERAL VOICES. Yes—Aslaksen! Bravo Aslaksen!

(DR. STOCKMANN *takes up his MS. and walks up and down the platform.*)

ASLAKSEN. Since my fellow-citizens choose to entrust me with this duty, I cannot refuse.

(*Loud applause.* ASLAKSEN *mounts the platform.*)

BILLING (*writing*). "Mr. Aslaksen was elected with enthusiasm."

ASLAKSEN. And now, as I am in this position, I should like to say a few brief words. I am a quiet and peaceable man, who believes in discreet moderation, and—and—in moderate discretion. All my friends can bear witness to that.

SEVERAL VOICES. That's right! That's right, Aslaksen!

ASLAKSEN. I have learnt in the school of life and experience that moderation is the most valuable virtue a citizen can possess—

PETER STOCKMANN. Hear, hear!

ASLAKSEN. —And moreover that discretion and moderation

are what enable a man to be of most service to the community. I would therefore suggest to our esteemed fellow-citizen, who has called this meeting, that he should strive to keep strictly within the bounds of moderation.

A MAN BY THE DOOR. Three cheers for the Moderation Society!

A VOICE. Shame!

SEVERAL VOICES. Sh!—Sh!

ASLAKSEN. No interruptions, gentlemen, please! Does anyone wish to make any remarks?

PETER STOCKMANN. Mr. Chairman.

ASLAKSEN. The Mayor will address the meeting.

PETER STOCKMANN. In consideration of the close relationship in which, as you all know, I stand to the present Medical Officer of the Baths, I should have preferred not to speak this evening. But my official position with regard to the Baths and my solicitude for the vital interests of the town compel me to bring forward a motion. I venture to presume that there is not a single one of our citizens present who considers it desirable that unreliable and exaggerated accounts of the sanitary condition of the Baths and the town should be spread abroad.

SEVERAL VOICES. No, no! Certainly not! We protest against it!

PETER STOCKMANN. Therefore I should like to propose that the meeting should not permit the Medical Officer either to read or to comment on his proposed lecture.

DR. STOCKMANN (*impatiently*). Not permit—! What the devil—!

MRS. STOCKMANN (*coughing*). Ahem!—ahem!

DR. STOCKMANN (*collecting himself*). Very well. Go ahead!

PETER STOCKMANN. In my communication to the "People's Messenger," I have put the essential facts before the public in such a way that every fair-minded citizen can easily form his own opinion. From it you will see that the main result of the Medical Officer's proposals—apart from their constituting a vote of censure on the leading men of the town—would be to saddle the ratepayers with an unnecessary expenditure of at least some thousands of pounds.

(*Sounds of disapproval among the audience, and some cat-calls.*)

ASLAKSEN (*ringing his bell*). Silence, please, gentlemen! I beg to support the Mayor's motion. I quite agree with him that there is something behind this agitation started by the Doctor. He talks about the Baths; but it is a revolution he is aiming at—he wants to get the administration of the town put into new hands. No one doubts the honesty of the Doctor's intentions—no one will suggest that there can be any two opinions as to that. I myself am a believer in self-government for the people, provided it does not fall too heavily on the ratepayers. But that would be the case here; and that is why I will see Dr. Stockmann damned—I beg your pardon—before I go with him in the matter. You can pay too dearly for a thing sometimes; that is my opinion.

(*Loud applause on all sides.*)

HOVSTAD. I, too, feel called upon to explain my position. Dr. Stockmann's agitation appeared to be gaining a certain amount of sympathy at first, so I supported it as impartially as I could. But presently we had reason to suspect that we had allowed ourselves to be misled by misrepresentation of the state of affairs—

DR. STOCKMANN. Misrepresentation—!

HOVSTAD. Well, let us say a not entirely trustworthy representation. The Mayor's statement has proved that. I hope no one here has any doubt as to my liberal principles; the attitude of the "People's Messenger" towards important political questions is well known to every one. But the advice of experienced and thoughtful men has convinced me that in purely local matters a newspaper ought to proceed with a certain caution.

ASLAKSEN. I entirely agree with the speaker.

HOVSTAD. And, in the matter before us, it is now an undoubted fact that Dr. Stockmann has public opinion against him. Now, what is an editor's first and most obvious duty, gentlemen? Is it not to work in harmony with his readers? Has he not received a sort of tacit mandate to work persistently and assiduously for the welfare of those whose opinions he represents? Or is it possible I am mistaken in that?

VOICES FROM THE CROWD. No, no! You are quite right!

HOVSTAD. It has cost me a severe struggle to break with a man in whose house I have been lately a frequent guest—a man who till to-day has been able to pride himself on the undivided goodwill of his fellow-citizens—a man whose only, or at all events whose essential failing, is that he is swayed by his heart rather than his head.

A FEW SCATTERED VOICES. That is true! Bravo, Stockmann!

HOVSTAD. But my duty to the community obliged me to break with him. And there is another consideration that impels me to oppose him, and, as far as possible, to arrest him on the perilous course he has adopted; that is, consideration for his family—

DR. STOCKMANN. Please stick to the water-supply and drainage!

HOVSTAD. —consideration, I repeat, for his wife and his children for whom he has made no provision.

MORTEN. Is that us, mother?

MRS. STOCKMANN. Hush!

ASLAKSEN. I will now put the Mayor's proposition to the vote.

DR. STOCKMANN. There is no necessity! To-night I have no intention of dealing with all that filth down at the Baths. No; I have something quite different to say to you.

PETER STOCKMANN (*aside*). What is coming now?

A DRUNKEN MAN (*by the entrance door*). I am a rate-payer! And therefore I have a right to speak too! And my entire—firm—inconceivable opinion is—

A NUMBER OF VOICES. Be quiet, at the back there!

OTHERS. He is drunk! Turn him out! (*They turn him out.*)

DR. STOCKMANN. Am I allowed to speak?

ASLAKSEN (*ringing his bell*). Dr. Stockmann will address the meeting.

DR. STOCKMANN. I should like to have seen anyone, a few days ago, dare to attempt to silence me as has been done to-night! I would have defended my sacred rights as a man, like a lion! But now it is all one to me; I have something of even weightier importance to say to you. (*The crowd presses nearer to him,* MORTEN KIIL *conspicuous among them.*)

DR. STOCKMANN (*continuing*). I have thought and pondered a great deal, these last few days—pondered over such a variety of things that in the end my head seemed too full to hold them—

PETER STOCKMANN (*with a cough*). Ahem!

DR. STOCKMANN. —but I got them clear in my mind at last, and then I saw the whole situation lucidly. And that is why I am standing here to-night. I have a great revelation to make to you, my fellow-citizens! I will impart to you a discovery of a far wider scope than the trifling matter that our water-supply is poisoned and our medicinal Baths are standing on pestiferous soil.

A NUMBER OF VOICES (*shouting*). Don't talk about the Baths! We won't hear you! None of that!

DR. STOCKMANN. I have already told you that what I want to speak about is the great discovery I have made lately—the discovery that all the sources of our *moral* life are poisoned and that the whole fabric of our civic community is founded on the pestiferous soil of falsehood.

VOICES OF DISCONCERTED CITIZENS. What is that he says?

PETER STOCKMANN. Such an insinuation—!

ASLAKSEN (*with his hand on his bell*). I call upon the speaker to moderate his language.

DR. STOCKMANN. I have always loved my native town as a man only can love the home of his youthful days. I was not old when I went away from here; and exile, longing and memories cast as it were an additional halo over both the town and its inhabitants. (*Some clapping and applause.*) And there I stayed, for many years, in a horrible hole far away up north. When I came into contact with some of the people that lived scattered about among the rocks, I often thought it would of been more service to the poor half-starved creatures if a veterinary doctor had been sent up there, instead of a man like me. (*Murmurs among the crowd.*)

BILLING (*laying down his pen*). I'm damned if I have ever heard—!

HOVSTAD. It is an insult to a respectable population!

DR. STOCKMANN. Wait a bit! I do not think anyone will charge me with having forgotten my native town up there. I was like one of the eider-ducks brooding on its nest, and what I hatched was—the plans for these Baths. (*Applause and protests.*) And then when fate at last decreed for me the great happiness of coming home again—I assure you, gentlemen, I thought I had nothing more in the world to wish for. Or rather, there was one thing I wished for—eagerly, untiringly, ardently—and that was to be able to be of service to my native town and the good of the community.

PETER STOCKMANN (*looking at the ceiling*). You chose a strange way of doing it—ahem!

DR. STOCKMANN. And so, with my eyes blinded to the real facts, I revelled in happiness. But yesterday morning—no, to be precise, it was yesterday afternoon—the eyes of my mind were opened wide, and the first thing I realised was the colossal stupidity of the authorities—. (*Uproar, shouts and laughter.* MRS. STOCKMANN *coughs persistently.*)

PETER STOCKMANN. Mr. Chairman!

ASLAKSEN (*ringing his bell*). By virtue of my authority—!

DR. STOCKMANN. It is a pretty thing to catch me up on a word, Mr. Aslaksen. What I mean is only that I got scent of the unbelievable piggishness our leading men had been responsible for down at the Baths. I can't stand leading men at any price!—I have had enough of such people in my time. They are like billy-goats in a young plantation; they do mischief everywhere. They stand in a free man's way, whichever way he turns, and what I should like best would be to see them exterminated like any other vermin—. (*Uproar.*)

PETER STOCKMANN. Mr. Chairman, can we allow such expressions to pass?

ASLAKSEN (*with his hand on his bell*). Doctor—!

DR. STOCKMANN. I cannot understand how it is that I have only now acquired a clear conception of what these gentry are, when I had almost daily before my eyes in this town such an excellent specimen of them—my brother Peter—slow-witted and hide-bound in prejudice—. (*Laughter, uproar and hisses.* MRS. STOCKMANN *sits coughing assiduously.* ASLAKSEN *rings his bell violently.*)

THE DRUNKEN MAN (*who has got in again*). Is it me he is talking about? My name's Petersen, all right—but devil take me if I—

ANGRY VOICES. Turn out that drunken man! Turn him out. (*He is turned out again.*)

PETER STOCKMANN. Who was that person?

1ST CITIZEN. I don't know who he is, Mr. Mayor.

2ND CITIZEN. He doesn't belong here.

3RD CITIZEN. I expect he is a navvy from over at—(*the rest is inaudible*).

ASLAKSEN. He had obviously had too much beer.—Proceed, Doctor; but please strive to be moderate in your language.

DR. STOCKMANN. Very well, gentlemen, I will say no more about our leading men. And if anyone imagines, from what I have just said, that my object is to attack these people this evening, he is wrong—absolutely wide of the mark. For I cherish the comforting conviction that these parasites—all these venerable relics of a dying school of thought—are most admirably paving the way for their own extinction; they need no doctor's help to hasten their end. Nor is it folk of that kind who constitute the most pressing danger to the community. It is not they who are most instrumental in poisoning the sources of our moral life and infecting the ground on which we stand. It is not they who are the most dangerous enemies of truth and freedom amongst us.

SHOUTS FROM ALL SIDES. Who then? Who is it? Name! Name!

DR. STOCKMANN. You may depend upon it I shall name them! That is precisely the great discovery I made yesterday. (*Raises his voice.*) The most dangerous enemy of truth and freedom amongst us is the compact majority—yes, the damned compact Liberal majority—that is it! Now you know! (*Tremendous uproar. Most of the crowd are shouting, stamping and hissing. Some of the older men among them exchange stolen glances and seem to be enjoying themselves.* MRS.

STOCKMANN *gets up, looking anxious.* EJLIF *and* MORTEN *advance threateningly upon some schoolboys who are playing pranks.* ASLAKSEN *rings his bell and begs for silence.* HOVSTAD *and* BILLING *both talk at once, but are inaudible. At last quiet is restored.*)

ASLAKSEN. As chairman, I call upon the speaker to withdraw the ill-considered expressions he has just used.

DR. STOCKMANN. Never, Mr. Aslaksen! It is the majority in our community that denies me my freedom and seeks to prevent my speaking the truth.

HOVSTAD. The majority always has right on its side.

BILLING. And truth too, by God!

DR. STOCKMANN. The majority *never* has right on its side. Never, I say! That is one of these social lies against which an independent, intelligent man must wage war. Who is it that constitute the majority of the population in a country? Is it the clever folk or the stupid? I don't imagine you will dispute the fact that at present the stupid people are in an absolutely overwhelming majority all the world over. But, good Lord! —you can never pretend that it is right that the stupid folk should govern the clever ones! (*Uproar and cries.*) Oh, yes— you can shout me down, I know! but you cannot answer me. The majority has *might* on its side—unfortunately; but *right* it has *not.* I am in the right—I and a few other scattered individuals. The minority is always in the right. (*Renewed uproar.*)

HOVSTAD. Aha!—so Dr. Stockmann has become an aristocrat since the day before yesterday!

DR. STOCKMANN. I have already said that I don't intend to waste a word on the puny, narrow-chested, short-winded crew whom we are leaving astern. Pulsating life no longer concerns itself with them. I am thinking of the few, the scattered few amongst us, who have absorbed new and vigorous truths. Such men stand, as it were, at the outposts, so far ahead that the compact majority has not yet been able to come up with them; and there they are fighting for truths that are too newly-born into the world of consciousness to have any considerable number of people on their side as yet.

HOVSTAD. So the Doctor is a revolutionary now!

DR. STOCKMANN. Good heavens—of course I am, Mr. Hovstad! I propose to raise a revolution against the lie that the majority has the monopoly on the truth. What sort of truths are they that the majority usually supports? They are truths that are of such advanced age that they are beginning to break up. And if a truth is as old as that, it is also in a fair way to become a lie, gentlemen. (*Laughter and mocking cries.*) Yes, believe me or not, as you like; but truths are by no means as long-lived at Methuselah—as some folks imagine. A normally constituted truth lives, let us say, as a rule seventeen or eighteen, or at most twenty years; seldom longer. But truths as aged as that are always worn frightfully thin, and nevertheless it is only then that the majority recognises them and recommends them to the community as wholesome moral nourishment. There is no great nutritive value in that sort of fare, I can assure you; and, as a doctor, I ought to know. These "majority truths" are like last year's cured meat—like rancid, tainted ham; and they are the origin of the moral scurvy that is rampant in our communities.

ASLAKSEN. It appears to me that the speaker is wandering a long way from his subject.

PETER STOCKMANN. I quite agree with the Chairman.

DR. STOCKMANN. Have you gone clean out of your senses, Peter? I am sticking as closely to my subject as I can; for my subject is precisely this, that it is the masses, the majority—this infernal compact majority—that poisons the sources of our moral life and infects the ground we stand on.

HOVSTAD. And all this because the great, broad-minded majority of the people is prudent enough to show deference only to well-ascertained and well-approved truths?

DR. STOCKMANN. Ah, my good Mr. Hovstad, don't talk nonsense about well-ascertained truths! The truths of which the masses now approve are the very truths that the fighters at the outposts held to in the days of our grandfathers. We fighters at the outposts nowadays no longer approve of them; and I do not believe there is any other well-ascertained truth except this, that no community can live a healthy life if it is nourished only on such old marrowless truths.

HOVSTAD. But instead of standing there using vague generalities, it would be interesting if you would tell us what these old marrowless truths are, that we are nourished on.

(*Applause from many quarters.*)

DR. STOCKMANN. Oh, I could give you a whole string of such abominations; but to begin with I will confine myself to one well-approved truth, which at bottom is a foul lie, but upon which nevertheless Mr. Hovstad and the "People's Messenger" and all the "Messenger's" supporters are nourished.

HOVSTAD. And that is—?

DR. STOCKMANN. That is, the doctrine you have inherited from your forefathers and proclaim thoughtlessly far and wide—the doctrine that the public, the crowd, the masses, are the essential part of the population—that they constitute the People—that the common folk, the ignorant and incomplete element in the community, have the same right to pronounce judgment and to approve, to direct and to govern, as the isolated, intellectually superior personalities in it.

BILLING. Well, damn me if ever I—

HOVSTAD (*at the same time, shouting out*). Fellow-citizens, take good note of that!

A NUMBER OF VOICES (*angrily*). Oho!—we are not the People! Only the superior folk are to govern, are they!

A WORKMAN. Turn the fellow out, for talking such rubbish!

ANOTHER. Out with him!

ANOTHER (*calling out*). Blow your horn, Evensen!

(*A horn is blown loudly, amidst hisses and an angry uproar.*)

DR. STOCKMANN (*when the noise has somewhat abated*). Be reasonable! Can't you stand hearing the voice of truth for once? I don't in the least expect you to agree with me all at once; but I must say I did expect Mr. Hovstad to admit I was right, when he had recovered his composure a little. He claims to be a freethinker—

VOICES (*in murmurs of astonishment*). Freethinker, did he say? Is Hovstad a freethinker?

HOVSTAD (*shouting*). Prove it, Dr. Stockmann! When have I said so in print?

DR. STOCKMANN (*reflecting*). No, confound it, you are right!—you have never had the courage to. Well, I won't put you in a hole, Mr. Hovstad. Let us say it is I that am the freethinker, then. I am going to prove to you, scientifically, that the "People's Messenger" leads you by the nose in a shameful manner when it tells you that you—that the common people, the crowd, the masses, are the real essence of the People. That is only a newspaper lie, I tell you! The common people are nothing more than the raw material of which a People is made. (*Groans, laughter and uproar.*) Well, isn't that the case. Isn't there an enormous difference between a well-bred and an ill-bred strain of animals? Take, for instance, a common barn-door hen. What sort of eating do you get from a shrivelled up old scrag of a fowl like that? Not much, do you! And what sort of eggs does it lay? A fairly good crow or a raven can lay pretty nearly as good an egg. But take a well-bred Spanish or Japanese hen, or a good pheasant or a turkey—then you will see the difference. Or take the case of dogs, with whom we humans are on such intimate terms. Think first of an ordinary common cur—I mean one of the horrible, coarse-haired, low-bred curs that do nothing but run about the streets and befoul the walls of the houses. Compare one of these curs with a poodle whose sires for many generations have been bred in a gentleman's house, where they have had the best of food and had the opportunity of hearing soft voices and music. Do you not think that the poodle's brain is developed to quite a different degree from that of the cur? Of course it is. It is puppies of well-bred poodles like that, that showmen train to do incredibly clever tricks—things that a common cur could never learn to do even if it stood on its head. (*Uproar and mocking cries.*)

A CITIZEN (*calls out*). Are you going to make out we are dogs, now?

ANOTHER CITIZEN. We are not animals, Doctor!

DR. STOCKMANN. Yes but, bless my soul, we *are*, my friend! It is true we are the finest animals anyone could wish for; but, even amongst us, exceptionally fine animals are rare. There is a tremendous difference between poodle-men and cur-men. And the amusing part of it is, that Mr. Hovstad quite agrees with me as long as it is a question of four-footed animals—

HOVSTAD. Yes, it is true enough as far as they are concerned.

DR. STOCKMANN. Very well. But as soon as I extend the principle and apply it to two-legged animals, Mr. Hovstad stops short. He no longer dares to think independently, or to pursue his ideas to their logical conclusion; so he turns the whole theory upside down and proclaims in the "People's Messenger" that it is the barn-door hens and street curs that are the finest specimens in the menagerie. But that is always the way, as long as a man retains the traces of common origin and has not worked his way up to intellectual distinction.

HOVSTAD. I lay no claim to any sort of distinction. I am the son of humble countryfolk, and I am proud that the stock I come from is rooted deep among the common people he insults.

VOICES. Bravo, Hovstad! Bravo! Bravo!

DR. STOCKMANN. The kind of common people I mean are not only to be found low down in the social scale; they crawl and swarm all around us—even in the highest social positions. You have only to look at your own fine, distinguished Mayor! My brother Peter is every bit as plebian as anyone that walks in two shoes—(*laughter and hisses*).

PETER STOCKMANN. I protest against personal allusions of this kind.

DR. STOCKMANN (*imperturbably*).—and that, not because he is, like myself, descended from some old rascal of a pirate from Pomerania or thereabouts—because that is who we are descended from—

PETER STOCKMANN. An absurd legend. I deny it!

DR. STOCKMANN. —but because he thinks what his superiors think and holds the same opinions as they. People who do that are, intellectually speaking, common people; and that is why my magnificent brother Peter is in reality so very far from any distinction—and consequently also so far from being liberal-minded.

PETER STOCKMANN. Mr. Chairman—!

HOVSTAD. So it is only the distinguished men that are liberal-minded in this country? We are learning something quite new! (*Laughter.*)

DR. STOCKMANN. Yes, that is part of my new discovery too. And another part of it is that broad-mindedness is almost precisely the same thing as morality. That is why I maintain that it is absolutely inexcusable in the "People's Messenger" to proclaim, day in and day out, the false doctrine that it is the masses, the crowd, the compact majority, that have the monopoly of broad-mindedness and morality—and that vice and corruption and every kind of intellectual depravity are the result of culture, just as all the filth that is draining into our Baths is the result of the tanneries up at Mölledal! (*Uproar and interruptions.* DR. STOCKMANN *is undisturbed, and goes on, carried away by his ardour, with a smile.*) And yet this same "People's Messenger" can go on preaching that the masses ought to be elevated to higher conditions of life! But, bless my soul, if the "Messenger's" teaching is to be depended upon, this very raising up the masses would mean nothing more or less than setting them straightway upon the paths of depravity! Happily the theory that culture demoralises is only an old falsehood that our forefathers believed in and we have inherited. No, it is ignorance, poverty, ugly conditions of life, that do the devil's work! In a house which does not get aired and swept every day—my wife Katherine maintains that the floor ought to be scrubbed as well, but that is a debatable question—in such a house, let me tell you, people will lose within two or three years the power of thinking or acting in a moral manner. Lack of oxygen weakens the conscience. And there must be a plentiful lack of oxygen in very many houses in this town, I should think, judging from the fact that the whole compact majority can be unconscientious enough to wish to build the town's prosperity on a quagmire of falsehood and deceit.

ASLAKSEN. We cannot allow such a grave accusation to be flung at a citizen community.

A CITIZEN. I move that the Chairman direct the speaker to sit down.

VOICES (*angrily*). Hear, hear! Quite right! Make him sit down!

DR. STOCKMANN (*losing his self-control*). Then I will go and shout the truth at every street corner! I will write it in other towns' newspapers! The whole country shall know what is going on here!

HOVSTAD. It almost seems as if Dr. Stockmann's intention were to ruin the town.

DR. STOCKMANN. Yes, my native town is so dear to me that I would rather ruin it than see it flourishing upon a lie.

ASLAKSEN. This is really serious. (*Uproar and cat-calls. MRS. STOCKMANN coughs, but to no purpose; her husband does not listen to her any longer.*)

HOVSTAD (*shouting above the din*). A man must be a public enemy to wish to ruin a whole community!

DR. STOCKMANN (*with growing fervour*). What does the destruction of a community matter, if it lives on lies! It ought to be razed to the ground, I tell you! All who live by lies ought to be exterminated like vermin! You will end by infecting the whole country; you will bring about such a state of things that the whole country will deserve to be ruined. And if things come to that pass, I shall say from the bottom of my heart: Let the whole country perish, let all these people be exterminated!

VOICES FROM THE CROWD. That is talking like an out-and-out enemy of the people!

BILLING. There sounded the voice of the people, by all that's holy!

THE WHOLE CROWD (*shouting*). Yes, yes! He is an enemy of the people! He hates his country! He hates his own people!

ASLAKSEN. Both as a citizen and as an individual, I am profoundly disturbed by what we have had to listen to. Dr. Stockmann has shown himself in a light I should never have dreamed of. I am unhappily obliged to subscribe to the opinion which I have just heard my estimable fellow-citizens utter; and I propose that we should give expression to that opinion in a resolution. I propose a resolution as follows: "This meeting declares that it considers Dr. Thomas Stockmann, Medical Officer of the Baths, to be an enemy of the people." (*A storm of cheers and applause. A number of men surround the DOCTOR and hiss him. MRS. STOCKMANN and PETRA have got up from their seats. MORTEN and EJLIF are fighting the other schoolboys for hissing; some of their elders separate them.*)

DR. STOCKMANN (*to the men who are hissing him*). Oh, you fools! I tell you that—

ASLAKSEN (*ringing his bell*). We cannot hear you now,

Doctor. A formal vote is about to be taken; but, out of regard for personal feelings, it shall be by ballot and not verbal. Have you any clean paper, Mr. Billing?

BILLING. I have both blue and white here.

ASLAKSEN (*going to him*). That will do nicely; we shall get on more quickly that way. But it up into small strips—yes, that's it. (*To the meeting.*) Blue means no; white means yes. I will come round myself and collect votes. (PETER STOCKMANN *leaves the hall.* ASLAKSEN *and one or two others go round the room with the slips of paper in their hats.*)

1ST CITIZEN (*to* HOVSTAD). I say, what has come to the Doctor? What are we to think of it?

HOVSTAD. Oh, you know how headstrong he is.

2ND CITIZEN (*to* BILLING). Billing, you go to their house —have you ever noticed if the fellow drinks?

BILLING. Well I'm hanged if I know what to say. There are always spirits on the table when you go.

3RD CITIZEN. I rather think he goes quite off his head sometimes.

1ST CITIZEN. I wonder if there is any madness in his family?

BILLING. I shouldn't wonder if there were.

4TH CITIZEN. No, it is nothing more than sheer malice; he wants to get even with somebody for something or other.

BILLING. Well certainly he suggested a rise in his salary on one occasion lately, and did not get it.

THE CITIZENS (*together*). Ah!—then it is easy to understand how it is!

THE DRUNKEN MAN (*who has got amongst the audience again*). I want a blue one, I do! And I want a white one too!

VOICES. It's that drunken chap again! Turn him out!

MORTEN KIIL (*going up to* DR. STOCKMANN). Well, Stockmann, do you see what these monkey tricks of yours lead to?

DR. STOCKMANN. I have done my duty.

MORTEN KIIL. What was that you said about the tanneries at Mölledal?

DR. STOCKMANN. You heard well enough. I said they were the source of all the filth.

MORTEN KIIL. My tannery too?

DR. STOCKMANN. Unfortunately your tannery is by far the worst.

MORTEN KIIL. Are you going to put that in the papers?

DR. STOCKMANN. I shall conceal nothing.

MORTEN KIIL. That may cost you dear, Stockmann. (*Goes out.*)

A STOUT MAN (*going up to* CAPTAIN HORSTER, *without taking any notice of the ladies*). Well, Captain, so you lend your house to enemies of the people?

HORSTER. I imagine I can do what I like with my own possessions, Mr. Vik.

THE STOUT MAN. Then you can have no objection to my doing the same with mine.

HORSTER. What do you mean, sir?

THE STOUT MAN. You shall hear from me in the morning. (*Turns his back on him and moves off.*)

PETRA. Was that not your owner, Captain Horster?

HORSTER. Yes, that was Mr. Vik the ship-owner.

ASLAKSEN (*with the voting-papers in his hands, gets up on to the platform and rings his bell*). Gentlemen, allow me to announce the result. By the votes of every one here except one person—

A YOUNG MAN. That is the drunk chap!

ASLAKSEN. By the votes of every one here except a tipsy man, this meeting of citizens declares Dr. Thomas Stockmann to be an enemy of the people. (*Shouts and applause.*) Three cheers for our ancient and honourable citizen community! (*Renewed applause.*) Three cheers for our able and energetic Mayor, who has so loyally suppressed the promptings of family feeling! (*Cheers.*) The meeting is dissolved. (*Gets down.*)

BILLING. Three cheers for the Chairman!

THE WHOLE CROWD. Three cheers for Aslaksen! Hurrah!

DR. STOCKMANN. My hat and coat, Petra! Captain, have you room on your ship for passengers to the New World?

HORSTER. For you and yours we will make room, Doctor.

DR. STOCKMANN (*as PETRA helps him into his coat*). Good. Come, Katherine! Come, boys!

MRS. STOCKMANN (*in an undertone*). Thomas, dear, let us go out by the back way.

DR. STOCKMANN. No back ways for me, Katherine. (*Raising his voice.*) You will hear more of this enemy of the people, before he shakes the dust off his shoes upon you! I am not so forgiving as a certain Person; I do not say: "I forgive you, for ye know not what ye do."

ASLAKSEN (*shouting*). That is a blasphemous comparison, Dr. Stockmann!

BILLING. It is, by God! It's dreadful for an earnest man to listen to.

A COARSE VOICE. Threatens us now, does he!

OTHER VOICES (*excitedly*). Let's go and break his windows! Duck him in the fjord!

ANOTHER VOICE. Blow your horn, Evensen! Pip, pip!

(*Horn-blowing, hisses, and wild cries. DR. STOCKMANN goes out through the hall with his family, HORSTER elbowing a way for them.*)

THE WHOLE CROWD (*howling after them as they go*). Enemy of the People! Enemy of the People!

BILLING (*as he puts his papers together*). Well, I'm damned if I go and drink toddy with the Stockmanns to-night!

(*The crowd press towards the exit. The uproar continues outside; shouts of "Enemy of the People!" are heard from without.*)

ACT V

(SCENE.—DR. STOCKMANN'S *study. Bookcases, and cabinets containing specimens, line the walls. At the back is a door leading to the hall; in the foreground on the left, a door leading to the sitting-room. In the right-hand wall are two windows, of which all the panes are broken. The* DOCTOR'S *desk, littered with books and papers, stands in the middle of the room, which is in disorder. It is morning.* DR. STOCKMANN *in dressing-gown, slippers and a smoking-cap, is bending down and raking with an umbrella under one of the cabinets. After a little while he rakes out a stone.*)

DR. STOCKMANN (*calling through the open sitting-room door*). Katherine, I have found another one.

MRS. STOCKMANN (*from the sitting-room*). Oh, you will find a lot more yet, I expect.

DR. STOCKMANN (*adding the stone to a heap of others on the table*). I shall treasure these stones as relics. Ejlif and Morten shall look at them every day, and when they are grown up they shall inherit them as heirlooms. (*Rakes about under a bookcase.*) Hasn't—what the deuce is her name?— the girl, you know—hasn't she been to fetch the glazier yet?

MRS. STOCKMANN (*coming in*). Yes, but he said he didn't know if he would be able to come to-day.

DR. STOCKMANN. You will see he won't dare to come.

MRS. STOCKMANN. Well, that is just what Randine thought —that he didn't dare to, on account of the neighbours. (*Calls into the sitting-room.*) What is it you want, Randine? Give it to me. (*Goes in, and comes out again directly.*) Here is a letter for you, Thomas.

DR. STOCKMANN. Let me see it. (*Opens and reads it.*) Ah! —of course.

MRS. STOCKMANN. Who is it from?

DR. STOCKMANN. From the landlord. Notice to quit.

MRS. STOCKMANN. Is it possible? Such a nice man—

DR. STOCKMANN (*looking at the letter*). Does not dare do otherwise, he says. Doesn't like doing it, but dare not do otherwise—on account of his fellow-citizens—out of regard for public opinion. Is in a dependent position—dare not offend certain influential men—

MRS. STOCKMANN. There, you see, Thomas!

DR. STOCKMANN. Yes, yes, I see well enough; the whole lot of them in the town are cowards; not a man among them dares do anything for fear of the others. (*Throws the letter on to the table.*) But it doesn't matter to us, Katherine. We are going to sail away to the New World, and—

MRS. STOCKMANN. But, Thomas, are you sure we are well advised to take this step?

DR. STOCKMANN. Are you suggesting that I should stay here, where they have pilloried me as an enemy of the people —branded me—broken my windows! And just look here, Katherine—they have torn a great rent in my black trousers too!

MRS. STOCKMANN. Oh, dear!—and they are the best pair you have got!

DR. STOCKMANN. You should never wear your best trousers when you go out to fight for freedom and truth. It is not that I care so much about the trousers, you know; you can always sew them up again for me. But that the common herd should dare to make this attack on me, as if they were my equals— that is what I cannot, for the life of me, swallow!

MRS. STOCKMANN. There is no doubt they have behaved very ill to you, Thomas; but is that sufficient reason for our leaving our native country for good and all?

DR. STOCKMANN. If we went to another town, do you suppose we should not find the common people just as insolent as they are here? Depend upon it, there is not much to choose between them. Oh, well, let the curs snap—that is not the worst part of it. The worst is that, from one end of this country to the other, every man is the slave of his Party. Although, as far as that goes, I daresay it is not much better in the free West either; the compact majority, and liberal public opinion, and all that infernal old bag of tricks are probably rampant there too. But there things are done on a larger scale, you see. They may kill you, but they won't put you to death by slow torture. They don't squeeze a free man's soul in a vice, as they do here. And, if need be, one can live in solitude. (*Walks up and down.*) If only I knew where there was a virgin forest or a small South Sea island for sale, cheap—

MRS. STOCKMANN. But think of the boys, Thomas!

DR. STOCKMANN (*standing still*). What a strange woman you are, Katherine! Would you prefer to have the boys grow up in a society like this? You saw for yourself last night that half the population are out of their minds; and if the other half have not lost their senses, it is because they are mere brutes, with no sense to lose.

MRS. STOCKMANN. But, Thomas dear, the imprudent things you said had something to do with it, you know.

DR. STOCKMANN. Well, isn't what I said perfectly true? Don't they turn every idea topsy-turvy? Don't they make a regular hotch-potch of right and wrong? Don't they say that the things I know are true, are lies? The craziest part of it all is the fact of these "liberals," men of full age, going about in crowds imagining that they are the broad-minded party? Did you ever hear anything like it, Katherine!

MRS. STOCKMANN. Yes, yes, it's mad enough of them, certainly; but—(PETRA *comes in from the sitting-room*). Back from school already?

PETRA. Yes. I have been given notice of dismissal.

MRS. STOCKMANN. Dismissal?

DR. STOCKMANN. You too?

PETRA. Mrs. Busk gave me my notice; so I thought it was best to go at once.

DR. STOCKMANN. You were perfectly right, too!

MRS. STOCKMANN. Who would have thought Mrs. Busk was a woman like that!

PETRA. Mrs. Busk isn't a bit like that, mother; I saw quite plainly how it hurt her to do it. But she didn't dare do otherwise, she said; and so I got my notice.

DR. STOCKMANN (*laughing and rubbing his hands*). She didn't dare do otherwise, either! It's delicious!

MRS. STOCKMANN. Well, after the dreadful scenes last night—

PETRA. It was not only that. Just listen to this, father!

DR. STOCKMANN. Well?

PETRA. Mrs. Busk showed me no less than three letters she received this morning—

DR. STOCKMANN. Anonymous, I suppose?

PETRA. Yes.

DR. STOCKMANN. Yes, because they didn't dare to risk signing their names, Katherine!

PETRA. And two of them were to the effect that a man, who has been our guest here, was declaring last night at the Club that my views on various subjects are extremely emancipated—

DR. STOCKMANN. You did not deny that, I hope?

PETRA. No, you know I wouldn't. Mrs. Busk's own views are tolerably emancipated, when we are alone together; but now that this report about me is being spread, she dare not keep me on any longer.

MRS. STOCKMANN. And some one who had been a guest of ours! That shows you the return you get for your hospitality, Thomas!

DR. STOCKMANN. We won't live in such a disgusting hole any longer. Pack up as quickly as you can, Katherine; the sooner we can get away, the better.

MRS. STOCKMANN. Be quiet—I think I hear some one in the hall. See who it is, Petra.

PETRA (*opening the door*). Oh, it's you, Captain Horster! Do come in.

HORSTER (*coming in*). Good morning. I thought I would just come in and see how you were.

DR. STOCKMANN (*shaking his hand*). Thanks—that is really kind of you.

MRS. STOCKMANN. And thank you, too, for helping us through the crowd, Captain Horster.

PETRA. How did you manage to get home again?

HORSTER. Oh, somehow or other. I am fairly strong, and there is more sound than fury about these folk.

DR. STOCKMANN. Yes, isn't their swinish cowardice astonishing? Look here, I will show you something! There are all the stones they have thrown through my windows. Just look at them! I'm hanged if there are more than two decently large bits of hardstone in the whole heap; the rest are nothing but gravel—wretched little things. And yet they stood out there bawling and swearing that they would do me some violence; but as for *doing* anything—you don't see much of that in this town.

HORSTER. Just as well for you this time, Doctor!

DR. STOCKMANN. True enough. But it makes one angry all the same; because if some day it should be a question of a national fight in real earnest, you will see that public opinion will be in favour of taking to one's heels, and the compact majority will turn tail like a flock of sheep, Captain Horster. That is what is so mournful to think of; it gives me so much concern, that—. No, devil take it, it is ridiculous to care about it! They have called me an enemy of the people, so an enemy of the people let me be!

MRS. STOCKMANN. You will never be that, Thomas.

DR. STOCKMANN. Don't swear to that, Katherine. To be called an ugly name may have the same effect as a pin-scratch in the lung. And that hateful name—I can't get quit of it. It is sticking here in the pit of my stomach, eating into me like a corrosive acid. And no magnesia will remove it.

PETRA. Bah!—you should only laugh at them, father.

HORSTER. They will change their minds some day, Doctor.

MRS. STOCKMANN. Yes, Thomas, as sure as you are standing here.

DR. STOCKMANN. Perhaps, when it is too late. Much good may it do them! They may wallow in their filth then and rue the day when they drove a patriot into exile. When do you sail, Captain Horster?

HORSTER. Hm!—that was just what I had come to speak about—

DR. STOCKMANN. Why, has anything gone wrong with the ship?

HORSTER. No; but what has happened is that I am not to sail in it.

PETRA. Do you mean that you have been dismissed from your command?

HORSTER (*smiling*). Yes, that's just it.

PETRA. You too.

MRS. STOCKMANN. There, you see, Thomas!

DR. STOCKMANN. And that for the truth's sake! Oh, if I had thought such a thing possible—

HORSTER. You mustn't take it to heart; I shall be sure to find a job with some ship-owner or other, elsewhere.

DR. STOCKMANN. And that is this man Vik—a wealthy man, independent of every one and everything—! Shame on him!

HORSTER. He is quite an excellent fellow otherwise; he told me himself he would willingly have kept me on, if only he had dared—

DR. STOCKMANN. But he didn't dare? No, of course not.

HORSTER. It is not such an easy matter, he said, for a party man—

DR. STOCKMANN. The worthy man spoke the truth. A party is like a sausage machine; it mashes up all sorts of heads together into the same mincemeat—fatheads and blockheads, all in one mash!

MRS. STOCKMANN. Come, come, Thomas dear!

PETRA (*to* HORSTER). If only you had not come home with us, things might not have come to this pass.

HORSTER. I do not regret it.

PETRA (*holding out her hand to him*). Thank you for that!

HORSTER (*to* DR. STOCKMANN). And so what I came to say was that if you are determined to go away, I have thought of another plan—

DR. STOCKMANN. That's splendid!—if only we can get away at once.

MRS. STOCKMANN. Hush!—wasn't that some one knocking?

PETRA. That is uncle, surely.

DR. STOCKMANN. Aha! (*Calls out.*) Come in!

MRS. STOCKMANN. Dear Thomas, promise me definitely—.
(PETER STOCKMANN *comes in from the hall.*)

PETER STOCKMANN. Oh, you are engaged. In that case,
I will—

DR. STOCKMANN. No, no, come in.

PETER STOCKMANN. But I wanted to speak to you alone.

MRS. STOCKMANN. We will go into the sitting-room in the
meanwhile.

HORSTER. And I will look in again later.

DR. STOCKMANN. No, go in there with them, Captain
Horster; I want to hear more about—.

HORSTER. Very well, I will wait, then. (*He follows* MRS.
STOCKMANN *and* PETRA *into the sitting-room.*)

DR. STOCKMANN. I daresay you find it rather draughty
here to-day. Put your hat on.

PETER STOCKMANN. Thank you, if I may. (*Does so.*) I
think I caught cold last night; I stood and shivered—

DR. STOCKMANN. Really? I found it warm enough.

PETER STOCKMANN. I regret that it was not in my power to
prevent those excesses last night.

DR. STOCKMANN. Have you anything particular to say to
me besides that?

PETER STOCKMANN (*taking a big letter from his pocket*). I
have this document for you, from the Baths Committee.

DR. STOCKMANN. My dismissal?

PETER STOCKMANN. Yes, dating from to-day. (*Lays the
letter on the table.*) It gives us pain to do it; but, to speak
frankly, we dared not do otherwise on account of public
opinion.

DR. STOCKMANN (*smiling*). Dared not? I seem to have
heard that word before, to-day.

PETER STOCKMANN. I must beg you to understand your
position clearly. For the future you must not count on any
practice whatever in the town.

DR. STOCKMANN. Devil take the practice! But why are you
so sure of that?

PETER STOCKMANN. The Householders' Association is cir-
culating a list from house to house. All right-minded citizens
are being called upon to give up employing you; and I can
assure you that not a single head of a family will risk refusing
his signature. They simply dare not.

DR. STOCKMANN. No, no; I don't doubt it. But what then?

PETER STOCKMANN. If I might advise you, it would be best
to leave the place for a little while—

DR. STOCKMANN. Yes, the propriety of leaving the place *has*
occurred to me.

PETER STOCKMANN. Good. And then, when you have had

six months to think things over, if, after mature consideration, you can persuade yourself to write a few words of regret, acknowledging your error—

DR. STOCKMANN. I might have my appointment restored to me, do you mean?

PETER STOCKMANN. Perhaps. It is not at all impossible.

DR. STOCKMANN. But what about public opinion, then? Surely you would not dare to do it on account of public feeling.

PETER STOCKMANN. Public opinion is an extremely mutable thing. And, to be quite candid with you, it is a matter of great importance to us to have some admission of that sort from you in writing.

DR. STOCKMANN. Oh, that's what you are after, is it! I will just trouble you to remember what I said to you lately about foxy tricks of that sort!

PETER STOCKMANN. Your position was quite different then. At that time you had reason to suppose you had the whole town at your back—

DR. STOCKMANN. Yes, and now I feel I have the whole town *on* my back—(*flaring up*). I would not do it if I had the devil and his dam on my back—! Never—never, I tell you!

PETER STOCKMANN. A man with a family has no right to behave as you do. You have no right to do it, Thomas.

DR. STOCKMANN. I have no right! There is only one single thing in the world a free man has no right to do. Do you know what that is?

PETER STOCKMANN. No.

DR. STOCKMANN. Of course you don't, but I will tell you. A free man has no right to soil himself with filth; he has no right to behave in a way that would justify his spitting in his own face.

PETER STOCKMANN. This sort of thing sounds extremely plausible, of course; and if there were no other explanation for your obstinacy—. But as it happens that there is.

DR. STOCKMANN. What do you mean?

PETER STOCKMANN. You understand very well what I mean. But, as your brother and as a man of discretion, I advise you not to build too much upon expectations and prospects that may so very easily fail you.

DR. STOCKMANN. What in the world is all this about?

PETER STOCKMANN. Do you really ask me to believe that you are ignorant of the terms of Mr. Kiil's will?

DR. STOCKMANN. I know that the small amount he possesses is to go to an institution for indigent old workpeople. How does that concern me?

PETER STOCKMANN. In the first place, it is by no means a

small amount that is in question. Mr. Kiil is a fairly wealthy man.

DR. STOCKMANN. I had no notion of that!

PETER STOCKMANN. Hm!—hadn't you really? Then I suppose you had no notion, either, that a considerable portion of his wealth will come to your children, you and your wife having a life-rent of the capital. Has he never told you so?

DR. STOCKMANN. Never, on my honour! Quite the reverse; he has consistently done nothing but fume at being so unconscionably heavily taxed. But are you perfectly certain of this, Peter?

PETER STOCKMANN. I have it from an absolutely reliable source.

DR. STOCKMANN. Then, thank God, Katherine is provided for—and the children too! I must tell her this at once—(*calls out*) Katherine, Katherine!

PETER STOCKMANN (*restraining him*). Hush, don't say a word yet!

MRS. STOCKMANN (*opening the door*). What is the matter?

DR. STOCKMANN. Oh, nothing, nothing; you can go back. (*She shuts the door.* DR. STOCKMANN *walks up and down in his excitement.*) Provided for!—Just think of it, we are all provided for! And for life! What a blessed feeling it is to know one is provided for!

PETER STOCKMANN. Yes, but that is just exactly what you are not. Mr. Kiil can alter his will any day he likes.

DR. STOCKMANN. But he won't do that, my dear Peter. The "Badger" is much too delighted at my attack on you and your wise friends.

PETER STOCKMANN (*starts and looks intently at him*). Ah, that throws a light on various things.

DR. STOCKMANN. What things?

PETER STOCKMANN. I see that the whole thing was a combined manœuvre on your part and his. These violent, reckless attacks that you have made against the leading men of the town, under the pretence that it was in the name of truth—

DR. STOCKMANN. What about them?

PETER STOCKMANN. I see that they were nothing else than the stipulated price for that vindictive old man's will.

DR. STOCKMANN (*almost speechless*). Peter—you are the most disgusting plebeian I have ever met in all my life.

PETER STOCKMANN. All is over between us. Your dismissal is irrevocable—we have a weapon against you now. (*Goes out.*)

DR. STOCKMANN. For shame! For shame! (*Calls out.*) Katherine, you must have the floor scrubbed after him! Let

—what's her name—devil take it, the girl who has always got soot on her nose—

MRS. STOCKMANN (*in the sitting-room*). Hush, Thomas, be quiet!

PETRA (*coming to the door*). Father, grandfather is here, asking if he may speak to you alone.

DR. STOCKMANN. Certainly he may. (*Going to the door.*) Come in, Mr. Kiil. (MORTEN KIIL *comes in.* DR. STOCKMANN *shuts the door after him.*) What can I do for you? Won't you sit down?

MORTEN KIIL. I won't sit. (*Looks around.*) You look very comfortable here to-day, Thomas.

DR. STOCKMANN. Yes, don't we!

MORTEN KIIL. Very comfortable—plenty of fresh air. I should think you have got enough to-day of that oxygen you were talking about yesterday. Your conscience must be in splendid order to-day, I should think.

DR. STOCKMANN. It is.

MORTEN KIIL. So I should think. (*Taps his chest.*) Do you know what I have got here?

DR. STOCKMANN. A good conscience, too, I hope.

MORTEN KIIL. Bah!—No, it is something better than that. (*He takes a thick pocket-book from his breast-pocket, opens it, and displays a packet of papers.*)

DR. STOCKMANN (*looking at him in astonishment*). Shares in the Baths?

MORTEN KIIL. They were not difficult to get to-day.

DR. STOCKMANN. And you have been buying—?

MORTEN KIIL. As many as I could pay for.

DR. STOCKMANN. But, my dear Mr. Kiil—consider the state of the Baths' affairs!

MORTEN KIIL. If you behave like a reasonable man, you can soon set the Baths on their feet again.

DR. STOCKMANN. Well, you can see for yourself that I have done all I can, but—. They are all mad in this town!

MORTEN KIIL. You said yesterday that the worst of this pollution came from my tannery. If that is true, then my grandfather and my father before me, and I myself, for many years past, have been poisoning the town like three destroying angels. Do you think I am going to sit quiet under that reproach?

DR. STOCKMANN. Unfortunately I am afraid you will have to.

MORTEN KIIL. No, thank you. I am jealous of my name and reputation. They call me "the Badger," I am told. A badger is a kind of pig, I believe; but I am not going to give them the right to call me that. I mean to live and die a clean man.

Dr. Stockmann. And how are you going to set about it?

Morten Kiil. You shall cleanse me, Thomas.

Dr. Stockmann. I!

Morten Kiil. Do you know what money I have bought these shares with? No, of course you can't know—but I will tell you. It is the money that Katherine and Petra and the boys will have when I am gone. Because I have been able to save a little bit after all, you know.

Dr. Stockmann (*flaring up*). And you have gone and taken Katherine's money for *this*!

Morten Kiil. Yes, the whole of the money is invested in the Baths now. And now I just want to see whether you are quite stark, staring mad, Thomas! If you still make out that these animals and other nasty things of that sort come from my tannery, it will be exactly as if you were to flay broad strips of skin from Katherine's body, and Petra's, and the boys'; and no decent man would do that—unless he were mad.

Dr. Stockmann (*walking up and down*). Yes, but I *am* mad; I *am* mad!

Morten Kiil. You cannot be so absurdly mad as all that, when it is a question of your wife and children.

Dr. Stockmann (*standing still in front of him*). Why couldn't you consult me about it, before you went and bought all that trash?

Morten Kiil. What is done cannot be undone.

Dr. Stockmann (*walks about uneasily*). If only I were not so certain about it—! But I am absolutely convinced that I am right.

Morten Kiil (*weighing the pocket-book in his hand*). If you stick to your mad idea, this won't be worth much, you know. (*Puts the pocket-book in his pocket.*)

Dr. Stockmann. But, hang it all! it might be possible for science to discover some prophylactic, I should think—or some antidote of some kind—

Morten Kiil. To kill these animals, do you mean?

Dr. Stockmann. Yes, or to make them innocuous.

Morten Kiil. Couldn't you try some rat's-bane?

Dr. Stockmann. Don't talk nonsense! They all say it is only imagination, you know. Well, let it go at that! Let them have their own way about it! Haven't the ignorant, narrow-minded curs reviled me as an enemy of the people?—and haven't they been ready to tear the clothes off my back too?

Morten Kiil. And broken all your windows to pieces!

Dr. Stockmann. And then there is my duty to my family. I must talk it over with Katherine; she is great on those things.

MORTEN KIIL. That is right; be guided by a reasonable woman's advice.

DR. STOCKMANN (*advancing towards him*). To think you could do such a preposterous thing! Risking Katherine's money in this way, and putting me in such a horribly painful dilemma! When I look at you, I think I see the devil himself—.

MORTEN KIIL. Then I had better go. But I must have an answer from you before two o'clock—yes or no. If it is no, the shares go to a charity, and that this very day.

DR. STOCKMANN. And what does Katherine get?

MORTEN KIIL. Not a halfpenny. (*The door leading to the hall opens, and* HOVSTAD *and* ASLAKSEN *make their appearance.*) Look at those two!

DR. STOCKMANN (*staring at them*). What the devil!—have *you* actually the face to come into my house?

HOVSTAD. Certainly.

ASLAKSEN. We have something to say to you, you see.

MORTEN KIIL (*in a whisper*). Yes or no—before two o'clock.

ASLAKSEN (*glancing at* HOVSTAD). Aha! (MORTEN KIIL *goes out.*)

DR. STOCKMANN. Well, what do you want with me? Be brief.

HOVSTAD. I can quite understand that you are annoyed with us for our attitude at the meeting yesterday—

DR. STOCKMANN. Attitude, do you call it? Yes, it was a charming attitude! I call it weak, womanish—damnably shameful!

HOVSTAD. Call it what you like, we could not do otherwise.

DR. STOCKMANN. You *dared* not do otherwise—isn't that it?

HOVSTAD. Well, if you like to put it that way.

ASLAKSEN. But why did you not let us have word of it beforehand?—just a hint to Mr. Hovstad or to me?

DR. STOCKMANN. A hint? Of what?

ASLAKSEN. Of what was behind it all.

DR. STOCKMANN. I don't understand you in the least.

ASLAKSEN (*with a confidential nod*). Oh yes, you do, Dr. Stockmann.

HOVSTAD. It is no good making a mystery of it any longer.

DR. STOCKMANN (*looking first at one of them and then at the other*). What the devil do you both mean?

ASLAKSEN. May I ask if your father-in-law is not going round the town buying up all the shares in the Baths?

DR. STOCKMANN. Yes, he has been buying Baths shares to-day; but—

ASLAKSEN. It would have been more prudent to get some one else to do it—some one less nearly related to you.

HOVSTAD. And you should not have let your name appear in the affair. There was no need for anyone to know that the attack on the Baths came from you. You ought to have consulted me, Dr. Stockmann.

DR. STOCKMANN (*looks in front of him; then a light seems to dawn on him and he says in amazement:*) Are such things conceivable? Are such things possible?

ASLAKSEN (*with a smile*). Evidently they are. But it is better to use a little *finesse*, you know.

HOVSTAD. And it is much better to have several persons in a thing of that sort; because the responsibility of each individual is lessened, when there are others with him.

DR. STOCKMANN (*composedly*). Come to the point, gentlemen. What do you want?

ASLAKSEN. Perhaps Mr. Hovstad had better—

HOVSTAD. No, you tell him, Aslaksen.

ASLAKSEN. Well, the fact is that, now we know the bearings of the whole affair, we think we might venture to put the "People's Messenger" at your disposal.

DR. STOCKMANN. Do you dare do that now? What about public opinion? Are you not afraid of a storm breaking upon our heads?

HOVSTAD. We will try to weather it.

ASLAKSEN. And you must be ready to go off quickly on a new tack, Doctor. As soon as your invective has done its work—

DR. STOCKMANN. Do you mean, as soon as my father-in-law and I have got hold of the shares at a low figure?

HOVSTAD. Your reasons for wishing to get the control of the Baths are mainly scientific, I take it.

DR. STOCKMANN. Of course; it was for scientific reasons that I persuaded the old "Badger" to stand in with me in the matter. So we will tinker at the conduit-pipes a little, and dig up a little bit of the shore, and it shan't cost the town a sixpence. That will be all right—eh?

HOVSTAD. I think so—if you have the "People's Messenger" behind you.

ASLAKSEN. The Press is a power in a free community, Doctor.

DR. STOCKMANN. Quite so. And so is public opinion. And you, Mr. Aslaksen—I suppose you will be answerable for the Householders' Association?

ASLAKSEN. Yes, and for the Temperance Society. You may rely on that.

DR. STOCKMANN. But, gentlemen—I really am ashamed to ask the question—but, what return do you—?

HOVSTAD. We should prefer to help you without any return

whatever, believe me. But the "People's Messenger" is in rather a shaky condition; it doesn't go really well; and I should be very unwilling to suspend the paper now, when there is so much work to do here in the political way.

DR. STOCKMANN. Quite so; that would be a great trial to such a friend of the people as you are. (*Flares up.*) But I am an enemy of the people, remember! (*Walks about the room.*) Where have I put my stick? Where the devil is my stick?

HOVSTAD. What's that?

ASLAKSEN. Surely you never mean—?

DR. STOCKMANN (*standing still*). And suppose I don't give you a single penny of all I get out of it? Money is not very easy to get out of us rich folk, please to remember!

HOVSTAD. And you please to remember that this affair of the shares can be represented in two ways!

DR. STOCKMANN. Yes, and you are just the man to do it. If I don't come to the rescue of the "People's Messenger," you will certainly take an evil view of the affair; you will hunt me down, I can well imagine—pursue me—try to throttle me as a dog does a hare.

HOVSTAD. It is a natural law; every animal must fight for its own livelihood.

ASLAKSEN. And get its food where it can, you know.

DR. STOCKMANN (*walking about the room*). Then you go and look for yours in the gutter; because I am going to show you which is the strongest animal of us three! (*Finds an umbrella and brandishes it above his head.*) Ah, now—!

HOVSTAD. You are surely not going to use violence!

ASLAKSEN. Take care what you are doing with that umbrella.

DR. STOCKMANN. Out of the window with you, Mr. Hovstad!

HOVSTAD (*edging to the door*). Are you quite mad!

DR. STOCKMANN. Out of the window, Mr. Aslaksen! Jump, I tell you! You will have to do it, sooner or later.

ASLAKSEN (*running round the writing-table*). Moderation, Doctor—I am a delicate man—I can stand so little—(*calls out*) help, help!

(MRS. STOCKMANN, PETRA *and* HORSTER *come in from the sitting-room.*)

MRS. STOCKMANN. Good gracious, Thomas! What is happening?

DR. STOCKMANN (*brandishing the umbrella*). Jump out, I tell you! Out into the gutter!

HOVSTAD. An assault on an unoffending man! I call you to witness, Captain Horster. (*Hurries out through the hall.*)

ASLAKSEN (*irresolutely*). If only I knew the way about here—. (*Steals out through the sitting-room.*)

MRS. STOCKMANN (*holding her husband back*). Control yourself, Thomas!

DR. STOCKMANN (*throwing down the umbrella*). Upon my soul, they have escaped after all.

MRS. STOCKMANN. What did they want you to do?

DR. STOCKMANN. I will tell you later on; I have something else to think about now. (*Goes to the table and writes something on a calling-card.*) Look there, Katherine; what is written there?

MRS. STOCKMANN. Three big *Noes*; what does that mean.

DR. STOCKMANN. I will tell you that too, later on. (*Holds out the card to* PETRA.) There, Petra; tell sooty-face to run over to the "Badger's" with that, as quick as she can. Hurry up! (PETRA *takes the card and goes out to the hall.*)

DR. STOCKMANN. Well, I think I have had a visit from every one of the devil's messengers to-day! But now I am going to sharpen my pen till they can feel its point; I shall dip it in venom and gall; I shall hurl my ink-pot at their heads!

MRS. STOCKMANN. Yes, but we are going away, you know, Thomas.

(PETRA *comes back.*)

DR. STOCKMANN. Well?

PETRA. She has gone with it.

DR. STOCKMANN. Good.—Going away, did you say? No, I'll be hanged if we are going away! We are going to stay where we are, Katherine!

PETRA. Stay here?

MRS. STOCKMANN. Here, in the town?

DR. STOCKMANN. Yes, here. This is the field of battle—this is where the fight will be. This is where I shall triumph! As soon as I have had my trousers sewn up I shall go out and look for another house. We must have a roof over our heads for the winter.

HORSTER. That you shall have in my house.

DR. STOCKMANN. Can I?

HORSTER. Yes, quite well. I have plenty of room, and I am almost never at home.

MRS. STOCKMANN. How good of you, Captain Horster!

PETRA. Thank you!

DR. STOCKMANN (*grasping his hand*). Thank you, thank you! That is one trouble over! Now I can set to work in earnest at once. There is an endless amount of things to look through here, Katherine! Luckily I shall have all my time at my disposal; because I have been dismissed from the Baths, you know.

MRS. STOCKMANN (*with a sigh*). Oh yes, I expected that.

DR. STOCKMANN. And they want to take my practice away from me too. Let them! I have got the poor people to fall back upon, anyway—those that don't pay anything! and, after all, they need me most, too. But, by Jove, they will have to listen to me; I shall preach to them in season and out of season, as it says somewhere.

MRS. STOCKMANN. But, dear Thomas, I should have thought events had showed you what use it is to preach.

DR. STOCKMANN. You are really ridiculous, Katherine. Do you want me to let myself be beaten off the field by public opinion and the compact majority and all that deviltry? No, thank you! And what I want to do is so simple and clear and straightforward. I only want to drum into the heads of these curs the fact that the liberals are the most insidious enemies of freedom—that party programmes strangle every young and vigorous truth—that considerations of expediency turn morality and justice upside down—and that they will end by making life here unbearable. Don't you think, Captain Horster, that I ought to be able to make people understand that?

HORSTER. Very likely; I don't know much about such things myself.

DR. STOCKMANN. Well, look here—I will explain! It is the party leaders that must be exterminated. A party leader is like a wolf, you see—like a voracious wolf. He requires a certain number of smaller victims to prey upon every year, if he is to live. Just look at Hovstad and Aslaksen! How many smaller victims have they not put an end to—or at any rate maimed and mangled until they are fit for nothing except to be householders or subscribers to the "People's Messenger"! (*Sits down on the edge of the table.*) Come here, Katherine—look how beautifully the sun shines to-day! And this lovely spring air I am drinking in!

MRS. STOCKMANN. Yes, if only we could live on sunshine and spring air, Thomas.

DR. STOCKMANN. Oh, you will have to pinch and save a bit —then we shall get along. That gives me very little concern. What is much worse is, that I know of no one who is liberal-minded and high-minded enough to venture to take up my work after me.

PETRA. Don't think about that, father; you have plenty of time before you.—Hullo, here are the boys already!

(EJLIF *and* MORTEN *come in from the sitting-room.*)

MRS. STOCKMANN. Have you got a holiday?

MORTEN. No; but we were fighting with the other boys between lessons—

EJLIF. That isn't true; it was the other boys were fighting with us.

MORTEN. Well, and then Mr. Rörlund said we had better stay at home for a day or two.

DR. STOCKMANN (*snapping his fingers and getting up from the table*). I have it! I have it, by Jove! You shall never set foot in the school again!

THE BOYS. No more school!

MRS. STOCKMANN. But, Thomas—

DR. STOCKMANN. Never, I say. I will educate you myself; that is to say, you shan't learn a blessed thing—

MORTEN. Hooray!

DR. STOCKMANN. —but I will make liberal-minded and high-minded men of you. You must help me with that, Petra.

PETRA. Yes, father, you may be sure I will.

DR. STOCKMANN. And my school shall be in the room where they insulted me and called me an enemy of the people. But we are too few as we are; I must have at least twelve boys to begin with.

MRS. STOCKMANN. You will certainly never get them in this town.

DR. STOCKMANN. We shall. (*To the boys.*) Don't you know any street urchins—regular ragamuffins—?

MORTEN. Yes, father, I know lots!

DR. STOCKMANN. That's capital! Bring me some specimens of them. I am going to experiment with curs, just for once; there may be some exceptional heads amongst them.

MORTEN. And what are we going to do, when you have made liberal-minded and high-minded men of us?

DR. STOCKMANN. Then you shall drive all the wolves out of the country, my boys!

(EJLIF *looks rather doubtful about it;* MORTEN *jumps about crying* "Hurrah!")

MRS. STOCKMANN. Let us hope it won't be the wolves that will drive you out of the country, Thomas.

DR. STOCKMANN. Are you out of your mind, Katherine? Drive me out! Now—when I am the strongest man in the town!

MRS. STOCKMANN. The strongest—now?

DR. STOCKMANN. Yes, and I will go so far as to say that now I am the strongest man in the whole world.

MORTEN. I say!

DR. STOCKMANN (*lowering his voice*). Hush! You mustn't say anything about it yet; but I have made a great discovery.

MRS. STOCKMANN. Another one?

DR. STOCKMANN. Yes. (*Gathers them round him, and says confidentially:*) It is this, let me tell you—that the strongest man in the world is he who stands most alone.

MRS. STOCKMANN (*smiling and shaking her head*). Oh, Thomas, Thomas!

PETRA (*encouragingly, as she grasps her father's hands*). Father!

The Wild Duck

The multiple strands of *The Wild Duck* make it one of Ibsen's most complex plays. Basically, the play is a study in the egotism of its two principal male characters: Hjalmar Ekdal, the impressionable weakling married to a strong, unimaginative woman; and his neurotic friend, Gregers Werle, who takes it upon himself to place Hjalmar's quite amiable marriage on new foundations of truth. At the play's beginning the Ekdal household exists in a state of beneficent illusion. When this harmonious and harmless illusion is willfully destroyed by the compulsive busybody Werle, the situation of the Ekdals turns bizarre and ultimately tragic.

Another strand in the tapestry concerns the lovely adolescent girl Hedvig who, starved for the affection of her egocentric, pseudo-artistic father, gives her love to a wounded wild duck which is, symbolically, herself. Still another strand is the way the elder Ekdal recovers his dignity by maintaining the illusion that he is still a mighty hunter, after he has endured imprisonment and disgrace because of another man's (Gregers' father's) guilt.

The Wild Duck is a profoundly beautiful play which interweaves scorn for moralistic meddlers in people's lives with a wealth of understanding for weak, fallible humanity. A vast pity for all the characters informs Ibsen's grim humor, and compassion vies with irony for primacy in the entire work. What Ibsen insists on is that the call of the absolute destroys human happiness and tranquillity. Though life is too hard to be endured without illusion, some people's illusions, like Gregers' messianic one, become vicious and destructive because they arise out of weakness rather than strength, out of blindness to their own and other people's natures rather than out of clarity of vision.

Some critics have considered *The Wild Duck* a comedy from start to finish. Hermann J. Weigand aptly points out, "The moralist in him [Ibsen] is for once put under lock and key, securely gagged and bound, while the intelligence of the artist contemplates from above with lingering minuteness the existence of the human animal that lives and thrives on lies, on sham, on make-believe!" But the co-existence of tragic and comic elements in the play justifies considering it the first masterpiece in the modern genre of mixed comedy and tragedy which the playwright and critic Lionel Abel termed "meta-theatre."

Two of Ibsen's greatest successors in the theatre, Maxim Gorky and Eugene O'Neill, returned to *The Wild Duck*'s theme in the twentieth century for two of their finest plays, *The Lower Depths* and *The Iceman Cometh*. Neither of the more modern plays, however, is as subtly textured nor as perfectly wrought as Ibsen's.

Ibsen wrote *The Wild Duck* in 1884 and the play was published the same year. Norwegian critical reaction to the book was largely bafflement, but on the stage the play won brilliant successes and has come to be regarded both in Norway and elsewhere as one of Ibsen's most interesting works.

DRAMATIS PERSONÆ

Werle, a merchant and manufacturer.
Gregers Werle, his son.
Old Ekdal.
Hjalmar Ekdal, his son, a photographer.
Gina Ekdal, Hjalmar's wife.
Hedvig, their daughter, aged fourteen.
Mrs. Sörby, the elder Werle's housekeeper.
Relling, a doctor.
Molvik, an ex-student of theology.
Graaberg, a bookkeeper in Werle's office.
Pettersen, Werle's servant.
Jensen, a hired waiter.
A Flabby Guest.
A Thin-haired Guest.
A Short-sighted Guest.
Six other Guests at Werle's dinner-party.
Several hired Servants.

(The first Act takes place in the elder Werle's house; the other four at Hjalmar Ekdal's.)

ACT I

(SCENE.—*A handsomely and comfortably furnished study
in* WERLE'S *house. Bookcases and upholstered furniture; a
desk, covered with papers and documents, in the middle of the
floor; the lamps are lit and have green shades, producing a soft
light in the room. At the back are folding doors which have
been thrown open and the portières drawn back. Through
these is visible a large and well-appointed room, brightly lit
with lamps and branch candlesticks. A small private door, on
the right-hand side of the study, leads to the office. On the
left is a fireplace, with a cheerful fire, and beyond it folding
doors leading to the dining-room.*

WERLE'S *servant* PETTERSEN, *in livery, and the hired
waiter* JENSEN *in black, are setting the study in order. In the
large room at the back two or three other waiters are moving
about, tidying the room and lighting more candles. From
within the dining-room the noise of the guests' talking and
laughing can be heard; someone raps on a glass with a knife,
silence follows and a toast is proposed; applause follows and
the hum of conversation begins again.*)

PETTERSEN (*lighting a lamp on the mantelpiece and putting a shade over it*). Hark at 'em, Jensen; the old man's up
now, making a long speech to propose Mrs. Sörby's health.

JENSEN (*moving a chair forward*). Do you think what
people say about those two is true, that there's something
between them?

PETTERSEN. Goodness knows.

JENSEN. He's been a gay old dog in his time, hasn't he?

PETTERSEN. Maybe.

JENSEN. They say this dinner-party is in honour of his son.

PETTERSEN. Yes, he came home yesterday.

JENSEN. I never knew old Werle had a son.

PETTERSEN. Oh yes, he has a son, but he sticks up at the

works at Höidal; he hasn't once been in the town all the years I have been in service here.

A WAITER (*in the doorway to the other room*). Pettersen, there is an old chap here who—

PETTERSEN (*muttering*). Devil take him, what is anyone coming now for!

(*Old* EKDAL *appears from the inner room. He is dressed in a weather-worn greatcoat with a high collar, carries a stick and a fur cap in his hands, and a paper parcel under his arm. He wears a dirty reddish-brown wig and a small grey moustache.*)

PETTERSEN (*going towards him*). Good Lord!—what do you want in here?

EKDAL (*in the doorway*). I want so badly to get into the office, Pettersen.

PETTERSEN. The office was closed an hour ago, and—

EKDAL. They told me that at the door, old man. But Graaberg is still there. Be a good chap, Pettersen, and let me slip in that way. (*Points to the private door.*) I've been that way before.

PETTERSEN. All right, you can go in. (*Opens the door.*) But, whatever you do, don't forget to go out the proper way, because we have got guests here.

EKDAL. Yes, yes—I know. Thanks, dear old Pettersen! My good old friend! Thanks! (*Under his breath.*) Old codfish! (*Goes into the office.* PETTERSEN *shuts the door after him.*)

JENSEN. Is that fellow one of the clerks?

PETTERSEN. No, he only does odd jobs of copying when there is any wanted. But I can tell you old Ekdal was a fine fellow in his day.

JENSEN. He looks as if he had seen better times.

PETTERSEN. That he has. He was a lieutenant, though you wouldn't think it.

JENSEN. The deuce he was!

PETTERSEN. True as I'm alive. But he took to the timber trade, or something. They say that he played old Werle a remarkably dirty trick once. The two of them were in partnership up at Höidal at that time. Oh, I know all about old Ekdal, I do. Many's the glass of bitters or bottle of beer we've drunk together at Mother Eriksen's.

JENSEN. I shouldn't have thought he had much to stand treat with.

PETTERSEN. Good Lord, Jensen, it's me that's stood the treat! Besides, I think one ought to be a bit civil to gentry that have come down in the world.

JENSEN. Did he go bankrupt, then?

PETTERSEN. No, it was a deal worse than that. He went to gaol.

JENSEN. To gaol!

PETTERSEN. Or perhaps it was the penitentiary—. (*Listens.*) Sh! they are getting up from table now.

(*The dining-room doors are thrown open by a couple of servants.* MRS. SÖRBY *comes out, talking to two of the guests. The others follow her by degrees, with the elder* WERLE *amongst them.* HJALMAR EKDAL *and* GREGERS WERLE *come last.*)

MRS. SÖRBY (*to the* SERVANT, *in passing*). We will take coffee in the music-room, Pettersen.

PETTERSEN. Very good, ma'am.

(MRS. SÖRBY *and the two gentlemen go into the inner room and out to the right of it.* PETTERSEN *and* JENSEN *follow them.*)

THE FLABBY GUEST (*to the* THIN-HAIRED GUEST). Whew! —it's hard work eating through a dinner like that!

THE THIN-HAIRED GUEST. Oh, with a little good-will, it's amazing what you can get through in three hours.

THE FLABBY GUEST. Yes, but afterwards, my dear sir, afterwards!

ANOTHER GUEST. I believe the coffee and liqueurs are to be served in the music-room.

THE FLABBY GUEST. Good! Then perhaps Mrs. Sörby will play us something.

THE THIN-HAIRED GUEST (*in a low voice*). So long as she doesn't make us dance to a tune we don't like.

THE FLABBY GUEST. Not a bit of it; Bertha would never go back on her old friends. (*They laugh and go into the inner room.*)

WERLE (*in a low and depressed voice*). I don't think anybody noticed it, Gregers.

GREGERS (*looking at him*). What?

WERLE. Didn't you notice it either?

GREGERS. What was there to notice?

WERLE. We were thirteen at table.

GREGERS. Really? Were we?

WERLE (*with a look towards* HJALMAR EKDAL). We are always accustomed to sit down twelve. (*Turns to the other guests.*) Come along in here, gentlemen. (*He leads the way out through the inner room, and is followed by all the others except* HJALMAR *and* GREGERS.)

HJALMAR (*who has heard what they were saying*). You shouldn't have invited me, Gregers.

GREGERS. What? This party is supposed to be in my honour. Why should I not invite my best and only friend?

HJALMAR. But I don't believe your father likes it. I never come to the house.

GREGERS. So I understand. But I wanted to see you and talk to you, because I expect to be going away again directly.— Well, we two old schoolfellows have drifted a long way apart from each other, haven't we? We have not met for sixteen or seventeen years.

HJALMAR. Is it so long?

GREGERS. It is indeed. And how is the world treating you? You look well. You have almost become corpulent!

HJALMAR. Well, I should hardly call it corpulent; but probably I look more of a man than I did then.

GREGERS. That you do; there is certainly more of your outer man.

HJALMAR (*sadly*). But the inner man, Gregers! Believe me, there is a vast difference there. You know what a disastrous blow has fallen on me and mine, since we two last met.

GREGERS (*lowering his voice*). How is your father getting on now?

HJALMAR. My dear fellow, don't let us talk about it. My poor unfortunate father lives at home with me, of course. He has not another creature in the world to cling to. But you can understand what torture it is to me to speak about it. Tell me, rather, how you have been getting on up there at the works.

GREGERS. It has been splendidly lonely. I have had a fine opportunity to ruminate over all sorts of things. Come here, let us make ourselves more comfortable. (*He sits down in an armchair by the fire and pushes* HJALMAR *into another beside him.*)

HJALMAR (*with feeling*). Anyway, Gregers, I am grateful to you for asking me here; it shows that you no longer bear me any grudge.

GREGERS (*astonished*). What should make you think I had any grudge against you?

HJALMAR. Just at first you certainly had.

GREGERS. When?

HJALMAR. After that miserable affair happened. And it was perfectly natural that you should, seeing that your own father was within a hair's breadth of being drawn into this—this terrible business.

GREGERS. Was that any reason for my bearing you a grudge? Who put that idea into your head?

HJALMAR. I know you did, Gregers; your father himself told me so.

GREGERS (*with a start*). My father! Did he, indeed? Ah!— And so that's why you never let me hear from you—not a single word?

HJALMAR. Yes.

GREGERS. Not even when you went and turned yourself into a photographer?

HJALMAR. Your father said I had better not write to you about anything at all.

GREGERS (*looking straight in front of him*). Well, perhaps he was right. But tell me now, Hjalmar, are you tolerably content with your present position?

HJALMAR (*with a slight sigh*). Oh yes, oh yes; I may say so, certainly. It was a bit difficult for me at first, as you can understand. It was such an entirely new life to take up. But then the old life could never have been the same any more. My father's hopeless disaster—the shame and disgrace, Gregers—

GREGERS (*feelingly*). Yes, yes—of course, of course.

HJALMAR. It was impossible to think of going on with my studies; we hadn't a shilling left—worse than that, there were debts, most of them owed to your father, I believe—

GREGERS. Hm!—

HJALMAR. So that it seemed to me the best thing was to drop the old life and all its associations, once and for all. It was chiefly due to your father's advice that I did so; and as he was so kind in helping me—

GREGERS. My father was?

HJALMAR. Surely you know he was? Where do you suppose I could find the money to learn photography and set myself up in a studio? That costs a bit, I can tell you.

GREGERS. And did my father pay for all this?

HJALMAR. Yes, my dear fellow, didn't you know that? I understood that he had written to you about it.

GREGERS. He never said a word about its being his doing. He must have forgotten. We have never written anything but business letters to each other. So it was really my father—!

HJALMAR. Yes, that it was, indeed. He has never wanted anyone to know anything about it, but it was he. And it was thanks to him, too, that I was able to marry. But perhaps that is news to you too?

GREGERS. I knew nothing whatever about it. (*Takes him by the arm.*) I can't tell you, my dear Hjalmar, how glad all this makes me—and how it pains me at the same time. I may have been unjust to my father after all, in some things. It shows at any rate that he has a heart. There is evidence of a conscience about it—

HJALMAR. Of a conscience—?

GREGERS. Well, call it what you like. I can't tell you how glad I am to hear this about my father.—And so you are a married man, Hjalmar. It will be a long time before I shall be able to say that of myself. Well, I hope you are happy in your marriage.

HJALMAR. Very happy. I have as pretty and as capable a wife as a man could wish, and she is by no means without education either.

GREGERS (*slightly surprised*). I should hope not!

HJALMAR. Well, life is an education, you see. Her daily companionship with me—and we see a few clever people now and then. I can assure you, you would hardly know it was the same Gina.

GREGERS. Gina?

HJALMAR. Yes, don't you remember her name was Gina?

GREGERS. What Gina? I don't know—

HJALMAR. Have you forgotten that she had a place in this house once?

GREGERS (*glancing at him*). Is it Gina Hansen?

HJALMAR. Of course it is Gina Hansen.

GREGERS. Who kept house for us that last year when my mother was ill?

HJALMAR. Certainly. But I thought, my dear fellow, that your father had written to you about my marriage.

GREGERS (*rising*). Yes, he did; but not that it was—. (*Walks up and down.*) Yes, wait a bit. I expect he did, now that I think of it. My father always writes me such brief letters. (*Sits down on the arm of* HJALMAR'S *chair.*) Tell me, Hjalmar—it's curious—how did you come to make Gina's— your wife's acquaintance?

HJALMAR. It was quite simple. Gina was not here any longer. Everything was upside down in the house then with your mother's illness; Gina could not put up with it, so she took herself off. That was the year before your mother died —or I daresay it was the same year.

GREGERS. It was the same year. I was up at the works then. And after that?

HJALMAR. Well, Gina went home to her mother, a very active and hard-working woman, who kept a small restaurant. And she had a room to let, a very nice, comfortable room—

GREGERS. And you were fortunate enough to get it, I suppose?

HJALMAR. Yes, and in fact it was your father who put the idea into my head. And that, you see, was the way I came to know Gina.

GREGERS. And it ended in your falling in love?

HJALMAR. Yes. Young people don't take long to fall in love, you know.

GREGERS (*rises again and walks about*). Tell me, was it when you were engaged that my father induced you—I mean, was it then that you began to think of taking up photography?

HJALMAR. Certainly. I was so anxious to get some settled occupation, and both your father and I thought photography offered the best chances. And Gina thought so too. Yes, and there was another reason, I must tell you; it turned out that, fortunately, Gina had taken some lessons in retouching photography.

GREGERS. It was extraordinarily lucky altogether.

HJALMAR (*in a pleased voice as he rises*). Yes, wasn't it! Don't you think everything happened wonderfully luckily for me?

GREGERS. I do, indeed. It looks as if my father had been a sort of providence to you.

HJALMAR (*heartily*). He did not forsake his old friend's son in the day of trouble. He has a heart, you see.

MRS. SÖRBY (*coming in on the elder* WERLE'S *arm*). Don't be obstinate, dear Mr. Werle. You must not stay in there any longer staring at all those lights. It is bad for your eyes.

WERLE (*slips his arm out of hers and passes his hand over his eyes*). Well, I really believe you are right.

MRS. SÖRBY (*to the guests, who are in the other room*). If anyone would like a glass of punch, he must come in here and get it.

THE FAT GUEST (*coming up to her*). Is it really true that you are determined to deprive us of the sacred right of smoking?

MRS. SÖRBY. Yes, it's forbidden in here, in Mr. Werle's sanctum.

THE THIN-HAIRED GUEST. When did you enact this cruel law about tobacco, Mrs. Sörby?

MRS. SÖRBY. After our last dinner, when certain persons allowed themselves to overstep the mark altogether.

THE THIN-HAIRED GUEST. Mayn't we overstep it just a wee bit?—not the least bit?

MRS. SÖRBY. Not the least bit in any direction, Mr. Balle.

(*Most of the* GUESTS *have come in by this time. The* SERVANTS *hand round the punch.*)

WERLE (*to* HJALMAR, *who is standing apart by a table*). What are you looking at there, Ekdal?

HJALMAR. I was just looking at an album, Mr. Werle.

THE THIN-HAIRED GUEST (*who is wandering about the room*). Ah, photographs! They must interest you, of course.

THE FAT GUEST (*who has settled himself in an armchair*). Haven't you brought any of your own with you?

HJALMAR. No, I haven't.

THE FAT GUEST. You should have; it's an excellent thing for the digestion to sit and look at pictures.

THE THIN-HAIRED GUEST. And it contributes to the general entertainment, you know.

THE SHORT-SIGHTED GUEST. And all contributions are thankfully received.

MRS. SÖRBY. They think that when one is asked out to dinner one ought to do something to earn it, Mr. Ekdal.

THE FAT GUEST. Which is a real pleasure when one gets a good dinner for it.

THE THIN-HAIRED GUEST. And when it is a case of a struggle for existence, then—

MRS. SÖRBY. You are right there! (*They go on laughing and joking.*)

GREGERS (*aside, to* HJALMAR). You must join in, Hjalmar.

HJALMAR (*wincing*). How on earth am I to join in?

THE FAT GUEST. Don't you think, Mr. Werle, that Tokay may be considered a comparatively wholesome drink?

WERLE (*standing by the fire*). I can vouch for the Tokay you had to-day, anyway; it is of one of the very finest years. But I have no doubt you noticed that.

THE FAT GUEST. Yes, it had a wonderfully delicate flavour.

HJALMAR (*hesitatingly*). Is there a difference between the years then?

THE FAT GUEST (*laughing*). Well, that's good!

WERLE (*with a smile*). It's evidently waste of money to give him a fine wine.

THE THIN-HAIRED GUEST. Tokay grapes are like photographs, Mr. Ekdal; they need sunshine. Isn't that so?

HJALMAR. Yes, the light is a great point, certainly.

MRS. SÖRBY. Then it is just the same with all you gentlemen in official positions; you all like to bask in the sunshine of Court favour.

THE THIN-HAIRED GUEST. Come, come!—that's a very ancient joke!

THE SHORT-SIGHTED GUEST. Mrs. Sörby is coming out!

THE FAT GUEST. And at our expense. (*Wags his finger.*) Madam Bertha! Madam Bertha!

MRS. SÖRBY. Another thing that is true of you, too, is that different years' vintages may differ vastly. The old vintages are the best.

THE SHORT-SIGHTED GUEST. Do you reckon me among the old ones?

MRS. SÖRBY. Far from it.

THE THIN-HAIRED GUEST. Listen to that! But what about me, dear Mrs. Sörby?

THE FAT GUEST. Yes, and me! What vintage do you consider us?

MRS. SÖRBY. Very sweet years, both of you! (*She puts a*

glass of punch to her lips; the GUESTS *continue laughing and joking with her.*)

WERLE. Mrs. Sörby can always get neatly out of a difficult position, if she likes. Don't put your glasses down; Pettersen, fill them up!—Gregers, come and have a glass with me. (GREGERS *does not move.*) Won't you join us, Ekdal? I had no opportunity of drinking with you at dinner.

(GRAABERG, *the bookkeeper, peeps into the room through the private door.*)

GRAABERG. I beg your pardon, sir, but I can't get out.

WERLE. Have you got locked in again?

GRAABERG. Yes, and Flagstad has gone off with the keys.

WERLE. All right, come out this way.

GRAABERG. But I have someone with me—

WERLE. Come along, come along, both of you. Don't mind us.

(GRAABERG *and old* EKDAL *come out of the office.* WERLE *gives an involuntary exclamation of disgust; the laughing and joking stops suddenly.* HJALMAR *starts at the sight of his father, puts down his glass and turns towards the fireplace.*)

EKDAL (*keeping his eyes on the ground and bowing awkwardly from side to side as he goes out, mumbling*). Excuse me! Come the wrong way—door's locked—door's locked—Excuse me!

[*Exit at the back, with* GRAABERG.

WERLE (*between his teeth*). Confound that Graaberg!

GREGERS (*with mouth hanging open and eyes staring, to* HJALMAR). Surely that was never—!

THE FAT GUEST. What is it? Who was that?

GREGERS. Nothing; only the bookkeeper and another man.

THE THIN-HAIRED GUEST (*to* HJALMAR). Was he a friend of yours?

HJALMAR. I don't know—I didn't notice—

THE FAT GUEST (*rising*). What the deuce is all this about? (*He joins some of the others, who are talking below their breath.*)

MRS. SÖRBY (*whispers to the* SERVANT). Give him something to take away with him—something good.

PETTERSEN (*nodding*). I will. [*Exit.*

GREGERS (*in a low and shaking voice, to* HJALMAR). So it was really he?

HJALMAR. Yes.

GREGERS. And yet you stood there and said you didn't know him!

HJALMAR (*in a loud whisper*). How could I—

GREGERS. Acknowledge your own father?

HJALMAR (*bitterly*). If you were in my place, you would—
(*The* GUESTS, *who have been talking in low tones, now raise their voices with an obvious effort.*)

THE THIN-HAIRED GUEST (*coming up genially to* HJALMAR *and* GREGERS). Well, I suppose you two are talking over old times at College, eh? Won't you smoke, Mr. Ekdal? Shall I give you a light? Ah, I forgot, we mustn't smoke.

HJALMAR. Thank you, I don't care to.

THE FAT GUEST. Can't you recite some charming little poem to us, Mr. Ekdal? You used to have a great talent for that.

HJALMAR. I am sorry I cannot remember anything.

THE FAT GUEST. What a pity. Well, what shall we do, Balle? (*The two* GUESTS *go together into the other room.*)

HJALMAR (*sadly*). Gregers, I must go away. When Fate has dealt a man such a blow as it has done to me, you know—. Say good-night to your father from me.

GREGERS. Yes, yes. Are you going straight home?

HJALMAR. Yes. Why?

GREGERS. Well, perhaps I may come along and see you presently.

HJALMAR. No, you mustn't do that. Don't come to my house. Mine is a sad home, Gregers—especially after a splendid entertainment like this. We can always find some place in the town to meet.

MRS. SÖRBY (*coming up to them, and speaking low*). Are you going, Mr. Ekdal?

HJALMAR. Yes.

MRS. SÖRBY. Remember me to Gina.

HJALMAR. Thank you.

MRS. SÖRBY. And tell her I shall be up to see her some day soon.

HJALMAR. Yes, thanks. (*To* GREGERS.) Stay here. I will slip out unobserved. (*He goes out through the other room.*)

MRS. SÖRBY (*to the* SERVANT *who has come back*). Well, did you give the old man something to take with him?

PETTERSEN. Yes, ma'am; I gave him a bottle of brandy.

MRS. SÖRBY. Oh, you might have found something better than that to give him.

PETTERSEN. No, indeed, ma'am. Brandy is what he likes best, I know.

THE FAT GUEST (*standing in the doorway with a piece of music in his hand*). Shall we play a duet, Mrs. Sörby?

MRS. SÖRBY. Certainly.

THE GUESTS. Bravo! Bravo! (*They and all the* GUESTS *go out of the room.* GREGERS *remains standing by the fire. His father is looking for something on the writing-table and seems anxious for* GREGERS *to go; as* GREGERS *does not move,* WERLE *goes towards the door.*)

GREGERS. Father, will you wait a moment?

WERLE (*stopping*). What is it?

GREGERS. I want a word with you.

WERLE. Can't it wait till we are alone?

GREGERS. No, it can't. Perhaps we shall never find ourselves alone.

WERLE (*coming nearer him*). What do you mean by that? (*During the following conversation the sound of the piano is heard faintly from the other room.*)

GREGERS. How could you let that family come so miserably to grief?

WERLE. You mean the Ekdals, I presume.

GREGERS. Yes, I mean the Ekdals. Lieutenant Ekdal and you were once so intimate.

WERLE. A great deal too intimate, unfortunately, and I have been paying for it these many years. It is him I have to thank for the fact that my good name and reputation have suffered to some extent too.

GREGERS (*in a low voice*). Was he really the only one guilty?

WERLE. Who else, if you please!

GREGERS. He and you were in partnership over that big purchase of timber—

WERLE. But you know that it was Ekdal who made the map of the ground—that misleading map. He was responsible for the illegal felling of timber on Government property. In fact, he was responsible for the whole business. I had no knowledge of what Lieutenant Ekdal was undertaking.

GREGERS. Lieutenant Ekdal seems to have had no knowledge himself of what he was undertaking.

WERLE. Maybe. But the fact remains that he was found guilty and I was acquitted.

GREGERS. Yes, I am quite aware there were no proofs.

WERLE. An acquittal is an acquittal. Why are you raking up these horrible old stories, which have whitened my hair before its time? Is this what your mind has been brooding upon up there all these years? I can assure you, Gregers, that here in town the whole story has been forgotten long ago, as far as I am concerned.

GREGERS. But what about that wretched family?

WERLE. What could you have expected me to do for them? When Ekdal regained his freedom he was a broken man, absolutely past help. There are some men who go under entirely if Fate hits them ever so little, and never come to the surface again. Believe me, Gregers, I could have done no more than I have, without exposing myself to all sorts of suspicion and gossip—

GREGERS. Suspicion—? Quite so.

WERLE. I got Ekdal copying to do at the office, and I pay him a great deal more for his work than it is worth.

GREGERS (*without looking at him*). I have no doubt of that.

WERLE. You smile? Perhaps you don't believe it is true? I am quite aware it doesn't appear in my accounts; I never enter such payments as that.

GREGERS (*with a cold smile*). I quite agree that there are certain expenses it is better not to enter in one's accounts.

WERLE (*with a start*). What do you mean?

GREGERS (*in a more confident tone*). Have you entered in your accounts what it cost you to have Hjalmar Ekdal taught photography?

WERLE. I? Why should I have entered that?

GREGERS. I know now that it was you who paid it. And I know, too, that it was you who made it possible for him to settle down as he has done.

WERLE. And, after all that, you say I have done nothing for the Ekdals! I can assure you that family has caused me enough expense, in all conscience.

GREGERS. Have you entered any one item of it in your accounts?

WERLE. Why do you ask that?

GREGERS. I have my reasons. Tell me this—didn't your great solicitude for your old friend's son begin just at the time he was contemplating getting married?

WERLE. Good Lord!—after all these years, how can I—?

GREGERS. You wrote to me at the time—a business letter, naturally—and in a postscript, in just one or two words, you told me Hjalmar Ekdal had married a Miss Hansen.

WERLE. Well, that was true; that was her name.

GREGERS. But you never mentioned the fact that this Miss Hansen was Gina Hansen, our former housekeeper.

WERLE (*laughs ironically, but in a constrained manner*). No, I didn't suppose you were so specially interested in our former housekeeper.

GREGERS. Nor was I. But (*lowering his voice*) there was someone else in this house who *was* specially interested in her.

WERLE. What do you mean? (*In an angry voice.*) You don't mean that you refer to me?

GREGERS (*in a low voice, but firmly*). Yes, I refer to you.

WERLE. And you dare—! You have the audacity to—! And as for this ungrateful photographer fellow—how dare he presume to come here and make such accusations!

GREGERS. Hjalmar has never said a single word of the kind.

I don't believe that he has even a suspicion of anything of the sort.

WERLE. Then where have you got it from? Who could have told you such a thing?

GREGERS. My poor unhappy mother told me, the last time I saw her.

WERLE. Your mother! I might have thought as much! She and you were always together in everything. It was she from the very first who drew you apart from me.

GREGERS. No, it was the suffering and humiliation she had to undergo, till at last it broke her down and drove her to such a miserable end.

WERLE. She had not the least suffering or humiliation to undergo—not more than many others, anyway! But there is no dealing with sickly and hysterical folk. I have good reason to know that. And so you have been brooding over such a suspicion as this!—you have been raking up all sorts of ancient rumours and slanders about your own father!—Let me tell you, Gregers, I really think at your age you might find something more useful to do.

GREGERS. Yes, I think it is quite time I did.

WERLE. And perhaps, if you did, you would be easier in your mind than you appear to be at present. What possible point is there in your drudging away at the works, year in and year out, like the merest clerk, and refusing to accept a shilling more than the ordinary wages? It is simply folly on your part.

GREGERS. Ah, if only I were as certain of that as you are!

WERLE. I think I understand. You want to be independent, not to be under the slightest obligation to me. Well, now there happens to be an opportunity for you to become independent, to be your own master entirely.

GREGERS. Indeed? and what may that be?

WERLE. When I wrote to you that I had urgent reasons for asking you to come to town at once—well—

GREGERS. Well, what is it exactly that you want? I have been waiting all day for you to tell me.

WERLE. I propose to offer you a partnership in the firm.

GREGERS. I!—a partner in your firm?

WERLE. Yes. It need not necessitate our always being together. You might manage the business here in town, and I would go up to the works.

GREGERS. You?

WERLE. Yes. You see, I am no longer as fit for my work as I used to be. I am obliged to be careful of my eyes, Gregers; they have begun to get a bit weak.

GREGERS. They were always that.

WERLE. Not as weak as they are now. And, besides that, circumstances might make it desirable for me to live up there, at any rate for a while.

GREGERS. Such an idea has never entered into my mind.

WERLE. Listen, Gregers; we seem to stand apart from each other in very many ways, but after all we are father and son. It seems to me we ought to be able to come to some kind of an understanding with one another.

GREGERS. To outward appearance, I suppose you mean?

WERLE. Well, at any rate that would be something. Think over it, Gregers. Doesn't it appear to you as a possibility? Eh?

GREGERS (*looking at him coldly*). There is something at the bottom of all this.

WERLE. What do you mean?

GREGERS. You probably intend to make use of me in some way.

WERLE. Two people as closely connected as we are can always be of use to one another.

GREGERS. Possibly.

WERLE. I want you to stay at home with me for a bit. I am a lonely man, Gregers; I have always felt lonely, all my life, and I feel it more than ever now that I am no longer young. I need some companionship.

GREGERS. You have Mrs. Sörby.

WERLE. Yes, that is true; and she has, to tell you the truth, become almost indispensable to me. She is clever and easygoing, and livens up the house—and I need that sort of thing badly.

GREGERS. Quite so; you seem to me to have just what you want.

WERLE. Yes, but I am afraid it can't last. Under such circumstances a woman is easily put into a false position in the eyes of the world. Indeed, one might almost say that the man is not much safer.

GREGERS. Oh, when a man gives such good dinners as you do, he can take considerable liberties with public opinion.

WERLE. Yes, but what about her, Gregers? I am so afraid she won't put up with it any longer. And even if she did—if out of attachment to me she were to disregard gossip and scandal, and so on—? You have a very strong sense of justice, Gregers; doesn't it seem to you that—

GREGERS (*interrupting him*). Tell me this, without beating about the bush; are you thinking of marrying her?

WERLE. And if I were, what then?

GREGERS. Exactly. What then?

WERLE. Would it be a thing you would find it impossible to countenance?

GREGERS. Not in the least. Not by any means.

WERLE. Well, I was not sure whether perhaps, out of respect for your mother's memory, you—

GREGERS. I am not sentimental.

WERLE. Well, whether you are or not, you have at any rate lifted a heavy weight off my mind. It is an immense pleasure to me that I can count on your sympathy in this matter.

GREGERS (*looking intently at him*). Now I understand how it is you want to make use of me.

WERLE. Make use of you? What an expression!

GREGERS. Oh, don't let us be so nice in our choice of words —at any rate when we are alone. (*With a short laugh.*) I see! This was the reason why it was absolutely necessary for me to come to town—to help you to make a pretence of family life here for Mrs. Sörby's edification!—a touching tableau, father and son! That would be something new.

WERLE. How dare you take that tone with me!

GREGERS. When was there any family life here? Never, as long as I can remember. But now, if you please, a little of that sort of thing is desirable. It would undeniably have a splendid effect if it could get about that the son has hastened home, on the wings of filial piety, to attend his old father's wedding. What becomes then of all the rumours of what his poor dead mother had suffered and endured? They are absolutely silenced; her son's action would do that.

WERLE. Gregers—I don't believe there is anyone living towards whom you feel as bitterly as you do to me.

GREGERS (*in a low voice*). I have seen you at too close quarters.

WERLE. You have seen me through your mother's eyes. (*Lowering his voice a little.*) But you ought to remember that her eyes were—were—clouded now and then.

GREGERS (*trembling*). I understand what you mean. But who is to blame for my mother's unfortunate weakness? You, and all your—! The last of them was this woman that was foisted upon Hjalmar Ekdal when you were tired of her. Faugh!

WERLE (*shrugging his shoulders*). Just the way your mother used to talk.

GREGERS (*without paying any attention to him*). And there he is now, like a big unsuspecting child, in the middle of all this deceit; living under the same roof with a woman like that, without the slightest idea that what he calls his home is built on a lie. (*Taking a step nearer his father.*) When I look back on all you have done, it is like looking at a battle-field strewn on every side with ruined lives.

WERLE. I am beginning to think the gulf between us two is too wide to be bridged.

GREGERS (*controls himself and bows*). I agree with you; and therefore I will take my hat and go.

WERLE. Go? Out of the house?

GREGERS. Yes, I see at last some object to live for.

WERLE. What may that be?

GREGERS. You would only laugh, if I told you.

WERLE. A lonely man doesn't laugh so readily, Gregers.

GREGERS (*pointing to the back of the room*). Look, father —Mrs. Sörby is playing blind man's buff with your guests. Good-night, and good-bye. (*He goes out. The* GUESTS *are heard merrily laughing as they come into the other room.*)

WERLE (*muttering scornfully after* GREGERS). Ha! Ha! Poor chap—and he says he is not sentimental!

ACT II

(Scene.—HJALMAR EKDAL'S *studio, a fairly large attic room. On the right, a sloping roof with large glass windows, half covered by a blue curtain. The door leading into the room is in the right-hand corner, and further forward on the same side is a door leading to a sitting-room. In the left-hand wall are two doors, with a stove between them. In the back wall are wide double doors, arranged so as to slide back on either side. The studio is simply but comfortably furnished. Between the doors on the right, near the wall, stands a sofa with a table and some chairs; on the table a shaded lamp is lit. An old armchair is drawn up by the stove. Photographic apparatus and instruments are scattered here and there about the room. Against the back wall, to the left of the double doors, is a bookcase, containing some books, boxes, bottles of chemicals, and a variety of instruments and tools. On the table are lying photographs, paint-brushes, paper, and so forth.* GINA EKDAL *is sitting on a chair by the table, sewing.* HEDVIG *is on the sofa reading a book, with her thumbs in her ears and her hands shading her eyes.*)

GINA (*who has glanced several times at* HEDVIG *with restrained anxiety, calls to her*). Hedvig! (HEDVIG *does not hear her.*)

GINA (*louder*). Hedvig!

HEDVIG (*puts her hands down and looks up*). Yes, mother?

GINA. Hedvig, you must be good and not sit there reading any longer.

HEDVIG. Mayn't I read a little more, mother? Just a little?

GINA. No, no, you must put your book away. Your father doesn't like it; he don't ever read in the evening himself.

HEDVIG (*shutting her book*). No, father doesn't care so much about reading.

GINA (*puts down her sewing anl takes up a pencil and a*
235

little note-book). Do you remember how much we paid for the butter to-day?

HEDVIG. One and ninepence.

GINA. That's right. (*Writes it down.*) It's frightful, the amount of butter we get through in this house. And then there was the smoked sausage and the cheese—let me see—(*writes*) —and then there was the ham—(*adds up*)—there, that lot alone comes to—

HEDVIG. And then there's the beer.

GINA. Yes, of course. (*Puts it down.*) It soon mounts up, but it can't be helped.

HEDVIG. But then you and I didn't need anything hot for dinner, as father was out.

GINA. No, that was lucky. And, what's more, I have taken eight and sixpence for photographs.

HEDVIG. As much as that!

GINA. Yes, eight and sixpence exactly.

(*Silence.* GINA *resumes her sewing.* HEDVIG *takes a piece of paper and a pencil and begins drawing, shading her eyes with her left hand.*)

HEDVIG. Isn't it funny to think of father at a big dinner-party at Mr. Werle's?

GINA. He is not, strictly speaking, Mr. Werle's guest, it was the son who invited him. (*After a pause.*) We have nothing to do with Mr. Werle.

HEDVIG. I wish most awfully he would come home. He promised to ask Mrs. Sörby for something nice to bring back to me.

GINA. Ah, there's plenty of good things going in that house, I can tell you.

HEDVIG (*resuming her drawing*). And I believe I am a bit hungry too.

(*Old* EKDAL *comes in, a roll of papers under his arm and a parcel sticking out of his pocket.*)

GINA. How late you are to-night, grandfather—

EKDAL. They had locked up the office. I had to wait for Graaberg; and then I was obliged to go through—hm!

HEDVIG. Did they give you some more copying, grand-father?

EKDAL. All this lot. Just look!

GINA. That's splendid.

HEDVIG. And you have got a parcel in your pocket, too.

EKDAL. Have I? Oh, that's nothing, that's nothing. (*Puts down his stick in a corner of the room.*) This will keep me busy for a long time, Gina. (*Pulls one of the sliding doors at the back a little open.*) Hush! (*He looks in through the door for a moment and then shuts it again carefully.*) Ha, ha!

They are all asleep together in there. And she has gone into
the basket of her own accord. Ha, ha!

HEDVIG. Are you quite sure she isn't cold in the basket,
grandfather?

EKDAL. What an idea! Cold? In all that straw? (*Goes to
the farther door on the left.*) Are there matches here?

GINA. There's some on the chest of drawers. (EKDAL *goes
into his room.*)

HEDVIG. Isn't it nice that grandfather has got all this fresh
copying to do!

GINA. Yes, poor old grandfather; he will be able to make
a little pocket-money.

HEDVIG. And won't be able to sit all the morning at that
horrid restaurant of Mrs. Eriksen's over there.

GINA. Yes, that's another thing.

HEDVIG (*after a short pause*). Do you think they are still at
dinner?

GINA. Goodness knows. Very likely they are.

HEDVIG. Just think what a lovely dinner father must be
having. I know he will be in such a good temper when he
comes home. Don't you think so, mother?

GINA. Yes, but just think how nice it would be if we could
tell him we had let the room.

HEDVIG. We don't need that to-night.

GINA. Oh, every little helps. And the room is standing
empty.

HEDVIG. I mean that we don't need to be able to tell him
that to-night. He will be in good spirits anyway. We shall be
all the better of the news about the room for another time.

GINA (*looking at her*). Do you like having some good news
to tell your father when he comes home of an evening?

HEDVIG. Yes, because things seem to go pleasanter then.

GINA (*thoughtfully*). There's something in that, certainly.
(*Old* EKDAL *comes in again, and is going out by the nearer
door on the left.*)

GINA (*turning in her chair*). Do you want something in the
kitchen, grandfather?

EKDAL. Yes, I do. Don't get up.   [*Exit.*

GINA. I hope he is not poking the fire, in there. (*After a
short pause.*) Hedvig, do see what he is up to.

(EKDAL *returns with a little jug of hot water.*)

HEDVIG. Have you been getting some hot water, grandfather?

EKDAL. Yes, I have. I want it for something—I have got
some writing to do, and my ink is all dried up as thick as
porridge—hm!

GINA. But you ought to have your supper first. It is all laid in there.

EKDAL. I can't bother about supper, Gina. I'm dreadfully busy, I tell you. I won't have anyone coming into my room, not anyone—hm! (*Goes into his room.* GINA *and* HEDVIG *exchange glances.*)

GINA (*in a low voice*). Can you imagine where he has got the money from?

HEDVIG. I expect he has got it from Graaberg.

GINA. Not a bit of it. Graaberg always sends his pay to me.

HEDVIG. Then he must have got a bottle on credit somewhere.

GINA. Poor grandfather, no one would give him credit.

(*Enter* HJALMAR EKDAL, *wearing an overcoat and a grey felt hat.*)

GINA (*throws down her sewing and gets up*). Back already, Hjalmar?

HEDVIG (*at the same time, jumping up*). Fancy your coming now, father!

HJALMAR (*taking off his hat*). Oh, most of the guests were leaving.

HEDVIG. So early?

HJALMAR. Yes, it was a dinner-party, you know. (*Begins taking off his coat.*)

GINA. Let me help you.

HEDVIG. And me too. (*They take off his coat, Gina hangs it on the wall.*) Were there many there, father?

HJALMAR. Oh no, not many. We were just twelve or fourteen at table.

GINA. And you had a chat with all of them?

HJALMAR. A little, yes; but Gregers practically monopolised me.

GINA. Is Gregers as ugly as ever?

HJALMAR. Well, he's not particularly handsome. Isn't the old man in yet?

HEDVIG. Yes, grandfather is busy writing.

HJALMAR. Did he say anything?

GINA. No, what about?

HJALMAR. Didn't he say anything about—? I fancied I heard he had been to Graaberg. I will go in and see him for a moment.

GINA. No, no, it's not worth while.

HJALMAR. Why not? Did he say he didn't want me to go in?

GINA. He doesn't want anyone to go in to-night.

HEDVIG (*making signs to her*). Hm—hm!

GINA (*taking no notice*). He came in and fetched himself some hot water.

HJALMAR. Then I suppose he is—?

GINA. Yes, that's it.

HJALMAR. Good heavens—my poor old grey-haired father! Well, anyway, let him have what little pleasure he can. (*Old* EKDAL *comes out of his room wearing a dressing-gown and smoking a pipe.*)

EKDAL. Ah, you are back. I thought I heard your voice.

HJALMAR. I have just come in.

EKDAL. You didn't see me, then?

HJALMAR. No, but they told me you had gone through—and so I thought I would come after you.

EKDAL. Nice of you, Hjalmar—hm! What were all those people?

HJALMAR. Oh, all sorts. Flor was there, and Balle, and Kaspersen, and what's-his-name—I don't remember—all of them men about the Court, you know.

EKDAL (*nodding*). Do you hear that, Gina? All of 'em men about the Court!

GINA. Yes, they are very fine in that house now.

HEDVIG. Did any of them sing, father—or recite?

HJALMAR. No, they only talked nonsense. They wanted me to recite to them, but I wasn't going to do that.

EKDAL. You weren't going to do that, eh?

GINA. I think you might have done that.

HJALMAR. No, I don't think one ought to be at everybody's beck and call. (*Walking up and down.*) Anyway, I am not going to be.

EKDAL. No, no, Hjalmar's not that sort.

HJALMAR. I fail to see why I should be expected to amuse others if I happen to go out for once. Let the others exert themselves a little. These fellows go from one house to another, eating and drinking, every day of their lives. I think they should take the trouble to do something in return for all the excellent meals they get.

GINA. But you didn't tell them that?

HJALMAR (*humming*). Hm—hm—hm; they heard something that astonished them, I can tell you.

EKDAL. And all of 'em men about the Court!

HJALMAR. That didn't save them. (*Casually.*) And then we had a little argument about Tokay.

EKDAL. Tokay, did you say? That's a grand wine, if you like!

HJALMAR. It *can* be a grand wine. But of course, you know, all vintages are not of the same quality; it entirely depends how much sunshine the vines have had.

GINA. There isn't anything you don't know, Hjalmar.

EKDAL. And did they want to argue about that?

HJALMAR. They tried to; but they were informed that it was just the same with Court officials. All years are not equally good in their case either, they were told.

GINA. I don't know how you think of such things!

EKDAL. Ha—ha! They had to put that in their pipes and smoke it?

HJALMAR. We let them have it straight between the eyes.

EKDAL. Do you hear that, Gina? Straight between the eyes! —and men about the Court too!

GINA. Fancy that, straight between the eyes!

HJALMAR. Yes, but I don't want you to talk about it. One doesn't repeat such things as that. The whole thing passed off quite amicably, of course. They were very genial, pleasant fellows. Why should I want to hurt their feelings? Not I.

EKDAL. But straight between the eyes—

HEDVIG (coaxingly). How funny it is to see you in dress clothes. You look very nice in dress clothes, father.

HJALMAR. Yes, don't you think so? And this really fits me beautifully. It looks almost as if it had been made for me— a little tight in the armholes, perhaps—help me, Hedvig. (Takes off the coat.) I would rather put on my jacket. Where have you put my jacket, Gina?

GINA. Here it is. (Brings the jacket and helps him on with it.)

HJALMAR. That's better! Be sure you don't forget to let Molvik have the suit back to-morrow morning.

GINA (folding it up). I will see to it.

HJALMAR (stretching himself). Ah, that's more comfortable. And I rather fancy a loose, easy coat like this suits my style better. Don't you think so, Hedvig?

HEDVIG. Yes, father.

HJALMAR. Especially if I tie my cravat with flowing ends, like this—what do you think?

HEDVIG. Yes, it goes so well with your beard and your thick curly hair.

HJALMAR. I don't know that I should call it curly; I should think "wavy" was a better word.

HEDVIG. Yes, it has beautiful waves in it.

HJALMAR. That's it—wavy.

HEDVIG (after a little pause, pulling his coat). Father!

HJALMAR. Well, what is it?

HEDVIG. You know quite well.

HJALMAR. No, indeed I don't.

HEDVIG (half laughing and half crying). Father, you mustn't tease me any longer.

HJALMAR. But what is it?

HEDVIG (*shaking him*). Don't pretend! Out with them, father—the good things you promised to bring home to me.

HJALMAR. There, just fancy my having forgotten all about it!

HEDVIG. No, you are only making fun of me, father! It's too bad. Where have you hidden it?

HJALMAR. Upon my word, I forgot all about it! But wait a bit, Hedvig, I have got something else for you. (*Rises, and hunts in the pockets of the dress coat.*)

HEDVIG (*jumping and clapping her hands*). Oh, mother! mother!

GINA. You see, if you only give him time—

HJALMAR (*holding out a bit of paper*). Look, here it is.

HEDVIG. That! It is only a piece of paper.

HJALMAR. It is the bill of fare, my dear—the whole bill of fare. Here is "Menu" at the top, that means the bill of fare.

HEDVIG. Is that all you have got?

HJALMAR. I forgot to bring anything else, I tell you. But I can tell you all these good things were a great treat. Sit down at the table now and read the list, and I will describe the taste of all the dishes to you. Look, Hedvig.

HEDVIG (*gulping down her tears*). Thank you. (*She sits down, but does not read it.* GINA *makes signs to her, and* HJALMAR *notices it.*)

HJALMAR (*walking up and down*). It is incredible what the father of a family is expected to be able to think about; and if he forgets the slightest little thing, he is sure to see glum faces at once. Well, one gets accustomed even to that. (*Stands by the stove beside his father.*) Have you taken a peep in there this evening, father?

EKDAL. Of course I have. She has gone into the basket.

HJALMAR. Has she gone into the basket? She is beginning to get accustomed to it, then.

EKDAL. Yes, I told you she would. But, you know, there are some little matters—

HJALMAR. Little improvements, eh?

EKDAL. Yes, but we must see to them.

HJALMAR. Very well, let us talk over these improvements, father. Come and sit on the sofa.

EKDAL. Quite so. But I think I will just attend to my pipe first—it wants cleaning. Hm! (*Goes into his room.*)

GINA (*smiling at* HJALMAR). Clean his pipe!

HJALMAR. Come, come, Gina—let him be. Poor, broken-down old fellow. Yes, these improvements—we had better get them off our hands to-morrow.

GINA. You won't have time to-morrow, Ekdal.

HEDVIG (*interrupting*). Oh yes, he will, mother!

GINA. Remember those prints that have got to be re-touched. They have asked for them over and over again.

HJALMAR. Bless my soul, those prints again! I'll finish those off easily enough. Are there any new orders?

GINA. No, worse luck. There are only the two appointments you booked for to-morrow.

HJALMAR. Nothing else? Well, of course, if people won't exert themselves—

GINA. But what am I to do? I am sure I advertise as much as I can.

HJALMAR. Yes, you advertise!—and you see how much good it does. I suppose nobody has been to look at the room either?

GINA. Not yet.

HJALMAR. What else could you expect? If people won't keep their wits about them—. You really must pull yourself together, Gina.

HEDVIG (*coming forward*). Shall I get you your flute, father?

HJALMAR. No, no; I have no room for pleasures in my life. (*Walking about.*) Work, work—I will show you what work means to-morrow, you may be sure of that. I shall go on working as long as my strength holds out—

GINA. My dear Hjalmar, I didn't mean you to take me up that way.

HEDVIG. Wouldn't you like me to bring you a bottle of beer, father?

HJALMAR. Certainly not, I don't want anything. (*Stops suddenly.*) Beer?—did you say beer?

HEDVIG (*briskly*). Yes, father; lovely cool beer.

HJALMAR. Well, if you insist on it, I don't mind if you bring me a bottle.

GINA. Yes, do, Hedvig; then we shall feel cosy.

(HEDVIG *runs towards the kitchen.* HJALMAR, *who is standing by the stove, stops her, looks at her, and draws her towards him.*)

HJALMAR. My little Hedvig!

HEDVIG (*with tears of joy in her eyes*). Dear, kind father!

HJALMAR. No, you mustn't call me that. There was I, sitting at the rich man's table, enjoying myself, sitting there filling myself with all his good things—. I might at least have remembered—!

GINA (*sitting down at the table*). Don't be absurd, Hjalmar.

HJALMAR. It's true. But you mustn't think too much of that. You know, anyway, how much I love you.

HEDVIG (*throwing her arms round him*). And we love you so awfully, father!

HJALMAR. And if sometimes I am unreasonable with you, you will remember—won't you—that I am a man beset by a host of cares. There, there! (*Wipes his eyes.*) No beer at such a moment as this. Give me my flute. (HEDVIG *runs to the bookcase and gets it for him.*) Thank you. That's better. With my flute in my hand, and you two beside me—! (HEDVIG *sits down at the table beside* GINA. HJALMAR *walks up and down, then resolutely begins playing a Bohemian country-dance, but in very slow time and very sentimentally. He soon stops, stretches out his left hand to* GINA *and says in a voice full of emotion.*) No matter if we have to live poorly and frugally, Gina—this is our home; and I will say this, that it is good to be at home again. (*He resumes his playing; shortly afterwards a knock is heard at the door.*)

GINA (*getting up*). Hush, Hjalmar—I think there is some one at the door.

HJALMAR (*laying down his flute*). Of course!

(GINA *goes and opens the door.*)

GREGERS WERLE (*speaking outside the door*). I beg your pardon—

GINA (*retreating a little*). Ah!

GREGERS (*outside*). Is this where Mr. Ekdal the photographer lives?

GINA. Yes, it is.

HJALMAR (*going to the door*). Gregers! Is it you after all? Come in, come in.

GREGERS (*coming in*). I told you I would come up and see you.

HJALMAR. But to-night—? Have you left all your guests?

GREGERS. I have left my guests and my home. Good evening, Mrs. Ekdal. I don't suppose you recognise me?

GINA. Of course I do; you are not so difficult to recognise, Mr. Werle.

GREGERS. I suppose not; I am like my mother, and no doubt you remember her a little.

HJALMAR. Did you say that you had left your home?

GREGERS. Yes, I have gone to an hotel.

HJALMAR. Indeed? Well, as you are here, take off your things and sit down.

GREGERS. Thank you. (*He takes off his coat. He has changed his clothes, and is dressed in a plain grey suit of provincial cut.*)

HJALMAR. Sit down here on the sofa. Make yourself at home.

(GREGERS *sits on the sofa and* HJALMAR *on the chair by the table.*)

GREGERS (*looking round him*). So this is where you live, Hjalmar. Do you work here too?

HJALMAR. This is the studio, as you can see—

GINA. It is our largest room, and so we prefer sitting in here.

HJALMAR. We used to live in better quarters, but these have one great advantage, there is such a splendid amount of space—

GINA. And we have a room on the other side of the passage, which we can let.

GREGERS (*to* HJALMAR). Ah!—have you any lodgers?

HJALMAR. No, not yet. It is not so easy, you know; one has to make an effort to get them. (*To* HEDVIG.) What about that beer? (HEDVIG *nods and goes into the kitchen.*)

GREGERS. Is that your daughter?

HJALMAR. Yes, that is Hedvig.

GREGERS. Your only child?

HJALMAR. Our only child, yes. She is the source of our greatest happiness and—(*lowering his voice*) also of our keenest sorrow.

GREGERS. What do you mean?

HJALMAR. She is dangerously threatened with the loss of her sight.

GREGERS. Going blind!

HJALMAR. Yes. There are only the first symptoms of it at present, and all may go well for some time yet. But the doctor has warned us. It is inevitable.

GREGERS. What a terrible misfortune! What is the cause of it?

HJALMAR (*sighing*). It is hereditary, apparently.

GREGERS (*starting*). Hereditary?

GINA. Hjalmar's mother had weak eyes too.

HJALMAR. Yes, so my father tells me; I can't remember her, you know.

GREGERS. Poor child! And how does she take it?

HJALMAR. Oh well, you will understand that we have not had the heart to tell her anything about it. She suspects nothing. She is as happy and careless as a bird, singing about the house, and so she is flitting through her life into the blackness that awaits her. (*Despairingly.*) It is terribly hard for me, Gregers.

(HEDVIG *comes in, bringing a tray with beer and glasses, and sets it down on the table.*)

HJALMAR (*stroking her hair*). Thank you, dear, thank you. (HEDVIG *puts her arms round his neck and whispers in his ear.*) No—no bread and butter, thanks—unless perhaps you would take some, Gregers?

GREGERS (*shaking his head*). No, thanks.

HJALMAR (*still speaking in a melancholy tone*). Well, you may as well bring in a little, all the same. If you have a crusty piece, I should prefer it—and be sure to see that there is enough butter on it. (HEDVIG *nods happily anl goes into the kitchen again.*)

GREGERS (*who has followed her with his eyes*). She seems well and strong in other respects.

GINA. Yes, thank heaven, she is quite well in every other way.

GREGERS. She looks as if she will be like you when she grows up, Mrs. Ekdal. How old is she now?

GINA. Hedvig is just fourteen; her birthday is the day after to-morrow.

GREGERS. She is tall for her age.

GINA. Yes, she has grown a lot this last year.

GREGERS. These young people growing up make us realise our own age. How long have you been married now?

GINA. We have been married—let me see—just fifteen years.

GREGERS. Can it be so long as that!

GINA (*looks at him watchfully*). It is indeed.

HJALMAR. Yes, that it is. Fifteen years all but a few months. (*Changes the subject.*) They must have seemed long years to you up at the works, Gregers.

GREGERS. They did seem so while I was getting through them; but now, looking back on them, I can scarcely believe it is all that time.

(*Old* EKDAL *comes in from his room, without his pipe, and wearing his old military cap. He walks a little unsteadily.*)

EKDAL. Now then, Hjalmar, we can sit down and talk over those—hm! What is it—what is it?

HJALMAR (*going towards him*). Father, some one is here—Gregers Werle. I don't know whether you remember him?

EKDAL (*looking at* GREGERS, *who has risen*). Werle? Do you mean the son? What does he want with me?

HJALMAR. Nothing; it is me he has come to see.

EKDAL. Oh, then there is nothing the matter?

HJALMAR. No, of course not.

EKDAL (*swinging his arms*). I don't mind, you know; I am not afraid, but—

GREGERS (*going up to him*). I only want to bring you a greeting from your old hunting-ground, Lieutenant Ekdal.

EKDAL. My hunting-ground?

GREGERS. Yes, from up there round the Höidal works.

EKDAL. Ah, up there. I was well known up there once.

GREGERS. You were a mighty hunter in those days.

EKDAL. Ah, that I was, I believe you. You are looking at my cap. I need ask no one's leave to wear it here indoors. So long as I don't go into the streets with it on—

(HEDVIG *brings in a plate of bread and butter, and puts it on the table.*)

HJALMAR. Sit down, father, and have a glass of beer. Help yourself, Gregers.

(EKDAL *totters over to the sofa, mumbling.* GREGERS *sits down on a chair beside him.* HJALMAR *sits on the other side of* GREGERS. GINA *sits a little way from the table and sews;* HEDVIG *stands beside her* FATHER.)

GREGERS. Do you remember, Lieutenant Ekdal, how Hjalmar and I used to come up and see you in the summertime and at Christmas?

EKDAL. Did you? No—no—I don't remember that. But I can tell you I was a fine sportsman in those days. I have shot bears, too—nine of 'em, I have shot.

GREGERS (*looking at him sympathetically*). And now you get no more shooting.

EKDAL. Oh, I don't know about that. I get some sport still now and then. Not that sort of sport, of course. In the forests, you know—the forests, the forests—! (*Drinks.*) Are the forests looking fine up there now?

GREGERS. Not so fine as in your day. A lot of them have been cut down.

EKDAL (*lowering his voice, as if afraid*). That's a dangerous thing to do. That brings trouble. The forests avenge themselves.

HJALMAR (*filling his* FATHER'S *glass*). Now, father—a little more.

GREGERS. How can a man like you, who were always accustomed to be in the open, live in a stuffy town, boxed in by four walls like this?

EKDAL (*looking at* HJALMAR *with a quiet smile*). Oh, it is not so bad here, not at all so bad.

GREGERS. But think of all you were always accustomed to —the cool, refreshing breezes, the free life in the woods and on the moors, among the beasts and birds—

EKDAL (*smiling*). Hjalmar, shall we show it to him?

HJALMAR (*hastily and with some embarrassment*). No, no, father—not to-night.

GREGERS. What does he want to show me?

HJALMAR. Oh, it is only a sort of—. You can see it some other time.

GREGERS (*continues talking to* EKDAL). What I had in my mind, Lieutenant Ekdal, was that you should come back up to the works with me; I am going back there very soon. You could easily get some copying to do up there too; and here you haven't a single thing to give you pleasure or to amuse you.

EKDAL (*staring at him in amazement*). I haven't a single thing to—!

GREGERS. Well, of course, you have Hjalmar; but then he has his own family ties. But a man like you, who has always felt so strongly the call of a free, unfettered life—

EKDAL (*striking the table*). Hjalmar, he *shall* see it!

HJALMAR. But, father, is it worth while now? It is dark, you know.

EKDAL. Nonsense, there is moonlight. (*Gets up.*) He *shall* see it, I say. Let me pass—and you come and help me, Hjalmar.

HEDVIG. Yes, do, father!

HJALMAR (*getting up*). Very well.

GREGERS (*to* GINA). What does he want me to see?

GINA. Oh, you mustn't expect to see anything very wonderful.

(EKDAL *and* HJALMAR *have gone to the back of the stage, and each of them pushes back one side of the sliding doors.* HEDVIG *helps the old man;* GREGERS *remains standing by the sofa;* GINA *sits quietly sewing. The open doors disclose a large, irregularly-shaped attic, full of recesses and with two stove-pipes running up through it. Through the little roof-windows the bright moonlight is pouring in upon certain spots in the attic; the rest of it is in deep shadow.*)

EKDAL (*to* GREGERS). Come close and have a look.

GREGERS (*going to him*). What is there for me to see?

EKDAL. Come and take a good look. Hm!

HJALMAR (*in a slightly constrained tone*). This is all my father's, you know.

GREGERS (*comes to the door and looks into the attic*). You keep poultry then, Lieutenant Ekdal!

EKDAL. I should think we did keep poultry. They are roosting now; but you should just see them in the daytime!

HEDVIG. And we have got a—

EKDAL. Hush! Hush! Don't say anything yet.

GREGERS. You have got pigeons too, I see.

EKDAL. Yes, I shouldn't wonder if we had got pigeons too! They have nesting-boxes up there under the eaves, you see; pigeons like to roost well above ground, you know.

GREGERS. They are not common pigeons, though.

EKDAL. Common pigeons! No, I should think not! We have got tumblers, and a pair of pouters too. But come and look here! Can you see that hutch over there against the wall?

GREGERS. Yes, what is it for?

EKDAL. That's where the rabbits sleep at night.

GREGERS. What, have you got rabbits too?

EKDAL. Yes, you bet we have rabbits! He is asking if we have got rabbits, Hjalmar! Hm! But now I will show you the great sight! Get out of the way, Hedvig. Just stand here; that's it; now look in there. Don't you see a basket with straw in it?

GREGERS. Yes. And I can see a bird lying in the basket.

EKDAL. Hm!—a bird!

GREGERS. Isn't it a duck?

HJALMAR. But what kind of a duck, should you say.

HEDVIG. It isn't an ordinary duck.

EKDAL. Sh!

GREGERS. It isn't a foreign bird either.

EKDAL. No, Mr.—Werle, that is no foreign bird, because it is a wild duck.

GREGERS. No! is it really? A wild duck?

EKDAL. Yes, that it is. The "bird," as you call it, is a wild duck. That's our wild duck.

HEDVIG. My wild duck. It belongs to me.

GREGERS. Is it possible it can live up here in the attic? Does it do well?

EKDAL. Of course it has a trough of water to splash about in.

HJALMAR. And gets fresh water every other day.

GINA (*turning to* HJALMAR). Hjalmar, dear, it is getting icy cold in here, you know.

EKDAL. Hm! we will shut it up then. We mustn't disturb their night's rest. Catch hold, Hedvig. (HJALMAR *and* HEDVIG *push the doors together.*) Some other time you shall see it properly. (*Sits down in the armchair by the stove.*) They are most remarkable birds, wild ducks, I can tell you.

GREGERS. But how did you manage to capture it?

EKDAL. I didn't capture it. It is a certain person in the town here, that we have to thank for it.

GREGERS (*with a slight start*). I suppose that man is not my father, by any chance?

EKDAL. You have hit it. Your father and no one else. Hm!

HJALMAR. It is funny you should guess that, Gregers.

GREGERS. You told me you were indebted to my father for so many different things; so I thought very likely—

GINA. But we didn't get the duck from Mr. Werle himself—

EKDAL. It is Haakon Werle we have to thank for it all the

same, Gina. (*To* GREGERS.) He was out in a boat, you see, and shot it. But your father's sight isn't good, you know, and it was only wounded.

GREGERS. I see, it was only slightly hit.

HJALMAR. Yes, only in two or three places.

HEDVIG. It was hit in the wing, so it couldn't fly.

GREGERS. I see; then I suppose it dived down to the bottom?

EKDAL (*sleepily in a thick voice*). Naturally. Wild duck always do that. They stick down at the bottom—as deep as they can get—bite fast hold of the weed and wrack and all the rubbish that is down there. And so they never come up again.

GREGERS. But, Lieutenant Ekdal, your wild duck came up again.

EKDAL. He had an extraordinarily clever dog, your father. And the dog—it dived after it and hauled it up again.

GREGERS (*turning to* HJALMAR). And then you got it?

HJALMAR. Not directly. It was brought to your father's house first, but it didn't thrive there; so Pettersen asked leave to kill it—

EKDAL (*half asleep*). Hm!—Pettersen—yes—old codfish!—

HJALMAR (*lowering his voice*). That was how we got it, you see. Father knows Pettersen a little, and heard this about the wild duck, and managed to get it handed over to him.

GREGERS. And now it thrives quite well in the attic there?

HJALMAR. Yes, perfectly well. It has grown fat. It has been so long in there now that it has forgotten all about its own wild life; and that was all that was necessary.

GREGERS. You are right there, Hjalmar. Only, never let it see the sky and the water.—But I mustn't stay any longer. I think your father has gone to sleep.

HJALMAR. Oh, don't go on that account.

GREGERS. But, by the way—you said you had a room to let, a room you don't use?

HJALMAR. Yes—why? Do you happen to know any one—?

GREGERS. Can I have the room?

HJALMAR. You?

GINA. What, you, Mr. Werle?

GREGERS. Can I have the room? If so, I will move in early to-morrow morning.

HJALMAR. Certainly, by all means—

GINA. But, Mr. Werle, it really isn't the sort of room to suit you.

HJALMAR. Gina, how can you say that!

GINA. Well, it isn't big enough or light enough, and—

GREGERS. That doesn't matter at all, Mrs. Ekdal.

HJALMAR. I should call it a very nice room, and not so badly furnished either.

GINA. But remember the couple that are lodging underneath.

GREGERS. Who are they?

GINA. One of them used to be a private tutor—

HJALMAR. Mr. Molvik—he has taken a degree—

GINA. And the other is a doctor of the name of Relling.

GREGERS. Relling? I know him a little; he used to practise up at Höidal at one time.

GINA. They are a regular pair of good-for-nothings. They are often out on the spree in the evening, and they come home late at night and not always quite—

GREGERS. I should easily get accustomed to that. I hope I shall settle down like the wild duck.

GINA. Well, I think you ought to sleep over it first, anyway.

GREGERS. You don't seem to like the idea of having me in the house, Mrs. Ekdal.

GINA. Gracious me! what makes you think that?

HJALMAR. I must say it is extremely odd of you, Gina. (*To* GREGERS.) Tell me, do you propose remaining here in town for the present?

GREGERS (*putting on his overcoat*). Yes, now I propose to remain here.

HJALMAR. But not at home with your father? What do you intend to do with yourself?

GREGERS. Ah, if only I knew that, it would be all plain sailing. But when one has had the misfortune to be christened "Gregers"—"Gregers," and "Werle" to follow—did you ever hear anything so hideous?—

HJALMAR. It doesn't sound so to me.

GREGERS (*shuddering*). I should feel inclined to spit on any fellow with a name like that. Once a man has had the misfortune to find himself saddled with the name of Gregers Werle, as I have—

HJALMAR (*laughing*). Ha, ha! Well, but if you weren't Gregers Werle, what would you like to be?

GREGERS. If I could choose, I would rather be a clever dog than anything else.

GINA. A dog!

HEDVIG (*involuntarily*). Oh no!

GREGERS. Yes, an extraordinarily clever dog; the sort of dog that would go down to the bottom after wild duck, when they dive down and bite fast hold of the weed and wrack in the mud.

HJALMAR. I will tell you what it is, Gregers—I don't understand a word of all this.

GREGERS. No, and I daresay the meaning is not very pretty either. Well, then, early to-morrow morning I will move in.

(*To* GINA.) I shan't give you any trouble; I do everything for myself. (*To* HJALMAR.) We will finish our chat to-morrow. Good-night, Mrs. Ekdal. (*Nods to* HEDVIG.) Good-night.

GINA. Good-night, Mr. Werle.

HEDVIG. Good-night.

HJALMAR (*who has lit a candle*). Wait a moment, I must give you a light; it is sure to be dark on the stair. (GREGERS *and* HJALMAR *go out by the outer room.*)

GINA (*staring in front of her, with her sewing lying on her lap*). A funny idea, to want to be a dog!

HEDVIG. Do you know, mother—I believe he meant something quite different by that.

GINA. What else could he mean?

HEDVIG. I don't know; but I thought he seemed to mean something quite different from what he said—all the time.

GINA. Do you think so? It certainly was queer.

HJALMAR (*coming back*). The lamp was still lit. (*Puts out the candle and lays it down*). Now, at last one can get a chance of something to eat. (*Begins to eat the bread and butter.*) Well, you see, Gina—if only you keep your wits about you—

GINA. How do you mean, keep your wits about you?

HJALMAR. Well, anyway we have had a bit of luck, to succeed in letting the room at last. And, besides, to a man like Gregers—a dear old friend.

GINA. Well, I really don't know what to say about it.

HEDVIG. Oh mother, you will see it will be lovely.

HJALMAR. You certainly are very odd. A little while ago you were so bent on letting the room, and now you don't like it.

GINA. Oh, I do, Hjalmar—if only it had been to some one else. What do you suppose his father will say?

HJALMAR. Old Werle? It is no business of his.

GINA. But you may be sure things have gone wrong between them again, as the young man is leaving his father's house. You know the sort of terms those two are on.

HJALMAR. That may be all very true, but—

GINA. And it is quite likely his father may think that you are at the bottom of it all.

HJALMAR. Let him think what he likes! Mr. Werle has done a wonderful lot for me; I am the last to want to deny it. But that is no reason why I should think myself bound to consult him in everything all my life.

GINA. But, Hjalmar dear, it might end in grandfather's suffering for it; he might lose the little bit of money he gets from Graaberg.

HJALMAR. I feel almost inclined to say I wish he might!

Don't you suppose it is a humiliating thing for a man like me, to see his grey-haired old father treated like an outcast? But I think that sort of thing is nearly at an end. (*Takes another piece of bread and butter.*) I have a mission in life, and I shall fulfil it!

HEDVIG. Oh yes, father, do!

HJALMAR (*lowering his voice*). I *shall* fulfil it, I say. The day will come when—when—. And that is why it is a good thing we got the room let; it puts me in a more independent position. And a man who has a mission in life must be independent of others. (*Stands by his father's chair and speaks with emotion.*) Poor old white-haired father! You may depend on your Hjalmar! He has broad shoulders—strong shoulders, at any rate. Some fine day you shall wake up, and—. (*To* GINA.) Don't you believe it?

GINA (*getting up*). Of course I do; but the first thing is to see about getting him to bed.

HJALMAR. Yes, come along then. (*They lift the old man carefully.*)

ACT III

(SCENE.—HJALMAR EKDAL'S *studio, the following morn-ing. The sun is shining in through the big window in the slop-ing roof, where the curtain has been drawn back.* HJALMAR *is sitting at the table busy retouching a photograph. Various other portraits are lying in front of him. After a few moments* GINA *comes in by the outer door, in hat and cloak, and carrying a covered basket.*)

HJALMAR. Back already, Gina?

GINA. Yes, I've no time to waste. (*She puts the basket down on a chair and takes her things off.*)

HJALMAR. Did you look in on Gregers?

GINA. Yes, that I did; and a nice sight too! He had made the room in a pretty state as soon as he arrived.

HJALMAR. How?

GINA. He said he wanted to do everything for himself, you know. So he tried to set the stove going; and what must he do but shut the register, so that the whole room was filled with smoke. Ouf!—there was a stink like—

HJALMAR. You don't mean it!

GINA. But that's not the best of it. He wanted to put the fire out then, so he emptied his ewer into the stove, and flooded the whole floor with a filthy mess.

HJALMAR. What a nuisance!

GINA. I have just got the porter's wife to clean up after him, the pig; but the room won't be fit to go into till the afternoon.

HJALMAR. What is he doing with himself in the meantime?

GINA. He said he would go out for a bit.

HJALMAR. I went to see him, too, for a minute, after you went out.

GINA. So he told me. You have asked him to lunch.

HJALMAR. Just for a snack of lunch, you know. The first

253

day he is here—we could hardly do less. You are sure to have something in the house.

GINA. I will go and see what I can find.

HJALMAR. Don't be too scrimpy, though; because I fancy Relling and Molvik are coming up too. I happened to meet Relling on the stair, you see, and so I had to—

GINA. Are we to have those two as well?

HJALMAR. Bless my soul!—a little bit more or less can't make much difference.

(*Old* EKDAL *opens his door and looks in.*)

EKDAL. Look here, Hjalmar— (*Seeing* GINA.) Oh!

GINA. Do you want something, grandfather?

EKDAL. No, no—it doesn't matter. Hm! (*Goes into his room again.*)

GINA (*taking up her basket*). Keep your eye on him, and see he doesn't go out.

HJALMAR. Yes, yes, I will. Look here, Gina—a little herring salad would be rather nice; I rather fancy Relling and Molvik were making a night of it last night.

GINA. So long as they don't come before I am ready—

HJALMAR. They won't do that. Take your time.

GINA. Very well, and you can get a little work done in the meantime.

HJALMAR. Don't you see I *am* working? I am working as hard as I can.

GINA. You will be able to get those off your hands, you see. (*Takes her basket into the kitchen.* HJALMAR *resumes his work on the photographs with evident reluctance.*)

EKDAL (*peeps in, and, after looking round the studio, says in a low voice*). Have you finished that work?

HJALMAR. I am working away at these portraits—

EKDAL. Well, well, it doesn't matter—if you are so busy— Hm! (*Goes in again, but leaves his door open.* HJALMAR *goes on working for a little in silence; then lays down his brush and goes to the door.*)

HJALMAR. Are you busy, father?

EKDAL (*from within, in an aggrieved voice*). If you are busy, I'm busy too. Hm!

HJALMAR. Quite so, quite so. (*Returns to his work. After a few moments* EKDAL *comes out of his room again.*)

EKDAL. Hm! Look here, Hjalmar, I am not so busy as all that.

HJALMAR. I thought you were doing your copying.

EKDAL. Deuce take Graaberg! Can't he wait a day or two? It's not a matter of life and death, I suppose.

HJALMAR. No; and you are not his slave, anyway.

EKDAL. And there is that other matter in there—

HJALMAR. Quite so. Do you want to go in? Shall I open the doors for you?

EKDAL. I don't think it would be a bad idea.

HJALMAR (*rising*). And then we shall have got *that* off our hands.

EKDAL. Just so, yes. It must be ready by to-morrow morning early. We did say to-morrow, didn't we? Eh?

HJALMAR. Yes, to-morrow.

(HJALMAR *and* EKDAL *each pull back a division of the sliding-door. The morning sun is shining in through the top-lights of the attic; some of the pigeons are flying about, others sitting cooing on the rafters; from time to time the sound of hens cackling is heard from the recesses of the attic.*)

HJALMAR. There—now you can start, father.

EKDAL (*going in*). Aren't you coming, too?

HJALMAR. Well, I don't know—I think I—. (*Seeing* GINA *at the kitchen door.*) No, I haven't time; I must work. But we must use our patent arrangement. (*He pulls a cord and lowers a curtain, of which the bottom part is made out of a strip of old sailcloth, while the upper part is a fisherman's net stretched out. When it is down, the floor of the attic is no longer visible.*) That's it. Now I can sit down in peace for a little.

GINA. Is he rummaging about in there again?

HJALMAR. Would you rather he had gone straight to the wine-shop? (*Sitting down.*) Is there anything you want? You look so—

GINA. I only wanted to ask if you thought we could have lunch in here?

HJALMAR. Yes; I suppose we have no sitters coming as early as that?

GINA. No, I don't expect anyone except the engaged couple who want to be taken together.

HJALMAR. Why the devil can't they be taken together some other day!

GINA. It is all right, Hjalmar dear; I arranged to take them in the afternoon, when you are having your nap.

HJALMAR. That's capital! Yes, then, we will have lunch in here.

GINA. Very well, but there is no hurry about laying the lunch; you can have the table for a good while yet.

HJALMAR. Can't you see that I am taking every opportunity that I can to use the table!

GINA. Then you will be free afterwards, you see. (*Goes into the kitchen again. Short pause.*)

EKDAL (*standing in the attic doorway, behind the net.*) Hjalmar!

HJALMAR. Well?

EKDAL. I am afraid we shall be obliged to move the water-trough after all.

HJALMAR. Exactly what I have said all along.

EKDAL. Hm—hm—hm! (*Moves away from the door.*)

(HJALMAR *goes on with his work for a little, then glances at the attic, and is just getting up when* HEDVIG *comes in from the kitchen; thereupon he sits down again promptly.*)

HJALMAR. What do you want?

HEDVIG. Only to come in to you, father.

HJALMAR (*after a moment's pause*). You seem to be very inquisitive. Were you sent to watch me?

HEDVIG. Of course not.

HJALMAR. What is your mother doing in there now?

HEDVIG. She's busy making a herring salad. (*Goes up to the table.*) Isn't there any little thing I could help you with, father?

HJALMAR. No, no. It is right that I should be the one to work away at it all—as long as my strength holds out. There is no fear of my wanting help, Hedvig—at any rate so long as my health doesn't give way.

HEDVIG. Oh, father—don't say such horrid things! (*She wanders about the room, then stands in the attic doorway and looks in.*)

HJALMAR. What is he about in there?

HEDVIG. I fancy he is making a new path to the water-trough.

HJALMAR. He will never be able to manage that by himself. What a nuisance it is that I am obliged to sit here and—

HEDVIG (*going to him*). Let me have the brush, father; I can do it, you know.

HJALMAR. Nonsense, you would only hurt your eyes.

HEDVIG. Not a bit of it. Give me the brush.

HJALMAR (*getting up*). Well, certainly it wouldn't take me more than a minute or two.

HEDVIG. Pooh! What harm can it do me? (*Takes the brush from him.*) Now then. (*Sits down.*) I have got one here as a model, you know.

HJALMAR. But don't hurt your eyes! Do you hear? I won't be responsible; you must take the responsibility yourself, understand that.

HEDVIG (*going on with the work*). Yes, yes, I will.

HJALMAR. Clever little girl! Just for a minute or two, you understand. (*He stoops under the net and goes into the attic.*

HEDVIG *sits still, working.* HJALMAR'S *voice and his* FATHER'S *are heard discussing something.*)

HJALMAR (*coming to the net*). Hedvig, just give me the pincers; they are on the shelf. And the chisel. (*Looks back into the attic.*) Now you will see, father. Just let me show you first what I mean. (HEDVIG *has fetched the tools, and gives them to him.*) Thanks. I think it was a good thing I came, you know. (*Goes into the attic. Sounds of carpentering and talking are heard from within.* HEDVIG *stands looking after him. A moment later a knock is heard at the outer door, but she does not notice it.*)

GREGERS WERLE (*who is bareheaded and without an over-coat, comes in and stands for a moment in the doorway*). Ahem!

HEDVIG (*turns round and goes to him*). Oh, good-morning! Won't you come in?

GREGERS. Thanks. (*Glances towards the attic.*) You seem to have workmen in the house.

HEDVIG. No, it's only father and grandfather. I will go and tell them.

GREGERS. No, no, don't do that; I would rather wait a little. (*Sits down on the sofa.*)

HEDVIG. It's so untidy here— (*Begins to collect the photographs.*)

GREGERS. Oh, let them be. Are they portraits that want finishing?

HEDVIG. Yes, just a little job I was helping father with.

GREGERS. Any way, don't let me disturb you.

HEDVIG. Oh, you don't. (*She draws the things to her again and sits down to her work.* GREGERS *watches her for a time without speaking.*)

GREGERS. Has the wild duck had a good night?

HEDVIG. Yes, thanks, I think it had.

GREGERS (*turning towards the attic*). In the daylight it looks quite a different place from what it did in moonlight.

HEDVIG. Yes, it has such a different look at different times. In the morning it looks quite different from in the evening, and when it rains you wouldn't think it was the same place as on a fine day.

GREGERS. Ah, have you noticed that?

HEDVIG. You couldn't help noticing it.

GREGERS. Are you fond of being in there with the wild duck, too?

HEDVIG. Yes, when I can—

GREGERS. But I expect you haven't much time for that. I suppose you go to school?

HEDVIG. No, I don't go to school any more. Father is afraid of my hurting my eyes.

GREGERS. I see; I suppose he reads with you himself, then?

HEDVIG. He has promised to read with me, but he hasn't had time so far.

GREGERS. But isn't there anyone else to give you a little help?

HEDVIG. Yes, there is Mr. Molvik, but he isn't always exactly—quite—that is to say—

GREGERS. Not quite sober?

HEDVIG. That's it.

GREGERS. I see; then you have a good deal of time to yourself. And, in there, I suppose, it is like a little world of its own, isn't it?

HEDVIG. Yes, exactly. And there are such lots of wonderful things in there.

GREGERS. Are there?

HEDVIG. Yes, there are great cupboards full of books, and in lots of the books there are pictures.

GREGERS. I see.

HEDVIG. And then there is an old desk with drawers and flaps in it, and a great clock with figures that ought to come out when it strikes. But the clock isn't going any longer.

GREGERS. So time has ceased to exist in there—beside the wild duck.

HEDVIG. Yes. And there is an old paint-box and things—and all the books.

GREGERS. And you like reading the books?

HEDVIG. Yes, when I can manage it. But the most of them are in English, and I can't read that; so then I look at the pictures. There is a great big book called *Harrison's History of London;* it is quite a hundred years old, and there's a tremendous lot of pictures in it. At the beginning there's a picture of Death, with an hour-glass, and a girl. I don't like that. But there are all the other pictures of churches, and castles, and streets, and big ships sailing on the sea.

GREGERS. But, tell me, where did you get all these wonderful things from?

HEDVIG. Oh, an old sea-captain lived here once, and he used to bring them home with him. They called him the Flying Dutchman; it was a funny thing to call him, because he wasn't a Dutchman at all.

GREGERS. Wasn't he?

HEDVIG. No. But one day he never came back, and all these things were left here.

GREGERS. Tell me this—when you are sitting in there looking at the pictures, don't you want to get away out into the big world and see it for yourself?

HEDVIG. Not I! I want to stay at home here always and help father and mother.

GREGERS. To finish photographs?

HEDVIG. No, not only that. What I should like best of all would be to learn to engrave pictures like those in the English books.

GREGERS. Hm! what does your father say to that?

HEDVIG. I don't think father likes it; he is so funny about that. Just fancy, he wants me to learn such absurd things as basket-making and straw-plaiting! I don't see any good in my doing that.

GREGERS. Nor do I.

HEDVIG. But father is right so far, that if I had learnt to make baskets, I could have made the new basket for the wild duck.

GREGERS. Yes, so you could; and it was your business to see it was comfortable, wasn't it?

HEDVIG. Yes, because it is my wild duck.

GREGERS. Of course it is.

HEDVIG. Yes, it's my very own. But I lend it to father and grandfather as long as they like.

GREGERS. I see, but what do they want with it?

HEDVIG. Oh, they look after it, and build places for it, and all that sort of thing.

GREGERS. I see; it is the most important person in there.

HEDVIG. That it is, because it is a real, true wild duck. Poor thing, it hasn't anyone to make friends with; isn't it a pity!

GREGERS. It has no brothers and sisters, as the rabbits have.

HEDVIG. No. The hens have got lots of others there, that they were chickens with; but it has come right away from all its friends, poor thing. It is all so mysterious about the wild duck. It has got no friends—and no one knows where it came from, either.

GREGERS. And then it has been down to the ocean's depths.

HEDVIG (looks quickly at him, half smiles and asks). Why do you say "the ocean's depths"?

GREGERS. What else should I say?

HEDVIG. You might have said "the bottom of the sea."

GREGERS. Isn't it just the same if I say "the ocean's depths"?

HEDVIG. It sounds so funny to me to hear anyone else say "the ocean's depths."

GREGERS. Why? Tell me why.

HEDVIG. No, I won't; it's only foolishness.

GREGERS. It isn't. Tell me why you smiled.

HEDVIG. It is because whenever I happen to think all at once —all in a moment—of what is in there, the whole room and all that is in it make me think of "the ocean's depths." But that's all nonsense.

GREGERS. No, don't say that.

HEDVIG. Well, it's nothing but an attic.

GREGERS (*looking earnestly at her*). Are you so sure of that?

HEDVIG (*astonished*). Sure that it's an attic?

GREGERS. Yes; are you so sure of that?

HEDVIG *is silent and looks at him open-mouthed.* GINA *comes in from the kitchen to lay the table.*)

GREGERS (*rising*). I am afraid I have come too early.

GINA. Oh, well, you have got to be somewhere; and we shall very soon be ready. Clear up the table, Hedvig. (HEDVIG *gathers up the things; she and* GINA *lay the table during the following dialogue.* GREGERS *sits down in the armchair and turns over the pages of an album.*)

GREGERS. I hear you can retouch photos, Mrs. Ekdal.

GINA (*glancing at him*). Mhm! I can.

GREGERS. That must have come in very handy.

GINA. How do you mean?

GREGERS. As Hjalmar has taken to photography, I mean.

HEDVIG. Mother can take photographs too.

GINA. Oh, yes, of course I got taught to do that.

GREGERS. I suppose it is you who run the business, then?

GINA. Well, when Hjalmar hasn't time himself, I—

GREGERS. His old father takes up a great deal of his time, I suppose?

GINA. Yes, and it isn't the sort of work for a man like Hjalmar to go taking rubbishin' portraits all day long.

GREGERS. Quite so; but still, when he had once gone in for the thing—

GINA. I will ask you to understand, Mr. Werle, that Hjalmar is not an ordinary photographer.

GREGERS. Just so, just so; but— (*A shot is fired within the attic.* GREGERS *starts up.*) What's that!

GINA. Bah! now they are at their firing again.

GREGERS. Do they use guns in there too?

HEDVIG. They go out shooting.

GREGERS. What on earth—? (*Goes to the attic door.*) Have you gone out shooting, Hjalmar?

HJALMAR (*inside the net*). Oh, are you there? I didn't know. I was so busy— (*To* HEDVIG.) To think of your not telling us! (*Comes into the studio.*)

GREGERS. Do you go shooting in there in the attic?

HJALMAR (*showing a double-barrelled pistol*). Oh, only with this old thing.

GINA. Yes, you and grandfather will do yourselves a mischief some day with that there gun.

HJALMAR (*angrily*). I think I have mentioned that a fire-arm of this kind is called a pistol.

GINA. Well, that doesn't make it much better, that I can see.

GREGERS. So you have become a sportsman too, Hjalmar?

HJALMAR. Oh, we only go after a rabbit or two now and then. It is principally to please my father, you know.

GINA. Men are funny creatures, they must always have something to bemuse them.

HJALMAR (*irritably*). Quite so, quite so; men must always have something to *a*muse them.

GINA. Well, that's exactly what I said.

HJALMAR. Well,—ahem! (*To* GREGERS.) It happens very fortunately, you see, that the attic is so situated that no one can hear us shooting. (*Lays down the pistol on the top shelf of the bookcase.*) Don't touch the pistol, Hedvig; one barrel is loaded, remember.

GREGERS (*looking through the net*). You have got a sporting gun too, I see.

HJALMAR. That is father's old gun. It won't shoot any longer, there is something gone wrong with the lock. But it is rather fun to have it there all the same; we can take it to pieces now and then and clean it, and grease it, and put it together again. Of course it's my father's toy, really.

HEDVIG (*going to* GREGERS). Now you can see the wild duck properly.

GREGERS. I was just looking at it. It seems to me to trail one wing a little.

HJALMAR. Well, no wonder; it was wounded.

GREGERS. And it drags one foot a little—isn't that so?

HJALMAR. Perhaps just a tiny bit.

HEDVIG. Yes, that was the foot the dog fixed its teeth into.

HJALMAR. But otherwise it hasn't the slightest blemish; and that is really remarkable when you consider that it has had a charge of shot in its wing and has been between a dog's teeth—

GREGERS (*glancing at* HEDVIG). And has been down so long in the ocean's depths.

HEDVIG (*with a smile*). Yes.

GINA (*standing by the table*). That blessed wild duck! The whole place is turned upside down for it.

HJALMAR. Ahem!—shall you soon have finished laying the table?

GINA. Yes, very soon. Come and help me, Hedvig. (*She and* HEDVIG *go into the kitchen.*)

HJALMAR (*in an undertone*). I think perhaps you had better not stand there watching my father; he doesn't like it. (GREGERS *comes away from the attic door.*) And I had better shut the doors, before the others arrive. Sh! sh! Get in with you! (*He hoists up the netting and pulls the doors together.*) That contrivance is my own invention. It is really quite an amusement to have things to contrive and to repair when they go wrong. Besides, it is an absolute necessity, you see, because Gina wouldn't like to have rabbits and fowls wandering about the studio.

GREGERS. Of course not, and I suppose the studio is really your wife's domain?

HJALMAR. I hand over the ordinary business as much as possible to her, for that enables me to shut myself up in the sitting-room and give my mind to more important matters.

GREGERS. What are they, Hjalmar?

HJALMAR. I wonder you haven't asked that before. But perhaps you haven't heard anyone speak of the invention?

GREGERS. The invention? No.

HJALMAR. Really? You haven't heard of it? Oh well, of course, up there in those outlandish parts—

GREGERS. Then you have made an invention?

HJALMAR. Not exactly made it yet, but I am working hard at it. You can surely understand that when I decided to take up photography, it was not with the idea of merely taking ordinary portraits.

GREGERS. No, that is what your wife was saying to me just now.

HJALMAR. I vowed to myself that, if I devoted my powers to this trade, I would so dignify it, that it should become both an art and a science. And so I decided to make this remarkable invention.

GREGERS. And what is the nature of the invention? What is the idea?

HJALMAR. My dear fellow, you mustn't ask me for details yet. It takes time, you know. And you mustn't suppose it is vanity that impels me. I assure you I don't work for my own sake. No, no; it is the object of my life that is in my thoughts night and day.

GREGERS. What object is that?

HJALMAR. Do you forget that poor old white-haired man?

GREGERS. Your poor father? Yes, but what exactly can you do for him?

HJALMAR. I can revive his dead self-respect by restoring the name of Ekdal to honour and dignity.

GREGERS. So that is the object of your life.

HJALMAR. Yes. I mean to rescue that poor shipwrecked being; for shipwrecked he was, when the storm broke over him. As soon as those horrible investigations were begun, he was no longer himself. That very pistol there—the same that we use to shoot rabbits with—has played its part in the tragedy of the Ekdals.

GREGERS. That pistol! Indeed?

HJALMAR. When the sentence of imprisonment was pronounced, he had his pistol in his hand—

GREGERS. Did he mean to—?

HJALMAR. Yes, but he did not dare. He was a coward; so dazed and so broken in spirit was he by that time. Can you conceive it? He, a soldier, a man who had shot nine bears and was the descendant of two lieutenant-colonels—one after the other, of course—. Can you conceive it, Gregers?

GREGERS. Yes, I can conceive it very well.

HJALMAR. I can't. And I will tell you how the pistol a second time played a part in the history of our house. When they had dressed him in prison clothes and put him under lock and key—that was a terrible time for me, my friend. I kept the blinds down on both my windows. When I peeped out, I saw the sun shining as usual. I could not understand it. I saw people going along the street, laughing and talking about casual matters. I could not understand that. It seemed to me as if the whole universe must be standing still as if it were eclipsed.

GREGERS. I felt exactly that when my mother died.

HJALMAR. It was at one of those moments that Hjalmar Ekdal pointed the pistol at his own heart.

GREGERS. Then you too meant to—?

HJALMAR. Yes.

GREGERS. But you didn't shoot?

HJALMAR. No. At that critical moment I gained the victory over myself. I went on living. But I can tell you it makes a call upon a man's courage to choose life under such conditions.

GREGERS. Well, that depends how you look at it.

HJALMAR. No, there is no question about it. But it was best so, for now I shall soon have completed my invention; and Relling thinks, and so do I, that my father will be allowed to wear his uniform again. I shall claim that as my only reward.

GREGERS. It is the matter of the uniform, then, that he—

HJALMAR. Yes, that is what he covets and yearns for most of all. You can't imagine how it cuts me to the heart. Every time we keep any little anniversary—such as our wedding-day, or anything of that sort—the old man comes in dressed in the uniform he used to wear in his happier days. But if he hears so much as a knock at the door, he hurries into his room again as fast as his poor old legs will carry him—because, you see, he daren't show himself like that to strangers. It is enough to break a son's heart to see it, I can tell you!

GREGERS. And about when do you suppose the invention will be ready?

HJALMAR. Oh, bless my soul!—you can't expect me to tell you to a day! A man who has the inventive genius can't control it exactly as he wishes. Its working depends in great measure on inspiration—on a momentary suggestion—and it is almost impossible to tell beforehand at what moment it will come.

GREGERS. But I suppose it is making good progress?

HJALMAR. Certainly it is making progress. Not a day passes without my turning it over in my mind. It possesses me entirely. Every afternoon, after I have had my lunch, I lock myself in the sitting-room where I can ruminate in peace. But it is no use trying to hurry me! that can do no good—Relling says so, too.

GREGERS. But don't you think all those arrangements in the attic there, distract you and divert your attention too much?

HJALMAR. Not a bit, not a bit; quite the contrary. You mustn't say that. It is impossible for me to be perpetually poring over the same exhausting train of ideas. I must have something as a secondary occupation, to fill in the blank hours when I am waiting for inspiration. Nothing that I am doing can prevent the flash of inspiration coming when it has to come.

GREGERS. My dear Hjalmar, I am beginning to think you have something of the wild duck in you.

HJALMAR. Something of the wild duck? How do you mean?

GREGERS. You have dived down and bitten yourself fast in the weeds.

HJALMAR. I suppose you refer to that well-nigh fatal blow that crippled my father, and me as well?

GREGERS. Not exactly that. I won't say that you have been wounded, like the duck; but you have got into a poisonous marsh, Hjalmar; you have contracted an insidious disease and have dived down to the bottom to die in the dark.

HJALMAR. I? Die in the dark? Look here, Gregers, you really must stop talking such nonsense.

GREGERS. Make your mind easy, I shall find a way to get you up to the surface again. I have got an object in life too, now; I discovered it yesterday.

HJALMAR. Maybe, but you will have the goodness to leave me out of it. I can assure you that—apart, of course, from my very natural melancholy—I feel as well as any man could wish to be.

GREGERS. That very fact is a result of the poison.

HJALMAR. Now, my dear Gregers, be good enough not to talk any more nonsense about diseases and poisons. I am not accustomed to conversation of that sort; in my house no one ever speaks to me about ugly things.

GREGERS. I can well believe it.

HJALMAR. Yes, that sort of thing doesn't suit me at all. And there *are* no marsh poisons, as you call them, here. The photographer's home is a humble one—that I know; and my means are small. But I am an inventor, let me tell you, and the breadwinner of a family. That raises me up above my humble circumstances.—Ah, here they come with the lunch!

(GINA *and* HEDVIG *bring in bottles of beer, a decanter of brandy, glasses, and so forth. At the same time* RELLING *and* MOLVIK *come in from the passage. They neither of them have hats or overcoats on;* MOLVIK *is dressed in black.*)

GINA (*arranging the table*). Ah, you have just come at the right moment.

RELLING. Molvik thought he could smell herring-salad, and then there was no holding him. Good-morning again, Ekdal.

HJALMAR. Gregers, let me introduce Mr. Molvik, and Doctor—ah, of course you know Relling?

GREGERS. Slightly, yes.

RELLING. Mr. Werle junior, isn't it? Yes, we have had one or two passages-at-arms up at the Höidal works. Have you just moved in?

GREGERS. I only moved in this morning.

RELLING. Molvik and I live just below you; so you haven't far to go for a doctor or a parson, if you should need them!

GREGERS. Thanks, it is quite possible I may; because yesterday we were thirteen at table.

HJALMAR. Oh, come—don't get on to ugly topics again!

RELLING. You may make your mind easy, Ekdal; it isn't you that events point to.

HJALMAR. I hope not, for my family's sake. But now let us sit down, and eat, drink, and be merry.

GREGERS. Shall we not wait for your father?

HJALMAR. No, he likes to have his lunch in his own room, later. Come along!

(*The men sit down at table, and eat and drink.* GINA *and* HEDVIG *move about, waiting on them.*)

RELLING. Molvik was disgracefully drunk again yesterday, Mrs. Ekdal.

GINA. What? Yesterday again?

RELLING. Didn't you hear him when I came home with him last night?

GINA. No, I can't say I did.

RELLING. It is just as well; Molvik was disgusting last night.

GINA. Is that true, Mr. Molvik?

MOLVIK. Let us draw a veil over last night's doings. Such things have no connection with my better self.

RELLING (to GREGERS). It comes over him like a spell; and then I have to go out on the spree with him. Mr. Molvik is a demoniac, you see.

GREGERS. A demoniac?

RELLING. Molvik is a demoniac, yes.

GREGERS. Hm!

RELLING. And demoniacs are not capable of keeping to a perfectly straight line through life; they have to stray a little bit now and then.—Well, and so you can still stand it up at those disgustingly dirty works?

GREGERS. I have stood it till now.

RELLING. And has your "demand," that you used to go about presenting, been met?

GREGERS. My demand? (Understanding him.) Oh, I see.

HJALMAR. What is this demand of yours, Gregers?

GREGERS. He is talking nonsense.

RELLING. It is perfectly true. He used to go round to all the cottagers' houses presenting what he called "the demand of the ideal."

GREGERS. I was young then.

RELLING. You are quite right, you were very young. And as for the "demand of the ideal," I never heard of your getting anyone to meet it while I was up there.

GREGERS. Nor since, either.

RELLING. Ah, I expect you have learnt enough to make you reduce the amount of your demand.

GREGERS. Never when I am dealing with a man who *is* a man.

HJALMAR. That seems to me very reasonable. A little butter, Gina.

RELLING. And a piece of pork for Molvik.

MOLVIK. Ugh! not pork!

(Knocking is heard at the attic door.)

HJALMAR. Open the door, Hedvig; father wants to come out.

(HEDVIG opens the door a little. Old EKDAL comes in, holding a fresh rabbit-skin. He shuts the door after him.)

EKDAL. Good-morning, gentlemen. I have had good sport; shot a big one.

HJALMAR. And you have skinned it without me—!

EKDAL. Yes, and salted it too. Nice, tender meat, rabbit's meat; and sweet, too; tastes like sugar. I hope you will enjoy your lunch, gentlemen! (*Goes into his room.*)

MOLVIK (*getting up*). Excuse me—I can't—I must go downstairs at once—

RELLING. Have some soda-water, you duffer!

MOLVIK (*hurrying up*). Ugh!—Ugh! (*Goes out by the outer door.*)

RELLING (*to* HJALMAR). Let us drink to the old sportsman's health.

HJALMAR (*clinking glasses with him*). To the old sportsman on the brink of the grave!—yes.

RELLING. To the grey-haired—(*drinks*)—tell me, is it grey hair he has got, or white?

HJALMAR. As a matter of fact, it is between the two; but, as far as that goes, he hasn't much hair of any kind left.

RELLING. Oh, well—a wig will take a man through the world. You are really very fortunate, you know, Ekdal. You have got a splendid object in life to strive after—

HJALMAR. And you may be sure I *do* strive after it.

RELLING. And you have got your clever wife, paddling about in her felt slippers, with that comfortable waddle of hers, making everything easy and cosy for you.

HJALMAR. Yes, Gina—(*nodding—to her*) you are an excellent companion to go through life with, my dear.

GINA. Oh, don't sit there making fun of me.

RELLING. And then your little Hedvig, Ekdal!

HJALMAR (*with emotion*). My child, yes! My child first and foremost. Come to me, Hedvig. (*Stroking her hair.*) What day is to-morrow?

HEDVIG (*shaking him*). No, you mustn't say anything about it, father.

HJALMAR. It makes my heart bleed to think what a meagre affair it will be—just a little festive gathering in the attic there—

HEDVIG. But that will be just lovely, father!

RELLING. Only wait till the great invention is finished, Hedvig!

HJALMAR. Yes, indeed—then you will see! Hedvig, I am determined to make your future safe. You shall live in comfort all your life. I shall demand something for you—something or other; and that shall be the poor inventor's only reward.

HEDVIG (*throwing her arms round his neck*). Dear, dear father!

RELLING (*to* GREGERS). Well, don't you find it very pleasant, for a change, to sit at a well-furnished table in the midst
of a happy family circle?

GREGERS. As far as I am concerned, I don't thrive in a
poisonous atmosphere.

RELLING. A poisonous atmosphere?

HJALMAR. Oh, don't begin that nonsense again!

GINA. Goodness knows there's no poisonous atmosphere
here, Mr. Werle; I air the place thoroughly every mortal day.

GREGERS (*rising from table*). No airing will drive away the
foulness I refer to.

HJALMAR. Foulness!

GINA. What do you think of that, Hjalmar!

RELLING. Excuse me, but isn't it more likely that you yourself have brought the foulness with you from the mines up
there?

GREGERS. It is just like you to suggest that what I bring to
a house is foulness.

RELLING (*going up to him*). Listen to me, Mr. Werle junior.
I have a strong suspicion that you are going about still with
the original unabridged "demand of the ideal" in your pocket.

GREGERS. I carry it in my heart.

RELLING. Carry the damned thing where you like; but I
advise you not to play at presenting demand notes here, as
long as I am in the house.

GREGERS. And suppose I do, nevertheless?

RELLING. Then you will go downstairs head first. Now you
know.

HJALMAR (*rising*). Really, Relling!

GREGERS. Well, throw me out, then—

GINA (*interposing*). You mustn't do any such thing, Mr.
Relling. But this I will say, Mr. Werle; it doesn't come well
from you, who made all that filthy mess with your stove, to
come in here and talk about foulness. (*A knock is heard at
the outer door.*)

HEDVIG. Somebody is knocking, mother.

HJALMAR. There now, I suppose we are going to be pes-
tered with people!

GINA. Let me go and see. (*She goes to the door and opens
it, starts, shudders and draws back.*) Oh, my goodness!

(*The elder* WERLE, *wearing a fur coat, steps into the doorway.*)

WERLE. Pardon me, but I fancy my son is living in this
house.

GINA (*breathlessly*). Yes.

HJALMAR (*coming up to them*). Mr. Werle, won't you be
so good as to—

WERLE. Thanks. I only want to speak to my son.

GREGERS. What do you want? Here I am.

WERLE. I want to speak to you in your own room.

GREGERS. In my own room—very well. (*Turns to go.*)

GINA. No, goodness knows it is not in a state for you to—

WERLE. Well, outside in the passage, then. I want to see you alone.

HJALMAR. You can do so here, Mr. Werle. Come into the sitting-room, Relling.

(HJALMAR *and* RELLING *go out to the right.* GINA *takes* HEDVIG *with her into the kitchen.*)

GREGERS. (*after a short pause*). Well, here we are, alone now.

WERLE. You made use of certain expressions last night—and, seeing that now you have taken up your abode with the Ekdals, I am driven to suppose that you are meditating some scheme or other against me.

GREGERS. I am meditating opening Hjalmar Ekdal's eyes. He shall see his position as it really is; that is all.

WERLE. Is this the object in life that you spoke of yesterday?

GREGERS. Yes. You have left me no other.

WERLE. Is it I that have upset your mind, Gregers?

GREGERS. You have upset my whole life. I am not thinking of what we said about my mother—but it is you I have to thank for the fact that I am harried and tortured by a guilt-laden conscience.

WERLE. Oh, it's your conscience that you are crazy about, is it?

GREGERS. I ought to have taken a stand against you long ago, when the trap was laid for Lieutenant Ekdal. I ought to have warned him, for I suspected then what the outcome of it would be.

WERLE. Yes, you should have spoken then.

GREGERS. I had not the courage to; I was so cowed and so scared of you. I can't tell you how afraid I was of you, both then and long after.

WERLE. You are not afraid of me now, apparently.

GREGERS. No, fortunately. The wrong that both I and—others have done to old Ekdal can never be undone; but I can set Hjalmar free from the falsehood and dissimulation that are dragging him down.

WERLE. Do you imagine you will do any good by that?

GREGERS. I am confident of it.

WERLE. Do you really think Hjalmar Ekdal is the sort of man to thank you for such a service?

GREGERS. Certainly.

WERLE. Hm!—we shall see.

GREGERS. And, besides, if I am to go on living, I must do something to cure my sick conscience.

WERLE. You will never cure it. Your conscience has been sickly from childhood. It is an inheritance from your mother, Gregers—the only thing she did leave you.

GREGERS (*with a bitter smile*). Haven't you managed yet to get over your mistaken calculation in thinking a fortune was coming to you with her?

WERLE. Don't let us talk about irrelevant matters. Are you determined on this course?—to set Hjalmar Ekdal on what you suppose to be the right scent?

GREGERS. Yes, quite determined.

WERLE. Well, in that case, I might have spared myself the trouble of coming here; because I suppose it isn't any use asking you to come home again.

GREGERS. No.

WERLE. And you won't come into the firm, either?

GREGERS. No.

WERLE. So be it. But now that I propose to make a new marriage, the estate will be divided between us.

GREGERS (*quickly*). No, I won't have that.

WERLE. You won't have it?

GREGERS. No, I won't have it. My conscience forbids it.

WERLE (*after a short pause*). Shall you go up to the works again?

GREGERS. No. I don't consider myself in your service any longer.

WERLE. But what are you going to do?

GREGERS. Only attain the object of my life; nothing else.

WERLE. Yes—but afterwards? What will you live on?

GREGERS. I have saved a little out of my pay.

WERLE. That won't last you long.

GREGERS. I think it will last out my time.

WERLE. What do you mean?

GREGERS. I shall answer no more questions.

WERLE. Good-bye, then, Gregers.

GREGERS. Good-bye. (WERLE *goes out.*)

HJALMAR (*peeping in*). Has he gone?

GREGERS. Yes. (HJALMAR *and* RELLING *come in; at the same time* GINA *and* HEDVIG *come from the kitchen.*)

RELLING. That lunch was a failure.

GREGERS. Get your things on, Hjalmar; you must come for a long walk with me.

HJALMAR. With pleasure. What did your father want? Was it anything to do with me?

GREGERS. Come along out; we must have a little talk. I will go and get my coat. (*Goes out.*)

GINA. You oughtn't to go out with him, Hjalmar.

RELLING. No, don't. Stay where you are.

HJALMAR (*taking his hat and coat*). What do you mean! When an old friend feels impelled to open his mind to me in private—?

RELLING. But, devil take it, can't you see the fellow is mad, crazy, out of his senses!

GINA. It is quite true. His mother had fits of that kind from time to time.

HJALMAR. Then he has all the more need of a friend's watchful eye. (*To* GINA.) Be sure and see that dinner is ready in good time. Good-bye just now. (*Goes out by the outer door.*)

RELLING. It's a great pity the fellow didn't go to hell in one of the mines at Höidal.

GINA. Good lord!—what makes you say that?

RELLING (*muttering*). Oh, I have my own reasons.

GINA. Do you think he is really mad?

RELLING. No, unfortunately. He is not madder than most people. But he has got a disease in his system, right enough.

GINA. What is the matter with him?

RELLING. I will tell you, Mrs. Ekdal. He is suffering from acute rectitudinal fever.

GINA. Rectitudinal fever?

HEDVIG. Is that a kind of disease?

RELLING. Indeed it is; it is a national disease; but it only crops up sporadically. (*Nods to* GINA.) Thanks for my lunch. (*Goes out by the outer door.*)

GINA (*walking about uneasily*). Ugh!—that Gregers Werle —he was always a horrid creature.

HEDVIG (*standing at the table and looking searchingly at her*). It all seems to me very odd.

ACT IV

(THE SAME SCENE.—*A photograph has just been taken; the camera, with a cloth thrown over it, a stand, a couple of chairs and a small table are in the middle of the floor. Afternoon light; the sun is on the point of setting; a little later it begins to grow dark.* GINA *is standing at the open door, with a small box and a wet glass plate in her hands, speaking to someone outside.*)

GINA. Yes, without fail. If I promise a thing, I keep my word. The first dozen shall be ready by Monday. Good-morning! (*Steps are heard going down the stair.* GINA *shuts the door, puts the plate in the box and replaces the whole in the camera.* HEDVIG *comes in from the kitchen.*)

HEDVIG. Are they gone?

GINA (*tidying the room*). Yes, thank goodness I have finished with them at last.

HEDVIG. Can you imagine why father hasn't come home yet?

GINA. Are you sure he is not downstairs with Relling?

HEDVIG. No, he isn't. I went down the back-stair just now to see.

GINA. And there is the dinner standing and getting cold for him.

HEDVIG. Think of father being so late! He is always so particular to come home in time for dinner.

GINA. Oh, he will come directly, no doubt.

HEDVIG. I wish he would; it seems so odd here to-day, somehow.

GINA (*calls out*). Here he is! (HJALMAR *comes in from the passage.*)

HEDVIG (*going to him*). Father, we have been waiting such a time for you!

GINA (*glancing at him*). What a long time you have been out, Hjalmar.

272

HJALMAR (*without looking at her*). I was rather long, yes. (*He takes off his overcoat.* GINA *and* HEDVIG *offer to help him, but he waves them aside.*)

GINA. Perhaps you have had your dinner with Mr. Werle.

HJALMAR (*hanging up his coat*). No.

GINA (*going towards the kitchen*). I will bring it in for you, then.

HJALMAR. No let it be. I don't want anything to eat now.

HEDVIG (*going up to him*). Aren't you well, father?

HJALMAR. Well? Oh, yes, well enough. Gregers and I had a very exhausting walk.

GINA. You shouldn't have done that, Hjalmar; you are not accustomed to it.

HJALMAR. Ah!—one has to get accustomed to a great many things in this world. (*Walks up and down.*) Has anyone been here while I was out?

GINA. No one but the engaged couple.

HJALMAR. No new orders?

GINA. No, not to-day.

HEDVIG. Someone is sure to come to-morrow, father, you will see.

HJALMAR. Let us hope so. To-morrow I intend to set to work as hard as I can.

HEDVIG. To-morrow! But—have you forgotten what day to-morrow is?

HJALMAR. Ah, that is true. Well, the day after to-morrow then. For the future I mean to do everything myself; I don't wish anyone to help me in the work at all.

GINA. But what's the good of that, Hjalmar? It will only make your life miserable. I can do the photographing all right, and you can give your time to the invention.

HEDVIG. And to the wild duck, father—and all the hens and rabbits.

HJALMAR. Don't talk such nonsense! From to-morrow I am never going to set foot in the attic again.

HEDVIG. But, father, you know you promised me that to-morrow we should have a little festivity—

HJALMAR. That's true. Well, from the day after to-morrow, then. As for that confounded wild duck, I should have great pleasure in wringing its neck!

HEDVIG (*with a scream*). The wild duck!

GINA. Did you ever hear such a thing!

HEDVIG (*pulling him by the arm*). Yes, but, father, it is my wild duck!

HJALMAR. That is why I won't do it. I haven't the heart—haven't the heart to do it, for your sake, Hedvig. But I feel in the bottom of my heart that I ought to do it. I ought not to tolerate under my roof a single creaure that has been in that man's hands.

GINA. But, good heavens, as it was from that ass Pettersen that grandfather got it—

HJALMAR (*walking up and down*). But there are certain claims—what shall I call them?—let us say claims of the ideal —absolute demands on a man, that he cannot set aside without injuring his soul.

HEDVIG (*following him about*). But think, father, the wild duck—the poor wild duck!

HJALMAR (*standing still*). Listen. I will spare it—for your sake. I will not hurt a hair of its head—well, as I said, I will spare it. There are greater difficulties than that to be tackled. Now you must go out for a little, as usual, Hedvig; it is dark enough now for you.

HEDVIG. No, I don't want to go out now.

HJALMAR. Yes, you must go out. Your eyes seem to me to be watering. All these vapours in here are not good for you. There is a bad atmosphere in this house.

HEDVIG. All right; I will run down the back-stair and go for a little stroll. My cloak and hat—? Oh, they are in my room. Father—promise you won't do the wild duck any harm while I am out.

HJALMAR. It shall not lose a feather of its head. (*Drawing her to him.*) You and I, Hedvig—we two!—now run along, dear. (HEDVIG *nods to her parents and goes out through the kitchen.* HJALMAR *walks up and down without raising his eyes.*) Gina!

GINA. Yes?

HJALMAR. From to-morrow—or let us say from the day after to-morrow—I should prefer to keep the household books myself.

GINA. You want to keep the household books too!

HJALMAR. Yes, or at any rate to keep account of what our income is.

GINA. Bless the man—that's simple enough!

HJALMAR. I am not sure; you seem to me to make what I give you go an astonishingly long way. (*Stands still and looks at her.*) How do you manage it?

GINA. Because Hedvig and I need so little.

HJALMAR. Is it true that father is so liberally paid for the copying he does for old Mr. Werle?

GINA. I don't know about its being so liberal. I don't know what is usually paid for that kind of work.

HJALMAR. Well, roughly speaking, what does he make? Tell me.

GINA. It varies; roughly speaking, I should say it is about what he costs us and a little pocket-money over.

HJALMAR. What he costs us! And you have never told me that before?

GINA. No, I couldn't. You seemed so pleased to think that he had everything from you.

HJALMAR. And in reality he had it from old Werle!

GINA. Oh, well, Mr. Werle has got plenty to spare.

HJALMAR. Light the lamp for me, please.

GINA (*lighting it*). Besides, we don't really know if it is Mr. Werle himself; it might be Graaberg—

HJALMAR. Why do you want to shift it on to Graaberg?

GINA. I know nothing about it; I only thought—

HJALMAR. Hm!

GINA. It wasn't me that got the copying for grandfather, remember that. It was Bertha, when she came to the house.

HJALMAR. Your voice seems to me to be unsteady.

GINA (*putting the shade on the lamp*). Does it?

HJALMAR. And your hands are shaking, aren't they?

GINA (*firmly*). Tell me straight, Hjalmar, what nonsense has he been telling you about me?

HJALMAR. Is it true—can it possibly be true—that there was anything between you and old Mr. Werle when you were in service there?

GINA. It's not true. Not then. Mr. Werle was always after me, true enough. And his wife thought there was something in it; and then there was the devil's own fuss. Not a moment's peace did she give me, that woman—and so I threw up my place.

HJALMAR. But afterwards?

GINA. Well, then I went home. And my mother—she wasn't what you thought her, Hjalmar; she talked a heap of nonsense to me about this, that and the other. Mr. Werle was a widower by that time, you know.

HJALMAR. Well, and then?

GINA. It's best you should know it. He never let me alone, till he had had his way.

HJALMAR (*clasping his hands*). And this is the mother of my child! How could you conceal such a thing from me?

GINA. It was wrong of me, I know. I ought to have told you about it long ago.

HJALMAR. You ought to have told me at the first,—then I should have known what sort of a woman you were.

GINA. But would you have married me, all the same?

HJALMAR. How can you suppose such a thing!

GINA. No; and that's why I didn't dare to tell you anything

then. I had got to love you so dearly, as you know. And I couldn't make myself utterly wretched—

HJALMAR (*walking about*). And this is my Hedvig's mother! And to know that I owe everything I see here— (*kicks at a chair*)—my whole home—to a favoured predecessor! Ah, that seducer, Werle!

GINA. Do you regret the fourteen—the fifteen years we have lived together?

HJALMAR (*standing in front of her*). Tell me this. Haven't you regretted every day—every hour—this web of lies you have enmeshed me in? Answer me! Haven't you really suffered agonies of regret and remorse?

GINA. My dear Hjalmar, I have had plenty to do thinking about the housekeeping and all the work there was to do every day—

HJALMAR. Then you never wasted a thought on what your past had been!

GINA. No—God knows I had almost forgotten all about that old trouble.

HJALMAR. Oh, this callous, insensate content! There is something so shocking about it, to me. Just think of it!—not a moment's regret.

GINA. But you tell me this, Hjalmar—what would have become of you if you hadn't found a wife like me?

HJALMAR. A wife like you!

GINA. Yes; I have always been a better business man than you, so to speak. Of course, it is true I am a year or two older than you.

HJALMAR. What would have become of me?

GINA. Yes, you had got into all sorts of bad ways when you first met me; you can't deny that.

HJALMAR. You talk about bad ways? You can't understand how a man feels when he is overcome with grief and despair —especially a man of my ardent temperament.

GINA. No, very likely not. And I oughtn't to say much about it anyway, because you made a real good husband as soon as you had a home of your own. And here we had got such a comfortable, cosy home, and Hedvig and I were just beginning to be able to spend a little bit on ourselves for food and clothes—

HJALMAR. In a swamp of deceit, yes.

GINA. If only that hateful fellow hadn't poked his nose in here!

HJALMAR. I used to think, too, that I had a happy home. It was a delusion. Where am I to look now for the necessary incentive to bring my invention into existence? Perhaps it will die with me; and then it will be your past, Gina, that has killed it.

GINA (*on the brink of tears*). Don't talk about such things, Hjalmar. I, that have all along only wanted what was best for you!

HJALMAR. I ask you—what has become of the dream of the bread-winner now? When I lay in there on the sofa, thinking over my invention, I used to have a presentiment that it would use up all my powers. I used to feel that when the great day came when I should hold my patent in my hands, that day would be the day of my—departure. And it was my dream, too, that you would be left as the well-to-do widow of the departed inventor.

GINA (*wiping away her tears*). You mustn't talk such nonsense, Hjalmar. I pray God I never may live to see the day when I am left a widow!

HJALMAR. Well, it is of no consequence now. It is all over now, anyway—all over now!

(GREGERS WERLE *opens the outer door cautiously and looks in.*)

GREGERS. May I come in?

HJALMAR. Yes, come in.

GREGERS (*advances with a beaming, happy face, and stretches out his hand to them*). Well, you dear people—! (*Looks alternately at one and the other, and whispers to* HJALMAR.) Haven't you done it yet?

HJALMAR (*aloud*). It is done.

GREGERS. It is?

HJALMAR. I have passed through the bitterest moment of my life.

GREGERS. But the most elevating too, I expect.

HJALMAR. Well, we have got it off our hands for the present, anyway.

GINA. God forgive you, Mr. Werle.

GREGERS (*greatly surprised*). But, I don't understand.

HJALMAR. What don't you understand?

GREGERS. After such a momentous enlightenment—an enlightenment that is to be the starting-point of a completely new existence—a real companionship, founded on truth and purged of all falsehood—

HJALMAR. Yes, I know; I know.

GREGERS. I certainly expected, when I came in, to be met by the light of transfiguration in the faces of you both. And yet I see nothing but gloomy, dull, miserable—

GINA (*taking off the lampshade*). Quite so.

GREGERS. I daresay you won't understand me, Mrs. Ekdal.

Well, well—you will in time. But you, Hjalmar? You must feel consecrated afresh by this great enlightenment?

HJALMAR. Yes, of course I do. This is to say—in a sort of way.

GREGERS. Because there is surely nothing in the world that can compare with the happiness of forgiveness and of lifting up a guilty sinner in the arms of love.

HJALMAR. Do you think it is so easy for a man to drink the bitter cup that I have just drained?

GREGERS. No, not for an ordinary man, I daresay. But for a man like you—!

HJALMAR. Good heavens, I know that well enough. But you mustn't rush me, Gregers. It takes time, you know.

GREGERS. You have a lot of the wild duck in you, Hjalmar.

(RELLING *has come in by the outer door.*)

RELLING. Hullo! are you talking about the old wild duck again?

HJALMAR. Yes, the one old Mr. Werle winged.

RELLING. Old Mr. Werle—? Is it him you are talking about?

HJALMAR. Him and—the rest of us.

RELLING (*half aloud, to* GREGERS). I wish the devil would fly away with you!

HJALMAR. What are you saying?

RELLING. I was breathing an earnest wish that this quack doctor would take himself off home. If he stays here he is capable of being the death of both of you.

GREGERS. No harm is coming to these two, Mr. Relling. I won't speak about Hjalmar; we know him. And as for his wife, I have little doubt that she, too, has the springs of trustworthiness and sincerity deep down in her heart.

GINA (*nearly crying*). Then you ought to have let me be as I was.

RELLING (*to* GREGERS). Would it be indiscreet to ask precisely what you think you are doing here?

GREGERS. I am trying to lay the foundation of a true marriage.

RELLING. Then you don't think Ekdal's marriage is good enough as it is?

GREGERS. Oh, it is as good a marriage as many others, I daresay. But a true marriage it has never yet been.

HJALMAR. You have never had your eyes opened to the demands of the ideal, Relling.

RELLING. Rubbish, my dear chap!—But, excuse me, Mr. Werle, how many "true marriages," roughly speaking, have you seen in your life?

GREGERS. I scarcely think I have seen a single one.

RELLING. Nor I either.

GREGERS. But I have seen such hundreds of marriages of the opposite kind, and I have had the opportunity of watching at close quarters the mischief such a marriage may do to both parties.

HJALMAR. A man's moral character may be completely sapped; that is the dreadful part of it.

RELLING. Well, I have never exactly been married, so I can't lay down the law on the matter. But this I do know, that the child is part of the marriage too—and you must leave the child in peace.

HJALMAR. Ah—Hedvig! My poor little Hedvig!

RELLING. Yes, you will have the goodness to keep Hedvig out of the matter. You two are grown people; goodness knows, you may play ducks and drakes with your happiness, for all I care. But you must walk warily with Hedvig, believe me; otherwise it may end in your doing her a great mischief.

HJALMAR. A great mischief?

RELLING. Yes, or it may end in her doing a great mischief to herself—and perhaps to others too.

GINA. But how can you know anything about it, Mr. Relling?

HJALMAR. There is no imminent danger for her eyes, is there?

RELLING. What I mean has nothing to do with her eyes at all. But Hedvig is at a critical age. She may take all sorts of strange fancies into her head.

GINA. There!—and to be sure she is doing that already! She has begun to be very fond of meddling with the fire, out in the kitchen. She calls it playing at houses-on-fire. Often and often I have been afraid she *would* set the house on fire.

RELLING. There you are. I knew it.

GREGERS (*to* RELLING). But how do you explain such a thing?

RELLING (*sulkily*). She is becoming a woman, my friend.

HJALMAR. So long as the child has me—! So long as my life lasts—! (*A knock is heard at the door.*)

GINA. Hush, Hjalmar; there is someone outside. (*Calls out.*) Come in! (MRS. SÖRBY, *dressed in outdoor clothes, comes in.*)

MRS. SÖRBY. Good-evening!

GINA (*going to her*). Bertha!—is it you!

MRS. SÖRBY. Certainly it's me! But perhaps I have come at an inconvenient time?

HJALMAR. Not at all; a messenger from *that* house—

MRS. SÖRBY (*to* GINA). To tell you the truth, I rather hoped I shouldn't find your men-folk at home just now; I just ran up to have a little chat with you and say good-bye.

GINA. Oh? Are you going away?

MRS. SÖRBY. Early to-morrow morning, yes—up to Höidal. Mr. Werle went this afternoon. (*Meaningly, to* GREGERS.) He asked to be remembered to you.

GINA. Just fancy—!

HJALMAR. So Mr. Werle has gone away?—and now you are going to join him?

MRS. SÖRBY. Yes, what do you say to that, Mr. Ekdal?

HJALMAR. Be careful what you are doing, I say.

GREGERS. I can explain. My father and Mrs. Sörby are going to be married!

HJALMAR. Going to be married!

GINA. Oh, Bertha! Has it come to that?

RELLING (*his voice faltering a little*). Is this really true?

MRS. SÖRBY. Yes, my dear Relling, it is perfectly true.

RELLING. Are you going to marry again?

MRS. SÖRBY. Yes, that's what it has come to. Mr. Werle has got a special licence, and we are going to be married very quietly up at the works.

GREGERS. Then I suppose I must wish you happiness, like a good stepson.

MRS. SÖRBY. Many thanks—if you mean it. And I am sure I hope it will mean happiness, both for Mr. Werle and for me.

RELLING. You can confidently hope that. Mr. Werle never gets drunk—so far as I know; and I don't imagine he is in the habit of ill-treating his wives, either, as the late lamented horse-doctor used to do.

MRS. SÖRBY. Sörby is dead; let him alone. And even he had his good points.

RELLING. Mr. Werle has points that are better, I expect.

MRS. SÖRBY. At any rate he hasn't wasted all that was best in him. A man who does that must take the consequences.

RELLING. To-night I shall go out with Molvik.

MRS. SÖRBY. That is wrong of you. Don't do that—for my sake, don't.

RELLING. There is nothing else for it. (*To* HJALMAR.) You can come too, if you like.

GINA. No, thank you. Hjalmar is not going with you to places of *that* kind.

HJALMAR (*half aloud in an irritated voice*). Oh, do hold your tongue!

RELLING. Good-bye, Mrs.—Werle. (*Goes out at the outer door.*)

GREGERS (*to* MRS. SÖRBY). You and Doctor Relling seem to know each other pretty well.

MRS. SÖRBY. Yes, we have known each other many years. At one time it looked as if our friendship were going to ripen into something warmer.

GREGERS. But, luckily for you, I suppose, it didn't.

MRS. SÖRBY. You may well say so. But I have always been chary of giving way to impulse. A woman mustn't absolutely throw herself away, either.

GREGERS. Are you not in the least afraid of my letting my father get a hint of this old acquaintance?

MRS. SÖRBY. Of course I have told him about it myself.

GREGERS. Indeed?

MRS. SÖRBY. Your father knows every single thing with a grain of truth in it that anyone could find to tell him about me. I have told him absolutely everything; it was the first thing I did when he made it evident what his intentions were.

GREGERS. Then you have been more frank than is usually the case, I expect.

MRS. SÖRBY. I always have been frank. It is the best way for us women.

HJALMAR. What do you say to that, Gina?

GINA. Oh, women are all so different. Some are built that way; some aren't.

MRS. SÖRBY. Well, Gina, I believe now that the wisest line to take is the one I have taken. And Mr. Werle hasn't concealed anything on his side, either. It is that, you see, that knits us so closely together. Now he can sit and talk to me as fearlessly as a child. That is a thing he has never had a chance of doing yet. All his young days, and for the best years of his life, when he was a healthy and vigorous man, he had to sit and listen to nothing but sermons on his sins. And very often the point of the sermons turned on the most imaginary offences—at least, so it seems to me.

GINA. Yes, it's quite certain that's true.

GREGERS. If you ladies are going into those subjects, I had better take my leave.

MRS. SÖRBY. Oh, you can stay, for that matter. I won't say a word more. But I wanted you to understand that I have done nothing deceitful or in the least degree underhand. Very likely you think I am coming in for a great slice of luck; and so I am, in a way. But, all the same, I don't believe I shall be taking more than I shall be giving. At any rate I shall never forsake him; and what I *can* do is to look after him and care for him as no one else can, now that he will soon be helpless.

HJALMAR. Soon be helpless?

GREGERS (*to* MRS. SÖRBY). Don't speak of that here.

MRS. SÖRBY. There is no use concealing it any longer, however much he would like to. He is going blind.

HJALMAR (*with a start*). Going blind? That is extraordinary. Is he going blind too?

GINA. A great many people do.

MRS. SÖRBY. And one can well imagine what that means to a business man. Well, I shall try to use my eyes for him as well as I can. But I mustn't stay any longer; I am frightfully busy just now.—Oh, I was to tell you this, Mr. Ekdal, that if there were anything in which Mr. Werle could be of service to you, you were just to go to Graaberg about it.

GREGERS. A message that I should think Hjalmar Ekdal would be *very* grateful for!

MRS. SÖRBY. Really? I rather think there was a time when—

GINA. He's quite right, Bertha. Hjalmar doesn't need to take anything from Mr. Werle now.

HJALMAR (*slowly and weightily*). Will you give my kind regards to your future husband, and say that I mean as soon as possible to call on Graaberg—

GREGERS. What! Do you really mean to do that?

HJALMAR. To call on Graaberg, I say, and ask for an account of the sum I owe his employer. I will pay that debt of honour—ha! ha! debt of honour is a good name for it!—but enough of that. I will pay the whole sum, with five per cent. interest.

GINA. But, my dear Hjalmar, we have no money to do that with, Heaven knows!

HJALMAR. Will you tell your *fiancé* that I am working busily at my invention. Will you tell him that what keeps up my strength for this exhausting task is the desire to be quit of a painful burden of debt. That is why I am working at this invention. The whole proceeds of it shall be devoted to freeing myself from the obligation under which your future husband's pecuniary advances have laid me.

MRS. SÖRBY. Something or other has happened in this house.

HJALMAR. You are right.

MRS. SÖRBY. Well—good-bye, then. I had something I wanted to talk over with you, Gina; but that must wait till another time. Good-bye! (HJALMAR *and* GREGERS *bow silently;* GINA *follows her to the door.*)

HJALMAR. Not farther than the door, Gina! (MRS. SÖRBY *goes out;* GINA *shuts the door after her.*) There, Gregers. Now I have got that load of debt off my hands.

GREGERS. Soon you will, any way.

HJALMAR. I think my attitude may be called correct.

GREGERS. You are the man I always took you for.

HJALMAR. In certain cases it is impossible to overlook the claim of the ideal. As breadwinner of the family, I have to writhe and smart under this. I can tell you it is by no means a joke for a man, who is not well off, to get free from a debt of many years' standing, over which the dust of oblivion, so to speak, has collected. But that makes no difference; the manhood in me demands its rights too.

GREGERS (*putting his hands on his shoulders*). Dear Hjalmar, wasn't it a good thing I came?

HJALMAR. Yes.

GREGERS. Hasn't it been a good thing that you have got a clear knowledge of the whole situation?

HJALMAR (*a little impatiently*). Of course it's a good thing. But there is one thing that goes against my sense of what is right.

GREGERS. What is that?

HJALMAR. It is this. I—well, I don't know whether I ought to speak so freely about your father?

GREGERS. Don't think of me in the matter at all.

HJALMAR. Very well. It seems to me a very aggravating thought that now it isn't I, but he, that will realise the true marriage.

GREGERS. How can you say such a thing?

HJALMAR. It certainly is so. Your father and Mrs. Sörby are entering upon a marriage which is based upon complete confidence, based upon an entire and unrestricted frankness on both sides; they conceal nothing from each other; there is no dissimulation at the back of things; they have proclaimed, if I may so express myself, a mutual forgiveness of sins.

GREGERS. Well, what if they have?

HJALMAR. Well, surely that is the whole thing. That is all that this difficult position needs, to lay the foundations of a true marriage—you said so yourself.

GREGERS. But this is a different thing altogether, Hjalmar. Surely you are not going to compare either you or your wife with these two—well, you know what I mean?

HJALMAR. Still I can't help feeling that in all this there is something that sorely injures my sense of justice. It looks for all the world as though there were no such thing as a just Providence at all.

GINA. Gracious, Hjalmar!—for heaven's sake don't say such a thing.

GREGERS. Ahem!—I think we had better not enter into that question.

HJALMAR. But, on the other hand, I certainly seem to see the directing finger of destiny in it, all the same. He is going blind.

GINA. Perhaps it isn't certain that he is.

HJALMAR. There is no doubt he is. We ought not to doubt that he will, anyway; for it is just that very fact that constitutes the just retribution. He himself, in his time, has blinded the eyes of a credulous fellow-creature.

GREGERS. Alas, he has done that to a good many!

HJALMAR. And now comes the inexorable, mysterious power, and demands this man's own eyes.

GINA. Hjalmar, how can you dare say such dreadful things! You make me all of a tremble.

HJALMAR. It is good for one sometimes to plunge down into the dark side of life. (HEDVIG, *in her hat and coat, comes in at the outer door, breathless and looking happy*.)

GINA. Are you back again?

HEDVIG. Yes, I didn't want to stay out any longer; and it was lucky I didn't, for I have just met some one at the door.

HJALMAR. Mrs. Sörby, I suppose.

HEDVIG. Yes.

HJALMAR (*walking up and down*). I hope you have seen her for the last time. (*A pause.* HEDVIG, *obviously disheartened, looks first at one and then at the other of them, as if to try and read their thoughts*.)

HEDVIG (*going up to her father coaxingly*). Father!

HJALMAR. Well, what is it, Hedvig?

HEDVIG. Mrs. Sörby had something with her for me.

HJALMAR (*standing still*). For you?

HEDVIG. Yes, it is something for to-morrow.

GINA. Bertha has always sent some little thing for her birthday.

HJALMAR. What is it?

HEDVIG. You mustn't know anything about it yet. Mother is to give it to me in bed the first thing to-morrow morning.

HJALMAR. All this mystery!—and I am to be kept in the dark, I suppose.

HEDVIG (*quickly*). No, you may see it if you like. It is a big letter. (*Takes a letter out of the pocket of her coat.*)

HJALMAR. A letter, too?

HEDVIG. She only gave me the letter. The rest of it is coming afterwards, I suppose. Just fancy—a letter! I have never had a letter before. And there is "Miss" on the envelope. (*Reads.*) "Miss Hedvig Ekdal." Think of it—that's me!

HJALMAR. Let me see the letter.

HEDVIG (*giving it to him*). There you are.

HJALMAR. It is old Mr. Werle's writing.

GINA. Are you sure, Hjalmar?

HJALMAR. See for yourself.

GINA. Do you suppose I know anything about such things?

HJALMAR. Hedvig, may I open the letter—and read it?

GINA. Not to-night, Hjalmar. It is for to-morrow, you know.

HEDVIG (softly). Oh, can't you let him read it! It is sure to be something nice, and then father will be happy and things will get pleasant again.

HJALMAR. Then I have leave to open it?

HEDVIG. Yes, please, father. It will be such fun to see what it is.

HJALMAR. Very well. (*He opens the letter, takes out a paper that is in it, and reads it through with evident astonishment.*) What on earth is this?

GINA. What does it say?

HEDVIG. Yes, father—do tell us.

HJALMAR. Be quiet. (*Reads it through again; he has turned pale, but collects himself.*) It is a deed of gift, Hedvig.

HEDVIG. Really? What am I getting?

HJALMAR. Read it for yourself. (HEDVIG *goes to the lamp and reads.* HJALMAR *clasps his hands and says half aloud.*) The eyes! The eyes!—and then this letter.

HEDVIG (*who stops reading*). Yes, but it seems to me it is grandfather who is getting it.

HJALMAR (*taking the letter from her*). Gina—can you understand this?

GINA. I know nothing whatever about it. Tell me what it is.

HJALMAR. Old Mr. Werle writes to Hedvig that her old grandfather need not bother himself with copying work any longer, but that for the future he will be entitled to five pounds a month paid from the office—

GREGERS. Aha!

HEDVIG. Five pounds, mother!—I read that.

GINA. How nice for grandfather!

HJALMAR. Five pounds a month, as long as he needs it; that means, naturally, till his death.

GINA. Well, then, he is provided for, poor old man.

HJALMAR. But that is not all. You didn't read the rest, Hedvig. Afterwards the gift is to be transferred to you.

HEDVIG. To me! All that?

HJALMAR. You are assured the same amount for the whole of your life, it says. Do you hear that, Gina?

GINA. Yes, yes, I hear.

HEDVIG. Just think of it—I am to get all that money. (*Shakes him.*) Father, father, aren't you glad?

HJALMAR (*moving away from her*). Glad! (*Walks up and down.*) What a future—what a picture it calls up to my eyes! It is Hedvig for whom he provides so liberally—Hedvig!

GINA. Yes, it's Hedvig's birthday—

HEDVIG. You shall have it all the same, father! Of course I shall give all the money to you and mother.

HJALMAR. To your mother, yes!—that's just the point.

GREGERS. Hjalmar, this is a trap he is laying for you.

HJALMAR. Do you think this is another trap?

GREGERS. When he was here this morning, he said: "Hjalmar Ekdal is not the man you imagine he is."

HJALMAR. Not the man—!

GREGERS. "You will see," he said.

HJALMAR. You will see whether I allow myself to be put off with a bribe—

HEDVIG. Mother, what does it all mean?

GINA. Go away and take your things off. (HEDVIG *goes out by the kitchen door, half in tears.*)

GREGERS. Yes, Hjalmar—now we shall see who is right, he or I.

HJALMAR (*tears the paper slowly across, and lays the two pieces on the table*). That is my answer.

GREGERS. That is what I expected.

HJALMAR (*goes over to* GINA, *who is standing by the stove, and speaks to her in a low voice*). No more lies, now. If everything was over between you and him when you—when you began to love me, as you call it, why was it that he put us in a position to marry?

GINA. I suppose he thought he would get a footing in the house.

HJALMAR. Only that? Wasn't he afraid of a certain possibility?

GINA. I don't understand what you mean.

HJALMAR. I want to know, whether—whether your child has the right to live under my roof.

GINA (*drawing herself up, with eyes flashing*). Can you ask that!

HJALMAR. You shall answer this question. Does Hedvig belong to me—or to—? Well?

GINA (*looking at him with cold bravado*). I don't know.

HJALMAR (*in a trembling voice*). You don't know?

GINA. How should I know? A woman like me—

HJALMAR (*quietly, as he turns away from her*). Then I have no longer any part in this house.

GREGERS. Think well what you are doing, Hjalmar!

HJALMAR (*putting on his overcoat*). There is nothing here for a man like me to think about.

GREGERS. Indeed there is a tremendous lot here for you to think about. You three must be together, if you are going to reach the goal of self-sacrificing forgiveness.

HJALMAR. I have no desire for that. Never! Never! My hat! (*Takes his hat.*) My home has fallen into ruins round me. (*Bursts into tears.*) Gregers, I have no child now!

HEDVIG (*who has opened the kitchen door*). What are you saying! (*Goes to him.*) Father! Father!

GINA. Now, what's to happen!

HJALMAR. Don't come near me, Hedvig! Go away—go away! I can't bear to see you. Ah—the eyes! Good-bye. (*Goes towards the door.*)

HEDVIG (*clings to him, screaming*). No, no! Don't turn away from me.

GINA (*crying out*). Look at the child, Hjalmar! Look at the child!

HJALMAR. I won't! I can't! I must get out of here—away from all this! (*He tears himself away from* HEDVIG *and goes out by the outer door.*)

HEDVIG (*with despair in her eyes*). He is going away from us, mother! He is going away! He will never come back!

GINA. Don't cry, Hedvig. Father will come back.

HEDVIG (*throws herself on the sofa, sobbing*). No, no,—he will never come back any more.

GREGERS. Will you believe that I meant all for the best, Mrs. Ekdal?

GINA. I almost believe you did; but, God forgive you, all the same.

HEDVIG (*lying on the sofa*). I think this will kill me! What have I done to him? Mother, you *must* get him home again!

GINA. Yes, yes; only be quiet, and I will go out and look for him. (*Puts on her coat.*) Perhaps he has gone down to Relling. But, if I go, you mustn't lie there crying. Will you promise me that?

HEDVIG (*sobbing convulsively*). Yes, I won't cry—if only father comes back.

GREGERS (*to* GINA, *as she goes out*). Would it not be better, anyway, to let him first fight his bitter fight to the end?

GINA. He can do that afterwards. First and foremost we must get the child quiet. (*Goes out.*)

HEDVIG (*sitting upright and wiping away her tears*). Now you must tell me what is the matter. Why won't father have anything to do with me any more?

GREGERS. You mustn't ask that until you are a big girl and grown up.

HEDVIG (*gulping down her tears*). But I can't go on being so wretchedly miserable till I am a big girl and grown up.

I believe I know what it is—perhaps I am not really father's child.

GREGERS (*uneasily*). How on earth could that be?

HEDVIG. Mother might have found me. And now perhaps father has found that out; I have read of such things.

GREGERS. Well, even if it were so—

HEDVIG. Yes, it seems to me he might love me just as much in spite of that—even more. We had the wild duck sent us as a present, too, but all the same I love it very dearly.

GREGERS (*to divert her thoughts*). The wild duck—that's true! Let's talk about the wild duck a little, Hedvig.

HEDVIG. The poor wild duck!—he can't bear to look at it any more, either. Just fancy, he wanted to wring its neck.

GREGERS. Oh, he won't do that.

HEDVIG. No, but he said so. And I think it was so unkind of him to say so, because I say a prayer every night for the wild duck, and pray that it may be preserved from death and anything that will harm it.

GREGERS (*looking at her*). Do you say your prayers at night?

HEDVIG. Of course.

GREGERS. Who taught you?

HEDVIG. I taught myself. It was once when father was very ill and had leeches on his neck, and said he was at the point of death.

GREGERS. Really?

HEDVIG. So I said a prayer for him when I had got into bed—and since then I have gone on doing it.

GREGERS. And now you pray for the wild duck too?

HEDVIG. I thought it would be best to put the wild duck in the prayer too, because it was so sickly at first.

GREGERS. Do you say prayers in the morning, too?

HEDVIG. No, of course I don't.

GREGERS. Why don't you say them in the morning as well?

HEDVIG. Because in the morning it is light, and there is nothing to be afraid of.

GREGERS. And your father wanted to wring the neck of the wild duck that you love so dearly?

HEDVIG. No, he said it would be a great pleasure to him to do it, but that he would spare it for my sake; and I think that was very nice of father.

GREGERS (*coming nearer to her*). But now, suppose you sacrificed the wild duck, of your own free will, for his sake?

HEDVIG (*getting up*). The wild duck?

GREGERS. Suppose now you gave up for him, as a free-will offering, the dearest possession you have in the world?

HEDVIG. Do you think it would help?

GREGERS. Try it, Hedvig.

HEDVIG (*gently, with glistening eyes*). Yes, I will try it.

GREGERS. Have you really the strength of mind to do it, do you think?

HEDVIG. I will ask grandfather to shoot the wild duck for me.

GREGERS. Yes, do. But not a word about anything of the kind to your mother.

HEDVIG. Why not?

GREGERS. She doesn't understand us.

HEDVIG. The wild duck! I will try it the first thing to-morrow morning. (GINA *comes in by the outer door.* HEDVIG *goes to her.*) Did you find him, mother?

GINA. No, but I heard he had gone out and taken Relling with him.

GREGERS. Are you certain?

GINA. Yes, the porter's wife said so. Molvik has gone with them too, she said.

GREGERS. And this, when his mind is so sorely in need of fighting in solitude—!

GINA (*taking off her things*). Oh, you never know what men are going to do. Heaven knows where Relling has taken him off to! I ran over to Mrs. Eriksen's, but they weren't there.

HEDVIG (*struggling with her tears*). Oh, suppose he never comes back any more!

GREGERS. He'll come back. I have a message to give him in the morning, and you will see how he will come home. You may go to sleep quite hopefully about that, Hedvig. Good-night. (*Goes out.*)

HEDVIG (*throws herself into* GINA'S *arms, sobbing*). Mother! Mother!

GINA (*patting her on the back and sighing*). Yes, yes,— Relling was right. This is what happens when mad folk come presenting these demands that no one can make head or tail of.

ACT V

(THE SAME SCENE.—*The cold grey light of morning is shining in; wet snow is lying on the large panes of the sky-light.* GINA *comes in from the kitchen wearing a high apron and carrying a broom and a duster, and goes towards the sitting-room door. At the same moment* HEDVIG *comes hurriedly in from the passage.*)

GINA (*stopping*). Well?

HEDVIG. Mother, I rather think he is downstairs with Relling—

GINA. Look at that, now!

HEDVIG. Because the porter's wife said she heard two people come in with Relling when he came home last night.

GINA. That's just what I thought.

HEDVIG. But that is no good if he won't come up to us.

GINA. At any rate I shall be able to go down and have a talk with him.

(*Old* EKDAL *comes in from his room, in dressing-gown and slippers and smoking his pipe.*)

EKDAL. Look here, Hjalmar—. Isn't Hjalmar at home?

GINA. No, he has gone out.

EKDAL. So early? and in such a heavy snowstorm? Well, well; that's his affair. I can take my morning stroll by myself. (*He opens the attic door;* HEDVIG *helps him. He goes in, and she shuts the door after him.*)

HEDVIG (*in an undertone*). Just think, mother—when poor grandfather hears that father wants to go away from us!

GINA. Nonsense—grandfather mustn't hear anything about it. It's God's mercy he wasn't here yesterday when all that rumpus was going on.

HEDVIG. Yes, but—

(GREGERS *comes in by the outer door.*)

GREGERS. Well? Have you any trace of him yet?

GINA. He is most likely downstairs with Relling, I am told.

GREGERS. With Relling! Can he really have been out with that fellow?

GINA. That he has, evidently.

GREGERS. Yes, but he—who so urgently needed solitude to pull himself seriously together—!

GINA. You may well say so.

(RELLING *comes in from the passage.*)

HEDVIG (*going up to him*). Is father in your rooms?

GINA (*at the same time*). Is he there?

RELLING. Certainly he is.

HEDVIG. And you never told us!

RELLING. Yes, I know I'm a beast. But first of all I had the other beast to keep in order—our demoniac gentleman, I mean—and after that I fell so dead asleep that—

GINA. What does Hjalmar say to-day?

RELLING. He doesn't say anything at all.

HEDVIG. Hasn't he talked to you at all?

RELLING. Not a blessed word.

GREGERS. Of course not; I can understand that very well.

GINA. But what is he doing with himself, then?

RELLING. He is lying on the sofa, snoring.

GINA. Is he? Hjalmar's a fine hand at snoring.

HEDVIG. Is he asleep? Can he sleep?

RELLING. Well, it looks like it.

GREGERS. It is easy to understand that; after the conflict of soul that has torn him—

GINA. Besides, he has never been accustomed to rambling out at night.

HEDVIG. I daresay it is a good thing he is getting some sleep, mother.

GINA. I think so, too; and it would be a pity to wake him up too soon. Many thanks, Mr. Relling. Now first of all I must get the house cleaned up and tidied a bit, and then—. Come and help me, Hedvig. (*She goes with* HEDVIG *into the sitting-room.*)

GREGERS (*turning to* RELLING). What do you think of the spiritual upheaval that is going on in Hjalmar Ekdal?

RELLING. As far as I am concerned, I haven't noticed any spiritual upheaval going on in him at all.

GREGERS. What! After such a crisis, when the whole of his life has been shifted on to a new basis? How can you suppose that a personality like Hjalmar's—

RELLING. Personality!—he? Even if he ever had any tendency to any such abnormality as you call "personality," it has been absolutely rooted out of him and destroyed when he was a boy. I can assure you of that.

GREGERS. It would certainly be very strange if that were

true, in the case of a man brought up with such loving care
as he was.

RELLING. By those two crazy hysterical maiden aunts of
his, do you mean?

GREGERS. Let me tell you that they were women who were
never oblivious to the demands of the ideal—but if I say
that, you will only begin making fun of me again.

RELLING. No, I am in no humour for that. Besides, I know
all about them. He has delivered himself to me of any amount
of rhetoric about these two "soul-mothers" of his. But I don't
think he has much to thank them for. Ekdal's misfortune is
that all his life he has been looked upon as a shining light
in his own circle—

GREGERS. And is he not that?—in profundity of mind, I
mean?

RELLING. I have never noticed anything of the sort. His
father believed it, I daresay; the poor old lieutenant has been
a simpleton all his days.

GREGERS. He has been a man with a childlike mind all his
days; that is a thing you can't understand.

RELLING. All right! But when our dear sweet Hjalmar
became a student of sorts, he was at once accepted amongst
his fellow-students as the great light of the future. Good-
looking he was, too, the nincompoop—pink and white—just
what common girls like for a lover; and with his susceptible
disposition and that sympathetic voice of his, and the facility
with which he declaimed other people's verses and other
people's thoughts—

GREGERS (*indignantly*). Is it Hjalmar Ekdal that you are
speaking of like this?

RELLING. Yes, by your leave; for that is the real man,
instead of the idol you have been falling on your knees to.

GREGERS. I venture to think I was not so blind as all that.

RELLING. Well, it's not far from the truth, anyway. You
are a sick man too, you see.

GREGERS. You are right there.

RELLING. Quite so. You are suffering from a complicated
complaint. First of all there is that debilitating rectitudinal
fever of yours; and then, what's worse, you are always in a
raving delirium of hero-worship—you must always have some
object of admiration that you really have no concern with.

GREGERS. I certainly can only find that by looking outside
of my own concerns.

RELLING. But you are so monstrously mistaken as to these
miraculous beings you think you find around you. This is
just another case of your coming to a workman's cottage to

present your "demands of the ideal"; but the people in this house are all insolvent.

GREGERS. If you haven't any higher opinion of Hjalmar Ekdal than that, how can you find any pleasure in being always hand-in-glove with him?

RELLING. Bless your heart—I am supposed to be a kind of doctor, though you mightn't think it; and it is only my duty to pay some attention to the poor invalids I live in the house with.

GREGERS. Really! Is Hjalmar Ekdal a sick man too, then?

RELLING. All the world is sick, pretty nearly—that's the worst of it.

GREGERS. And what treatment are you using for Hjalmar?

RELLING. My usual one. I am trying to keep up the make-believe of life in him.

GREGERS. The make-believe? I don't think I heard you aright?

RELLING. Yes, I said make-believe. That is the stimulating principle of life, you know.

GREGERS. May I ask what sort of a make-believe enters into the scheme of Hjalmar's life?

RELLING. No, you mayn't. I never disclose secrets like that to quacks. You were making an even worse mess of his case than I. My method has stood the test of trial. I have applied it in Molvik's case too. I have made a "demoniac" of him. That is the blister I have put on *his* neck.

GREGERS. Isn't he a demoniac, then?

RELLING. What in heaven's name do you mean by "being a demoniac"? That is only a bit of make-believe I invented to keep the life in him. If I hadn't done that, the poor honest wretch would have given way to self-contempt and despair years ago. And the same with the old lieutenant there! But he has happened to hit upon the cure by himself.

GREGERS. Lieutenant Ekdal? what of him?

RELLING. Well, what do you make of an old bear-stalker, like him, going into that dark attic there to shoot rabbits? There isn't a happier sportsman in the world than that poor old man playing about in there in that scrap-heap. The four or five withered Christmas trees that he has kept are the same to him as the great tall live trees in the Höidal forests; the cocks and hens are the wild-fowl in the tree-tops; and the rabbits, that lop about all over the attic floor, are the big game this famous backwoodsman used to pit himself against.

GREGERS. Poor old man! Yes, he has indeed had to endure the quenching of all his youthful ideals.

RELLING. And, while I think of it, Mr. Werle junior—don't

use that outlandish word "ideals." There is a good home-grown word—"falsehoods."

GREGERS. Do you really think the two things are the same?

RELLING. Just as nearly as typhus and putrid fever are.

GREGERS. Doctor Relling, I won't give in till I have rescued Hjalmar from your clutches.

RELLING. So much the worse for him. If you take away make-believe from the average man, you take away his happiness as well. (*To* HEDVIG, *who has come in from the sitting-room.*) Well, little wild-duck mother, I am going down now to see whether your daddy is still lying pondering over the wonderful invention. (*Goes out by the outer door.*)

GREGERS (*going up to* HEDVIG). I can see by your face that the deed isn't done yet.

HEDVIG. What deed? Oh, the wild duck. No.

GREGERS. Your courage failed you when the time came to do it, I suppose?

HEDVIG. No, it's not that. But when I woke up early this morning and remembered all we said, it all seemed so strange to me.

GREGERS. Strange?

HEDVIG. Yes, I don't know—. Last night, when we were talking about it, it seemed such a splendid idea; but, after my sleep, when I remembered it again, it all seemed different.

GREGERS. I see; I suppose it was impossible for you to grow up here without something being injured in you.

HEDVIG. I don't care anything about that; if only father would come up, then—

GREGERS. Ah, if only your eyes had been opened to what makes life worth living—if you possessed the true, happy, courageous spirit of self-sacrifice—you would see how you would be able to bring him up to you. But I have faith in you still, Hedvig. (*Goes out by the outer door.* HEDVIG *walks up and down; she is just going into the kitchen, but at the same moment a knock is heard on the attic door; she goes and opens it a little, and old* EKDAL *comes out, after which she shuts the door again.*)

EKDAL. Hm! There's not much pleasure in taking one's morning walk alone.

HEDVIG. Haven't you felt inclined for any shooting, grand-father?

EKDAL. It isn't the weather for shooting to-day. Too dark in there, you can hardly see a hand's length.

HEDVIG. Have you never felt inclined to shoot anything else but the rabbits?

EKDAL. Why? Aren't the rabbits good enough sport?

HEDVIG. Yes, but the wild duck?

EKDAL. Ho! ho!—are you afraid I shall shoot your wild duck for you? Never in the world: I would never do that.

HEDVIG. No, I suppose you couldn't; wild duck must be very hard to shoot.

EKDAL. Couldn't! I should rather think I could.

HEDVIG. How would you manage it, grandfather?—not my wild duck, I mean, but with others?

EKDAL. I would see that I shot them in the breast, you know, because that is the surest place. And you must shoot against the lie of the feathers, do you understand—not with the lie of the feathers.

HEDVIG. Do they die then, grandfather?

EKDAL. Certainly they do, if you shoot properly. Well, I must go in and make myself tidy. Hm!—you understand— hm! (*Goes into his room.* HEDVIG *waits a little; glances at the door, then goes to the bookcase, stands on tiptoe, and takes the pistol down from the shelf and looks at it.* GINA *comes in from the sitting-room, with her broom and duster.* HEDVIG *hastily puts down the pistol unnoticed.*)

GINA. Don't go rummaging among your father's things, Hedvig.

HEDVIG (*moving away from the bookcase*). I only wanted to put things straight a little.

GINA. You had much better go into the kitchen and see if the coffee is keeping hot; I will take his tray with me, when I go down to him.

(HEDVIG *goes out.* GINA *begins to sweep and clean the studio. After a while the outer door is opened slowly, and* HJALMAR *looks in. He is wearing his overcoat, but is without his hat; he is unwashed and his hair is ruffled and untidy; his eyes are dull and heavy.* GINA *stands still with the broom in her hand and looks at him.*)

GINA. Well there, Hjalmar!—have you come after all?

HJALMAR (*walks in and answers in a dull voice*). I have come—but only to go away again directly.

GINA. Yes, yes—I suppose so. But, mercy me, what a sight you are!

HJALMAR. What a sight?

GINA. And your good overcoat too! It *has* had a doing!

HEDVIG (*from the kitchen doorway*). Mother, shall I—? (*Sees* HJALMAR, *screams with joy and runs to him.*) Father! father!

HJALMAR (*turning away and waving her back*). Go away, go away! (*To* GINA.) Make her go away from me, I tell you!

GINA (*in an undertone*). Go into the sitting-room, Hedvig. (HEDVIG *goes in silently.*)

HJALMAR (*pulling out the table-drawer, with a show of*

being busy). I must have my books with me. Where are my books?

GINA. What books?

HJALMAR. My scientific works, of course—the technical journals I use for my invention.

GINA (*looking in the bookcase*). Are they these unbound ones?

HJALMAR. Of course they are.

GINA (*laying a pile of magazines on the table*). Shan't I get Hedvig to cut them for you?

HJALMAR. I don't need to have them cut. (*Short silence.*)

GINA. Is it settled that you leave us, then, Hjalmar?

HJALMAR (*rummaging among the books*). I should think that was evident.

GINA. Yes, yes.

HJALMAR (*vehemently*). I can't come here and get a knife into my heart every hour of the day!

GINA. God forgive you, for saying such hard things of me.

HJALMAR. Prove to me—

GINA. I think it is you should prove to me.

HJALMAR. After a past like yours? There are certain demands—one might almost call them demands of the ideal—

GINA. But what about grandfather? What is to become of him, poor old man?

HJALMAR. I know my duty; the helpless old man will go with me. I shall go into the town and make my arrangements. —Hm—(*hesitatingly*)—has anyone found my hat on the stairs?

GINA. No. Have you lost your hat?

HJALMAR. Of course I must have had it when I came in last night, there's no doubt of that; but this morning I couldn't find it.

GINA. Good Lord!—wherever did you go with those two scamps?

HJALMAR. Don't ask silly questions. Do you suppose I am in a condition to remember details?

GINA. I only hope you haven't caught cold, Hjalmar. (*Goes into the kitchen.*)

HJALMAR (*talks to himself in an angry undertone while he empties the table drawer*). You are a scoundrel, Relling! You are a blackguard!—a shameless seducer!—I should like to murder you! (*He puts some old letters on one side, comes upon the torn paper of the day before, takes it up and looks at the pieces, but puts it down hastily as* GINA *comes in.*)

GINA (*putting down a breakfast tray on the table*). Here is a drop of something hot, if you could fancy it. And some bread and butter and a little salt meat with it.

HJALMAR (*glancing at the tray*). Salt meat? Never under this roof!—It is true I haven't tasted a bit of food for four-and-twenty hours, but that makes no difference.—My notes! The beginning of my memoirs! Where on earth are my diary and my important papers? (*Opens the sitting-room door, but draws back.*) There she is again!

GINA. Good gracious, the child must be somewhere!

HJALMAR. Come out. (*Stands aside, and* HEDVIG *comes out into the studio, looking frightened.* HJALMAR *stands with his hand on the door-handle.*) In these last moments I am spending in my former home, I wish to be protected from those who have no business here. (*Goes into the room.*)

HEDVIG (*goes with a bound towards her mother and speaks in a low trembling voice*). Does he mean me?

GINA. Stay in the kitchen, Hedvig; or, no—better go into your own room. (*Talks to* HJALMAR, *as she goes in to him.*) Wait a minute, Hjalmar; don't turn all the drawers upside down; I know where all the things are.

HEDVIG (*stands motionless for a moment frightened and irresolute, biting her lips to keep back the tears. Then she clenches her hands convulsively and says softly.*) The wild duck! (*She creeps over and takes the pistol from the shelf, opens the attic door a little, slips in and shuts the door after her.* HJALMAR *and* GINA *are heard wrangling in the sitting-room.* HJALMAR *comes out carrying some note-books and old loose papers which he lays on the table.*)

HJALMAR. That portmanteau won't nearly hold them! There are a hundred and one things I must take with me.

GINA (*following him with the portmanteau*). Well, let the rest wait. Just take a shirt and a pair of drawers with you.

HJALMAR. Poof!—these exhausting preparations—! (*Takes off his overcoat and throws it on the sofa.*)

GINA. And there is the coffee getting all cold, too.

HJALMAR. Hm! (*Drinks a mouthful absently and then another.*)

GINA (*dusting the backs of the chairs*). You will have a job to find another big attic like this for the rabbits.

HJALMAR. What! Have I got to take all the rabbits with me too?

GINA. Yes, grandfather can't live without his rabbits, I am sure.

HJALMAR. He will have to get accustomed to it. I have got to renounce what is of a deal more vital importance than rabbits.

GINA (*dusting the bookcase*). Shall I put your flute in the portmanteau for you?

HJALMAR. No. No flute for me. But give me the pistol.

GINA. Are you going to take that there gun with you?

HJALMAR. Yes. My loaded pistol.

GINA (*looking for it*). It isn't here. He must have taken it in with him.

HJALMAR. Is he in the attic?

GINA. No doubt he is.

HJALMAR. Hm—poor lonely old fellow. (*Takes a piece of bread and butter, eats it and drinks up his cup of coffee.*)

GINA. If only we hadn't let our other room, you might have moved in there.

HJALMAR. I should be living under the same roof with—! Never—never!

GINA. But couldn't you put up for a day or two in the sitting-room? You should have it all to yourself.

HJALMAR. Never within these walls.

GINA. Well, then, downstairs, with Relling and Molvik?

HJALMAR. Don't mention those fellows' names! The very thought of them almost takes my appetite away. No, no—I must go out into the storm and snow—go from house to house seeking shelter for my father and myself.

GINA. But you have no hat, Hjalmar! You know you have lost your hat.

HJALMAR. Oh, those scum of the earth, steeped in every vice!—I must get a hat as I go. (*Takes another piece of bread and butter.*) I must make the necessary arrangements. I am not going to endanger my life. (*Searches for something on the tray.*)

GINA. What are you looking for?

HJALMAR. Butter.

GINA. I will get some in a moment. (*Goes into the kitchen.*)

HJALMAR (*calling after her*). Oh, it's of no consequence. Dry bread will do just as well for me.

GINA (*bringing in a butter-dish*). See, this is fresh churned. (*She pours out another cup of coffee for him; he sits down on the sofa, puts more butter on his bread, and eats and drinks for a little while in silence.*)

HJALMAR. If I decided to do so, could I—without being exposed to intrusion on anyone's part—put up for a day or two in the sitting-room there?

GINA. Of course you could, if only you would.

HJALMAR. Because I don't see there is any possibility of getting all father's things out in a moment.

GINA. And, besides that, you have got to tell him first that you don't mean to live here with us any longer.

HJALMAR (*pushing his cup away*). Yes, that's another thing; I have got to open up all this complicated question again—I must consider the situation; I must have time to breathe; I cannot sustain all these burdens in a single day.

GINA. No, and in such vile weather as it is, too.

HJALMAR (*turning over* MR. WERLE'S *letter*). I see this paper is still lying here.

GINA. Yes, I haven't touched it.

HJALMAR. The rubbish is no concern of mine—

GINA. Well, I am sure *I* had no idea of doing anything with it.

HJALMAR. But it might be as well not to let it get out of sight altogether. In all the upset of my moving, it might so easily—

GINA. I'll take care of it, Hjalmar.

HJALMAR. The deed of gift, after all, belongs first and foremost to my father, and it is his affair whether he chooses to make any use of it.

GINA (*sighing*). Yes, poor old father.

HJALMAR. Just for the sake of safety—where can I find some paste?

GINA (*going to the book-shelf*). Here is the paste-pot.

HJALMAR. And a brush.

GINA. Here is a brush too. (*Brings them to him.*)

HJALMAR (*taking up a pair of scissors*). Just a strip of paper along the back—. (*Cuts and pastes.*) Far be it from me to want to do anything amiss with other people's property—least of all with what belongs to a poor old man—and, indeed, to someone else as well. There we are! Let it lie there for a little. And when it is dry, take it away. I don't wish ever to set eyes on the paper again. Never!

(GREGERS WERLE *comes in from the passage.*)

GREGERS (*slightly astonished*). What—are you sitting here, Hjalmar?

HJALMAR (*getting up hurriedly*). I had sunk down from exhaustion.

GREGERS. You have been having some breakfast, I see.

HJALMAR. The body makes its claims felt sometimes, too.

GREGERS. What have you decided to do?

HJALMAR. For a man like me, there is only one thing to be done. I am just engaged in putting my most important things together. But it takes time, as you may suppose.

GINA (*a little impatiently*). Well, am I to get the room ready for you, or pack your portmanteau?

HJALMAR (*with a glance of irritation towards* GREGERS). Pack—and get the room ready as well!

GREGERS (*after a short pause*). I should never have thought this would be the end of it. Is there really any necessity for you to leave house and home?

HJALMAR (*walking about uneasily*). What do you want me to do, then?—I am not fit to stand unhappiness, Gregers. I need a sense of security and peace about me.

GREGERS. But can't you have that here? Just make the trial. It seems to me that now you have firm ground to build upon —and to begin afresh. Remember, too, you have your invention to live for.

HJALMAR. Oh, don't talk to me about my invention. I shouldn't wonder if that were a very long way off.

GREGERS. Really?

HJALMAR. Good heavens! Yes. Just tell me what you suppose I am going to invent? Other people have invented most things already. It becomes harder every day—

GREGERS. But you, who have worked so hard at it—

HJALMAR. It was that scoundrel Relling who set me on to it.

GREGERS. Relling?

HJALMAR. Yes, it was he that first called my attention to my talent for making some remarkable discovery in photography.

GREGERS. Aha!—it was Relling!

HJALMAR. I got so much happiness out of it, Gregers. Not so much for the sake of the invention itself, as because Hedvig believed in it—believed in it with a child's whole-hearted enthusiasm. Perhaps I should say that I have been fool enough to go and fancy she believed in it.

GREGERS. Can you really suppose that Hedvig has not been genuine about it?

HJALMAR. I can suppose anything now. It is Hedvig that stands in my way. She has taken all the sunshine out of my life.

GREGERS. Hedvig? Can you say that of Hedvig? How can she have done anything of the sort?

HJALMAR (*without answering him*). How unspeakably I have loved that child! How unspeakably happy I have felt every time I came home into my poor room, and she ran to meet me with her sweet little half-closed eyes!—Credulous fool! I loved her so unspeakably, that I deluded myself with the dream that she loved me just as much.

GREGERS. Do you say that was a delusion?

HJALMAR. How can I tell? I can get nothing whatever out of Gina, and she is so utterly lacking in any sense of the ideal side of all these complications. But to you I feel forced to open my mind, Gregers. There is that terrible doubt— perhaps Hedvig has never really honestly loved me.

GREGERS. It is possible you may have proof of that. (*Listens.*) What is that? I thought I heard the wild duck cry.

HJALMAR. It is the wild duck quacking. Father is in the attic.

GREGERS. Is he? (*A look of happiness lights up his face.*) I tell you, you may have proof yet that your poor misunderstood Hedvig loves you.

HJALMAR. What proof can she give me? I daren't believe in any assurances from that quarter.

GREGERS. There is not an atom of deceitfulness in Hedvig.

HJALMAR. Ah, Gregers, that is just what I am not so certain about. Who knows what Gina and that Mrs. Sörby may have sat here whispering and gossiping about? And Hedvig is generally all ears, I can tell you. Perhaps the deed of gift did not come so unexpectedly, after all. Indeed, I thought I noticed something.

GREGERS. What sort of spirit is this that has taken hold of you?

HJALMAR. I have had my eyes opened. Just you wait. You will see the deed of gift is only a beginning. Mrs. Sörby has all along been very thick with Hedvig, and now she has it in her power to do whatever she pleases for the child. They can take her from me whenever they like.

GREGERS. Hedvig will never leave you.

HJALMAR. Don't be so sure of that. If they come beckoning to her with their hands full of gifts——. And I have loved her so unspeakably! I, who would have thought it my greatest joy to take her carefully by the hand and lead her through life—just as one leads a child, who is frightened of the dark, through a great empty room! Now I feel such a gnawing certainty that the poor photographer, up in his garret here, has never really and truly been anything to her. She has only been cunningly careful to keep on a good footing with me till the time came.

GREGERS. You don't really believe that, Hjalmar?

HJALMAR. That is just the cruellest part of it—that I don't know what to believe—and that I shall never know. But can you really doubt that it is as I say? Ha! ha! You rely far too much on your "demands of the ideal," my good Gregers! If the others were to come, with their hands full, and call to the child: "Come away from him: you will learn what life is with us—"

GREGERS (*hastily*). Well, what then, do you suppose?

HJALMAR. If I asked her then: "Hedvig, are you willing to give up this life they offer you, for my sake?" (*Laughs derisively.*) Thank you!—you would just hear what answer I should get.

(*A pistol shot is heard from within the attic.*)

GREGERS (*with a happy shout*). Hjalmar!

HJALMAR. Listen to that. He must needs go shooting too.

GINA (*coming in*). Hjalmar, I think grandfather is blundering about in the attic by himself.

HJALMAR. I will look in—

GREGERS (*quickly and with emotion*). Wait a moment! Do you know what that was?

HJALMAR. Of course I know.

GREGERS. No, but you don't. I know. That was the proof you wanted.

HJALMAR. What proof?

GREGERS. That was a child's act of sacrifice. She has got your father to shoot the wild duck.

HJALMAR. Shoot the wild duck!

GINA. Fancy that, now!

HJALMAR. What for?

GREGERS. She wanted to sacrifice, for your sake, what she prized most in the world; because she believed it would make you love her again.

HJALMAR (*tenderly with emotion*). Poor child!

GINA. What things she thinks of!

GREGERS. She only wanted your love again, Hjalmar; she did not feel as if she could live without it.

GINA (*struggling with her tears*). There you are, Hjalmar!

HJALMAR. Gina, where is she?

GINA (*sniffing*). Poor thing, she is sitting out in the kitchen, I expect.

HJALMAR (*crosses the room and opens the kitchen door*). Hedvig—come! Come here to me! (*Looks round.*) No, she is not there.

GINA. Then she must be in her own little room.

HJALMAR (*who has gone out to look*). No, she is not here either. (*Comes in.*) She must have gone out.

GINA. Yes, you wouldn't have her anywhere in the house.

HJALMAR. If only she would come home soon, so that I could let her know—. Everything will go well now, Gregers; now I believe we can begin life over again.

GREGERS (*quietly*). I knew it was through the child that reparation would be made.

(*Old* EKDAL *comes to the door of his room; he is in full uniform, and is occupied in trying to buckle on his sword.*)

HJALMAR (*in astonishment*). Father! are you there!

GINA. Was it in your room that you fired?

EKDAL (*indignantly as he approaches*). So you go shooting alone, do you, Hjalmar?

HJALMAR (*anxious and perplexed*). Wasn't it you, then, that was shooting in the attic?

EKDAL. I shooting? Hm!

GREGERS (*calls to* HJALMAR). She has shot the wild duck herself, don't you see?

HJALMAR. What can it mean! (*Hurries to the attic door, tears it aside, looks in, and gives a loud scream.*) Hedvig!

GINA (*running to the door*). Heavens! what is it?

HJALMAR (*going in*). She is lying on the floor!

GREGERS. Hedvig on the floor! (*Goes in to* HJALMAR.)

GINA (*at the same time*). Hedvig! (*From within the garret.*) Oh, no! no! no!

EKDAL. Ho! ho! does she go out shooting too!

HJALMAR, GINA *and* GREGERS *carry* HEDVIG *into the studio; the pistol is clasped tight in the fingers of her right hand, which is hanging down.*)

HJALMAR (*distractedly*). The pistol has gone off—and she has been shot. Call for help! Help!

GINA (*runs into the passage and calls out*). Relling! Relling! Doctor Relling! come up as quickly as ever you can! (HJALMAR *and* GREGERS *lay* HEDVIG *on the sofa.*)

EKDAL (*quietly*). The forests avenge themselves.

HJALMAR (*on his knees beside* HEDVIG). She is coming to now. She is coming to—yes, yes, yes.

GINA (*who has come in again*). Where has she been shot? I can't see anything. (RELLING *comes in hurriedly with* MOLVIK *at his heels; the latter is without waistcoat or necktie, and with his coat flying open.*)

RELLING. What is the matter?

GINA. They say Hedvig has shot herself.

HJALMAR. Come here and help!

RELLING. Shot herself! (*Pushes the table aside and begins to examine her.*)

HJALMAR (*looking anxiously up at him*). It can't be dangerous, Relling? What? She hardly bleeds at all. It can't be dangerous?

RELLING. How did it happen?

HJALMAR. I can't imagine—!

GINA. She wanted to shoot the wild duck.

RELLING. The wild duck?

HJALMAR. The pistol must have gone off.

RELLING. Hm! Quite so.

EKDAL. The forests avenge themselves. But I am not afraid, anyway. (*Goes into the attic and shuts the door after him.*)

HJALMAR. Well, Relling—why don't you say something?

RELLING. The ball has entered the breast.

HJALMAR. Yes—but she's coming to!

GINA (*bursting into tears*). My child, my child!

GREGERS (*in a choked voice*). In the ocean's depths—

HJALMAR (*springing up*). Yes, yes, she *must* live! Oh, for God's sake, Relling—just for a moment—just long enough for me to let her know how unspeakably I have loved her all the time!

RELLING. The heart has been hit. Internal hæmorrhage. She died on the spot.

HJALMAR. And I hunted her away from me! And she crept like a frightened animal into the attic and died for love of me. (*Sobbing.*) I can never make it right now! I can never tell her—! (*Clenches his fists and cries up to heaven.*) Thou who art there above us—if indeed Thou *art* there! Why hast Thou done this to me!

GINA. Hush, hush! you mustn't take on in that terrible way. We had no right to keep her, I suppose.

MOLVIK. The child is not dead, but sleepeth.

RELLING. Rubbish!

HJALMAR (*goes more calmly over to the sofa and, folding his arms, looks down at* HEDVIG). There she lies, so stiff and still.

RELLING (*trying to take the pistol from her fingers*). She holds so tight, so tight.

GINA. No, no, Relling, don't hurt her fingers; let the thing alone.

HJALMAR. She shall take it with her.

GINA. Yes, let her. But the child mustn't lie out here for a show. She shall go into her own little room, she shall. Carry her with me, Hjalmar. (*She and* HJALMAR *take her up.*)

HJALMAR (*as they carry her out*). Oh, Gina, Gina—can you ever get over this?

GINA. We must help one another. Now, I think, we each have a share in her.

MOLVIK (*stretches out his arms and babbles*). Blessed be the Lord! Earth to earth, dust to dust—

RELLING (*whispering*). Shut up, you fool—you're drunk.

(HJALMAR *and* GINA *carry the body out through the kitchen.* RELLING *stands looking after them.* MOLVIK *sneaks out into the passage.*)

RELLING (*going over to* GREGERS). No one will ever persuade me this was an accident.

GREGERS (*who has stood terror-stricken, his face twitching convulsively*). No one can say how the dreadful thing happened.

RELLING. The flame has scorched her dress. She must have held the pistol to her breast and fired.

GREGERS. Hedvig has not died in vain. You saw how his grief called out all the best that was in him.

RELLING. Most people show their best side in the presence

of death. But how long do you suppose this turn for the better will last in his case?

GREGERS. Surely it will last and increase as long as he lives!

RELLING. In eight or nine months little Hedvig will be no more to him than a beautiful theme to declaim upon.

GREGERS. Do you dare to say that of Hjalmar Ekdal?

RELLING. We will talk of it again as soon as the grass has grown over her grave. Then you will hear him pumping up his fine phrases about "the child torn prematurely from her father's loving heart"; you will see him wallowing in emotional fits of self-admiration and self-compassion. Just you wait and see!

GREGERS. If you are right, and I am wrong, life is no longer worth living.

RELLING. Oh, life would be all right if we could only be rid of these infernal fools who come to poor people's doors presenting their "demands of the ideal."

GREGERS (*looking in front of him*). If that is so, I am glad my destiny is what it is.

RELLING. Excuse me, but—what *is* your destiny?

GREGERS (*turning to go*). To be the thirteenth at table.

RELLING. So I should imagine!

Bibliography

Bradbrook, Muriel C., *Ibsen, The Norwegian*. New York, 1948.

Downs, Brian W., *Ibsen: The Intellectual Background*. New York, 1947.

Fjelde, Rolf, *Ibsen: A Collection of Critical Essays*. Englewood Cliffs, 1965.

Knight, G. Wilson, *Henrik Ibsen*. New York, 1962.

Koht, Halvdan, *The Life of Ibsen*. (2 vols.) New York, 1931.

Lavrin, Janko, *Ibsen: An Approach*. London, 1950.

Northam, John, *Ibsen's Dramatic Method*. London, 1953.

Shaw, George Bernard, *The Quintessence of Ibsenism*. New York and London, 1913.

Tennant, P.F.D., *Ibsen's Dramatic Technique*. Cambridge, 1948.

Weigand, Hermann J., *The Modern Ibsen*. New York, 1925.

Zucker, A.E., *Ibsen the Master Builder*. New York, 1929.

See also:

Brustein, Robert, *The Theatre of Revolt: An Approach to the Modern Drama*. Boston, 1964.

Fergusson, Francis, *The Idea of a Theatre*. Princeton, 1949.

Gassner, John, *Masters of the Drama*. New York, 1940, 1945, 1954.

Huneker, James, *Iconoclasts*. New York, 1905.

James, Henry, *The Scenic Art*. New Brunswick, 1948.

Krutch, Joseph Wood, *"Modernism" in the Modern Drama*. Ithaca, 1953.

Nicoll, Allardyce, *World Drama*. New York, 1950.

Valency, Maurice, *The Flower and the Castle: An Introduction to the Modern Drama*. New York, 1963.